Alternative realities:
a study of communes and their members

International Library of Sociology

Founded by Karl Mannheim

Editor: John Rex, University of Warwick

Arbor Scientiae
Arbor Vitae

A catalogue of the books available in the **International Library of Sociology** and other series of Social Science books published by Routledge & Kegan Paul will be found at the end of this volume.

Alternative realities:
a study of communes and their members

Andrew Rigby
Department of Sociology,
University of Aberdeen

Routledge & Kegan Paul
London and Boston

First published in 1974
by Routledge & Kegan Paul Ltd
Broadway House, 68–74 Carter Lane,
London EC4V 5EL and
9 Park Street,
Boston, Mass. 02108, U.S.A.
Printed in Great Britain by
Unwin Brothers Limited
The Gresham Press
Old Woking, Surrey

ISBN 0 7100 7715 7

Library of Congress Catalog Card No. 73–86577

Contents

Preface

In recent years there has been a growth of interest in the creation of alternative life styles based upon various forms of communal living. At one level this study represents an attempt to examine the nature of this contemporary social movement, the commune movement. It is an attempt to examine the sources of recruitment to the movement and to analyse the various types of living experiment that it encompasses. At another level, however, the study reflects my interest in anarcho-pacifism and non-violence and a concern to examine non-violent means of revolutionary change that can be deemed relevant to our contemporary society. Given this perspective, then, I cannot claim to have written this work from the point of view of the impartial, isolated, and non-involved observer. I do not believe that this invalidates the study in any way, however. What I have sought to do in the following pages is to portray the commune scene in Britain as it is seen and interpreted by those who are involved in it. I have been concerned to portray *their* reality and not some artificial reality constructed by the allegedly scientific observer, which is then presented as the 'real' reality, when in fact it is nothing more than the scientist's own personal version of that reality. Some words on my field research methods might be relevant here.

To use that hackneyed phrase much beloved by symbolic interactionists, my concern during the period of field research was to 'take the actor's point of view'. Given that people construct their action on the basis of the interpretations they make of the situations in which they find themselves, it seems to me imperative that sociologists, in their attempt to understand why people do the things they do, must base their work on these interpretations that people make of situations, that they make of the actions of others and of their own actions. It was this kind of thinking which led me to pursue in this study what many social scientists will no doubt consider 'soft' research methods. The bulk of the information upon which the study is based was obtained through conversations with commune members and aspiring communards. Occasionally, in my role as guest/friend/observer/participant observer during my stay at communes I would tape-record conversations and more structured interviews, otherwise notes were taken after the interaction had ceased. The other major source of information was the writings of the communards themselves: in the general 'underground' press, in their own publications, and in specialist commune journals such as *Communes*.

After the bulk of the field research had been completed I decided to send out a short questionnaire to fifty commune members with whom I had established contact previously, as an attempt to obtain additional information. Of the fifty questionnaires sent out, only twenty were returned completed. This figure reflects in part the understandable reluctance commune people have for being 'typed' or 'processed' in any way. This low response rate also indicated to me that any attempt I might have made to carry out the research solely on the basis of the standardized type of questionnaire so highly regarded by certain social scientists would have been doomed to failure. Sociologists must learn to adapt their research methods to the subject of their study, and not vice versa, if they are to remain faithful to the phenomena that they seek to understand.

One problem which confronts any field researcher is the question of the generalizability of his findings. How can one generalize about communes in Britain on the basis of research into what was quite possibly a small and unrepresentative cross section of them? In fact, over the period 1969–71 I made contact with, and spent time at, sixteen communes in Britain. In addition I established personal contact with the members of six other groups, although for one reason or another I never managed to spend time at the commune itself. Such contact was made typically at various 'gatherings' of one sort or another. I also had considerable contact with three other groups who were seeking to form communes but who, at the time of my research, had not succeeded in their aim. So, to what extent can this sample, to a significant degree self-selected, be considered representative of communes as a whole in Britain? I do not think anyone can come up with a definitive answer to this question. No adequate census of communes exists and so it is impossible to estimate with any great degree of accuracy the exact number of communes of one sort or another in Britain. It is impossible to take anything like a random sample of such ventures. All I can do is state my belief that the different types of communes and communards that I encountered during the course of my research were representative of the relevant population during that period. Whether this belief is correct or not will only be shown through others pursuing their own enquiries and investigations.

At every stage during the research process that led to the completion of this work I have relied upon the help, support and assistance of a host of people. In particular I should like to acknowledge the friendly support of the people at the Richardson Institute in London who provided me with a desk and a 'home' during 1969–70. I am deeply indebted to Nigel Young who, in his capacity as supervisor, friend, and fellow 'peace-nik', provided critical support at every stage. Deepest thanks, however, are due to all those people in and around the commune scene who suffered my questioning and enquiries. In particular I should like to thank Anna, Betty, Charles, Dave and friends in Liverpool, David Horn, Ian and Val, Jill and John, 'Jill the Weaver', Miranda and Peter, Nicholas and friends at BIT, Owen and Anne, Pat, Peter and friends at Findhorn, Rosemary and Michael. Special thanks are due to Tony in Wales for all his help and encouragement. To all these people and many more— thank you. From them I have learnt much, not only about communes but also about myself.

I also wish to thank Apple Publishing Limited for permission to quote from 'Space Cowboy' by Steve Miller, and *IT* for permission to quote Julian Beck's poem 'Paradise Now'.

Finally, I should like to acknowledge the valiant efforts made by Carol, Eileen, and Val in the typing of this work.

Throughout the work the terms 'commune', 'community', and 'intentional community' are used interchangeably, as are the terms 'communard' and 'communitarian'.

This book is based on research largely carried out during 1969–70. The bulk of the text was written during 1970–1. Since that time a number of the communal ventures referred to in the text have changed, not only in membership composition but also in general orientation. Other projects have ceased to exist. As a result, much of the descriptive detail contained in the book will appear outdated to those with anything like a familiar knowledge of the contemporary commune scene in Britain. So be it.

1 Introduction

Pacifists have traditionally argued that political power does not stem from the barrel of a gun, but rather that 'all power, of all groups and all governments, derives from sources in the society, and the availability of these is determined by the degree of cooperation and obedience offered by the people.'[1] That is, in any power relationship in which the power holder seeks to exert his influence over the apparently less powerful, there must come a stage in the interaction where, if the will of the power holder is to prevail, the less powerful must agree with the demands or requests made of them, they must agree to do what is demanded of them if the power holder is to be successful in his attempts to influence their actions. Basic to the non-violent position is the view that men create their own tyrants by granting them obedience, and that once this obedience is undercut or withheld, then tyranny will collapse. This view, that tyranny rests on voluntary servitude, was expressed by Gandhi, when he wrote, 'All exploitation is based on co-operation, willing or forced, of the exploited . . . there would be no exploitation if people refused to obey the exploiter.'[2]

A similar perspective can be adopted with regard to the problem which has traditionally concerned sociologists: the problem of social order. That is, it can be argued that the social order can persist, and social chaos be avoided, only for as long as the members of society continue to share roughly complementary definitions of the most important situations that they encounter in their social life and continue to view the social world that they occupy as natural, requiring neither explanation nor justification. The social order persists because, as Berger has argued, 'For most of us, as we grow up, and learn to live in society, its forms take on the appearance of structures as self evident and as solid as those of the natural cosmos.'[3] In other words, no society has existed as it does at the present since the beginning of time. Rather, each of its institutions, its patterns of social relationships, its networks of social roles, its hierarchies of power and authority, and so on, has been created at some stage or another by the actions of men in the world. Although all social systems have been created by men, and can also be changed by men, it can be argued that they persist largely because the members of such systems lose sight of this fact. Society, for the bulk of its members, appears as something 'out there' which existed before they were born, will continue to exist after their death, and, as such, is viewed as comparable to the physical universe which surrounds man, as an 'external, subjectively opaque and coercive facticity'.[4] In other words, society can be viewed as persisting due largely to the fact that it is taken for granted by the majority of its members as the natural and only way that social life could be ordered. As Berger has phrased it, 'Society can maintain itself only if its fictions . . . are accorded ontological status by at least some of its members some of the time.'[5] The persistence of social order can thus be said to rest upon the voluntary servitude of its members.

Thus, the majority of society's members can be defined as alienated in so far as they view the social order in which they live as the natural order of things, and view their own personal lives as subject to the pressures of impersonal forces beyond their control. However, just as society has been made by men, it can also be changed by them. There are occasions when the apparently objective status of social reality is revealed as resting on the precarious basis of fiction. As Schutz remarked:[6]

What has been beyond question so far and remained unquestioned up to now may always be put in question: things taken for granted then become problematical. This will be the case, for example, if there occurs in the individual or social life an event or situation which cannot be met by applying the traditional and habitual pattern of behaviour or interpretation.

There are occasions when the role of the human agent in the construction of social reality can become apparent to individuals and social groups, frequently as a consequence of some individual or group experience which has shattered their previously taken for granted worlds. Such people are frequently to be found in the ranks of radical social movements, defined by Blumer as 'collective enterprises to establish a new order of life'.[7] Blumer argued that social movements 'have their inception in a condition of unrest, and derive their motive power on the one hand from dissatisfaction with the current form of life, and on the other hand, from wishes and hopes for a new scheme or system of living'.[8] One can reason that before a person commits himself to working towards what he defines as the creation of a new social order, he must not only be disaffected from the existing order, but also view that order as amenable to change. The possible origins of such disaffection would appear to be almost as varied and numerous as the number of disaffected individuals. Possible sources of estrangement from the existing order include the collapse of an individual's previously taken for granted world as a consequence of such experiences as sudden economic hardship through unemployment, the break-up of a marriage or the loss of a loved one, or a religious conversion-type experience. Other sources of estrangement and disaffection can be traced to the early life of the individual—an unhappy childhood within an authoritarian family can lead to an individual rebelling against the society personified by his parents; just as the socialization of a child within a family where the parents hold radical ideas and beliefs, and are themselves estranged from the existing society, can inspire the individual with a desire to transform the social world. The perception of apparent injustices inflicted upon other individuals, groups, nationalities and races can also act as a catalyst leading to the adoption of a radical career by the individual.

Whatever the sources of an individual's estrangement and disaffection from the existing order of society, once the precarious nature of the existing social order has become apparent to him, and the urge to transform this system has been implanted, then it becomes possible to trace the career of the radical in terms of his recruitment to particular types of social movements, his acceptance of certain types of revolutionary ideologies and belief systems, and his involvement in particular projects of action typically viewed as radical by himself and his peers. One such form of action has traditionally involved the formation of intentional communities, such projects having been described by one writer[9] as 'utopian colonies' consisting of

> a group of people who are attempting to establish a new social pattern based upon a vision of the ideal society and who have withdrawn themselves from the community at large to embody that vision in experimental form. The purpose is usually to create a model which other colonies and eventually mankind in general will follow.

Such ventures can be described as utopian in so far as they have generally been founded by people who have perceived a gap between the nature of social life as it appeared to them, and the nature of social life as they felt it ought to be. As such, they have typically set about the task of transforming what was then the existing order in the direction of their ideal society. The means chosen was what might be termed 'revolution by life style'. They have sought to realize their ideal society through the process of establishing small-scale, living examples of their utopia, and through their exemplary actions have attempted to convert the members of the wider society to their systems of belief and modes of living. The participants in such experiments can be described as utopian to the extent that their orientation to the world conforms to Mannheim's definition of the utopian mentality as one which 'transcends reality and which at the same time breaks the bonds of the existing order'.[10]

Mannheim argued that[11]

> those social strata which represent the prevailing social and intellectual order will experience as reality that structure of relationships of which they are the bearers, while the groups driven into opposition to the present order will be oriented towards the first stirrings of the social order for which they are striving and which is being realized through them.

From this perspective, then, it can be argued that communitarians have traditionally sought to transform the existing social order and create an 'alternative society' through the presentation of what might be termed counter-definitions of reality for the consideration of society's members.

In recent years there has been a growth of interest in the creation of alternative life styles based on such counter-definitions of reality, and increasing numbers of people have pursued their interest to the extent of involving themselves in community ventures of one sort or another. Thus, it has been estimated by one observer that in the United States in 1970 there were over two thousand rural communes along with several thousand urban groups.[12] In Japan there are some fifty communes and approximately three hundred co-operative villages.[13] On the continent of Europe communes have sprung up in most of the major cities, inspired to some extent by the example of Kommune 1 which was founded in Berlin in March 1967, and whose members received a great amount of publicity as a consequence of their activities.[14] In Holland it has been estimated that there are approximately two hundred community ventures run by members of the Roman Catholic Church.[15] In Israel the kibbutz movement has continued to grow to the point where there are some 235 kibbutzim with a total population of over ninety thousand, about 4 per cent of the Jewish population in Israel.[16] In Britain it has been estimated that there are approximately fifty communal ventures of one sort or another. There is a formal Commune Movement with a membership of around three hundred, and which publishes a bi-monthly magazine, *Communes*, with sales of over two thousand per issue.

It is this contemporary British movement which is the subject of this study. What follows in the ensuing chapters is an attempt to

4

examine the nature of this movement, its membership, the communal activities in which they are involved, and their views of the world which inspire such activities. In addition to being an essay in sociological fieldwork, an attempt to provide descriptive data of a contemporary social movement, the study represents an attempt to explain why increasing numbers of people, particularly among the young (although their total number is still relatively minute compared with the total population) are apparently opting out of society and seeking to embody, through their commune ventures, what they tend to define as the nucleus of a new and alternative social order.

The stated object of the formal Commune Movement is 'To create a federal society of communities wherein everyone shall be free to do whatever he wishes provided only that he doesn't transgress the freedom of another.' This aim would appear to be shared to a greater or lesser degree by all members of communes in Britain, whether such people are actually fee-paying members of the Commune Movement or not. There is a general agreement that through the formation of communes each group will be establishing something akin to 'a colony in a new world, the first outpost of a new society', as one respondent phrased it. Now, in order to understand why such people have resorted to such a strategy in order to create what one commune member described to me as 'a society in which each individual can have the right and the space to exercise their creative autonomy', it is necessary first of all to locate the origins of their estrangement from the existing order, the sources of their discontent with the status quo. However, it is not sufficient merely to ask and to try and answer the simple question: 'what aspects of life in modern Britain do commune members find particularly unbearable and intolerable?' One must enquire further and ask the question: Why? Why do certain groups of people find different aspects of life in modern Britain unbearable, when other groups of people appear to find such conditions acceptable?

It is one of the arguments of this book that the answers to such questions lie in the particular life problems encountered by members of particular social groups, located in particular areas of the social structure, such as the young from middle-class social and economic backgrounds. That is, one cannot begin to understand the present-day commune movement without considering the impact of certain social forces upon the social structure of modern Britain in general, and without considering how these social forces have had different consequences for the lives of members of different social groups in particular.

Thus, it can be argued that what has rendered increasing numbers of middle-class youth available for recruitment to the commune movement has been their experience of what Klapp has termed the

5

problem of personal identity, 'an inability to define oneself successfully in a milieu of inadequate symbolism':[17] a situation experienced
by the people as a consequence of such forces as the high rate of
technologically induced social change and the loss of traditional
sources of personal identity and self-affirmation that has accompanied the development of large-scale, hierarchically organized, institutions of economic, political, and social life. It can be argued that the
operations of such public institutions have largely been determined
by norms and standards that have been rationalized in so far as they
have been determined solely by the functional requirements of the
institution as a whole. For many, it can appear that in such institutions the individual has little opportunity to develop a meaningful
sense of his own worth, and is treated more like a cog in a machine
than an autonomous creative human being. The prospect of such an
occupational role for those such as the middle-class young, who have
been accustomed to think of themselves as worthy of respect as
individuals, can be particularly repugnant. As a result, many young
people feel at a loss as to what they should seek to become. They
can perceive no attractive role models for them within the conventional occupational structure. Consequently, increasing numbers of
middle-class young are attempting to 'find themselves' in a commune,
attempting to discover what one correspondent has described as 'a
life style in which work for money is irrelevant and undesired work
is minimised, thus permitting concentration on the objectives of
developing every individual to his maximum capacity'.[18]

To stay with the example of the middle-class young, one can argue
that it is not sufficient merely to examine the problems of life
encountered by such people, for the joining of a commune only
represents one way of resolving such problems. Although increasing
numbers of young people are joining communes, the vast majority of
them do not do so. Thus, in order to discover why the minority do
choose to form communes or join existing ones it is necessary to
enquire into their personal biographies. Through tracing the paths
to community followed by individuals it is possible to construct
models of the typical careers followed by different types of commune
members which have led them to the stage of dropping out of
conventional society. This concept of a career can be used, as it has
been done by Goffman and others, in order to[19]

refer to any social strand of any person's course through life.
The perspective of natural history is taken: unique outcomes
are neglected in favour of such changes over time as are basic
and common to the members of a social category, although
occurring independently to each of them.

Thus it is possible to argue that, for any individual to join a commune, he must not only feel dissatisfaction with his life in conventional society and feel estranged from society in general, he must also be aware that such phenomena as communes have existed in the past and exist in the present. He must also have had some experience which has caused him to think that such a style of life might be suitable for individuals like himself. Furthermore, he must also become aware that particular communes are at present in existence where he may be able to discover an environment suitable for the achievement of his personal ambitions and goals, and he must establish contact with such communes by some means in order for him to gain acceptance as a member. Finally, it can be argued that he must define his social situation as sufficiently free for him to drop out of society in order to commence his new life. Of course, if an individual is unable to discover any existing communes that fit his particular vision, then he must attempt to contact by some means other individuals who share his dream and who possess sufficient resources to help him found a new commune. In order to remain as a member of a commune, the individual must view his life there as sufficiently rewarding in various ways to enable him to resist whatever temptations he might feel to return to a more conventional form of existence. He must view the advantages of communal life as outweighing the advantages and the anticipated consequences of a return to normal life. Through the use of this concept of the career, insight can be obtained into the various types of processes by which individuals have become commune members.[20]

To summarize the above: in order to understand why certain individuals seek to form or join communes it is necessary not only to explain how the impact of certain social forces on society results in certain groups encountering various types of life problems which make them relatively available for recruitment to the commune movement. We also need to examine the processes of recruitment by which the individual actually becomes a member of a commune.

Members of communes have, of course, come from different social groups in society, have become interested in the idea of communal living in response to different types of life problems, and have followed different types of pathways or careers which have led to their joining different types of communal ventures. Thus in order to fully understand the nature of the contemporary commune movement it is necessary to distinguish between different types of communitarians and different forms of commune ventures.

One can choose various sets of criteria from which to derive a classificatory framework of communes: for instance, the rural-urban continuum or the length of time the commune has been in existence, the degree of communality within the commune with regard to income-sharing, the degree of private property within the commune

7

as opposed to communal property and so on. However, as a major concern of this study is with attempting to explain why certain types of people feel the need to drop out of society to some extent and live their daily life in a communal setting, the distinctions made between different types of communes is based on the members' definitions of the goals or purposes of their ventures. Most communitarians have some conception of their particular experiment as having some sort of purpose or aim—hence the term 'intentional community'. It is upon the different intentions underlying different ventures that the typology adopted in this book is based. Thus, in Chapters 5 and 6 a basic six-fold typology is presented.

1 *Self-actualizing communes* By this type it is intended to refer to those experiments in communal living that are seen by their members as contributing towards the creation of a new social order by providing, within the community, that environment in which the individual members feel most free to discover themselves, and develop their individual creative potentialities, through the exercise of individual freedom.

2 *Communes for mutual support* The intention underlying this second type of communal experiment is typically viewed by its members primarily in terms of providing a setting of mutual support, a sense of brotherhood for themselves.

3 *Activist communes* The members of this type of commune typically define the purpose of their institution in terms of providing an urban base from which they can directly involve themselves in social and political action oriented towards the wider community.

4 *Practical communes* This label is used to refer to those experiments in communal living which are defined by their members primarily in terms of the economic and practical material advantages to be obtained through such a style of life, such as the saving on living costs, rather than in terms of the revolutionary potential of communities, etc.

5 *Therapeutic communes* These communes are those which are seen by their members as having the prime purpose of therapy. They are aimed primarily at the creation of that social, physical and spiritual environment within which particular types of people who are sick or considered to be in need of care and attention can be looked after, and prepared for what is considered to be a more rewarding kind of life by the staff of the commune.

6 *Religious communes* These are those communes whose goal is

defined by their members primarily in religious terms. That is, the commune is viewed as fulfilling some purpose or other which the members feel to be in accordance with their religious beliefs, a purpose which they consider to be at least partly inspired and possibly guided by supra-empirical or sacred forces. Within this category of religious commune, however, one can distinguish between two basic types according to the different types of religious belief system. That is, one can distinguish between ascetic and mystic religious communes. The ascetic venture is typically inspired by a belief in a transcendent deity and the desire to serve God through seeking to resolve the conflict between His injunctions and the ways of the world, by living a life in accordance with God's word, within a community. The mystic experiment is generally guided by a belief in an immanent divine power and the desire on the part of the members of the community to attain oneness with this power. As such, the members of mystic communes are generally more concerned with the development of what they define as their spiritual consciousness and awareness, than with the project of transforming worldly life in accordance with the dictates of the ascetic's transcendent God.

Just as the commune movement in Britain encompasses different types of community ventures, so the membership of such projects is made up of different types of individuals. Thus, in order to explain why such individuals have rejected the conventional forms of social existence taken for granted by most people as the natural way to live in a modern urban-industrial capitalistic society such as Britain, it is necessary to distinguish, initially, between these different types of communitarians who have become involved in what can be considered a unique form of radical social action for different reasons and for different motives, and to relate the individual ideal-types to the different sorts of community ventures in which they are involved.

The approach to this problem is one that draws heavily upon the insights provided by Alfred Schutz.[21] Thus an individual's actions in the world are viewed as an ongoing process which is devised by the actor in advance. Human conduct is viewed as motivated behaviour based on the actor's preconceived project. Schutz distinguished between two types of motives: he termed motives which involve ends to be achieved, goals sought for, as 'in order to' motives, and motives which can be explained on the basis of the actor's social and economic background, psychic disposition and past history, he labelled 'because' motives. It is upon the basis of a communitarian's consciously held 'in order to' motives with regard to the question of the personal goal sought through the practice of communal living that the following distinctions between different types of commune member are based.

9

A six-fold typology of commune ventures was suggested above, and on *a priori* grounds one would expect individuals with particular personal ends in view to gravitate towards those communes which appeared to them most likely to further these ends. Thus, a basic classification of commune members could conceivably be based upon the typology of commune ventures already presented. The typology presented below, however, is a three-fold rather than a six-fold one. To the extent that the typology and the analysis in Chapter 7 which is based upon it does not embrace every type of individual involved in all six types of commune venture, then the examination of the members of the commune movement in contemporary Britain that follows is a restricted one. The major reason for this self-imposed limitation on the scope of the work stems from the fact that my interest in the commune movement as a subject of study was first aroused by the claims made by the representatives of the movement with whom I first came into contact that they were involved in projects aimed ultimately at the creation of a new social order. Mainly as a consequence of my own personal interest in alternative styles of living and the creation of alternative structures, one of my major concerns in the research project was with trying to understand why increasing numbers of people were apparently dropping out of society as part of a conscious attempt to transform the nature of their own lives as a step towards the radical transformation of the existing social order.

As a result of this personal orientation on my part, my interest as a researcher in those commune members whose orientation and involvement in communes was 'less' than this was limited. Thus, for example, those people living and working in therapeutic communities who defined their involvement in such experiments primarily in terms of providing a caring and supportive environment for particular social groups who suffered from what they viewed as physical and mental disorders, were of only marginal interest from the point of view of the research project. Similarly, peripheral to what was defined as the major area of research interest were those members of practical communes who viewed their involvement in communal living primarily in terms of the economic advantages to be obtained through such a style of life, and who were not interested in experimenting with alternative forms of family life, occupational pursuits and so forth. This is not to say that I was not interested in the members of therapeutic and practical communes as such. Where the members of such ventures defined their motives not solely in terms of servicing the remedial function of the commune as a whole or in terms of the economic advantages to be obtained through communal living arrangements, but stressed the importance of what they considered to be their attempt to radically transform their own lives and the life of society in general through their involvement in such projects, then their self-identification as individuals working towards the creation of a new social order caused me to consider them as such.

On the basis of such self-imposed restraints upon the area of research which formed the basis for this thesis, the typology presented below is restricted to those individuals who claimed that one of their consciously held motives for becoming involved in commune ventures was the belief that through such a form of action they could work towards the creation of a new social order, an alternative society. Within this broad category, however, distinctions emerged between three ideal-types of communitarian: the activist, the freedom-seeker, and the security-seeker, which mirrored to some extent the distinctions referred to above between the activist, the self-actualizing, and the mutual support communities. Thus, one class of communitarians consisted of those individuals who were concerned to bring about radical social change at the societal level through direct involvement in political and social affairs, particularly at the local community level, and who viewed the commune as an important base for such activities and also as an important revolutionary strategy to the extent that the commune itself acted as an example to other people of the quality of social relationships that it was possible to create within such an institution. Such activists were generally to be located in the urban communes of the activist type. This type of commune member could be distinguished from those who placed little or no emphasis on transforming the existing social order through such direct action measures. Typically, the occupants of rural communes sought to pursue their declared aim of creating an alternative society primarily by creating within the commune that kind of environment within which they themselves, as individuals, could be happiest, and which in turn could act as an example for other people to follow in the reshaping of their own lives, and thus, eventually, the reshaping of society. Within this broad category, however, a distinction can be made on the basis of the different personal, intermediate, goals which they sought as individual members of communes. Thus, the freedom-seekers were seeking, through the means of communal living, to create a social world for themselves that they hoped would provide them with a sufficient degree of personal freedom to enable them to follow their own pursuits, 'thus permitting concentration on the objectives of developing every individual to his maximum capacity'. The security-seekers, on the other hand, were seeking to create within a commune a social world within which they could develop strong and affective bonds with other individuals, from which they could obtain that sense of belongingness and the accompanying sense of emotional, psychological, and social security that they felt they were unable to obtain as members of 'straight' society. One such commune member informed me frankly that one of the motives underlying his decision to join a commune was, 'I want to live in a commune where people will look after me'. Such security-seekers were generally to be found in mutual support communes, whilst the freedom-seekers were to be found predominantly in the self-actualizing communes.

Now it can be argued that, despite the differences in approach to communal living displayed by such types, and despite the diversity in the form of communal ventures that characterizes the contemporary commune movement in Britain, this variety is contained by certain unifying factors. Thus it would appear that all communes represent the attempts of groups of individuals who possess, in varying degrees, the utopian mentality, with regard to their orientation towards the conventional forms of social existence that characterizes a modern, urban industrial society such as Britain, sufficient to say 'no' to society and to choose to live their lives according to their own inclinations and wishes. They have realized that, although it might appear that man in society has little choice but to follow the social demands made of him in his various roles, in fact man does have a choice in so far as he can step outside of his social roles and the taken-for-granted routines of society.

At the same time, the response of such people to these insights, and the strategies chosen to further their attempts to realize a new social order through the formation of communes, is not a response unique to the present age. Withdrawal from the world into communities of believers has been a traditional response of those of past ages who have seen a gap between their ideal and reality, and who have sought to transform that reality. There exists a long history of community experiments, and a variety of belief systems which have, in the past, inspired such ventures. To the extent that all radicals draw upon bodies of revolutionary knowledge that have been accumulated over the years, and have become institutionalized into various revolutionary schools of thought, the contemporary experimenters in communal living continue to be influenced by their predecessors. All social actors, whether they consider themselves to be radicals or not, depend to an overwhelming extent upon what Schutz termed 'socially derived knowledge' in their attempts to interpret the social world in general and their own experiences in particular. Thus:[22]

It seems to be a mere truism to state that only an exceedingly small part of our actual and potential knowledge originates in our own experience. The bulk of our knowledge consists in experiences which not we but our fellow-men, contemporaries or predecessors, have had, and which they have communicated or handed down to us.

The social actor has available to him a body of socially derived knowledge which he can draw upon in order to define and interpret the various situations in which he finds himself on his journey through life. For some people, however, the commonly accepted knowledge of the world that is accepted without question as an adequate and sufficient stock of recipes for social guidance by the majority of people, is deemed inadequate as an explanation and justification of the perceived social world. Such people, the radicals, are those who question the commonly accepted view of the world. They are cognitive deviants in so far as they hold knowledge of the world which is not generally shared, and seek to attribute new meanings to situations and events.

Now, while the source of disillusionment with the commonly accepted and generally shared body of knowledge might well be unique to each individual, the nature of the 'deviant' knowledge which he acquires is likely to be shared by others who together constitute what can be termed a cognitive minority. Moreover, the body of knowledge is likely to be socially derived also. It can be argued that any individual who begins to doubt the validity and relevance of the world view held by the majority of his contemporaries is susceptible to the appeals of an alternative body of knowledge which its adherents present as the truth. This is so, if for no other reason than the fact that the threat of personal chaos that faces the individual who has lost his faith is a terrible one of being adrift in a world which he no longer understands. The particular faith which the individual eventually adopts will depend on a variety of factors such as the kinds of books he reads, the people and groups with whom he comes into contact, the nature of his past beliefs, his position in the social structure, the nature of his complaints against society and the world view that serves to legitimate the existing social order, and so on. However, whatever the faith that he adopts, it will undoubtedly be one which has originated in the past and has been carried into the present, whether in its original purity or as an amended version, by various individuals, organizations, or other agencies of communication such as the written word. Such belief systems can present the individual with an alternative interpretation of the world, provide him with a theoretical basis and justification for his complaints against society, explain the nature of that society, provide an image of an alternative society, and present a variety of strategies by which this utopia can be attained. Thus, the radicals of the present draw upon the work and examples of their forebears, sometimes to the extent of taking the name of one of their mentors from the past as a label for their own radical philosophy and movement, such as the Marxists, or Tolstoyans.

The members of the contemporary commune movement would

13

appear to be no exception to this. An examination of the literature on past community experiments reveals a number of interesting themes that characterized the belief systems of such experimenters as the early Anabaptist sects, the mystic groups who practised communal living, the utopian socialists of the nineteenth century, and the anarcho-pacifists of the late nineteenth and early twentieth centuries.[23] Despite the obvious differences between these different types of communitarians, they would appear to have shared certain common tenets of belief, tenets which present-day communitarians also share. Amongst such shared articles of faith, one can point to the common desire to create those social conditions that would ensure man's happiness and full development. This utopian end was, for the Anabaptists, the millennium; for the Owenites it was the new 'moral order'; for the contemporary commune members it can be referred to as the 'Age of Aquarius' by those with mystic inclinations, or as the 'alternative society' by others, one of whom described it as

> a society where we think first of our fellow-man's needs and do not exploit him. And where an individual can grow and develop his full potential, and not live a life based on fear of others. A society where love and co-operation with others are the prime qualities, and not the selfishness and power seeking of our present structure.

The means chosen to pursue this end, through the establishment of communities as positive alternatives to the existing order, involves, for most contemporary commune members, just as much as it did for previous generations, a belief in the possibility and desirability of non-violent change through exemplary action based on the power of love and personal example. This orientation towards the question of social change also involves, for the modern proponents of communal living, a rejection of the philosophy that the end justifies the means. They believe, as did the communitarians of the past, that the choice of means determines the nature of the end achieved, and that the only way one can be sure of creating a non-coercive social order based on the brotherhood of man is through pursuing non-coercive means of change based on the premise of the brotherhood of man. This perspective naturally involves a rejection of the Marxist belief in the inevitability of class conflict, and the associated belief in class conflict as the motor force of historical change.[24] Just as communitarians of past ages sought to transform the nature of all aspects of social life within the context of an experimental community, so the modern commune membership denies the adequacy of merely political change alone as a means of bringing about significant social change. As one respondent phrased it:

Perhaps where political thinkers of the past have come unstuck is in that they have tried to separate economic policy from the moral structure of society. They have been concerned solely with economic and political issues. You need to completely revolutionise people's whole way of thinking and way of life, and point out to them what they consider as cherished values are, in fact, a load of rubbish.

Perhaps the key to an understanding of the projects and activities of contemporary commune members, and the experiments of their historical predecessors, lies in the belief that one member expressed to me that 'You are changing society every day as you live your life. . . . I now know that by living and acting the way I do I influence people, and if they in turn influence others, then it spreads.' This is the belief in the attainment of societal wide change through individual change. The belief that, through the individual refusing to take part in what are viewed as the rituals of conventional society, and through living a way of life in which are implemented the values that are to characterize life in the new social order, established conceptions of society and social life are challenged and the seeds of the new social order are sown.

Thus, in order to understand the utopian mentality of the contemporary commune member, and in order to explain the nature of such utopian ventures as the formation of communes in the present age, it is necessary to look at the impact of particular social forces within contemporary society upon particular social groups and individuals. It is also necessary to examine the different revolutionary traditions that such people draw upon in order to understand and explain what they view as the problematic nature of conventional life and society, and which present models of action and strategy to be pursued in order to transform the existing society and create a new social order.

Therefore the strategy adopted in the ensuing chapters is as follows:

Chapter 2 An examination of the various communitarian traditions of thought and practice available to modern-day commune members.

Chapters 3 and 4 An examination of the impact of certain social forces in contemporary society upon the lives of individuals in general, and upon the young in particular, and of some of the typical responses to what are perceived as the problems of life in conventional society.

Chapters 5 and 6 An examination of the contemporary commune movement in Britain in terms of the different types of ventures in which communitarians in general are involved.

Chapter 7 An examination of the different paths to community followed by different types of commune members.

Chapter 8 An examination of the world view of the communitarian. Accepting W. I. Thomas's statement that 'If men define their situations as real, then they are real in their consequences', this chapter represents an attempt to examine the manner in which the members of the contemporary commune movement define their situation.

Chapter 9 An examination of the claim made by many commune members that the commune represents an alternative institution to that of the nuclear family, which is typically viewed as one of the major bulwarks of the existing social order. This chapter concludes with an examination of some of the major problems encountered by communitarians in their efforts to form new ventures and maintain existing ones as ongoing enterprises.

Chapter 10 The concluding chapter attempts to examine the relevance of the commune movement as a revolutionary social movement aimed at the creation of an alternative society.

2 The communitarian tradition

The definitive feature of any deviant view of the world is that it differs from the normal, traditionally sanctioned and taken-for-granted world view prevalent in that society. Now in any complex social system there generally exists a variety of enforceable and evaluative standards and rules of conduct to guide and direct social action from one situation to the next. Objectively similar objects and events that the actor recognizes, judges and acts upon do not necessarily possess the same meaning for the actor from one situation to the next. In the social world the ordinary competent person is required to use practical wisdom to interpret the relevance of a general rule to a particular instance of the typified situation to which the rule usually pertains. The majority of people, armed with their stock of practical, common-sense wisdom and knowledge about the world, would appear to live in this world without consciously experiencing too great a strain. They are able to live with the ambiguities and contradictions inherent within the commonly accepted world view. It is taken for granted. Thus, for instance, they can accept without question that, while the generally accepted value-system might urge us to love our neighbour, in certain situations this injunction loses its validity and relevance as a guide for action, so that our neighbour in one social situation becomes our enemy in another situation, such as in time of war. Thus, while it might be generally accepted that this rule of conduct should have general relevance in some ideal, utopian world, at the level of the theory of everyday practical action in the world as it is, it is generally recognized that this rule is only applicable to a limited number of situations. In a similar manner, the ordinary competent actor on the social scene learns to distinguish between the types of situations where the telling of an untruth constitutes a blatant lie and as such is reprehensible, and those types of situations where the telling of an

17

untruth is merely a display of tact and, as such, is to be commended.

However, while the majority of people appear to be able to live with such ambiguities and problems, the radicals of society are those who view the nature of social life as problematic, and who seek to question the validity of whole areas of common-sense social knowledge. The radicals are those who ask, 'If all men are created equal, why are the terms of life so unequally loaded against so many in society?' and 'If all men are brothers, then what justification is there for people acting as if the opposite were true, as if all men were born enemies?' Seen in this light, radicals are to be found amongst those who question the taken-for-granted view of the social world, who hold knowledge of the world which is not generally shared, who seek to attribute new meanings to situations and events. Radicals are frequently those who seek a unified and internally consistent interpretation of the meaning of the world, who adopt as binding an internally consistent scheme of interpretation and who are thus obliged to reason from a rigidly supreme set of principles to all occasions of actual conduct.[1]

It is the function of radical ideologies to provide the theoretical basis and justification for such critiques of the ambiguous and hetero-geneous standards of thought and behaviour traditionally taken for granted in society. The adherents of such internally consistent interpretative schemes, when organized into collectivities and groups, have been labelled sectarians in the religious field, political and social radicals or revolutionaries in the secular field.[2] Now while a variety of forms of concrete action can result from the application and translation of such radical belief systems into the realm of general social action, the concern here is with one particular type of radical action—the establishment of communities of believers, frequently withdrawn from the world as experienced by the majority of conventional people, in which the faithful seek to create for them-selves that social life which is seen to be in accordance with the precepts, standards and injunctions of their belief system. In pursuing such a course of action they have usually sought to remould the world into greater conformity with their ideal, frequently seeking to create in microcosm the ideal social structure and mode of life, a heaven on earth, to act as a model for others to follow, so eventually leading to the creation of the ideal social order and social world.

This form of radical social action is rendered more understandable when one considers the peculiar position of the radical as a deviant. It is socially shared and taken-for-granted knowledge that allows us to move with varying degrees of confidence through our everyday life. It is the fact that the meanings which we attribute to the various situations in which we find ourselves are roughly congruent with the meanings that other relevant actors attribute to such situations that enables us to live our lives as social beings. Stable interaction depends on the actors sharing complementary definitions of objectively similar situations, on their sharing a common body of knowledge. When actors hold knowledge which is not socially shared, when they constitute a cognitive minority, then their position is inevitably an uncomfortable one in so far as the majority refuses to accept the minority's definitions of reality as relevant knowledge. Hence the plausibility of such minority knowledge is constantly threatened in the mind of the cognitive deviant.[3] Unless the members of the cognitive minority can insulate themselves in some way from the challenges of the majority to their deviant, taken-for-granted reality, then they will inevitably begin to doubt the validity of their particular version. There are various organizational strategies that can be adopted to meet this problem, generally involving some attempt on the part of the leaders of the cognitive minority to control whole areas of the everyday lives of their followers in order to prevent contamination by non-believers and sceptics. One strategy involves the creation of counter-communities, alternative societies, within which the radicals or cognitive deviants may maintain the plausibility of their knowledge. It can be argued that only through the creation of a strong sense of brotherhood and solidarity, such as is possible within a community of believers, can the challenges of the cognitive antagonists be repelled.

The following extract is taken from an account of the formation of an urban commune in Scotland which illustrates this point:[4]

The attitudes of the people in the group towards the idea of living communally are not all the same. Some people see it mainly as a functional base for a lot of people to live their own lives according to their different commitments, whereas others see it as being something for its own sake as well, an attempt at a different life style which tries to overcome some of the destructive effects of the capitalist system on ourselves— e.g. private property instincts, individualism, cynicism, apathy, lack of creativity, lack of real communication with other people. I personally feel that while it is absolutely necessary to engage oneself in the class struggle, it is also necessary to develop in one's personal life the human values of socialism.

Most of us have either recently finished University, or are nearing the end of our courses, *and some of us feel that, now that we are more exposed to the compromising forces of the broader social order, living in a group of like-minded people will help us to retain our ideological integrity and sustain an ongoing educative process.*

19

In Britain increasing numbers of people are dropping out of conventional society, a society with which they no longer feel able to identify themselves. This act of dissociating themselves from the taken-for-granted social world of the majority of people, however, is not solely a negative one of fleeing from the world. The typical drop-out sees himself as opting out of the prevailing system in order to create a new version of reality, to establish advance posts for a new social order through the formation of communes.[5] The life styles of the communards are largely based on a set of values which are counter to those typically accepted without question in modern society, such as the deferred gratification of rewards, long-term planning, the acquisition of material goods, monogamy, private property, and many others. From one point of view it is possible to see this modern movement as a collective response of certain individuals to the stresses, strains, ambiguities and contradictions that have been generated within modern urban-industrial societies such as Britain. However, to understand more fully the nature of the modern commune movement, it is necessary to see it not only in the context of modern industrialized societies, but to view this phenomenon as the most recent manifestation of a number of radical traditions with which it has certain important characteristics in common.

The formation of communes or intentional communities has been a course of action adopted by religious and secular radicals, and cognitive deviants in general, throughout history. As Margaret Mead has written:[6]

The belief that a small group of determined, like-minded idealists could set out to construct a little closed society, whose members, sharing everything, would be a living demonstration that the good life (however defined) was within the reach of dedicated human beings has recurred in almost every period of social turmoil and change.

Thus, in Britain it is possible to trace in very general terms a fairly continuous historical tradition of community building, starting with the attempts of Gerrard Winstanley and the Diggers in the mid-seventeenth century upon St George's Hill, Weybridge, to provide a practical answer to their question, 'Why may we not have our Heaven here (that is a comfortable livelihood in the Earth) and Heaven hereafter too?'[7] The attempts of Winstanley and his friends to establish a 'Heaven on Earth' were frustrated by the hostile activities of the inhabitants of Cobham Common, to where the Diggers had moved from St George's Hill. However, some indication of their influence on later experiments is evidenced by the fact that the members of a contemporary commune, sited on an island off the coast of Eire, have taken as their name the 'Diggers' Action Movement'.

From the original Diggers the thread can be followed through the Quakers and the various religious sectarian groups such as the Philadelphians, the Moravians, and the Transcendentalists in Britain; and the Shakers, the Rappites, the Hutterites, and Perfectionists abroad. In addition, the more secular threads of Robert Owen, Fourier and the utopian socialist schemes of the nineteenth century can be traced through to the anarchist and pacifist ventures of the first half of the twentieth century in Britain and America. The kibbutz movement in Israel can be viewed as a twentieth-century example of this tradition, sharing with the communitarians of previous ages the belief in the desirability and possibility of 'a renewal of society through a renewal of its cell tissue'.[8]

For a person to feel estranged from the existing order, he is likely to possess some vision of an alternative social order, a better way of life for himself and people like him. Such a vision is typically contained in the belief system adhered to by the radical. Radical belief systems generally contain two further components: an analysis and explanation of the world as it is, and an elaboration and justification of the type of strategies and means to be used in order to transform the status quo. In examining those radicals of the past who have resorted to the creation of communes as a course of action oriented towards social change, four distinct types of belief systems can be distinguished as having inspired them. A brief examination of these will serve to throw light on the different types of community ventures of the past, and how such experiments have influenced the beliefs and actions of the modern-day proponents of such a mode of life. The roots of the present movement can be discerned most clearly in the religious traditions of communal living inspired by the belief systems of world-rejecting asceticism and mysticism respectively, and in those ventures inspired by the secular traditions of utopian socialism and anarcho-pacifism.

Before going on to consider these traditions, however, mention ought to be made of another tradition of communal living inspired by both ascetic and mystic religious belief systems: that of monasticism. The origin of monasticism, like that of many non-monastic religious communities, was connected with the belief that the world is evil, and that to achieve salvation the soul must be delivered from matter and the true self be attained. To reach this end, groups of men and women have formed communities separated from other men for the purpose of seeking the quiet deemed necessary for simple devotion and contemplation. Typically, in pursuing the aim of personal sanctification, monks have adopted the three vows of poverty, chastity, and obedience. Such an orientation towards life is not commonly found in contemporary communities.[9] But to the extent that the various monastic orders have kept alive the tradition of withdrawal from the world of men by the religiously committed, a response adopted by certain of the modern-day religiously inspired communitarians, then the monastic tradition can be viewed as constituting another influence on the contemporary commune movement. To my knowledge, however, one existing monastic order has had a more direct influence on the modern movement—this is the Buddhist monastery of Samye-Ling in Scotland.[10] Founded by some Tibetan monks, this religious group has close connections with the Findhorn Centre of Light, a religious community in the north of Scotland.[11] With the growth of interest in mysticism and the religions of the Orient amongst certain sections of contemporary youth in particular, there has been a steady flow of guests and visitors to the monastery in recent years. Among such visitors has been a number of present members of the Findhorn community. It was at Samye-Ling that the existence of the Centre was first brought to their notice and their interest in the possibility of their living at Findhorn was aroused. In this way the monastic tradition associated with the Buddhist religion of Tibet has had a fairly direct, if limited, influence on the contemporary commune movement in Britain.

It is however to a consideration of the four major traditions of communal living which would appear to have had an influence on the present movement that attention will now be turned.

In March 1971 a community in London drew up a manifesto which began:[12]

> We recognise that it is our Father's will—it is in the nature of the earth—for all men's needs to be covered. Therefore we repudiate the mere financial structure of society, and we work to give food and shelter and fellowship, as rights, to our neighbour in need. And, in the service of Christ, we are serviceable one to another and bold to heal and recreate society.

In seeking in this way to 'create a society moved and sustained by the example of Christ'[13] the members of the Kingsway Community revealed certain similarities with such communitarians of the past as the Hutterites and Doukhobors, in so far as they share a similar set of religious beliefs—those of the world-rejecting ascetic, whose goal is the establishment of the kingdom of God on earth.

For the ascetic, the ways of the world are sinful and evil. He sees an inevitable and essential conflict between the ways and laws of man and the ways and the laws of God. God, for the ascetic, is a supra-mundane being who stands outside and above the world in which the human condition is situated, and which He created. God is a transcendent and omnipotent Power to whom men, as His creatures, are utterly subordinate and whose ways and injunctions must be followed if men are to attain salvation. Thus the ascetic seeks salvation through actively pursuing God's ways and living his life according to God's word in the world. Such a course of action has led, and continues to lead, to a formal withdrawal from the world of ordinary men, from 'the mere financial structure of society', into a community of believers, in so far as participation in the affairs of the world of ordinary men is viewed as inevitably implying one's acceptance of that sort of world, and therefore inevitably leading to one's estrangement from God. However, whilst the world-rejecting ascetic seeks to renounce the world and its ways, he also seeks actively to follow the sacred road, deriving assurance of his state of grace from his awareness that through his actions he serves God as an instrument of His divine will. As such, the ascetic's rejection of the world is typically seen not as a negative flight from the world, but as a positive act involving the renunciation of the world and its ethical temptations to sin, material greed, creaturely desires and appetites. Thus, while in one sense the world-rejecting ascetic is denying the world its claim on him through living in a community, at the same time it is recognized that only rational, ethical activity within the world, serving God, can enable the ascetic to attain that for which he strives—salvation.[14]

Seeking to follow the ways of God, the ascetic typically turns to the Bible, and to the New Testament in particular, as the source of insight into the path that must be followed in order to attain salvation. Thus, Cohn has written of the early sixteenth-century Anabaptist groups who formed themselves into communities of believers:[15]

> In general the Anabaptists attached relatively little importance either to theological speculations or to formal religious observances. In place of such practices as church-going they set a meticulous, literal observance of the precepts which they thought they found in the New Testament. In place of theology they cultivated the Bible—which however they were apt to interpret in the light of the direct inspirations which they believed they received from God. Their values were primarily ethical; for them religion was above all a matter of active brotherly love. Their communities were modelled on what they supposed to have been the practice of the early Church and were intended to realise the ethical ideal propounded by Christ.

The members of these Anabaptist groups generally consisted of those craftsmen and peasants who found themselves displaced by a changing economy. A confession of faith adopted by the Swiss Anabaptists in 1527 gives some idea of the major tenets of their belief: it endorsed adult baptism, the use of the ban on all members who fell into 'error and sin', the observance of communion 'in remembrance of the broken body of Christ', the authority of the elected minister of the church, and rejected the primacy of the temporal over the spiritual power in the form of the rejection of the oath and the use of the sword. For them the New Testament was the sole authority in spiritual matters. They believed that if a person felt that the directive from the Scripture was unequivocal, then he had no other choice but to follow the dictates of divine guidance. Since only a mature adult could bear such a responsibility, they rejected infant baptism.

Some of the Anabaptist communal groups formed in those days have remained faithful to their original beliefs up to the modern age. Thus it has been estimated that there were approximately 17,800 Hutterites in North America in 1965, living in 164 communities known as Bruderhöfe.[16] The spiritual roots of the Hutterites can be traced to the Swiss Brethren who had fled from Switzerland in 1528 in order to avoid persecution from the state. Taking their name from one of their early leaders, Jacob Huter, the Hutterian Brethren viewed, and continue to view, the world as carnal, corrupt, idolatrous, fun-seeking, and therefore removed from God. To live in the world would necessarily involve the compromising of the literal observation of the teachings of the early Christian Church. Their aim was, and is, to emulate as closely as possible the life of the early Christians as related in the Acts of the Apostles, and in order to fulfil this aim they have sought to withdraw from the world. This rejection of the world takes the form of a refusal to accept public office, the refusal to participate in the election of public officials, and the refusal to involve themselves in litigations based on man-made laws.[17] More generally, the rejection of the world involves the rejection of those modern innovations such as the radio and television which they see as threatening the seclusion of the colony. At the same time, the Brethren must make money to live, and are therefore forced to arrive at some accommodation with the world of men in general, and the market economy in particular. However, even in this department of communal life their activities are guided by their religious precepts. They are allowed to make money by selling the agricultural goods that they produce with their own hands, but they are forbidden to buy and sell the same goods for profit. Moreover, they do not produce manufactured goods for profitable sale as such a commercial practice would bring them too close to the ways of the world, and divorce them from the ways of God.

The Hutterites share with other Anabaptist groups, such as the Mennonites and the Amish, the belief that all Christians must be united in the bond of love for Christ and each other. A belief reflected in the claim of the members of the Kingsway Community in London that 'We intend to create a society, moved and sustained by the example of Christ, in which we deal with each other as brothers and sisters'.[18] In order to maintain the bond of love and self-effacement, the Hutterites seek to organize their society and economy according to egalitarian principles. This aim is expressed in the concept of *Gelassenheit*—a term which implies the submission of one's whole nature to God's will, as the instrument of His transcendent authority. The community of all goods which is the basis of the Hutterite economic organization is based on the literal interpretation of Acts 2: 41–5:

Then they that gladly received his word were baptized . . .
And they continued stedfastly in the apostles' doctrine
and fellowship, and in breaking of bread, and in prayers . . .
And all that believed were together, and had all things
common; And sold their possessions and goods, and parted
them to all men, as every man had need.

Each Hutterite colony is organized and administered along similar lines. All important decisions concerning the running of the colony are arrived at by a majority vote of all adult male members. Women are not permitted to participate in their assemblies or to vote. A council of about half a dozen senior members of the community, including among its members the minister, the colony steward and the farm foreman, constitutes the executive arm of the colony. In keeping with the emphasis on egalitarianism, however, no position in the colony entails the right to be exempted from manual labour. Moreover, the authority of the elders and heads is rarely made manifest. For the Hutterites, the leaders show the way and it is rare for them to chide others for shoddy work. Instead, they set the pace, while group pressure is almost invariably sufficient to prevent individual acts of deviance.

In seeking to set themselves apart from the rest of the world in communities of believers, the Hutterites appear to represent an excellent example of what Wilson has defined as the 'utopian sect', whose response to the world consists[19]

Partly in withdrawing from it, and partly in wishing to remake
it to a better specification. . . . It sets out through its activities
to construct the world on a communitarian basis. It does not

seek only to establish colonies but also proposes a programme
for the reorganisation of the world along community lines.

However, the Hutterites can also be viewed as a particular type of
utopian sect, those inspired by a religious belief system that can be
described as world-rejecting asceticism, those inspired by the
example of Christ and the belief in the relevance and validity of the
moral injunctions contained in the New Testament for the attainment of salvation through the performance of God's will. I have
attempted to show that certain communes and commune members
in contemporary Britain are inspired by a similar set of beliefs.[20]
However, while it is possible for the sociologist to stand outside
the communitarian tradition, so to speak, and perceive similarities
between the beliefs and practices of experimenters in communal
living of different epochs, it is a different question altogether as to
whether actual members of contemporary communes feel themselves
and their actions to have been influenced in any way by the examples
of those who have trodden similar types of paths before them.
What one generally discovers, in fact, is that very few members of
contemporary communes, inspired by Christian beliefs or not,
reveal any detailed awareness of such groups as the Hutterites.
Rather, one finds a general awareness, particularly among those who
feel that through living in a commune they are fulfilling their
obligations as Christians, that the formation of communes has been
one possible course of action that has been pursued by sectarian-
type Christians of previous generations, including the members of
monastic orders, and a view of themselves as comparable with the
apostles of the early Christian Church and the life of Christian
purity which the apostles attempted to lead. The path followed by
ideas is not a simple and direct one. Such groups as the Hutterites
can be said to have had an influence on contemporary communes
such as the Kingsway Community in so far as they have kept alive a
particular type of Christian response to the world, the withdrawal
from conventional society into communities of believers. What this
has meant is that such a form of action enters into the realm of
possible solutions considered by those members of contemporary
society who experience particularly acutely the tension and conflict
between the ways of the world and the ways of God. Even if such
people have little or no detailed knowledge about particular experiments in communal living of the past, they generally possess an
awareness that the formation of communes has been one solution
pursued by people of the past who, like them, felt themselves to be
faced by the problem of being 'in' the world at the same time as not
wishing to be 'of' the world.

However, during the course of my research I did come into contact with two people who had spent some years of their lives living in religious communities which were partly inspired and certainly influenced in their actual organization and relationship to the world by the example of the Hutterites. One of these was a housewife in her thirties who was involved in an attempt to form a commune in the south-west of England, the other was a farmer who had apparently given up all hope of ever changing the world by any form of collective action. Both of them had lived as members of a communitarian sect known as the Society of Brothers, whose colonies were generally known by the same label as that applied to the colonies of the Hutterites—the 'Bruderhof'.

The Bruderhof was a communitarian group founded by Eberhard Arnold in Germany in 1920 after he had become convinced, through reading the Acts of the Apostles, that any truly Christian community had to be based on full economic communism. The beliefs that led Arnold to this decision identify him very clearly with the tradition of world-rejecting asceticism as represented by the Hutterites. He wrote:[21]

> I tried by means of Bible study and talks to lead people to Jesus.
> But there came a time when this was no longer enough. . . .
> I recognised more and more the need of men, the need of their
> bodies and souls, their material and social needs, their
> humiliation, their exploitation and their enslavement. I
> recognised the tremendous power of Mammon, of discord, of
> hate, and of the sword. . . . I felt that I had to find a way to
> come to an actual service of mankind; to a dedication which
> not only was a meeting of individual souls, but a dedication
> which would establish a monument in real life by which men
> could recognise the cause for which Jesus died . . . it became
> clear to me that the first Christian community in Jerusalem was
> more than a historical happening; rather, it was here that the
> Sermon on the Mount came to life.
>
> It is necessary today as it never has been that we renounce the
> last vestige of our privilege and rights, and let ourselves be won
> for this way of total love; the love that will pour itself out over
> the land from the breath of the Holy Spirit; the love that was
> born out of the first church-community.

Arnold sought to emulate in his community the lives led by the early Christians, one characterized by openness, communism, purity, pacifism, simplicity and unity.[22] As such, he realized in 1928, after reading about the Hutterites, the similarity between his conception of the Christian life and the life led in the colonies of the Hutterites. In the 1930s Arnold and his followers were accepted into the Hutterite Church. In 1936 the members of the group purchased a farm in the Cotswolds, moving to Britain to escape the Nazi threat in Germany. In Britain they were joined by British converts, including the two people I met during the course of my research. They were given support in Britain by various Quaker groups. However, by 1966 the property which the Bruderhof had bought near Gerrard's Cross had been sold, and today the Society of Brothers consists of three communities in the eastern U.S.A. with a total population of around a thousand members. Before 1966, however, both the housewife who was involved in trying to form a commune and the farmer had left, and for similar reasons. They had both found the regime within the Bruderhof too rigid for their personal tastes. They had felt that within the colony every aspect of their life was dominated by group pressure towards conformity. Their experience was that to live in a Bruderhof demanded the complete surrender of the self to the community and the group as a whole—a sacrifice which they felt, eventually, that they could not make. This conflict between the desire for brotherhood and community and the desire for privacy and individual freedom constitutes one of the major problems of community living. It is a problem that is constantly raised in discussion with members of contemporary communes.[23] However, the housewife had felt her experiences at the Bruderhof to have been valuable, she was still concerned to form a commune in which she could live a life according to her beliefs, but she stressed to me that she would never again live in a commune where the authority of the group was paramount and where the autonomy of the individual was threatened. In her person, however, she could be viewed as representing a concrete link between the communes of contemporary Britain and the communes of the world-rejecting ascetics of the past.

However, certain contemporary communes and commune members in Britain bear the marks of a religious tradition other than that of world-rejecting asceticism—that of mysticism. Whilst the members of the Kingsway Community and similar ventures in Britain[24] view themselves as the inheritors of the sacred knowledge that stems from God and his Son, Jesus Christ, and the early Christians, other people in other communes appear to have turned towards the religious traditions of the Orient for guidance and inspiration. Briefly stated, the ideal-typical world view of the mystic is of God or divine power standing within and throughout the world, an immanent force. The personal quest of the mystic is to achieve that subjective condition which may be enjoyed as possession of, or mystic union with, the divine. He desires to become a vessel, rather than an instrument, of the divine. Man is seen as possessing a dual nature, a worldly ego and an eternal self. The latter is viewed as that part of the divine power which is called the soul. The individual attains oneness with the divine by identifying himself with this eternal self and forgetting his worldly ego. Thus, for the mystic, activity within this world can never give him certainty of his state of grace, and might serve to divert his attentions from his attempts to attain oneness with the divine. Thus, the mystic can be led to reject the world of men, to remove himself from it and to form communities withdrawn from the world of everyday people as a means of avoiding the world and associated subjective desires and temptations.

Whilst the mystic orientation towards the sacred world has been more typical of the Orient than of the Occident, the West has had its own tradition of mystics. Meister Eckhardt in the fourteenth century, Jakob Boehme in the seventeenth, Emanuel Swedenborg in the eighteenth, and Friedrich Von Scheeling in the nineteenth were all exemplars of this mode of viewing the relationship between man and the divine, as were Madame Blavatsky, Gurdjieff, Ouspensky, Annie Besant, and Rudolf Steiner who spanned the nineteenth and early twentieth centuries. Boehme and Swedenborg appear to have exerted a particularly marked influence on the development of early community ventures in Britain. Thus one of the leading Diggers of the seventeenth century, William Everard, had also been a member of a community at Bradfield under John Pordage. Pordage, as a consequence of reading the work of Boehme, had 'received from the Lord a stamp and strong impression of power moving our wills to follow the light through the death of all things, to come up into the perfect life and image of God'.[25] Winstanley, the leader of the Diggers, later joined a group led by George Fox. The early Quakers, with their message that stressed the personal experience of the inner light and an immanent God that was recognizable and could be inwardly known by all, can also be considered as belonging to the spiritual ancestors of certain types of modern communitarians.

Coleridge, who with his friend Southey had entertained serious thoughts of settling in America to form a community, paid tribute to the influence Fox and Boehme had exerted on him: 'the writings of these mystics acted in no slight degree to prevent my mind from being imprisoned within the outline of any single dogmatic system. They contributed to keep alive the heart in the head.'[26] William Blake, who believed that 'God is Man and exists in us and we in him', and who sought to 'build Jerusalem in England's green and pleasant land', had also absorbed significant aspects of Swedenborg's doctrines. Blake is now firmly established as one of the prophets of the contemporary 'underground' movement, from whose members the modern communitarians are largely drawn. Indeed, one commune member quoted to me Blake's vision of Jerusalem when he was seeking to express the nature of his ideal, alternative society. Swedenborg's influence also made itself felt, indirectly, in Rochdale in 1844 when the twenty-eight 'Rochdale Pioneers' established their co-operative. Their aim was:[27]

> As soon as practicable, this society shall proceed to arrange the powers of production, distribution, education and government, or in other words to establish a self-supporting home colony of united interest, or assist other societies in establishing such colonies.

One of the movers behind this experiment, which was to grow into the giant Co-operative Wholesale Society, was a local preacher for the Swedenborgians, John Scowcroft.

In such a fashion the thread of mysticism linked different types of community ventures in Britain through the seventeenth, eighteenth and nineteenth centuries. This thread was to continue into the twentieth century with a disciple of Jakob Boehme arguing for the revival of 'the small country community', for people to desert the urban centres of population where 'overpopulation and over organisation' have made 'a fully human life of multiple relationships . . . almost impossible'.[28] This was Aldous Huxley, whose own utopian vision portrayed in *Island* has continued to inspire contemporary utopians.

Huxley's own experiences with hallucinogenic drugs, which he interpreted in terms of mysticism, meant that he became one of the first public figures to present such drugs as mescaline and lysergic acid (LSD) as chemical aids to the attainment of oneness with what he termed the 'Divine Ground' and 'Ultimate Reality'.[29] In fact, many of the tenets of the mystic's view of the nature of life and the divine are shared by the drug-using members of the contemporary underground movement who have been instrumental in the formation and expansion of a number of communes in contemporary Britain. For many of them, drug experiences are defined in pantheistic terms, and the goals of drug-taking are expressed in terms of expanding the consciousness in order to attain that level of awareness whereby the individual becomes one with the divine. Likewise, the pride of place given by many 'heads' to development of their inner psychic state with the associated devaluation of active involvement in the material world mirrors the mystic's awareness that the purpose of life is not to conquer the material world but is rather to conquer the ego and to discover one's true self, and so become one with God. Moreover, many trippers claim to have become aware, through their drug experiences, of the essential unity of all things, of the universal link that is immanent throughout all things, especially between the brotherhood of man. The attempt to form a commune follows quite naturally for those who seek to pursue the twin goals of realizing one's essential self and demonstrating the unity of all life, especially when such motives are combined with a devaluation of active involvement with the world.

Very frequently, in communes, one finds young people who have defined their drug experiences in such terms, and who have embarked upon a self-imposed course of study of the writings of mystics of previous ages such as Gurdjieff, Ouspensky, Blavatsky and Steiner, as well as the traditional works of the Eastern mystics. For example, I remember talking at some length with one member of a commune that was established in Middlesex who asked me with great excitement whether I had ever read any of the works of Madame Blavatsky, the founder in 1875 of the Theosophical Society.[30] On another occasion, at the Camphill-Rudolf Steiner School for handicapped children near Aberdeen, I met a young worker who told me of his wide experiences with drugs, but who had ceased to rely on such chemical aids to the expansion of consciousness since he had become interested in the work of Steiner. Generally, it is only when such people start reading the works of such figures of the past that they realize that the goals they are seeking through the formation of communes in the present age place them quite clearly as the contemporary carriers of a long tradition of community ventures inspired by the world-view of the mystic.

Not all communes of the past, of course, were inspired by religious belief systems, just as only a minority of contemporary communes can comfortably be slotted into one of the two religious types suggested above. In fact, a number of communes of the past were inspired by world views that were specifically anti-religious. Among such ventures one can include those labelled originally by the Marxists as experiments in utopian socialism. Marx and Engels contemptuously dismissed the systems propounded by such figures as St Simon, Fourier, and Robert Owen as the fruits of an epoch in which industry and the capitalist system of property ownership had not fully matured, and hence, 'the proletariat, as yet in its infancy, offers to them the spectacle of a class without any historical initiative or any independent political movement.'[31] While recognizing the value of the criticisms of the existing conditions on which these utopian systems were built, they argued that all their positive recommendations were condemned to lose all practical value and theoretical justification in the course of historical development.[32]

However, the growth of communes in America and Britain in recent years, comparable to the growth of similar ventures in these countries in the nineteenth century under the impact of Owen and Fourier in particular, would appear to indicate that such schemes have retained some of their relevance for the present day. In seeking to explain this, one would have to take into account the spread of disillusionment among many radicals with what appear to many as the only alternative roads to socialism: the Marxist model involving the dictatorship of the proletariat as practised/distorted in the Soviet Union and Eastern Europe, and the Fabian model as exemplified by the British Labour Party.

In recent years there has been a growing loss of faith by British radicals in the possibility of the Labour Party ever proving itself to be a genuine radical alternative to the Conservative Party. Increasing numbers of people, especially amongst the ranks of the commune members, have lost any belief in the Labour Party as a socialist party concerned with the creation of a society characterized by social, political and economic egalitarianism. This disillusionment with the Labour Party has frequently become generalized into a disenchantment with the parliamentary system of government itself. As one commune member expressed his feelings to me:

> Before 1964 I threw everything into the Labour Party. I was a delegate and secretary for the local branch. At one point it did look as if we would transform Labour from within, locally we were very strong. I left about a year ago through disillusionment with the party and with party politics as well. There is a complete lack of understanding of the needs of the people. Once a person becomes a professional politician, he loses contact with the people completely. The idea of socialism died overnight when Labour got in.

At the same time, such people are revolted by the path to utopia adopted by the socialists of such states as the Soviet Union. The Stalinist purges, the denial to individuals of their civil liberties, as exemplified particularly in the trials of Daniel and Sinyavski, the suppression of the Hungarian Revolution in 1956, and the invasion of Czechoslovakia in 1968 have all contributed to a disillusionment with the state socialist strategy for social change. Such people have been brought to a position where they share the view of Martin Buber, that with 'scientific socialism'[33]

> a yawning chasm opens out before us which can only be bridged by that special form of Marxist utopics, a chasm between, on the one side, the transformation to be consummated sometime in the future—no one knows how long after the final victory of the Revolution—and, on the other, the road to the Revolution and beyond it, which road is characterised by a far-reaching centralisation that permits no individual features and no individual initiative. Uniformity as a means is to change miraculously into multiplicity as an end; compulsion into freedom.

Like Buber they are attracted by a third alternative which for them has involved the formation of communes and which, for Buber, was characterized as that of the utopian or non-Marxist socialist who[34]

> desires a means commensurate with his ends; he refuses to believe
> that in our reliance on the future 'leap' we have to do now the
> direct opposite of what we are striving for; he believes rather
> that we must create here and now the space *now* possible for the
> thing for which we are striving, so that it may come to fulfilment
> *then*; he does not believe in the post-revolutionary leap, but he
> does believe in a continuity within which revolution is only the
> accomplishment, the setting free and extension of reality that has
> already grown to its true possibilities.

Although Buber wrote this in 1949, he might well have been describing the strategy for social change envisaged by certain contemporary commune members who view their activities in terms of constructing an alternative society. The desirability of non-violent social change, the need to destroy the existing system by gradually replacing it by a brand new and alternative society—these are the themes emphasized by contemporary commune members, just as they were stressed by the utopian socialists such as Owen.

There is the same belief in the possibility of transforming society through the agency of model experimental communities, a strategy which involves a strong emphasis on the decentralization of power and control in society. As one respondent expressed it, when asked what he understood by the term 'alternative society':

> it means this sort of germ of a new society within the old which
> is based on a very different system of values and norms which
> are in a sense socialist, in the sense of being anti-capitalist, but
> at the same time not political . . . it is basing economic action
> and such like on a different set of motives than profit and
> money. It is because of other people that you do something and
> not because of the profit you are going to get out of it.

This same respondent, talking about the possibility of achieving social change through violent means, typified the view of violence held by many of the nineteenth-century utopian socialists and the twentieth-century communitarians:

> I used to think so [that violence can bring meaningful social
> change] but now I tend not to. You can achieve a goal but not
> satisfactorily. It [violence] can achieve what you want but if it
> is bred out of violence it will not be what it should be.

Another perspective common to both commune members of the present age and the utopian socialists of the past is the view of the nuclear family as one of the major bulwarks of the existing social order, and that any attempt to transform society must also involve an attempt to transform the pattern of family life in society.[35] Thus, the view of Owen that 'separate interests and individual family arrangements with private property are essential parts of the existing irrational system. They must be abandoned with the system'[36] can be seen reflected in the words of such commune members as the respondent who informed me that

> I am a radical in that I think that the social structure is rotten and needs to be changed. A commune is my way. You have to start with the family, and whilst this might take a generation or so there will be communes flourishing all over the place.

Another respondent wrote of his motives for wanting to form a commune in somewhat similar terms: 'we believe that man is really a social animal and needs to live in a wilder and less fragmented way than the usual system we live in this society of individuals and married couples interacting with other such couples and individuals.'[37]

Another characteristic attitude shared by contemporary communitarians with certain utopian socialists of the past is the romantic strain of pastoralism that can be discerned in the writings of Owen in particular. Thus, Harrison has written:[38]

> At the back of most Owenite plans for community was a utopian vision of a propertyless, equalitarian society; of men working together in the fields, taking from the common stock according to their needs, and engaging in intellectual pursuits in their ample leisure time. In such a society there was a source of satisfaction and independence; and feelings of anger, envy and all uncharitableness were dismissed as unworthy of a rational being.

The same utopian vision can be located in the thoughts of contemporary communitarians. Thus, the respondent last quoted also wrote in the same letter to *Communes*:

> At the risk of being accused of wanting to 'get back to nature' or 'back to the land', let us admit that that is indeed just what we want. It seems to us, and we don't pretend to be unique in this, that we have come too far from natural things, from growth and air and light, from the seasons of fruiting and decay and from the sources of creativity, maturity, and self-knowledge. While not particularly wanting to live a 'primitive' life in any sense, we do feel that a closer relationship with plants, trees, and unpolluted air than that possible in a town is desirable and essential.

Other parallels between the utopian socialists and the modern-day utopians of the commune movement can be drawn. For instance, whereas Marx viewed class conflict as one of the major motor forces of history, and socialism was seen as the necessary outcome of the struggle between the 'two great classes directly facing each other: bourgeoisie and proletariat', for Owen the belief in class antagonism was irrational and irrelevant. The task for the working classes, as defined by Owen, was to know themselves so that they might discover what other men were. He believed that for the first time in human history, in the early nineteenth century, there existed the necessary basis for the good environment, that environment which would be productive of human happiness. Thus in an address he delivered on 1 January 1816 he remarked:

> What ideas individuals may attach to the term Millennium, I know not; but I know that society may be formed so as to exist without crime, without poverty, with health greatly improved, with little, if any, misery, and with intelligence and happiness increased a hundred-fold; *and no obstacle whatsoever intervenes at this moment except ignorance, to prevent such a state of society from becoming universal.*

In similar fashion the members of the contemporary commune movement in general do not emphasize the role of the working classes as the human agents through which the new social order will be realized. More typical of their perspective was the remark made by one respondent who argued, 'I don't see the proletariat rising up and throwing off their chains, because half the time they are very tightly holding the chains on.' Reminiscent of the utopian socialists, they emphasize the role of education and exemplary action as the non-coercive means necessary for the attainment of a new social order, a new order to be achieved through the transformation of society from the bottom up rather than from the top down. As one commune member phrased it:

> I don't think you can remould society by taking it en bloc.
> But one can do so, I think, by setting up lots of little examples.
> If they are good, people will follow them, if not and they don't,
> well they don't deserve to be followed.

For the vast majority of commune members the key lever for social change was defined as residing in the consciousness of individuals, problems of social change were seen as revolving around the 'question of awareness, of gradually trying to make others more aware'.

In emphasizing their view that social change can be obtained mainly through the agency of change at the level of the individual, in stressing, as one respondent phrased it, that 'you are changing society every day as you live your life', many contemporary communitarians revealed themselves to be the inheritors of a fourth tradition of thought and practice concerning intentional communities —that represented by the anarcho-pacifists.

Anarchism has typically been associated in the public mind with political terrorism, 'propaganda by the deed'. However, the anarchist tradition in which one can locate certain roots of the modern commune movement was associated with a particular form of non-violent propaganda by the deed: the creation of libertarian communities. It is possible to argue that the only political philosophy that is consistent with the non-violent philosophy of life is anarchism. Such anarcho-pacifists as Tolstoy have traditionally accepted the moral supremacy of the injunctions contained in the Sermon on the Mount, and have determined to live their lives in accordance with the moral code contained therein. For the anarcho-pacifist, the acceptance of the non-violent philosophy of life entails an attempt to resist evil with good and a refusal to impose one's will upon another. Non-violence for the anarcho-pacifist is not just an alternative means of attaining specific goals, but is rather a philosophy of life which, if taken seriously, can frequently lead to the formation of libertarian communities. Such a course of action follows naturally from Tolstoy's injunction that one must cease to co-operate with that which one condemns. The refusal of the individual to obey any laws or pursue any conventions felt to be unjust was the greatest revolutionary force in Tolstoy's eyes. This view was echoed by Gandhi when he wrote that 'it is possible for a single individual to defy the whole might of an unjust empire to save his honour, his religion, his soul, and lay the foundation for that empire's fall or regeneration'.[39]

One of the most powerful statements of the anarcho-pacifist position can be found in the writings of R. Sampson, a British pacifist who has had a considerable influence on a number of pacifists in contemporary Britain. He has written:[40]

The purpose of life is to exemplify goodness at the expense of badness, and thus to strengthen the force of goodness in the world. . . . Violence itself is the outcome of the will to power in man. . . . It is this will to power which is the source of most of the evils which threaten to overwhelm us.

To abstain, therefore, from the quest for power is logically entailed by an understanding of the evil of violence. To renounce power means abandoning all idea of getting power, of seeking to overthrow the rulers, of bringing about a revolution, of devising blue-prints for new institutions. In their stead, anarchists seek to eradicate the evil potentialities in themselves and by so doing to change the nature of their relations with other men. When enough people succeed in doing this, the social institutions which reflect existing human beliefs and relations, will of necessity begin to change.

Such a statement is echoed by those commune members who share the belief expressed by one member that 'By living a different way of life, we can make some people sit up and think "maybe there is another way of life, maybe we ought to change our way of life. . . ." If people want to follow, that is fair enough.'

This perspective, in fact, appeared to be typical of that held by the majority of commune members whom I encountered during the course of my research. They shared with the members of the general social movement, the underground, the emphasis on 'doing your own thing' and the stress on the importance of individual freedom. Indeed, one respondent went so far as to define the alternative society, towards the creation of which he felt himself to be working, in terms of its being a society where 'everyone can have the right and the space to exercise their creative autonomy'. Another respondent defined the alternative society as

a society in which the alternative is always open. Present society is monolithic. I regard the alternative society as one where, if you don't like where you are, there are always a few choices available. . . . Freedom of choice is the prime criterion. Do what you like and it made easy to do what you like.

In this emphasis on the importance of individual freedom, the contemporary communitarians display what many commentators have stressed is the essence of anarchist thought. Thus they share with the anarcho-pacifists of the past a rejection of the attempts by the utopian socialists to create static blueprints of the future society, the models for which were embodied in their experimental communities. As Woodcock remarked:[41]

In fact the very idea of utopia repels most anarchists, because it is a rigid mental construction which, if successfully imposed, would prove as stultifying as any existing state to the free development of those subjected to it. Moreover, utopia is conceived as a perfect society, and anything perfect has automatically ceased growing.

The refusal of anarchists to entertain rigid schemes or blueprints about the perfect society has not, however, deterred them from embarking upon their own attempts to create for themselves more ideal forms of life through the creation of communities. One such venture was founded at Whiteway in the Cotswolds at the beginning of this century by some ex-members of a Tolstoyan community that had a brief life at Purleigh in Essex in the 1890s. Of his motives for joining the experiment at Whiteway, one of the founders was later to write:[43]

> It is hard to say if it was the horror of industrial cities or the degradation of the workers, or shame in my participation in an evil system that gave me a passionate desire to escape to some spot where I and my friends could settle and cultivate land.

True anarchists, the founder members of Whiteway considered the private ownership of property not only immoral but also nonsensical. However, they felt obliged to meet the requirements of the law with regard to the drawing-up of ownership deeds for their land. Three of them agreed to sign the necessary document, and then the group proceeded to burn it in ritualistic fashion over an open fire.[44] From mainly middle-class backgrounds, like the members of contemporary communes, their aims reflected the influence of such anarcho-pacifists as Tolstoy and Thoreau:[45]

> To live a happy, idyllic life, free from carking care and the responsibility of property? Yes, that and something more. We do not set ourselves up as reformers of society, but try to reform ourselves. If we cannot be actively useful and good we can at least cease doing evil by competing with others, or spending our energies in some useless way. . . . To live as far as possible up to our ideals is what we are striving for.

The anarchist leanings of the members was further revealed in their refusal to map out blueprints for the future society or to lay down dogmatic rules about the organization of the colony.[46]

> At no time did we formulate any creed or define our position. No one was asked what his opinions were or required to subscribe to any doctrine. It was believed that all who joined would quite naturally wish to do their share of the necessary work. We had a simple child-like belief in the inherent goodness of human nature, and imagined that, given good conditions, equal and loving treatment, people would respond and give of their best.

Unfortunately, things did not work out that way. The inevitable problems that stem from the gathering together of a group of heterogeneous individuals with different levels of commitment to different sets of ideas plagued the life of the community. Possessions were stolen, people refused to work the communal land, emotional problems beset the group and lost them many sympathizers, particularly when one young couple separated and the wife began living with another member. One member took away some livestock which he considered to be his private property, while another member gave away a whole variety of communally-owned goods. Eventually it was decided to virtually abandon the original communalistic principles and to allow each member to take possession of an individual plot of land. On this basis new settlers continued to arrive until all the available land was taken up. On this individualistic basis the settlement has continued up to the present day.

Just as the problems encountered by the members of the Whiteway colony correspond with the problems now faced by contemporary communitarians,[47] so important aspects of their world view which inspired the venture are reflected in the perspectives of the members of the modern movement. One finds the same emphasis upon the desirability of a life led close to nature, the same rejection of any attempt to devise blueprints for new institutions, the same idealization of the simple life where a man can live by the fruits of his own labour in a state of dignified poverty as was shared by Tolstoy, Thoreau and Gandhi. Perhaps most significant of all, one finds among contemporary communitarians the emphasis upon the right of the individual to do his own thing, to follow his own path;[48] along with an equal emphasis upon the prime need for the individual to transform his own life if meaningful social change is to be attained.[49]

Thus it is possible to discern certain important similarities between the ideas and actions of communitarians of the present age and their predecessors. In particular it can be argued that the modern-day exemplars of this radical form of social action share with the world-rejecting ascetics of the past a concern to live a life according to a higher set of moral principles than those normally accepted and taken for granted by members of conventional society; they share with the mystics of the past a concern with developing self-awareness through a variety of yogic methods. The recognition by many of the contemporary commune members of the apparent unity and link between all things and their feeling for nature, also mirrors the concern of many mystics of the past. Like the utopian socialists of the nineteenth century the contemporary utopians seek to change the world through exemplary action by non-violent, non-coercive means, emphasizing the role of education in the creation of a new social order. The emphasis of the members of the modern movement upon individual autonomy, upon the need for social change through individual change, and the attainment of social liberation through individual liberation, mirrors the traditional concerns of the anarcho-pacifists, as does their reluctance to devise rigid blueprints for their alternative society.

That there are important similarities between the world views of contemporary communitarians and those of the past would appear to be beyond doubt. However, it is to a rather different problem that attention will be turned in concluding this chapter: that is, to what extent are the members of contemporary communes aware of whether or not they have been influenced in any way with regard to their beliefs and courses of action by the examples of their predecessors, whether ascetic, mystic, utopian socialist or anarcho-pacifist?

Whatever the protestations that might be made by the members of any particular experiment that all the members are of equal status as individuals, to the observer it often appears that a crude distinction can be made in the membership between the founders, opinion leaders, or spokesmen of the group and the 'joiner' or rank-and-file members. That is, in most communes one discovers one or two individuals who to some extent act as spokesmen and opinion leaders for their group. They are the ones responsible mainly for the writing of the manifestos, the letters, and so on. They are the people whose voice is given most weight in the group discussions. They are frequently those who were directly involved in the formation of the group, in getting the commune together. The opinions they help to shape, not always intentionally, are those of their fellow commune members who have joined the original nucleus of founder members. Thus, even in the largest of communes, such as the now deceased Eel Pie Island Commune, one would frequently be informed of the latest experiences or statements of belief or observations made by certain key individuals whom some of the rank-and-file members considered to be the 'gurus' of the venture.

In general it would appear, from my observation, that such spokesmen are far more aware of the past history of community experiments and of the variety of traditions associated with this history as personified in the lives and thoughts of certain key historical figures than are the more rank-and-file members. They are also more likely to admit to being influenced by the work and writings of such people as Jesus Christ, Tolstoy, Gandhi, Thoreau, Robert Owen, William Morris, Rudolf Steiner, Gurdjieff, Ouspensky, Huxley, Madame Blavatsky and so on. Very often such people are a year or two older than the other members, with a wider experience and perspective upon the relationship between commune ventures and conventional society derived from their previous involvement in secular and religious movements of a radical or 'deviant' nature. They are more likely to adhere to an internally consistent interpretative schema of the world derived from their personal experiences and original thoughts, and their reading of the thoughts and practices of previous generations of communitarians. It is among such people that one can discover fairly direct links between the various traditions of thought and practice associated with the history of community experiments and the present-day movement.

In contrast to the ideal-typical spokesman or opinion leader, the typical rank-and-file member or 'joiner' is younger and does not share the former's length of experience in social movements or his breadth of knowledge of the various communitarian traditions. Typically, the 'joiner' has become a member of a commune through a general feeling of dissatisfaction with the nature of his life in conventional society. Through some experience or other he has become aware that others share his feelings, and that many of them, with whom he feels some kind of identity, have sought a solution through dropping out of society to form communes. The examples of the kibbutz in Israel and the communes in contemporary America, the coverage of community experiments in Britain and abroad in the underground press and the mass media in general, are the kinds of things that can make the dissident member of society aware of the possibility of seeking a solution to the kinds of problems he experiences himself through joining a commune. Finally, such experiences as an encounter with a member of an existing group or with someone who is attempting to start a group, or a visit to an existing commune, help the individual to crystallize in his own mind a project of action involving him in joining a communal group.

Generally speaking, at this stage of joining a commune the individual possesses only a limited knowledge of the communitarian traditions of thought and practice. Greater significance is granted to the writings in the underground press and the feelings and thoughts expressed in contemporary popular music than to the writings of representatives of previous generations. Once an individual has joined a commune, however, it is highly likely that his awareness of the history of community experiments and the influence of previous utopians upon his own thoughts and actions will grow, as he comes into contact with fellow members who have been influenced by the examples from the past and who talk with the new member, lend him books, and so on. For such people, then, the influence of their predecessors in communal living is transmitted through the agencies of the contemporary underground press, and the spokesmen and opinion leaders of the communes of which they are members. The influence of the past is brought to bear upon the majority of commune members of the present through a multi-stage process, a simple model of which is outlined below.

Stage 1 The thoughts and practical activities of past exemplars of the communitarian tradition are recorded in books, etc.

Stage 2   Certain of these works are read by a number of individuals of later generations.

Stage 3   The world views of such individuals are influenced by their reading, as are their practical activities inspired by such world views.

Stage 4   The views of such people, as expressed in their writings, discussions, activities in general, and possibly as expressed in their attempts to form a commune, serve to influence certain of their contemporaries. In their role as commune leaders they act as significant others in the socialization of certain of their peers into the deviant, radical subculture and its associated world view.

Stage 5   Through the influence of such significant others as commune leaders individuals are made aware of the writings, works, and experiments of previous generations of communitarians and begin to define themselves as contemporary carriers of the traditions which are represented by them.

It is through such processes that the influence of past communitarians has been brought to bear, frequently in indirect fashion, upon the members of the contemporary movement. However, in order to understand why certain individuals are dropping out of contemporary society in order to form communes, it is necessary not only to examine the various radical traditions of thought and practice which have influenced them in choosing such a course of action, one must also examine the origins and nature of their estrangement from the existing order of society. It is to this problem that attention is turned in the following chapters.

3 Man in society

The formation of intentional communities has traditionally been associated with an attitude of world rejection and flight from the realities of conventional existence. To the extent that members of communes in contemporary Britain are seeking to opt out of conventional life, then they too can be viewed as fleeing from the world. One does not drop out of society to join a commune in the hope of contributing towards the creation of an alternative society without experiencing some forms of estrangement and disaffection from the existing order. The purpose of this chapter and the next is to present a tentative analysis of the sources of the estrangement of contemporary commune members from what they define as conventional society.

Most forms of radical social action have their origins in some felt estrangement on the part of the individual from the prevailing social order. One might hypothesize that the type of radical action pursued provides some clue as the particular aspects or dimensions of the perceived social world from which the actor feels estranged. Thus, one would expect that those who are prepared to drop out of the existing social order with the expressed intention of working towards the creation of an entirely new society would be estranged not merely from what they defined as specific and limited abuses but from the social system as a whole, and in particular from the fundamental values and core ideas which they viewed as underpinning the entire social structure. Evidence to support such a hypothesis would appear to be provided in the following extract taken from the writings of one commune member:[1]

> If civilization is what we make it, then there is no need for
> intentional community for such would be civilization. But it isn't.
> It is largely what others have made for us, and while it might

have suited somebody at some time, and not necessarily those taking part in it, it certainly doesn't suit all of us now, and if we're thinking in optimum terms, it doesn't really suit any of us particularly well. . . . Civilization in the mass is basically a dictatorship, autocratic in some cultures, and democratic in others, and in order to impose a particular culture on a great diversity of a great many people it must be so. . . . If we must live in a macroculture, then we must be content with being manipulated by that culture, but if our views differ radically from contemporary collective prejudice or *if we see life in terms of a different scale of values*, then intentional community offers the only way in which we can put our ideas into practice, whether for experiment or for experience, and in the company of like-minded people.

In interviews and conversations with commune members about their attitudes towards straight society, very few of them mentioned such specific social wrongs as the distribution of wealth and property in society. Rather, their attacks on the grey world were aimed largely against what they tended to view as the basic values upon which the institutions and social forms of life were based. If one were to adopt the analogy of the game, then very few complained about the distribution of prizes in the game of life. Their social criticisms were concentrated upon the game of life itself and the rules according to which they felt it was played, and the power-lessness of the individual player to create his own rules to follow.

Materialism, the concern with acquiring more and more con-sumer goods and status symbols, the competitive individualism and the associated lack of concern for one's fellow men, the routine and machine-like quality of daily life and the loss of opportunity for the expression of one's individuality and creativity, the concern with technical efficiency at the cost of self-fulfilment and human control—these are the features of life in urban-industrial society that commune members tend to define as unbearable and insuffer-able. As the writer quoted above has expressed it in his indictment of the mass culture:[2]

Before we turn our back on mass culture let's take a hard look at it—at its injustices, stupidities, prejudices, and callousness. We see societies based on the accumulation of capital, *competitive in the extreme,* and depending for their maintenance on a vast number of underprivileged people who were losers in this competition. . . . We see societies pledged to distribute the wealth of the community equitably among its people, and we see in those very societies *the ruthless suppression of individuality* and the lack of any opportunity to express originality unless the individual is fortuitously favoured at birth by a superior mind or an ability to assert himself. . . . What of the masses who provide the labour and the mental stress around which this monolith we still call civilization winds its stifling shackles? What say have they in the progress of the community or indeed in the organisation of their own lives? Who among herded humanity is fortunate enough to discover adventure and what mind is still free enough to see inspiration amongst the mass of mediocrity and subjugation of individuality?

We have, sadly, reached that stage of evolution where *few individuals are valued in themselves* in such a way that they cannot be readily replaced. It is too expensive to be unique. In the time it takes a craftsman to create an object which is a thing of beauty as well as utility, a machine will produce a thousand stamped out with unerring precision and monotony and fed on the vast conveyor belts which are the life blood of this *regimented society* to the *stereotyped minds* that lie like doomed prisoners in the gloomy shades of bodies tied to *an endless round of work, sleep and play.* . . . There's the ever present feeling of insecurity and dissatisfaction. We feel we want to do something of real value, but there is nothing we can do . . . whatever we would like to become active in, we find the ground already covered by a whole army of experts with supporting administrative and executive teams. . . . *We feel utterly inferior and impotent in the face of this social monolith. We have no feeling of belonging.* . . . We can't be adjusted both to a natural code of living and to the code of a repressed and consequently prejudiced society. Maladjustment to one or the other is inevitable. Maladjustment to our own natural yearnings—once they have emerged from near obliteration—is preposterous, and if we're thereby maladjusted to society, we can only create a more enlightened society. Such is intentional community.

Similar sentiments were expressed to me by other commune members and respondents. One person who had worked as a librarian told me of her hatred for the rat-race, which she saw as the most unbearable aspect of conventional life, 'the feeling that you have got to trample everyone else down in order to get on. I don't think it's worth it. I would rather not get on if you have to do that.' Another respondent, who had worked as a machine-tool operator, told me of his view of the human condition:

Life in straight society is all so bloody pointless. People largely spend their lives doing something they don't particularly enjoy. All the wives work. The whole system stinks. . . . They all live in these little boxes. They have another little box on wheels for

Sundays. They are just not using their abilities. . . . And there's
the bloody television—that's another box—and the women go to
bingo—I think I am going mad.

This view that 'the whole system stinks' and 'life is all so bloody
pointless' was stressed by another respondent, although in rather
different terms. His view of the human condition was that

Capitalism generally destroys the souls of people—it turns them
into machines—even though people themselves are not aware of
this fact. At school they are conditioned to accept authority;
they leave school and are conditioned to the fact that they have
to find a job; they are conditioned to thinking they must get
married and settle down and buy a house; and once they have
settled down and bought their house they are trapped for the
rest of their lives. Capitalism has then got another cog in its
machine. Everybody seems to fall into this rut.

Theorizing about the human condition or about man in general
is an extremely hazardous venture. It is more meaningful to talk of
some men and of certain types of men than of man in general, for
one's statements and hypotheses are more readily falsifiable. Despite
this, however, certain sociologists and writers have observed the
contemporary urban-industrial world and have written about what
they have seen in terms not too different from the language used by
certain commune members. Such writers as Stein, Riesman, Fromm
and many others have written of the meaninglessness of modern
life spent in the pursuit of status symbols of one sort or another.
Thus, Stein has written of life in American suburbia:[3]

no one in the suburb really has to know anyone else as long as
appearances are kept up. Housewives, taught to desire careers,
are trapped in the home. Husbands, trapped in careers which
drain their best energies, must look forward to a fate that has
become as dreaded as death—that of retirement and free time.
Looking ahead to their own prospective life cycles, the children
soon learn to submerge the specter of a life that lacks rooted
values and creative meanings by throwing themselves into the
struggle for status. All of the vital roles wherein the human
drama used to be played out—mother-son, father-daughter,
worker-player, adult-child, male-female—now tend to be levelled.
Their specific contents which had previously made them into
channels for realising a particular set of human possibilities have
been bartered for an ephemeral and empty sense of status. Not
to perform these roles is to lose one's place but, sadly enough,
performing them can never give one a place.

At the basis of such analyses of the nature of contemporary social life, a life which is characterized as consisting of little more than empty role-playing without purpose or meaningful reward for the individual, there lie, I believe, certain fundamental assumptions about the essential nature of man as a potentially creative being. Just as one respondent informed me of his basic faith in humanity and his belief that people are basically good, so another respondent proclaimed his belief that everyone is an artist, and Fromm has written of his feeling that one must not succumb to the[4]

> grave error . . . of a sociological relativism in which man is nothing but a puppet, directed by the strings of social circumstances. Man's inalienable rights of freedom and happiness are founded in inherent human qualities: his striving to live, to expand and to express the potentialities that have developed in him in the process of historical evolution.

For such people it is not only desirable but also possible for man to possess a true sense of identity, and to fulfil his innate creative potential, a possibility which contemporary society appears to deny man. They share Marx's view of man as a being with a wide range of creative potentialities, or 'species powers' whose 'self-realization exists as an inner necessity, a need'.

For Marx, the alienation of man in capitalist society lay in the organization of work, in which process man became an object used by others and was therefore unable to obtain satisfaction in his own activities and thereby was denied the possibility of realizing his creative potentialities. To quote Marcuse:[5]

> The social division of labour, Marx declares, is not carried out with any consideration for the talents of individuals and the interests of the whole, but rather takes place entirely according to the laws of capitalist commodity production. Under these laws, the product of labour, the commodity, seems to determine the nature and end of human activity. In other words, the materials that should serve life come to rule over its content and goal, and the consciousness of man is completely made victim to the relationships of material production.

Marx explained the alienation of labour as exemplified, first of all, in the relation of the worker to the product of his labour. The worker labours for the capitalist, to whom he surrenders, through the wage contract, the product of his labour. Viewing capital as the power to dispose over the products of labour, the more the worker produces, the greater the power of capital becomes and the smaller the worker's own means for appropriating his products. Labour thus becomes the victim of a power it has itself created. The worker alienated from his product is at the same time alienated from himself. For Marx, labour in its true form is a medium for man's self-fulfilment and the full development of his potentialities. Where the worker is separated from his product, however, instead of developing his physical and mental energies, he cripples his body and ruins his mind. He feels he is truly himself when he is away from work, and apart from his true self when he is at work. His work is not done willingly and, far from being the satisfaction of a creative need, is merely a means for the satisfaction of wants outside it. Man's alienation from himself is simultaneously an estrangement from his fellow men. Just as man is not what he should be as a creative being, but finds himself treated as a means, a tool, so he is alienated from his fellow men since he treats them also as means. All personal relations between men take on the form of objective relations between things. Thus:[6]

> The alienation of labour creates a society split into opposing classes. Any social scheme that effects a division of labour without taking account of the abilities and needs of individuals in assigning them their roles tends to shackle the activity of the individual to external economic forces. The mode of social production, the way in which the life of the whole is maintained, circumscribes the life of the individual and harnesses his entire existence to relations prescribed by the economy, without regard to his subjective abilities or wants.

The Marxist notion of alienation thus refers to the relationship of the individual both to his social and natural environment and to his relationship with himself. The alienated individual is one who fails to recognize his actions and the results of his actions as his own, but believes in the existence of impersonal, determinate forces that shape and control individual and social life. The alienated in capitalist society are like objects rather than creative subjects. For the alienated, one could argue, the ways of the world are natural and inevitable, and for such individuals there would appear no other choice but to follow these ways. As one of the communards quoted above phrased it, 'capitalism generally destroys the souls of people—*it turns them into machines*—even though people are not aware of this fact'.

For Marx also, the roots of this condition lay in the private ownership of the means of production: under the capitalist system of ownership the worker is separated from his essential being. The liberation of man from this condition could only be attained through creative action (praxis) within the social world and directed towards the establishment of the communist society where men would be able to work for themselves and in which the necessary preconditions would be laid for the development of the kind of labour that would be the expression of the human capacities of the individual. Thus, for Marx, the abolition of the private ownership of property was the necessary means for the abolition of alienated labour.

Thus there would appear to exist a definite similarity between the conclusions reached by Marx in his analysis of the human condition in capitalist societies, and that reached by certain of the more articulate members of the contemporary commune movement. When communards depict the contemporary human condition as 'bloody pointless', with people 'just not using their abilities', 'trapped for the rest of their lives' as cogs in the capitalist machine, they are describing that condition which Marx depicted as the alienation of man in capitalist society.

The relevant issue becomes, then, one of examining why at this stage in the development of urban-industrial societies there has been a resurgence in the popularity of the Marxian concept of alienation and an associated development among significant sectors of the population of a view of the human condition as machine-like and meaningless. The answer lies at least partly in the discovery of Marx's earlier writings and in what can be termed the profound identity crisis that confronts significant sections of the population in general, and certain sections of the young in particular, in the modern world.

Before going on to expand on this theme, however, I think the point should be made that the alienated individual is not necessarily a psychologically estranged social being who does not feel at home in society. It can in fact be argued that the alienated individual is far more likely to feel at home in society than the unalienated. On *a priori* grounds it can be argued that, for social life to exist in the form of regular, ordered, and meaningful relationships between discrete individuals and groups, it is necessary that those sharing the same objective situation should also share complementary subjective definitions of that situation in order that they can meaningfully relate to each other. In so far as the alienated members of society view the human constructs that together make up the institutions and social structures of the social world as alien objects possessing independent existences beyond the control of mere mortals, then in the face of such objectified social structures it would appear, to such people, that the individual has no option but to follow the dictates and rules of the natural order of things. The objectivation of the social structure helps to perform the necessary function of providing the regulative channels that must be followed by actors on the social scene if they are to avoid the threat of social chaos, where nothing is certain and where the actions of others appear as random occurrences rather than predictable and meaningful actions. That is, to the extent that the alienated individual is surrounded by constructs and objects which guide and direct his actions, then he is saved from the threat of anomie or normlessness, of living in a world which fails to make sense, a world in which one's expectations are unfulfilled and in which one feels lost and alone.

Such a perspective differs radically from the conception of alienation adhered to by non-Marxist writers who use the term to apply to those members of society whom they define as being unattached, normless, isolated and so on. Nisbet, for instance, has written of his interpretation of the concept as follows:[7]

> By alienation I mean the state of mind that can find a social order remote, incomprehensible, or fraudulent; beyond real hope or desire; inviting apathy, boredom, or even hostility. The individual not only does not feel a part of the social order; he has lost interest in being a part of it.

According to such a perspective, the members of the contemporary commune movement could be labelled as 'alienated' as opposed to

TABLE 1 *Individuals' view of the social world*

Psychological condition of the individual	Alienated	Unalienated
estranged	(2) Alienated individuals, estranged from existing social order but unable to conceive of the possibility of social change.	(3) The utopians at odds with society but able to conceive of the possibility and desirability of social change.
unestranged	(1) Alienated individuals but feeling at one with the existing order of things. They are unable to conceive of any alternative social order.	(4) Those who are aware of man's ability to control his social environment but who are attached to the status quo and who do not seek radical social change.

the communards' labelling of the members of conventional society as 'alienated' and of themselves as 'unalienated'. In fact, it would appear that what such writers as Nisbet, Seeman, Nettler and others are referring to when they use the concept of alienation with all its various dimensions, is merely the subjective experience of estrangement from the social world, and the various ways in which this can be made manifest. This contrasts markedly with the essentially

Marxist perspective presented above of the alienated individual as one who is unaware that one possesses any control over life, for whom the ways of the world stem from the natural and inevitable order of things which individuals cannot choose but to follow. A condition which Kafka expressed so well when he wrote of 'the conveyor belt of life which carries you on, no one knows where. One is more of an object, a thing, than a living creature.'

On the basis of a distinction between alienation and estrangement, a four-fold schema of social types suggests itself as a possible heuristic device for considering the 'human condition' of modern man. This framework is shown in Table 1.

Type one: alienated but not estranged

For those members of society who, according to the perspective presented above, are alienated but not estranged from society, for such 'happy robots', society appears as 'something out there'. The complex of institutions, roles, social identities and so on appears separate from the individual who can do nothing but play the parts expected of him as an actor on the social scene. In so far as he has internalized as his own the conventional view of the world and of his place in that world, then it is taken for granted as the natural order of things by him. For such an individual, the life he leads and the institutions in which he is enmeshed appear as the only conceivable way life could possibly be led and ordered. It does not enter into his consciousness that such a structure could be questioned. For him there is no felt disjunction between how the life of an individual such as himself is ordered, and how it ought to be ordered. This status of the happy robot is that occupied by the majority of people in conventional society according to many commune members. Thus one respondent replied, when asked why he thought that many people appeared to be content to live out their lives in a society which, according to him, had little to commend it:

> This question has been hanging me up a hell of a lot. I have been thinking and thinking about it. Perhaps it is just awareness—lots of those who are contented haven't thought about it, they have just accepted it as the norm, they haven't questioned it—'What other way is there for us to live? Our parents and everybody have been doing it so why should we change?'

Type two: alienated and estranged

For most sociologists, society is understood as an interrelated set of institutions, roles and social identities. For ordinary mortals,

51

however, society appears as a set of typifications about what kinds of people one meets in certain sorts of social situations, general images about the sort of attitudes and actions expected from such situations; typifications about the kinds of attitudes and behavioural patterns expected of himself as the holder of a certain stock of social identities—as a skilled plumber, as a husband and father, as a middle-aged man past his prime or whatever. For the alienated individual who is at home in society, these socially-provided typifications structure his world and conform, isomorphically, with his own personal constructs—they are one and the same thing. For the alienated individual who is estranged and at odds with society, however, there is a felt disjunction between his objective social identity, his position in society, the kinds of attitudes and behavioural patterns expected of him and so on, and his own personal evaluation of these things. At the same time there appears to be nothing he can do to alter this state of affairs. His life is led in 'bad faith', to use Sartre's term. To his way of thinking, it is unfortunate that he was not cast in a role which would have provided him with a more personally rewarding mode of existence, but there appears to be nothing he can do about it. He is estranged from society and estranged from what he might feel to be his real self, but his alienated view of the relationship between the individual and society causes him to deny himself whatever world-creating ability he might possess. For him, what will be will be, and there is nothing, unfortunately, that one can do about it.

Carlo Levi, in his description of peasant life in a region of southern Italy prior to the Second World War, described the peasant attitude towards the government of Mussolini in terms which convey the alienated condition of the peasants; they appear as individuals who are alienated but estranged from the existing social order:[8]

> They were not Fascists, just as they would never have been Conservatives or Socialists, or anything else. Such matters had nothing to do with them; they belonged to another world and they saw no sense in them. What had the peasants to do with Power, Government and the State? The State, whatever form it might take, meant 'the fellows in Rome'. 'Everyone knows', they said, 'that the fellows in Rome don't want us to live like human beings. There are hailstorms, landslides, droughts, malaria, and . . . the State. These are inescapable evils; such there always have been and there always will be. They make us kill off our goats, they carry away our furniture, and now they're going to send us to the wars. Such is life.' To the peasants the State is more distant than heaven and far more of a scourge, because it is always against them. . . . Their only defence against the State and

the propaganda of the State is resignation, the same gloomy resignation, alleviated by no hope of paradise, that bows their shoulders under the scourges of nature.

A fatalistic 'gloomy resignation' to the ways of nature and the world is the typical response, then, of those individuals who are alienated and estranged from the social order. Unlike the happy robots who are alienated but at one with the existing order, the alienated and estranged do perceive a gap between the ways of the world as they are and how they ought to be. Like the alienated but unestranged, however, they can conceive of no possibility of ever changing the world. For them, the existing social, political and economic relationships of society are given, and all the individual can aspire to is to make do within this objective structure.

Type three: the utopians: estranged from society but aware of man's world-creating ability

Such individuals possess the utopian mentality in the sense that they perceive a gap between how society appears to be and how they feel society ought to be, and envisage the possibility of radical social change through the agency of human actors. They are generally at odds with the prevailing social order in this respect, but are concerned with attempting to move society and/or themselves towards something approaching their ideal. The nature of this ideal and the paths chosen to obtain it can vary widely. Among their number one can locate the radical activists of society, including communitarians, who are estranged from the dominant cultural and institutional patterns of society and who, far from accepting the prevailing order as the only possible state of things as natural, refuse to take it for granted. They seek to create a new social order within which men will be able to create what the communitarians would consider more rewarding lives for themselves. This aim was expressed by the majority of commune members with whom I came into contact. As one respondent expressed it:

I don't know if people in straight society are reasonably content. If they are, they are probably not being honest with themselves. I think in a lot of cases, like the young, they do not see any way out. They cannot conceive of anything different. Maybe this is something we can do—given an example—show that there is a way out.

Another commune member expressed a similar orientation. 'By living a different way of life we can make some people sit up and think, "maybe there is another way of life, maybe we ought to change our way of life".' Using the terminology of this chapter one could argue that a general aim of commune members is to transform the estranged but alienated individuals of society into utopian agents of social and personal change.

Type four: individuals at one with a man-made world

In this box one would find, if such people actually existed, those individuals who are aware of the extent to which the social world is created and maintained by human agents but who feel at one with the prevailing state of affairs. One might expect to find such individuals among the 'top-dogs' of society—the power-holders and members of the élite groups who can see the effects of their decisions and actions reverberating through society. Among their number one would expect to find those individuals who, consciously or unconsciously, help to perpetuate the myth of the reified state of the social order through their control of the means of communication, production and decision-making, in order to serve their own group interests, which they interpret as equivalent to the national interest.

In this typology are presented four ideal types, three of which have been labelled at different times by different writers as alienated. The purpose behind the exercise has been two-fold. First of all, it is hoped that it might help to throw some clarity on to the confused state of affairs concerning the use of the concept of alienation as an all-embracing concept which has, to quote Nisbet, 'become nearly as prevalent as the doctrine of enlightened self-interest was two generations ago'.[9] Secondly, and of more direct relevance to the study of the relationship between communitarians and the conventional social world, it is hoped that this typology may provide a meaningful framework within which this relationship can be studied. That is, it has been argued in Chapter 1 that in order to understand why increasing numbers of people are seeking to join or to form new communes it is first of all necessary to examine the impact of certain social forces upon the social structure of modern Britain in general, and how such social forces have generated particular life problems for the members of different social groups. Only through such an exercise can one begin to locate the origins of a particular group's estrangement from the status quo and the relative availability of its members for recruitment to movements which appear to provide solutions to their particular life problems. The typology presented in this chapter represents an attempt to provide the conceptual armoury with which to approach this task.

In considering the relationship between modern man and his society it is possible to point to a general historical trend beginning with the Reformation and continuing into the present day. Using the typology presented above, medieval man can be characterized as being of the happy robot type, type one, alienated but not estranged from the social system in which he lived. The process of man's emergence as an individual with the severance of the ties that connected him to his church and his social caste has been traced by many writers.

Fromm, for example, typified medieval man as being characterized by[10]

> lack of individual freedom. Everybody in the earlier period was chained to his role in the social order. . . . But although a person was not free in the modern sense, neither was he alone and isolated. In having a distinct, unchangeable, and unquestionable place in the social world from the moment of birth, man was rooted in a structuralised whole, and thus life had a meaning which left no place and no need for doubt. A person was identical with his role in society; he was a peasant, an artisan, a knight, and not an individual who happened to have this or that occupation. The social order was conceived as a natural order and being a definite part of it gave man a feeling of security and of belonging. . . . Within the limits of his social sphere the individual actually had much freedom to express his self in his work and in his emotional life. Although there was no individualism in the modern sense of the unrestricted choice between many possible ways of life, (a freedom of choice which is largely abstract), there was a great deal of concrete individualism in real life.

From such accounts it would seem that, for man in the medieval world, the social system and his place in it appeared as given—his was an alienated view of the social world. At the same time it would appear that he was very much at one with this world. Whatever suffering he underwent was made tolerable by the Church that explained it as the result of the original sin of Adam and the individual's own sins, but assured the individual of his eventual forgiveness by God.

In the late Middle Ages the unity and the structured whole of medieval society was weakened. A new moneyed class began to develop as individual economic initiative and competition grew. On the other hand, the breakdown of the old feudal castes led to the growth of the urban masses of exploited and politically suppressed workers. In the process of this development it is possible to discern the emergence of the three remaining social types. On the one side the growth of capitalism freed man from the bonds of the corporate system, allowing him to stand on his own feet as an individual and seek to take his fate in his own hands. For the wealthy capitalists it

C

was shown that individual effort could lead to success and economic independence. In this process, baldly stated here, one can discern the emergence of the fourth social type referred to above—those 'top dogs' attached to the social order and with a belief that life was there for them to take hold of and to shape as they could.[11]

At the same time, the increasing role of the market and competition meant that for the majority of the urban masses and the urban élites, capital assumed the quality of a suprapersonal force that appeared to determine their economic and thereby their personal fate. In this sense, the majority of the members of capitalist society were alienated. But this process whereby the medieval social system was destroyed, destroyed with it the stability and relative security it had offered the individual, undermining the traditional communal sense of identity. For the urban poor and the peasantry, these trends resulted in greater exploitation and impoverishment. In this process can be discerned the emergence of the second social type referred to above—alienated individuals estranged from the social order.

Just as one can discern, with the development of capitalism, the emergence on a mass scale of estranged but alienated individuals (type two), so one can also see the development of utopian types, estranged but not alienated, including revolutionaries such as Marx. Marx sought to transform the social question of the material want and deprivation of man in capitalist society into a political force by persuading the poor and the deprived that poverty was not a natural phenomenon, but was rather the result of exploitation and violence on the part of the ruling classes, and as such was a political rather than a natural phenomenon. In emphasizing the power of men to shape their own history, Marx differed from the religious utopians of an earlier age who legitimated their millennial claims by reference to some supernatural, sacred realm. Such people could be viewed as constituting a fifth social type—that of the alienated utopian— according to the degree to which they denied man his world-creating ability and located this power in some superhuman entity or power. This, indeed, is a guise in which some vulgar Marxists appear when they view the working class as the embodiment of some historical necessity, seemingly denying man his status as an active and creative force in the making of history.

Marx envisaged the working classes leading in the revolutionary transformation of society from the age of necessity into the age of freedom because, under capitalism, they represented the most dehumanized and potentially the most powerful section of society— they had nothing to lose but their chains of material deprivation and economic and political exploitation. However, in interviews with contemporary commune members, few placed any great emphasis on the working class as a revolutionary force, just as very few of them considered material deprivation to be the major social problem of man in modern society. As one respondent phrased it:

O.K., there are material problems, but there are other more important problems such as 'Who am I? What am I here for?' It is amazing how many people you would think thick do ask these questions—but then give up or become satisfied with cars and so on.

For such people, the pursuit of consumer goods that they saw as being the major feature of life for contemporary man, including the members of the working class, represented a search for a substitute for their failure to achieve a meaningful sense of personal identity. For the communitarians, the members of the working class are bound to the existing order not so much by the chains of economic and political exploitation, as by the chains of materialism and their own lack of awareness of any attractive alternative to the existing order. This feeling was expressed by one respondent in the following words: 'I don't see the proletariat rising up and throwing off their chains, because half the time they are very tightly holding the chains on.'

For an individual to become a utopian, in the sense of the term used in this chapter, he must not only believe that social change is desirable, but also believe that it is possible. The task for the communitarians, as many of them defined it, was to make people aware, to get them to question the nature of their individual lives, the society in which such lives are led, and the values by which they were led.

The major problems associated with the human condition of man in modern industrial societies, as defined by the communitarians, involved such issues as the need to attain a meaningful sense of personal identity on the part of the individual, the individual's need to express his own creative autonomy, and the need to achieve brotherly co-operation between men. It was the perception of modern technological society as presenting serious obstacles to the fulfilment of such quests that lay at the core of the rejection of such a social order by many communitarians. In the remainder of this chapter an attempt will be made to locate the social processes through which such themes have come to occupy such a central place in their world view.[12]

With the development and transformation of capitalism in societies such as Britain and America, there has developed that phenomenon which can be characterized as bureaucratic capitalism: a class society based on wage labour, in which the management of collective activities is in the hands of an impersonal apparatus, hierarchically organized with recruitment according to impersonal and universalistic rules, and directed by rational criteria. The concentration and rationalization of production has led to the appearance of a bureaucratic apparatus with large-scale industrial enterprise which manages, from the outside, the whole labour process: defining tasks, imposing rhythms and methods of work, controlling the quantity and quality of the product. The bureaucratic apparatus of the state, at the same time, has developed as an instrument of control and management in an ever-increasing number of sectors of economic and social life. The bureaucratization of such traditional working-class organizations as the trade unions has also proceeded apace. The processes of geographical and social mobility that began with the breakdown of medieval society have continued. Increasing numbers of people have felt the need to leave their traditional home areas and environments in pursuit of work, higher wages and better living conditions, losing in the process the friendship and company of their original peers and companions. There has been a general centralization of national life that has accompanied the decline of community.

The combined effect of these trends of modern industrialization, urbanization, bureaucratization, and the related centralization of political and economic power, upon the individual member of society, it can be argued, has been one of creating a profound identity crisis. Mead and Cooley argued that the individual's identity consisted of a configuration of self conceptions that originated in social processes. According to this perspective the identity of an individual (the answers he gets when he asks himself, 'Who am I? What am I?'), is as much a social construct as it is an individual one, emerging through an interaction of the two. To a large extent, therefore, the individual's sense of his own identity and personal worth is largely dependent on the various reflected images of himself that he perceives in the way significant others treat him.

Now with the development of large-scale, hierarchically organized institutions of economic, social and political life, the norms governing the operations and activities within these spheres have become increasingly rationalized, in so far as they have tended to be determined primarily by the functional requirements of the institutions as a whole, as defined by the central decision-makers of the institutions. The norms are thus rational only in relation to the final objective of the institution as such. They have become restricted in their ability to provide meaning for the existence of the individual located within the structure. This contrasts with the situation that characterized medieval life as described by Tawney:[13]

> Much that is now mechanical was then personal, intimate and direct and there was little room for an organisation on a scale

too vast for the standards that are applied to individuals, and for the doctrine that silences scruples and closes all accounts with the final plea of economic expediency.

While these trends have been going on in the institutions shaping the individual's public life, there has been a corresponding decline in the significance of the institutions traditionally concerned with the individual's private sphere of existence. This trend is perhaps best illustrated by the decline in the relevance and significance of organized religion and its values as guidelines for the average individual's life style. As MacIntyre has expressed it:[14]

What the urbanization of the Industrial Revolution meant was the destruction of the older forms of community, in many cases rapidly, and in particular the destruction of those features of them to which religion had given symbolic expression. There is first of all the loss of the background of a given and largely unalterable social order within whose limits men of different social rank all have to live. There is secondly the disappearance of the relative continuity and stability of social order, a stability which makes that order appear continuous with the order of nature. There is thirdly an end to the existence of shared and established norms, common to all ranks in the community, in the light of which everyone stands either vindicated or convicted by their own conduct. Religion, when it is the religion of a whole society, may have functions other than the expression of the natural and social order, but it is always at least an expression of a society's moral unity, and it lends to that unity **a** cosmic and universal significance and justification.

For the individual this means that, whereas in the primary public institutions he is expected to play narrowly defined functionary roles, he is left to fend for himself in his private life.
In the words of Berger and Luckmann:[15]

As an actor on the social scene he moves through a series of situations defined bureaucratically. Subjectively he is forced to define himself as a 'cog in the machine' . . . the primary public institutions tend to seem meaningless to the individual; their functional rationality cannot be converted into individual sense. . . . The paradox of total conformity in one sector of individual existence and seemingly absolute autonomy in the other, therefore, has its structural roots in total performance control by the primary institutional domains, combined with their indifference to the person.

Berger and Luckmann go on to argue that, with the decline of the traditional sources of the individual's sense of identity, an alleged need for 'essential identities' on the part of individuals has to be met from other quarters than work. They argue that a market of secondary institutions has grown up to supply this need in modern industrial societies. In their eyes the individual has now become a consumer of identities offered on this market by the mass media and advertising, football teams, religious organizations, psychoanalysts, and other supply agencies.

Correspondingly, it can be argued, the consequence for many people in contemporary society of the social and geographical mobility that increasing numbers are experiencing has been a change of social milieu which has involved a weakening of the individual's relationships with the primary groups that socialized him and of his relationships with his lifelong peers. As a consequence, the norms and standards according to which the individual was originally reared, and his past identities, are no longer reaffirmed in his new social relationships—they become less real. There appears a cleavage between past and present identities so that, inevitably, there develops an increased dependency on the reaffirmation of one's identity and personal worth from those with whom the individual shares his present social situation. However, high social and geographical mobility, the nature of the work task and the hours spent at work, the nature of modern urban and suburban communities and so on, has meant that the individual usually fails to establish the network of intimate social relationships that are necessary for the reaffirmation through social interaction of the individual's sense of his own inner worth.

This nature of 'man alone' in modern society helps to account for the materialism of the consumer culture. Material goods become perceived as visible symbols of one's inner worth. According to Berger and Luckmann the 'sacramentalism of consumption'[16]

> is necessitated structurally by high geographical mobility, as a result of which conspicuous patterns of consumption take the place of continuous interpersonal contacts within an individual biography. That is, material objects rather than human beings must be called upon to testify to the individual's worth . . . an important part of identity re-affirmation is directly played by material objects rather than by human beings.

Unable to find meaning in his work task, unable to gain reaffirmation of his own inner worth through interpersonal relationships, unable to find solace in a religion whose traditional emphasis on brotherhood and love has become increasingly divorced from the competitive realities of economic life, seemingly becoming increasingly separated from the centres of political power and decision-making, and having had much of his sense of personal autonomy eroded by his experience of such events as the great economic depression and the Second World War—the response of the individual has been a natural turning inward, so to speak. The decisive identity confirmations and sources of meaning and pleasure are now expected from the private worlds of the family and home. The response of most people to the experience of being treated as small cogs in the big wheels of industry, community and polity, has been to heed the wisdom of sticking to one's own business and letting the uncomfortable and complex problems of society alone—particularly if one remembers the days of physical and material deprivation and hardship of the years prior to the Second World War. The typical response has been that of 'privatization', in the form of an increasingly abstract and attenuated relationship to the larger social forces affecting one's job and the community and the focusing of one's attentions on the personal strategy of piloting oneself and one's family through the storm of life.

This turning inwards and sticking to one's business is the privatized response of significant sections of society to the problem of personal identity encountered in modern life. It is the response of those alienated individuals who are to a greater or lesser degree estranged from the existing social order (types one and two). It is the response of those individuals for whom the social world 'out there' is like some big machine over which mere individuals have little control. It is not, however, the response of all sections of society. The identity problem that confronts people in modern society is one that appears to be experienced particularly acutely by the young, and it is largely from the ranks of the estranged young that commune members are drawn. Such people can be considered as modern day utopians (type three) in so far as they refuse to accept the prevailing social order as 'thing-like' and unchangeable and seek to create a new social world for themselves and others. It is to the position of youth in contemporary urban industrial society and to some of the collective forms of action pursued by the utopians amongst them that attention is turned in the next chapter.

4 Youth, the youth culture and the underground

In the previous chapter it was argued that one of the key problems faced by the individual in modern industrial societies was that involved in the development of a rewarding sense of personal identity. Orrin Klapp has written in somewhat similar terms of the problems confronting modern man in the United States.[1] For Klapp, the major forms of unrest and dissent displayed in America represent the collective response of certain social groups to what he has described as 'the identity problem, an inability to define oneself successfully in a milieu of inadequate symbolism'.[2] He distinguished five major forms of what he termed the 'collective search for identity': contagious ghetto violence, new left activism, radical right extremism, style rebellion, and the drop-out movement associated with the hippies.

The development of a commune movement in Britain can be viewed as a counterpart to the drop-out movement of America referred to by Klapp. Klapp argued that the drop-outs of America could be considered as 'only part of a larger, more persuasive (and older) movement, including beatniks, hipsters, surfers, some folk singers, dandies, poseurs, jacket boys, and other style rebels'.[3] In similar fashion, it is possible to view the commune movement in Britain as a specific social movement that has grown out of that general, broad, social movement of dissident youth that has been labelled by its leaders and by the mass media as the 'underground'.

In making this distinction between the underground and the commune movement, it is useful to draw upon Blumer's distinction between general and specific social movements.[4] According to Blumer, the general movement lacks the well-defined objectives and goals which the specific movement seeks. It is relatively undirected in this sense. It lacks the developed organization and structure, with the associated formalized division of labour, that the specific movement possesses. The leaders of a general movement are not so much directors as pace-makers, pioneers, whose example helps develop the awareness, sensitivity, aspirations and dreams of the others. The followers in such a movement are not so much formal members of an established association, but are rather partisans—individuals who share a certain group consciousness in so far as they share similar positions within the social structure and see themselves as facing similar life-problems. They share similar ideas, particularly with regard to the conceptions they hold of themselves, and of their rights and privileges. Such images tend, however, to be vague and unstructured, and consequently the actions associated with such images tend to be vague and uncertain. Collective action tends to take the form of unco-ordinated efforts representing slow and hesitant steps towards some hazily conceived objective. Whereas interaction within the specific social movement, apart from informal contact between members, is likely to be structured within the framework of official conferences, newsletters, meetings and activities—the main media of interaction for the members of the general movements, according to Blumer, are likely to be informal conversations, 'get-togethers' and the reading of that literature which expresses the general ethos of the movement, and the individual perception of the examples set by the pioneers of the movement.

Richard Neville has written that the 'unpopular label, "Underground" embraces hippies, beats, mystics, madmen, freaks, yippies, crazies, crackpots, communards and anyone who rejects rigid political ideology ("it's a brain disease"), and believes that once you have blown your own mind, the Bastille will blow up itself'.[5]

That it is legitimate to treat the commune movement as a specific movement which is part of this general underground movement is evidenced by the constant reference made to such experiments in living by the correspondents of the various underground papers and magazines that have flourished in recent years.[6] At the same time, the members of many communal ventures read such literature and advertise for new members in them.[7] In addition, a number of commune members have claimed that they first became interested in the idea of communal living through reading of community ventures in the columns of the underground press. Thus, one respondent informed me of how she first became interested in the idea of communal living:

I had seen a television programme a few years ago about one of the communes in America . . . it really struck me. . . . I thought it was a great idea living off the excess of society. And that idea must have stayed with me even though I didn't realize it. We didn't really talk about it, and then we both read the article in 'Gandalph's Garden' on Selene, and it started the discussion between us and we both realized we felt the same.

The members of the underground constitute a general movement by the fact that they share a common set of values and ideas, and possess a certain group-consciousness. The agreement is on the primacy of such values as individual freedom and the desirability of productive and co-operative relationships between individuals rather than any definite and specific objective. However, the movement does have a general aim, the creation of an alternative society. This vision of an alternative society was described to me by a number of respondents. For one respondent it meant

the germ of the new society within the old which is based on a very different system of values and norms which are, in a sense, socialist—in the sense of anticapitalist—but at the same time is not political. This love bit can be artificial but it is basing economic action and such on a different sort of motives than profit or money. It is because of other people that you do something and not out of the profit you are going to get out of it,

while for another commune member

it means an alternative society to the one we have got now. It means a different sort of way of looking at other people and treating them, and responding to people. A different way of growing food and producing things. Practically everything would be different.

Another respondent informed me that 'The alternative society means people caring about one another and sharing. In straight society they are all competing and thinking only about themselves.' There is also a general agreement upon the possibility and desirability of bringing about social change and the creation of the alternative society through individual exemplary action and counter-institutional building, through the creation of cells of the new society within the shell of the old.

In so far as the members of the underground share a set of values and orientations to the world which are counter to those held by the members of other social groups in society, then they can be described as constituting a sub-cultural group, a body of cognitive deviants whose knowledge of the world is not generally shared by the rest of society, who together share a counter-culture.[8] Blumer, in fact, has argued that the background to a general social movement[9]

is constituted by gradual and pervasive changes in the values of people—changes which can be called cultural drifts. Such cultural drifts stand for a general shifting in the ideas of people, particularly along the line of the conceptions which people have of themselves, and of their rights and privileges. Over a period of time many people may develop a new view of what they believe they are entitled to—a view largely made up of desires and hopes. It signifies the emergence of a new set of values, which influence people in the way in which they look upon themselves. . . . They acquire new dispositions and interests and, accordingly, become sensitized in new directions; and, conversely, they come to experience dissatisfaction where before they had none. These new images of themselves, which people begin to develop in response to cultural drifts, are vague and indefinite; and correspondingly, the behaviour in response to such images is uncertain and without definite aim. It is this feature which provides a cue for the understanding of general social movements.

Thus, in order to understand the emergence of the underground movement in Britain and the associated growth of the commune movement, it is necessary first of all to examine briefly the type of process by which subcultural groups emerge in society.

Society can be viewed as consisting of groups of people, each group possessing its own stock of knowledge about the world in general, the norms and values internalized by the members of the group being embodied in this stock of socially accepted knowledge. Part of this shared body of group knowledge of and about the world consists of commonly accepted solutions to the problems typically experienced by the members of the group in their quest to attain those ends that are valued by the group members. One can generally locate explanations and justifications for such ends in the body of group knowledge, along with the accounts of the approved means of overcoming the obstacles that can hinder one's progress towards them. This body of knowledge constitutes part of the culture of the group. However, there occasionally occurs a breakaway from this cultural tradition by certain members of the group. Such people adopt a different body of knowledge as their own. They develop new definitions of the situations which they perceive themselves occupying as individuals and as a group in relation to the wider society. This development of a counter-culture, described by Berger as 'an island of deviant meanings within the sea of its society',[10] generally occurs when the cultural tradition within which people have been brought up is perceived by them as inadequate for the solution of certain life-problems which they see as confronting them. When it becomes apparent to individuals that the aspirations which they have internalized as their own with regard to positions in such areas of life as work, family and sex are no longer attainable by socially approved means, then it is probable that such people will respond to such problems by seeking out new ways of achieving their goals and/or developing a new stock of goals and personal ends. The holders of this new body of knowledge about the nature of society and the purpose of individual social life will thus come to constitute a sub-cultural or counter-cultural group. Such a group can form the basis of a general social movement such as the underground.

Thus in order to explain the emergence of the underground in Britain it is necessary to look at the wider processes occurring in society in general. In particular, it is necessary to examine the problems faced by the members of the underground, problems for which they have been unable to find solutions within the existing culture and which have led them to seek out new solutions in new forms of action such as communal living, on the basis of a set of subterranean or counter-cultural values.

It was suggested above that the key problem that confronts the members of the underground was one of personal identity, and that it could be viewed as a movement whose members are involved in a search for identity. The nature of this search, and the felt need for it, becomes more readily apparent when one considers the fact that the underground is very much a youth movement. There is a feeling among its members that the major form of social conflict is no longer drawn along class lines, but along generational and racial ones. Thus, one can read in Joseph Berke's essay, *Counter-Culture: The Creation of an Alternative Society*, the following diatribe:[11]

> Son: Father, how can I achieve enlightenment?
> Father: Kill me.
> And this is the minimum requirement for survival—the struggle to escape THEIR death, to avoid incorporation into THEIR body—which is 'SOCIETY', run by the old for the old— authoritarian and impotent. THEIR's is the constant stimulation— money, sex, food, cars and so forth, but only open to the middle-aged—a mammoth conspiracy against the young.
> We see this—which is what THEY cannot see—that they are turned off and would have the same happen to us. We see, and fight THEM and turn on.

Before going on to consider in more detail the nature of this general movement, it is important to consider the position of youth in modern society, with particular reference to the identity problems which have always been associated with the passage of the individual from youth to adulthood, but which appear to have become particularly acute in the modern age. Only through a consideration of this issue can one come to an understanding of what makes certain sections of modern youth particularly available for recruitment to such a movement as the underground.

In Erikson's terms, the period of youth is one of psychosocial moratorium, during which a lasting pattern of inner identity is scheduled for relative completion. During this period, through free role experimentation, the individual has the opportunity to try out a range of new cultural models of himself with regard to sexual, occupational roles and so forth. If he finds the right 'mix', then the young adult gains a sense of inner continuity, a natural link between what he was as a child and what he is about to become as a member of the adult world. This assured sense of inner identity will enable him to reconcile his conception of himself, and his community's recognition of him—his personal and social identity.

The taking on of a particular adult identity presupposes, however, that there are meaningful and attractive models to follow. For many of the young in modern industrial societies, however, the social types available as adult exemplars are frequently deemed either undesirable or just plain irrelevant. As Nuttall has written:[12]

> The people who had not yet reached puberty at the time of the
> bomb were incapable of conceiving of life *with* a future. . . .
> Dad was a liar. He lied about the war and he lied about sex.
> He lied about the bomb and he lied about the future. He lived
> his life on an elaborate system of pretence that had been going
> for hundreds of years. The so-called 'generation gap' started
> then and has been increasing ever since.

The modern phenomenon of rapid and continuous technical change and the related changes in social institutions and practices is one major factor which has increased the unpredictability of the future and the life situation to be shared by all members of any generation. One consequence of this, for the young, has been a new emphasis on the present and the short term, rather on long-term planning for the future. As one commentator has written:[13]

> Why prepare if there will be so few satisfying jobs to prepare
> for? Why defer if there will be a super-abundance of inex-
> pensively produced goods to choose from? Why plan if all
> plans can disintegrate into nuclear dust?
> Premature or exaggerated as these questions may seem they
> are being asked, especially by young people. And merely to ask
> them is to prompt a radical shift in time perspective—from what
> *will* be to what *is*, from future promise to present fulfilment,
> from the mundane discounting of present feeling and mood to a
> sharpened awareness of their contours and the possibilities for
> instant alteration.

This attitude towards time was expressed by one respondent who argued that it was no use planning for the future, because one would then distort what was to be. He then explained his reluctance to be interviewed. 'You must live for each moment as it comes. I don't want to be interviewed because that's the past and it's over, and I don't want to go over it again.'

The impact of technically induced social change subjects different age spans to different pressures and stresses. The least affected are those relatively 'outside' society: the very young and the very old. The young, who are in the process of making their life-long commitment to the future, are particularly affected. If the only thing that one knows about the future is that, in the first place, it will be vastly different from the present, and, in the second place, man's future itself is threatened by the possibilities of nuclear war and ecological catastrophe, then the models of the adult world offered to the young are inevitably deemed as irrelevant to the kinds of life situation that they will encounter in the future. Generational discontinuity is extreme in modern industrial societies not so much because parents and other adult models are poor examples for the young, but because they are increasingly seen as irrelevant. The result is that relationships between parents and child are frequently not so much those of hostility as lack of understanding and comprehension. As one respondent described his relationship with his parents, 'I get on o.k. with them, but they don't really understand where my head is at.' The result is that many of the young are at a real loss as to what they should seek to become—there would appear to be few valid and relevant models for the as-yet-to-be-imagined world in which they will live.

Particularly for those young brought up within middle-class families where the values of social responsibility and service are emphasized and the desirability of attaining self-fulfilment through one's work is stressed, the modern technological society can appear repulsive in so far as the likelihood of ever attaining a position in society where one can enjoy individual autonomy and self-expression in one's work seems remote. The problem that can face such people has been expressed by Keniston:[14]

The growing fragmentation of our technological society makes three heavy demands on individuals: that they choose without adequate criteria between the many social roles, 'opportunities' and organisations that have been fractioned out of traditional society; that they work not because their work makes sense but merely to earn a 'living' somewhere else with its proceeds; and that they somehow integrate—or live without being able to integrate—the fractured roles and organisations which fail to define and unify them. These demands are heavy ones; and among the common responses to them are to experience choice as a burden and seek an escape from freedom, to expect and therefore find no fulfilment and satisfaction in work, to feel psychologically divided and socially homeless. Moreover, like all heavy social demands, these are potentially alienating forces. In alienated youths . . . the demand to choose without criteria, to work only for a 'living', and to integrate one's life unaided—these demands cannot or will not be met: they help inspire a rejection of American society and a determination to find another way of life. And even for those who are not alienated, these demands can cause vacillation and indecision, a feeling of emptiness and lack of meaning, a sense of being inwardly divided and outwardly homeless.

The social changes of the post-war era have affected the young in another way: they have contributed to a special sensitivity to the discrepancy between principle and practice. No society, of course, ever fully lives up to its professed dominant ideals: there is always some gap between the articulated central values and their actual implementation in practice. In every society the recognition of this gap constitutes a powerful lever for social change. However, this gap between principle and practice is often blurred in societies where social change is slow and social institutions relatively strong and unchanging.

In such societies there develops what Keniston has termed the 'institutionalisation of hypocrisy'. There develops a stock of common-sense knowledge or wisdom about when and where it is reasonable to expect people to adhere strictly to certain central values, and when and where it is unreasonable to hold such expectations. It is this stock of common-sense knowledge that makes it acceptable and legitimate for the 'honest and sincere' businessman who professes an attachment to one set of values by which he seeks to lead his private and family life, to ignore them in his business life and public activities. The kinds of processes by means of which the young member of society is expected to become familiar with the taken-for-granted hyprocrisy of everyday life is illustrated particularly well in the following passage from Norman Mailer's *The Naked and the Dead*.[15]

The sermon ends in church. We are all children of the Lord Jesus and God, instruments of His compassion, committed unto earth to enact the instruments of His goodness, to sow the seeds of brotherhood and good works.

A fine sermon, the mother says.

Yeahp.

Was he right? Edward asks.

Certainly, Cyrus says, only you got to take it with a grain of caution. Life's a hard thing and nobody gives you nothing. You do it alone. Every man's hand is against you, that's what you also find out.

Then he was wrong, Father.

I didn't say that. He's right and I'm right, it's just in religion you act one way, and in business, which is a lesser thing, well, you go about things in another way. It's still Christian.

In times of rapid social and value change, however, this institutionalization of hypocrisy seems to break down. New situations and practices develop with the result that the areas of value-exemption have not had time to be defined and generally accepted. The universal gap between principle and practice appears with unusual clarity. This is particularly apparent to the middle-class young who are to be found amongst the ranks of the student radicals and the underground. Flacks has written of the situation that confronts those members of the young generation who have been reared in middle-class families where the values of egalitarianism and personal autonomy were stressed and a sceptical attitude towards authority encouraged. Such people are, he has written, 'likely to be particularly sensitive to the hypocrisies, rigidities, and injustices of particular institutions and of the society as a whole as they experience it'.[16]

The ability of many of today's youth to perceive the conflict between values deemed relevant as guides for action in some situations and irrelevant in others, and the conflict between formal values and practice, and their questioning of such apparent contradictions, is enhanced as a consequence of their educational experiences. With the expansion of higher education, increasing numbers of young people, especially those from middle-class backgrounds, are staying on at college and university until their early and mid-twenties. Whereas primary and secondary education is generally characterized by the fairly straight and uncritical transmission of generally accepted knowledge, in the later stages of secondary and tertiary education there is a greater emphasis upon stimulating the student's critical judgment and rational scepticism. Thus, on the one hand, young people are likely to internalize many of the central values and abstract ideals of society through exposure to them through their teachers, while at the same time a degree of critical awareness is fostered. Thus students particularly are likely to be highly sensitized to any apparent divorce between ideals and reality.

In the light of these observations, it does not seem so surprising that for many young people in the modern world, particularly those from middle-class backgrounds, the transition from youth to adulthood appears as either extremely problematic or downright undesirable. Given the unattractiveness or irrelevance of the majority of adult role-models available, given the apparent moral corruption and hyprocrisy of adult society, and given the fact that many of today's youth, particularly those from affluent middle-class origins, want something more out of life than material success—given these facts, then it is not surprising that many young people are relatively available for recruitment to movements which appear to present possible solutions to their personal identity problem and their estrangement from the existing order of society.

The relative availability of young people to movements that appear to be predominantly age-related rather than related to such factors as class, geographical locale, or nationality, is made more understandable if reference is made to the argument presented in the previous chapter. It was argued that one factor which has contributed towards the emergence of the phenomenon of profound identity crises for the individuals embroiled in society was the extent of individual geographical and social mobility with the resulting loss and break-up of the traditional community of birth and origin. One of the results of this increasingly common trend for the parental generation, it was argued, was that sacramentalism of consumption whereby the display function of consumer goods starts to replace intimate and honest interpersonal relationships as the major source of reaffirmation and assurance of the individual's worth. It is possible to argue that the groping activities and enterprises of the young members of the underground represents not only a reaction against the perceived emptiness of such a way of life, but is also comparable to the sacramentalism of consumption in so far as they represent efforts to create symbols which give meaning to the individual's life, the focusing of one's thoughts and activities on some pursuit which gives meaning to one's existence.

For the young, subjected to this geographical and social mobility, the loss of the home community has meant that they have also been deprived of the traditional, local role-models that existed as examples to be followed or avoided in the process of growing up. The loss of this support in the identity search of certain sections of modern youth has meant that increasing numbers are more available to be influenced by more cosmopolitan age-related reference groups. Partly as a consequence of the growth of the 'global village', which has meant that what California does today Aberdeen hears about a few hours later, partly as a consequence of the realization on the part of the consumer industry of the actual size of the young population and its importance as a section of the market to be attacked and exploited,[17] and partly as a consequence of the use of the media by the genuine pace-makers of the youth movements to spread the word, the sources of identity available to modern youth are far more cosmopolitan, trans-national, and more specifically age-related, than those that were available for earlier generations.

In going on to consider the nature of the underground as a general social movement, an attempt will be made to approach it from three perspectives, each of which, it is hoped, will throw some light on certain salient features of the movement. The perspectives are as follows: (a) the underground as a movement of fashion, (b) the underground as a movement of individuals seeking self-realization, and (c) the underground as a movement for radical, social and cultural change.

The underground as fashion

I had been at the Roundhouse, Chalk Farm, London, N.W.1 on the afternoon of 2 August 1970 for the Festival of Communes which had been advertised as 'a big informal information-exchanging and food-sharing Meal and Meeting for Communes and people interested in Communes, plus (perhaps) chanting and other signs of togetherness, plus (perhaps) Quintessence and Third Ear Band . . .' I, and a number of friends, were watching the procession of young people queueing for the Implosion Benefit Concert for the Commune Movement which followed the general get-together. We were discussing the events of the afternoon. Some of us felt that a great opportunity might have been missed that afternoon for groups and individuals genuinely interested in forming or joining communes, and who had never had the opportunity to meet before, to get together, discuss plans, exchange ideas, and so forth. Instead, the information-exchanging function of the Festival had somehow appeared to have been swamped by the 'signs of togetherness' aspect. We had witnessed and participated in a three-hour-long 'happening' dominated by a group around the stage playing an assortment of bongo drums, tambourines, beer cans, sticks, and anything else they could get their hands on to beat out an African-style rhythmic pattern to which people danced, ate, wandered and tried to talk. It was a marvellous experience of togetherness and an expression of joy in life, movement, song, music and 'Being'; but, at the back of our minds, as we watched the people filing back into the Roundhouse, was the feeling that the whole thing had been a bit too much like some great publicity stunt for the benefit of the mass media of straight society, and to be heralded by the underground press as the Commune Movement's own equivalent to Woodstock.

As we watched the queues of women dressed in standard variations of the common theme of maxi-length dresses, second-hand clothes, and bare feet, and the men with their levi jeans, long hair, beards and sandals, one of us remarked, 'I wonder how many of them will be dressed like that and show the same interest if this was to happen again in ten years' time.' Behind this remark was the thought that, for many of the people there, to be a member of the underground and to display the standard assortment of modes of dress, styles of speech and so on, was merely a matter of fashion—the 'in' thing to be doing that year for young people, particularly if you lived in Notting Hill, with the implication that it was for many of them a merely temporary and tenuous commitment to the movement which they would grow out of in time.

To understand this fashionable 'trendy' aspect of the underground movement, it is necessary first of all to understand how the particular nature of the identity problem associated with the age span of youth makes the members of this age-range particularly available to movements of fashion. I have described how the identity problem of youth in the modern world appears to be increasingly acute. This sort of problem is shared to a greater or lesser degree by the majority of the members of the youthful age span, and hence there exists a latent community of interest. If this becomes articulated as a collective awareness of shared positions and problems, then there develops an age-related group consciousness—an age group.

I have suggested that modern youth are particularly available to cosmopolitan age-related sources of identity provided by élite groups, pace-makers and the mass media. However, there is a problem inherent in the taking on of an age-related social identity, with its implication that there is something unique and special about the holders of this identity as compared with older age-groups. If the uniqueness is over-specified, and the contrast between the roles associated with the young age-group and those associated with the adult age-group is over-drawn, then it makes it rather difficult for the individual to make smoothly the transition, which appears as so necessary to many, into one of the currently available adult role-models with the passing of youth. In other words: if the distinctive-ness of the identity associated with a particular age span is over-specified, then the individual's passage on to occupy roles associated with subsequent age spans can become problematic.

As a consequence of this problem, the most common means of age-group differentiation tend to be, on the one hand, readily visible and easily recognizable by the on-looking public but, at the same time, superficial, in the sense of not provoking too much value-dissensus between age-groups. Fashion meets the bill perfectly with regard to these two criteria, enabling the individual by his dress style, appearance and language to assert his unique identity without placing himself in a position which will make it difficult for him to return to the fold of adult roles later in life.[18]

The range of material that is subject to fashion and available to be used and copied as identity-props in the social world is rapidly expanding. Apart from clothes and styles of appearance, speech styles, areas to live in, the kind of car to have, the type of food to be eaten, the type of cigarette to be smoked, the points of view to be held—one gets the impression that the choice of one's mate, the nature of one's sex life and the type of child to be reared is increasingly a subject of fashion for people of all ages.

Just as for increasing numbers of adults their mode of life is to a large extent determined by the models offered for their consumption and adoption by the advertising media, so for increasing numbers of young people their style of dress, mode of speech, forms of music and art to be appreciated, and kinds of activities to be participated in, are merely matters of fad and fashion. While many participants in the underground can be seen as experimenting with the social identities offered by membership in the general movement, they are 'plastic heads' in so far as the identities they act out are merely copies of the original as offered by the pace-makers and trend-setters of the movement. The dabbling with drugs, mystical religion, the participation in arts labs, the watching of underground films, the attendance at pop festivals, the display of the latest underground magazine under the arm and the frequent use of certain key expressions of speech such as 'beautiful', 'straight' and so on, are matters of display to the public audience, artificial supports for their lack of a sense of a meaningful identity. They are playing at the role of being a member of the underground. They are poseurs.

Klapp has referred to the fact that it is possible to locate various levels of posing amongst beatniks—in some ways the forerunners of the underground in the bohemian tradition. Among the different levels he refers to we find[19]

> the regular beatniks, whose style is as correctly beatnik as a
> society woman's is chic; weekend beatniks, who have two
> styles supported by separate groups; unsupported—one might
> call them cookbook—beatniks, who get their ideas about the
> role not from their fellows but from the copious literature; and
> 'fashionable' or 'partly' beatniks, for whom the style is merely
> a costume.

That he should find these different levels of posing should not surprise us—we are all poseurs to some extent or other in so far as we all seek to project a particular image of ourselves to onlookers and so enable them to identify us as a particular sort of person from whom they can expect certain typical beliefs, attitudes and behavioural patterns. The difference lies in the degree to which one consciously plays the role, without investing any deep personal commitment and involvement in it, the degree to which the public face is a false mask as opposed to something which is genuinely felt to be an expression of the 'real me'.[20]

Members of the underground can be located on all points of this scale. For some, their public face as a member of the underground is a confidence trick which they play because they get rewards and pleasure from it; for the vast majority, however, there is genuine feeling of identification with the movement, as personified by the opinion leaders of the pop groups, the writers in the underground press and so on. This feeling becomes all the stronger when such figures are, as the members of the underground might define it, pilloried by the Establishment for alleged drug offences, as in the case of John Lennon and Mick Jagger, and for alleged obscenity as in the case of Richard Neville and the editors of *Oz* magazine. At the same time, there is for many young people the awareness of a certain shallowness of commitment, of the fact that identification with the movement is merely a temporary stopping-off point on their passage through life into the adult roles and identities that are waiting for them, however reluctant they might be, when the time comes. For them, the underground is merely a fashion.

However, even if a large proportion of the people who, while young, identify with the bohemian culture of the underground return to the welcoming arms of conventional society, they are almost certain to take with them certain of the attitudes and expectations that they have acquired from the movement. Such attitudes will colour their approach to their future jobs, careers, sex and family life. While the underground is no more than a fashion for many, its influence on the subsequent life patterns and modes of looking at the world of those who have passed through it is likely to be substantial. Fred Davis has written of one of the likely long-term effects on American society of the hippies' sub-culture, and has come to a similar conclusion, that[21]

> even among those youth who remain in conventional society in some formal sense, a very large number can be expected to hover so close to the margins of the hippie subculture as to have their attitudes and outlooks substantially modified. Indeed, it is probably through some such muted, gradual, and indirect process of social conversion that the hippie subculture will make a lasting impact on American society, if it is to have any at all.

The underground as a movement of individuals seeking self-realization

Buckman has written that[22]

> To be a member of the protesting underground, I consider, is an essentially behavioural phenomenon. It is living by what you

believe, with a set of attitudes shared by, but not sacred to, a number of people intent on challenging their society to live up to its promise. . . . It is a movement of social liberation through individual liberation. Everyone must be free to do their own thing. The Underground puts self at the centre of its spectrum. That is, no form of social or political liberation, however desirable, can take place unless its first priority is to allow each individual to determine his own desires, free from psychological, political or conventional pressures.

This is certainly how many of the pace-makers of the movement view it, anyway. But what is the defining creed of the underground? What is its programme? As one would expect from a general movement, it is almost impossible to delineate such features—the underground has more the character of a mood, a general mode of looking at the world and the individual, than any firm set of premises. It is the agreement on a set of values which are counter to those generally taken for granted as valid and relevant by the bulk of society that defines the parameters of the underground. The values of productivity, work, delayed gratification, the accumulation of wealth and consumer goods, competition, the sanctity of marriage and pre-marital chastity, 'my country right or wrong', strong government and so on—it is the questioning of such values which is perhaps the key characteristic of the underground membership.

Perhaps above all, the members reject what they view as the over-routinized, over-managed quality of individual life in the modern world—the life of the happy robot leading an empty existence made meaningful only by the pursuit of consumer goods and material wealth. The question they ask is an old one: 'What gain, then, is it for a man to win the whole world and ruin his life?' (Mark 8:36). As one commune member informed me, 'Each individual's life should be a search for self-fulfilment. You don't necessarily know what it is but you will know when you arrive. When you've arrived—start again—create a new reality.' The members of the underground seek to restore man as the controller of his own environment, to assert the primacy of the individual self over the claims of society and its institutions, and in the process restore meaning to individual existence. As such they are 'utopians' in the sense that they view the social world as a human product which is amenable to change through human agencies, rather than as an objective reality which is 'given' to man and as such cannot be transformed, and in so far as they actively seek to bring about change.

For the members of the underground, man is typically seen as a potentially creative, expressive and pleasure-seeking creature. Man in modern society is viewed as being repressed. It is only through giving vent to one's essential nature that one can realize one's true identity, and only through the awareness of one's true identity that one can go on to develop to the full one's innate potentialities. In pursuing this goal, the members of the underground have resorted to a number of techniques and courses of action, including communal living, sexual experimentation, and so on. Of course, the idea of 'Make Love, Not War' is not new. I can remember enquiring of an old friend as to the reason why he went on the Aldermaston marches. After a pause, he replied, 'Because it was the one place where you could be guaranteed an easy lay every night.' In similar fashion, Richard Neville quoted the American editor of an underground paper who explained, 'I'm only in the movement to meet chicks and get laid anyway.'[23]

Not all members of the underground are so honest. Many will justify their sexual experimentation in terms of rejecting the repressive morality of the straight society and in terms of putting into practice their belief in the family of man. Basically, however, such a search for a more varied sex life on the part of the members of the underground is a reflection of their belief in the immediate gratification of one's needs, rather than deferment of the fulfilment of one's sexual needs until after marriage. Few would go as far as William Blake, but many would sympathize with his injunction that one should 'sooner murder an infant in its cradle than nurse an unacted desire'.[24]

Related to this involvement in sexual experimentation as part of the quest for individual freedom and self-realization is the use by many members of the underground of hallucinogenic drugs in general, and marijuana and LSD in particular. The fact that the use of such hallucinogens is so widespread within the underground is simply a reflection of the fact that they are viewed as facilitating the quest for one's true identity and the fulfilment of one's creative potential.

The problem that confronts the individual who seeks to discover his essential self is one of knowing how to transcend the constraints of the straight world in general, and in particular the problem of how to break out of the traditional taken-for-granted view of the world that is held by the majority of the members of society in order to, as a respondent phrased it, 'create a new reality'. The use of hallucinogenic drugs, it is claimed, is one way of solving this problem. As Allen Ginsberg has remarked, quoting Dr Roubichek, 'LSD inhibits conditioned reflexes.'[25] In other words, the psychedelic trip is viewed as one way by which the individual can transcend the alienated state of the happy robots of society, as described in the preceding chapter, whose view of the world denies the richness of worldly possibilities open to man and thereby denies them their chance of discovering their true selves. The use of awareness-increasing drugs such as marijuana and LSD is viewed as an important means of attaining that utopian mentality which enables the individual to perceive that 'what has been beyond question so far and remained unquestioned up to now may always be put in question'.[26] It is argued that the psychedelic removes the 'filters' from the rational-functional section of the brain and thereby enables the individual to view the world and his own existence with new eyes, so facilitating his escape from the repression of the conventionally taken-for-granted view of the world and its associated alienated condition. Freed from the constraints of workaday reality, the individual can look within himself in order to discover his true self, as a first step towards the realization of his full potentialities as an autonomous and creative human being in a man-made world. To quote one writer:[27]

> The manner in which the hallucinogens make transparent the relative nature of seemingly absolute standards of conduct make them attractive to a culture which views contemporary man as alienated and social mores as mere games to be played. Culture is a game because it consists of rules created by man and sustained only by his adherence. It is alienating because these rules are thought of as existing apart from, and superordinate to, individual desires for self-expression. Identity is therefore sought in a subterranean reality. Moreover, the drugs which are vehicles to this realm promise insight into the social basis of identity; they invite an exciting exploration, a trip through the esoteric pathways of the psyche.

Of course, drugs are not the only means of altering one's consciousness. The yogic traditions of the Hindu and Buddhist offer non-chemical means of transcendence through meditation, breathing exercises, chanting, diet, and so on. As William James phrased it, 'all the different steps in yoga are intended to bring us scientifically to the superconscious state of Samadhi',[28] that state where the mystic achieves liberation from illusion and 'the truth shines in all its effulgence, and we know ourselves'.[29]

There would appear to be little doubt that the effects of attaining liberation from the 'game' of life is common to both the psychedelic 'tripper' and the mystic.[30] Thus:[31]

> The irreligious man and the man who is religious in the con-ventional sense both differ radically from the mystic because they are enmeshed—not in their own unconscious and its imperious demands—but in the unexamined purposes of the hierarchically ordered external world. The tribal super-ego, which forces its compulsions on the collectivity under the guise

of freely chosen pragmatisms . . . is the flux from which the
mystic is determined to detach himself.

Given the continuity of mystical and drug experiences in terms of
the nature of the actual experiences and the aims claimed by the
mystics and the 'heads', it is not surprising that many users of drugs
have become involved in mystic and esoteric religious groups and
communities.[32] Thus many members of contemporary communes,
whether they use drugs or not, emphasize the important role of such
yogic methods as meditation as a means of heightening self-awareness as a basis for the creation of a rewarding form of communal
life. As one person has written:[33]

Because one is inextricably related to everything else in the
universe it isn't really accurate to speak of 'founding a community' as if community did not exist. . . . What I am suggesting is that when we speak of 'founding or joining a community'
we really mean that we wish to involve ourselves in more
creative relationships. . . . But better relationships can only
happen when we are no longer at loggerheads with ourselves
and our environment. For a beginning has to be made with
ourselves in the here and now. . . . And this is where I think
meditation comes in, or any other practice which heightens our
self-awareness and enables us to relate ourselves more creatively
to our circumstances. This, I believe, is the growing point of
true community and I think that any community that grows out
of the light that meditation practice can throw on a person's
path will be more solidly founded than one which is at the
mercy of well-intentioned blundering in the dark of our own
unaware ignorance and insensitivity.

It was not unusual to discover, during the course of my research,
that those commune members who practised meditation and other
non-chemical means of increasing one's awareness had typically had
a wide experience of various forms of drug use but had ceased to use
them as their interest in meditation and the religious traditions of
the Orient had increased. This was what one would have expected
however, given that drugs have been generally resorted to by the
user as one means of overcoming the life-problems that appeared to
confront him in general, and in particular, the problem of personal
identity. One would expect that, once an individual discovered
alternative solutions to his problems that did not involve the use of
drugs, his reliance on drugs as a problem-solver would decline.

Just as the involvement of members of the underground with drug
experimentation and with mystic religions can be understood in
terms of their response to the problem of personal identity which
many of them feel, and their search for their essential self as a

means of attaining self-realization, so their interest and involvement in a peculiarly western form of yoga, the encounter group, can be understood. Such encounter-groups or awareness sessions generally consist of a group of people who meet together and, having sought to create an atmosphere of complete honesty and trust, seek to develop their awareness of themselves, others, and life in general, through such methods as game-playing, psycho-drama, exercises, and group encounters when individual members are subjected to the experience of group criticism and group praise. The idea behind such sessions is to create an environment within which the participants can step out of the strait-jackets represented by their social roles, and so be left free to discover their true selves through the means of game-playing and so on. Interest in such activities is not, however, confined to members of the underground. Indeed, the Esalen Institute in California, where the technique was developed, runs a great number of courses for people involved in industry and commerce.[34] However, the yogic method represented by such encounter groups has attracted the interest of members of the underground in general, and the commune movement in particular. Thus an important part of the group life at a community in London revolved around the group encounter sessions, which were seen, along with the group meditation sessions and the experience of group living in itself, as important means of obtaining true consciousness of the self.[35]

Such techniques of 'consciousness expansion' as drug use, mysticism and meditation, and involvement in encounter groups frequently involve a certain degree of withdrawal from active social involvement. As such, they must appear to many people as essentially private, apolitical forms of deviance with little relevance to the promotion of radical social change and the creation of an alternative society. However, in the minds of the members of the underground such activities are viewed as revolutionary, in so far as they believe that one cannot attain that social order within which freedom for all will be possible without first experimenting with what freedom means for the individual, and that one cannot discover true freedom as an individual until one has first of all examined the inner recesses of one self and discovered one's essential nature. Thus they believe that the revolution must start with one's own head and in one's own daily life. One of the founder members of a commune has written:[36]

The centre has come into existence as a response to the problems created by modern life in the West, a way of life which is increasingly unsatisfactory and frustrating to all sorts of people and which seems to threaten the survival of man on this planet. It is not difficult to see that it is the individual who is the source of energy and life in society, that society has no volition or life apart from that of its individual members, that the ecological problems which now face us are created by individual acts from minute to minute all over the world. And it is not difficult to see that these same problems can only be solved in so far as the individual can change his modus vivendi so that he no longer contributes to their causes.

Apart from being an excellent illustration of what has been termed above the 'utopian mentality', with the belief 'that society has no volition or life apart from that of its individual members', this quotation illustrates the intrinsic link that is seen to exist by the members of the underground between societal change and individual transformation, the former being achieved by means of the latter. Only through the discovery of one's own inner identity, through drug use or some other means, it is argued, can the individual hope to realize his true self and thereby make his contribution to radical social change. This emphasis on the importance of the individual in the process of revolutionary change reveals a peculiarly anarchist element in the contemporary underground, and it is to a consideration of this aspect of the movement that attention is turned in the next section.

The underground as a revolutionary movement: the revival of anarchism

It is not the purpose of this section to provide a comprehensive account of the development of that revolutionary movement among a minority of the young of the Western world that has come to be labelled the 'underground', nor is it intended to provide any appraisal of the revolutionary potential of this movement.[37] Rather, an attempt will be made to set the scene for the following chapters by pointing to the essential continuity that exists between certain wings of the contemporary movement and the anarcho-pacifist tradition, and then providing a brief descriptive account of some of the major features of the contemporary movement.

Woodcock, in the epilogue to his standard work on anarchism, wrote of 1939 as the date of the death of the anarchist movement. Since that time such anarchist groups as have existed have formed, he wrote, 'only the ghost of the historical anarchist movement, a ghost that inspires neither fear among governments nor hope among peoples nor even interest among newspaper men'.[38] However, Woodcock was here referring to the anarchist movement as founded by Bakunin a century earlier. The anarchist idea, that had existed for centuries before Bakunin, continued to live on, and at the very end of the book Woodcock concluded with what might now seem a rather prophetic comment, although one senses that it was written more in hope than in genuine anticipation:[39]

To acknowledge the existence and the over-bearing force of the movement toward universal centralization that still grips the world is not to accept it. If human values are to survive, a counter-ideal must be posed to the totalitarian goal of a uniform world, and that counter-ideal exists precisely in the vision of pure liberty that has inspired the anarchist and near-anarchist writers from Winstanley in the seventeenth century . . . it (the anarchist ideal) can help in the urgent task of mere survival, of living out the critical decades ahead until the movement of world centralization loses its impetus like all historical movements, and the moral forces that depend on individual choice and judgement can reassert themselves in the midst of its corruption.

That the anarchist idea has come again to the fore in the new youth movement that began to emerge with the beatniks of the 1950s has been commented upon by a number of writers.[40] What also appears to be happening is that a viable anarchist movement seems to be emerging, even if the members do not necessarily think of themselves as anarchists. It is, in fact, interesting to note that, just as the traditional anarchist movement was divided into opposing schools of thought with regard to the use of violent means as a mechanism of change, so the younger generation of radicals is split in a similar manner. This division is perhaps best illustrated by the contrast between the following two poems, the first written by Julian Beck of the 'Living Theatre', the other taken from 'Space Cowboy' by the Steve Miller Band.[41]

it is 1968
i am a magic realist
i see the adorers of che

i see the black man
forced to accept
violence

i see the pacifists
despair
and accept violence

i see all all all
corrupted
by the vibrations

vibrations of violence of civilization
that are shattering
our only world
. . . .

we want
to zap them
with holiness

we want
to levitate them
with joy

we want
to open them
with love vessels
we want
to clothe the wretched
with linen and light

we want
to put music and truth
in our underwear

we want
to make the land and its cities glow
with creation

we will make it
irresistible
even to racists
. . . .

we want to change
the demonic character of our opponents
into productive glory.

In direct contrast:[42]

Let me tell you people that I've found a new way
And I'm tired of all this talk about love. . . .
You back-room schemers, star-struck dreamers
Better find something new to say;
It's the same old story, same old song
And you've got some heavy dues to pay. . . .
. . . I've been travelling through space
Since the moment I first realized
What all you fast-talking cats would do if you could
I'm ready for the final surprise.

Despite such manifest differences of approach between the modern
day Tolstoyans and Bakuninites they share, among other things, that

peculiarly anarchist rejection of conventional political procedures combined with a passionate sense of the political responsibility of the individual. They meet on common anarchist ground in their radical critique of the technocratic society, their ascetic attitude towards property and worldly goods in general, and in their desire to simplify life. However, in this section I am not concerned with 'Street Fighting Men' such as the 'Weathermen' in the U.S.A. and the 'Angry Brigade' in Britain, but with those who seem to have come to the conclusion that freedom and moral self-realization are interdependent, that neither can be attained within the confines of the prevailing society, and who have therefore set about creating their own alternative society. I am concerned with those who are involved with the arts laboratories, the craft co-operatives, the free universities, the free schools, the alternative press, the community action projects and, of course, the communes.

The vision that all these individuals share is Shelley's dream of a society in which man may rise to his full glory:

Sceptreless, free, uncircumscribed, but man
Equal, unclassed, tribeless, and nationless,
Exempt from awe, worship, degree, the king
Over himself, just, gentle, wise . . .

The way to bring this world into being is one of exemplary action, the creation of alternative structures and institutions counter to those of the dominant society, and, above all, to work upon oneself and to transform oneself and one's relationships with others and thereby to change the social world. This was a point emphasized by the editor of an American underground magazine:[43]

Neither dropping out to set up ideal societies nor making
bombs for the revolution makes much sense in my book.
Self-awareness comes first. Opening up, being honest with
others, exposing oneself in interaction with friends—that's the
beginning of the real revolution. If we are to have a more
humanistic and ideal social structure, we have to work on our
own hang-ups just as hard as we work on changing the system.

These modern-day anarchists share with Tolstoy and Thoreau a belief that the moral strength of a single man who is prepared to speak and to live the truth as he sees it is greater than that of a multitude of silent slaves.

The anarchist tradition is found not only in their vision of man, their rejection of established authority, and their abhorrence of orthodox organizations, but also in their adoption of a form of 'propaganda of the deed' in the shape of a determination to offer as many constructive alternatives to what they see as current problems and abuses as the mind can bear. Such a strategy of change, involving the creation of meaningful counter-institutions as alternative structures to the institutions of straight society, follows quite naturally from the analysis of the human condition typically held by members of the underground. While recognizing the importance of the social question, the problems of material deprivation and economic exploitation faced by large numbers of people in modern society, their major concern, which perhaps reflects their own largely middle-class social origins, is with another aspect of the human condition—the quality of life in society, a life which they see as meaningless, spent largely in the execution of boring, repetitive, pointless work-tasks for the sake of acquiring the consumer goods and all the other trappings of our materialistic age. Thus communitarians, when asked what particular aspect of life in modern society they found particularly unbearable, found great difficulty in specifying one particular aspect, but were far more likely to view life as a whole in modern society as unbearable. As one respondent expressed what she found most unbearable, 'The whole nine-to-five business. You are like a machine. It is no life.'

Intrinsically linked with this is a parallel concern with the question of freedom—the view that life as typically led by man in society is increasingly subjected to the control and regulation of the 'powers out there'. Man is seen as having been deprived, or as having deprived himself, of the will to control his own life and destiny. He is viewed as the happy robot leading an over-routinized life made meaningful solely by the selfish pursuit of material goods.

Given this view that it is the quality of life as a whole in straight society which is so repugnant, the aim of the underground is frequently viewed not so much in terms of righting particular wrongs or the promotion of specific causes as in terms of the creation of a completely new social order, an alternative society. As various members have described it to me, it is a society 'in which each individual can have the right and the space to exercise his creative autonomy', 'a society in which the Brotherhood of Man is realized', with 'people caring for each other and sharing', and 'a society in which the alternative is always open . . . where, if you don't like where you are, there are always a few choices available. . . . Freedom of choice is the prime criterion.'

This utopia is to be attained largely through the non-coercive means of individual change and exemplary action, aimed at demonstrating to the straights that alternative and more meaningful modes of life and institutional arrangements are possible and within the reach of all. The aim of the counter-institutions is to provide a challenge and a threat to existing social structures seeking to challenge their legitimacy. Given the belief typically held by members of the underground that the majority of non-believers are tied to the prevailing order of things not so much by the coercive power of the state as by their blinkered vision, that they are unable to conceive of an alternative reality because of the conditioning processes they have undergone through their educational experiences, it is natural that many of the experiments in counter-institution building have been concerned with presenting alternatives to the conventional educational process. Free universities and free schools are just two types of venture that are being experimented with by members of the underground.

In Britain free universities have not developed to the same extent that they have in the U.S.A., but there have been one or two notable experiments. One of these was the Anti-University of 1968 that grew out of the Dialectics of Liberation Congress that was held in London in the summer of 1967. Among the proposed goals of this venture were that it would not use labels such as 'student' and 'teacher' that would structure and constrain human relations within the institution; that it would act as a centre for radical politics; and that it would provide 'an alternative to the contemporary university, with its "battery student" gobbling information fed him to produce eggs for the system'.[44]

Although by no means an unparalleled success, this experiment appeared to bear more fruit than an earlier venture that Jeff Nuttall has described.[45]

The free university movement, well established in the United States and the backbone from which the strength of the Underground must ultimately spring, consists largely of voluntary week-end schools at which radical academics can meet their non-academic counterparts and pool their ideas. Joe Berke, a New York psychiatrist who had conducted a free coffee bar clinic, appeared at the Kingsley Hall in London as soon as the Philadelphia Foundation took over in 1965. Immediately he wanted to start the same activities there as had been taking place in the Free University of New York. Unfortunately he hadn't accounted for the yawning gaps existing between the English Underground, the English left-wing liberals, and his 'professionally' defensive colleagues in the Philadelphia Foundation, who refused to allow him to use Kingsley Hall for his weekend schools. The London Free School moved, then, to a disused cellar in Notting Hill Gate where John Hopkins and Rhaunic Lasslet struggled, in opposite directions, to make it into a kind of local spontaneous Centre 42. . . . Ultimately the Free School did nothing constructive but put out a local Underground newsletter and organise the two

Notting Hill Gate Festivals, which were, admittedly, models of exactly how the arts should operate—festive, friendly, audacious, a little mad and all taking place on demolition sites, in the streets, and in a magnificently institutional church hall in Powis Gardens.

In 1968 the University of Birmingham was the scene of an attempt to create a free university as an alternative to the existing university. A distinctly personal version of the origins of 'FUB' (Free University of Birmingham) has been written by one of the early activists, Richard Bluer.[46]

The event responsible, more than any other single one, for any expanded political consciousness on the campus was the sit-in of 1968. . . . Although nothing concrete emerged from the sit-in . . . many people came to realise the tyrannical and unjust way that the university is run, and turn-ons of all natures were had by all. Those of us who were sick of retching up the bad trips doled out by the university had a collective hallucination of a non-coercive, joyful way of learning which people would follow because their humanity bade them to, not because their frightened desire for security told them to. Like a body of hot gas condensing into a star, the hallucination stopped eluding us and made the painful, degrading journey into the realms of reality, germinating in one final wriggle as the Free University of Birmingham.

However, the Free University of Birmingham had, by 1971, failed in one of its original aims, which was to involve members of the general Birmingham public in the courses. As Richard Bluer has commented:[47]

Where FUB most obviously failed was in not involving the population of the 'real' world. The first courses were made up almost entirely of people connected with the Old University, substantially post-graduates and staff at that, with a concomitant 'high-brow' academic approach to most topics which alienated those of the community outside who did turn up.

This emphasis on community involvement, on acting as a catalyst for social change in the wider community, is a theme that is to be found running through other experiments in counter-institution building. One example, again within the field of alternative educational institutions, is that of the Scotland Road Free School, an attempt to create an alternative type of school along the lines of A. S. Neill's Summerhill in the Scotland Road area of Liverpool.[48] The following extract from their introductory pamphlet reveals the

D   87 emphasis placed on encouraging the free and creative development of the child within a libertarian educational system, and the felt need to create an alternative to the present state system of education, in the belief that the example displayed by such an experiment will contribute to the creation of a new and far-reaching system of education, at the same time as encouraging the inhabitants of the local community to take control of their own lives and their immediate environment through community self-help ventures.

There will be set up in the Scotland Road–Vauxhall area of Liverpool, an alternative type of school to be known as the Scotland Road Free School. The school will be a community school which will be totally involved with its environment. The nature of this involvement will be such that the school will be in the vanguard of social change in the area. By accepting this role, the school will not seek to impose its own values, but will have as its premise a total acceptance of the people and the area. It is felt that the organisation of education is insensitive, unaware and in content largely irrelevant to the needs of the children and their future role as adults in the society. Particularly in the Scotland Road–Vauxhall area, it has not provided for the aspirations, life and culture of the people, who have a social heritage worthy of itself which must be given an identity and expression of its own. We do not seek to alienate people from their backgrounds but seek to enrich and intensify their lives. Only those who are educated in the fullest sense of the word, imaginative and creative; mature and tolerant; aware and concerned can hope to cope with the pressures and complexities of modern society. It is only those schools that consciously create an atmosphere of understanding and tolerance that best allow these qualities to develop.

The ultimate aim of the free school is to bring about a fragmentation of the state system into smaller, all age, personalised, democratic, locally controlled community schools which can best serve the immediate needs of the area in which they are situated. It is felt that the state system in contemplating change considers only innocuous reforms which do not question the total structure. We are obliged therefore to step outside the system in order to best demonstrate the feasibility and fulfilment of the free school idea. Having achieved this demonstration we are sure that society will enforce the adoption of the free school idea.

The school will not have a headmaster or hierarchy, nor will it recognize any central authority, but will be controlled by the parents, children and teachers together. This would be achieved democratically through a school council.

The school will operate as a day school but will never close whilst people desire to use its facilities. Lessons will not be compulsory, the onus will be upon the teacher to stimulate the children sufficiently to attend. . . . A major area of activity for the Scotland Road Free School will be to demonstrate how a community school can continue the educational process into all areas of life throughout life.

Another specific movement within the general underground movement which displays a similar emphasis on seeking to develop the creative potential of the individual and the promotion and encouragement of participatory democracy through people controlling their own physical and social environment, is the Arts Laboratory movement. There is also the same emphasis on the need to develop new institutions outside of the established institutions of the arts. Typical of many such ventures, although more successful than most, was the Birmingham Arts Laboratory which came into existence in the spring of 1969. This experiment developed out of a felt need on the part of the original founders for new institutions in the arts based around the idea of community orientation, believing as they did that existing institutions had proved themselves too structured and rigid to cope with new movements inside the arts, and with the large numbers of young people wishing to experiment in these fields. The general aims of the arts laboratories are three-fold. First, to provide centres for the experimental arts. Second, to become communities of creative young people in complete control of their physical and social environment. Third, to use the situation thus established as a base for work both in and for the larger community, and to provide a realistic alternative to the commercialized arts.

The following extract taken from a statement of intent distributed by the Birmingham Arts Laboratory in June 1969 will give some indication of the types of activities with which most arts laboratories are involved.

Since April 1st progress has been steady. As well as continuing and expanding our weekend activities, (we booked a series of 'Angry Arts' films from London, not previously shown in the Midlands), we initiated a number of 'workshops' during the week. These are in kinetic art, 'political theatre' (in conjunction with the Free University of Birmingham), free form jazz; the writer's group, meeting on Fridays, has already produced six poetry broadsheets. The Lab has also been used regularly by a film unit on Saturdays, a group of West Indian singers, and

Tea and Symphony—one of the most interesting and talented groups in the country. A number of posters have been produced by screen-printing processes; an electronics workshop is moving in, and the photographic group is building a dark room. All these groups of people find the Lab useful and the atmosphere reasonably stimulating. Most importantly we have been a place where people could contact each other with a view to working together in the arts. For example, musical groups have been provided with light shows; singers with musicians; directors with actors; sculptors with sources of material; and so on. Many of the results of these contacts have gone out into the city to enrich its cultural life. . . . Today's problem is to cope with a social environment moving too fast and in too many directions for most people to assimilate. We believe that the applied arts are the best means of reaching people and giving them the tools to cope with their life more competently. . . . We want to try to reach individuals and groups through the media of music, theatre, mime, poetry, painting, films, and all the newly developing combined art forms. We believe that for an increasing number of people these are far more direct and powerful means of communication than the structured situations prevalent in bureaucratic organisations. . . .

Just as the Arts Labs can be seen as attempts to develop alternative institutions separate from the 'straight' institutions of the theatre, cinema, music concert and so on, and just as the free universities and free schools represent attempts to develop alternative educational institutions, so there have also been tentative attempts to develop alternative institutions to the conventional health services of society. One of the more successful of such projects has been P.N.P., People Not Psychiatry, which was formed in July 1969. This movement was established to provide an alternative form of service and treatment for the mentally ill and disturbed. It represented an attempt to take an individual psychiatric problem into a fresh group setting. It existed primarily to facilitate people with psychiatric problems to meet and talk with small groups of people who would present an understanding and sympathetic arena for the unburdening of troubles, outside of the official institutions for psychiatric care. The aim was to encourage the setting up of close and trusting relationships between two or three *people*, as opposed to *doctors*, *patients* and other stereotyped roles, within which environment people could speak openly about their 'hang-ups' and, through the feelings of acceptance and confirmation received from the others present in the group, learn to cope with their problems and overcome them.

Just as straight society, has its citizens' advice bureaux and other bodies, to advise them of their statutory rights and to provide them with help and information on a whole range of issues, so the members of the underground are developing their own alternative institutions to make more readily available for its members information and advice concerning the alternative society and the straight society. Amongst such counter-institutions one could mention BIT, which has been in existence for some years with the aim of acting as an alternative information/ideas/advisory/social work agency. Based in London, BIT's example has been instrumental in leading to the development of similar ventures in other centres of population such as Brighton, Manchester, Glasgow, Leeds, Bath and Cardiff. Other associated activities include the attempts to develop alternative career advisory services for those people who do not seek employment within the conventional occupational fields of business and industry.[49] There has also been a tremendous growth in the number of claimants' unions which have been established by people on supplementary benefits to advise others of their statutory rights with regard to the Supplementary Benefits Commission in particular and the social services in general.[50] There has also been in recent years a rapid growth in the numbers of underground newspapers and magazines. The growth of such papers throughout Britain is especially significant in so far as they represent not only an important means of communication for the members of the underground, but also provide their readers with a sense of belonging to a coherent and recognizable movement, and ensuring the spread of ideas and information not generally available in the 'overground' press. The birth of such newspapers and magazines has been greatly facilitated by the emergence of what can be termed underground printing and publishing institutions such as the Moss Side Press in Manchester, Open Press in Liverpool and Aberdeen Peoples Press.

In the area of the production of food, goods and services, the attempts of the members of the underground to develop alternative institutions to those of straight society which are concerned with such functions are only in the early stages of development. Many of the rural and urban communes discussed in the ensuing chapters are seeking to develop alternative means of producing food, particularly by organic farming methods, and goods such as clothing, furniture, pottery, candles, jewellery and such like. For those members of the underground who are involved in the processes of production, there is no shortage of outlets for their products. In almost any town in Britain one can find at least one 'head shop' concerned mainly with the sale and exchange of underground products of one sort or another. On the consumer side of things there has also been the development of food co-operatives by members of the underground. Such institutions provide for their members a means whereby they can reduce the cost of food and groceries through the establishment of an alternative service to that of the straight retail trade. In any given locality a group of people can get together and agree to pool their regular grocery orders. This enables them to purchase the total food order from a local 'cash and carry' wholesaler, thereby denying the retailer his profit.

Despite the diversity of such activities and projects, they are all concerned with the development of alternative or counter-institutions to those function-performing institutions of the straight society. As such, they have been created not solely to meet specific and practical needs but also to act as vanguards or frontier posts of the new age, the alternative society, which their participants seek to herald into existence through their exemplary action. It is now time attention was turned to a more detailed consideration of a specific social movement which can be viewed as engaged in a similar quest—the Commune Movement.

5 The commune movement in Britain

The approach presented in the previous chapter was of the underground, as a general movement from which has emanated specific social movements such as the commune movement. In this chapter I am concerned with attempting to map out some of the major features of this specific movement and its history before going on in later chapters to consider in more detail the nature of its membership and the world-views of its activists. In addition, a brief overview is given of some of the community experiments in modern Britain.

The commune movement as a specific social movement

One of the characteristics of specific social movements is that they have a formal organization or structure, with a formal membership, publications, stated aims and purposes. In Britain at the moment there is in existence a formal Commune Movement, the stated object of which is 'To create a federal society of communities wherein everyone shall be free to do whatever he wishes provided only that he doesn't transgress the freedom of another'.

The secretaries of the movement publish a bi-monthly journal, *Communes*, available free of charge to members; and in addition publish occasional newsletters for members containing information about the movement in general, current projects, points for discussion and correspondence, and which act as the main means of communication for the members of this movement.

In keeping with this stated object of the movement with its emphasis on the importance of individual autonomy as a desirable goal, the constitution contains several clauses designed to ensure that this is achieved with regard to the operations of the movement itself. Thus with regard to the literature published by the movement, it is stated in the constitution that 'No restriction will be imposed in the movement's literature, or in any other channel of expression, funds permitting, on discussion of sociological issues relevant to the objects of the movement'.

Again, with regard to membership, the constitution states that 'Subject to payment of membership subscription, and the attainment of 16 years of age, no application for membership may be refused. No members may be expelled or suspended.'

Further evidence of the value placed on individual freedom is the presence of a special clause in the constitution concerning 'Personal Autonomy' which concerns the right of members to preserve their anonymity if they so desire, otherwise the secretary used to publish each member's name and address in the journal after the member joined.[1]

In keeping with the anarchic emphasis of the stated object, the administration of the movement is vested in the entire membership, with decisions being reached on the basis of the results of a postal ballot of all the members, although the general level of participation is very low. The executive officers, first, second and third secretaries deal with most of the correspondence, publication of the journal and newsletter and so forth. They are elected annually by a ballot of all the members. Candidature is open to any member. Again, however, participation is very low.

The Commune Movement emerged in the mid-1960s out of what was then the Vegan Communities Movement. This original movement had as its stated objects:[2]

1 To establish and support vegan and progressive vegetarian communities.
2 To initiate and support humanitarian social experiments.
3 To propagate the principle of ahimsa, that is, the principle of complete avoidance of exploitation of all sentient life forms.

The rationale underlying the objects of the Vegan Communities Movement was clearly stated by Tony Kelly in the June 1965 issue of their journal *Ahimsa Communities* (no. 3)—the forerunner of the current journal *Communes*—in an article entitled 'The Need for Urgency'. In this article, fears of the impending world food shortage were raised, and the main answer suggested to meet this threat was the general adoption of the vegan diet. The article went on:[3]

This country and Europe are the most densely populated areas in the world, and we are going to feel the effects of world food shortage first . . . food prices will begin to climb . . . with accelerating pace. With food prices claiming an ever greater share of our income, there will be a rush to acquire a stake in our own diminishing acres and land prices will soar out of

reach. . . . Apart from the urge to acquire the means of maintenance of life, and apart too from the attraction of land as a
purely financial investment, town life is degenerating so that
those who can escape are doing so and adding to land price
inflation, while those who can't are taking refuge in alcohol, a
phenomenal consumption of tranquilizers, or displays of mass
violence and petty destruction. Government legislation to
favour small families would, at least at this stage, merely
ensure the overthrow of the government by an uneducated mass
prejudice, and rationalisation of our eating habits is still too
dangerous for a government to tackle if it hopes to stay in
office—and it certainly can do nothing effective out of office.
The new attitude must come from within rather than above,
and since the measures required are drastic by popular standards
we can only succeed by establishing small models and showing
that they work—both practically in terms of adequate food
production, and psychologically in terms of providing a meaningful, satisfying, and challenging environment. . . . At present
a few pioneers such as we can still afford to make mistakes,
and while making them, learn to render our shrinking acres
more productive. If groups such as we undertake a hundred
experiments and only one succeeds, that one will make the
hundred worthwhile, and the only viable economy—a vegan
one—will be established as a pattern upon which to base future
efforts at averting the famine.

At this time the number of journals sold was only in the region of
twenty to thirty and the membership of the movement in April 1966
was sixteen in number.

Towards the end of 1966 Tony Kelly, Betty Kelly and Pat Blackmore, who had been living together as a group at Wheathampstead
in Hertfordshire, completed purchase of a plot of land in Carmarthenshire, Wales, as the proposed site for their rural commune—the
Selene Community. By Easter 1967 the move from the home counties
to Wales was complete. But whilst the Vegan Communities Movement
could boast of the existence of one pioneer community, the membership of the movement was by this time down to fifteen.

It was in the December 1967 issue of *Ahimsa* that an article
appeared entitled 'Reappraisal' by Tony Kelly, who was at this time
Second Secretary (with two other members of Selene—Pat Blackmore
and John Hopkins—as First and Third secretaries respectively).
Membership was still as low as nineteen and Tony explained this as
being due largely to two factors: lack of advertising and a lack of
activity within the movement by its members. There was also the
feeling that

D*

despite the fact that a movement such as ours serves a very real need in modern society, we are simply not getting through because of lack of understanding of our purpose and to rectify this the movement needs to devote a considerable amount of energy to making its sociological ideals manifest. Let us break away from our one-sided attachment to the vegetarian and other animal welfare societies and declare much more forcefully our feeling of identity with all social reform, whether human or animal. (p. 1.)

In the journal's August issue an article appeared entitled 'Vegan Ethic Reappraised'—an account of a discussion at the Selene Community between Pat Blackmore, Betty and Tony Kelly and Ian Wood, as a result of which the members of Selene decided to give up their vegan ethic to become omnivores. This change resulted in the twenty-third issue of the journal appearing under the title of *Communes*—the Journal of the Commune Movement. However, at this time, October 1968, membership was still only twenty-four, despite the change in the nature of the movement and the resulting widening of its scope and appeal. It was also around this time that the Selene Community moved to their present home—a hill farm near Ffarmers in Carmarthenshire (Sir Gaerfyrddin).[4] Pat Blackmore and Tony Kelly, secretaries at this time, were responsible for most of the material in the journal, and in December 1968 Tony Kelly allowed himself a despairing moan in that month's issue. The movement at this time was still a minute one, confined to the members of Selene and a few others who had read of the movement in such journals as *Peace News* and *Gandalf's Garden*, and most of the administrative work was being carried by the members of Selene. Thus Tony Kelly moaned:

Selene Community needs help—urgently. When we appealed for newspaper cuttings the response was hardly noticeable. When we appealed for co-operation with our advertising campaign the response was absolutely nothing. The response to our suggestion regarding a federation fund was complete silence. There have been complaints that too much of the journal is about the Selene Community. We agree. Looking back over our four years' existence, material contributed by members of Selene Community amounted in 1965 to 79%, in 1966 to 32%, in 1967 to 90% and in 1968 to 93%.

These figures give some indication of the extent to which the Commune Movement, largely the creation of the people at Selene, was dependent on them for its continued existence.

In 1969 John Driver, from Taunton in Somerset, took over the first secretaryship, and it was in 1969 that the first signs appeared of a slow but steady growth in the fortunes of the movement, as evidenced by the size of the membership and the sale of journals. The figures in Table 2 might help to give some indication of the growth in the size of the movement. They are taken from the figures published in the journal.[5]

In 1970 the first secretaryship was taken over by Nicholas Albery, who spent his hours working for the underground information service 'BIT'. That Nicholas should have been executive officer of the

TABLE 2 *Journal and membership numbers*

Date	Journal: issue number	Member-ship	Additional journal subscriptions	Total number of journals distributed	Number of free copies	No. printed
Vegan Communities Movement						
Aug. 1965	4	22	10	41	9	
Apr. 1966	8	16	11	36	9	
Oct. 1966	11	23	17	50	10	
Dec. 1966	12	28	17	55	10	
Apr. 1967	14	15	9	31	7	
Jun. 1967	15	18	9	34	7	
Aug. 1967	16	19	10	35	6	
Oct. 1967	17	19	10	35	6	
Dec. 1967	18	19	11	36	6	
Feb. 1968	19	8	3	14	3	
Apr. 1968	20	8	5	16	3	
Aug. 1968	22	19	14	36	4	
Commune Movement						
Oct. 1968	23	24	18	46	4	
Dec. 1968	24	26	18	48	4	
Feb. 1969	25	23	4	45	18	
Apr. 1969	26	26	10	56	20	
Jun. 1969	27	32	15	72	25	200
Aug. 1969	28	61	17	107	29	300
Oct. 1969	29	92	18	160	50	450
Dec. 1969	30	108	19		49	700
Feb. 1970	31	129	21		55	1,000
Apr. 1970	32	125			55	1,500
Jun. 1970	33	170			56	2,500
Sep. 1970	34	214			70	2,500
Dec. 1970	35	286			70	2,500
Jan. 1971	36	310			70	1,000
Mar. 1971	37	354			70	3,000

Commune Movement and at the same time a long-serving member of the underground's twenty-four-hour information and co-ordinating service,[6] was significant. With Nicholas Albery taking up the office, it meant that links between the specific Commune Movement and the more general underground scene, centred as it was and is in the Notting Hill–Ladbroke Grove area of West London, were made more firm and tight. It was largely through the efforts of Nicholas and helpers that the sales of the journal grew from 700 at the end of 1969 to 2,500 by the middle of 1970. In the windows of most of the 'head' shops of London during 1970 could be seen copies of *Communes*, alongside *Oz, IT, Gandalf's Garden, Peace News* and other underground journals. In some ways 'BIT' is the linchpin of the London underground scene, the communication centre of what is an expanding range of activities—and Nicholas was well placed there to ensure that visitors and friends all became aware of the existence of the Commune Movement and its publications.

As the size of the membership has grown, and the sales of the journal increased along with the growth in the number of commune experiments in existence, it would appear that the movement has now reached its 'take-off' stage. Its role has been essentially one of bringing people together, of providing a means of communication between all those individuals interested in forming or joining a commune. At the same time, the movement has been able to provide a sense of solidarity and of not being alone to those members who have been particularly conscious of their status as cognitive deviants and have felt particularly threatened by the non-believers around them. That this feeling is a fairly common one can be judged by glancing at the letter columns of the journal. One correspondent expressed his position as follows:[7]

My position of living near to the destructive effects of modern 'life' which are ever blinding people to real experience of natural organic forces and sinking them into the areas of apathy and stagnation, often puts me in the need of reassurance from others. This usually comes in the form of books (also in the form of all art which flies on the creative wings of love, and also in small glimpses of the presence of love and beauty in my acquaintances under the coverings of much ugliness).

The role of the movement in helping the individual to overcome this sense of aloneness has been recognized by certain members. For instance:[8]

We only learned of the Commune Movement several months after we started planning our venture. It has been helpful in giving us contacts and ideas, but also in giving a kind of security, a feeling that we're not going it alone and that there are many others who feel the same as we do. Also it could become very useful as a source of information, financial aid and inter-communal activity.

Certainly it is one of the aims of the movement to provide the kind of financial aid referred to, and to this end a fund, the Federation Fund, has been established. This is a voluntary fund to which members are invited to contribute, the money to be used for the purpose of establishing communes. By the end of 1970, however, the fund had only reached just over £200.

While those involved in trying to form a commune might well stand in need of reassurance and financial aid, they may well be in need of practical help and advice also. It was with this thought in mind that Joan Harvey of Cambridge formed the Commune Services agency in February 1970. The aim was to create an agency that would be able to draw upon a pool of practical skills and technical knowledge to help those communes and individuals in need of such assistance. The importance of this service is likely to increase as the number of communes in existence grows.[9]

With these developments, the role of the people at Selene in the administration of the movement and the production of the journal has naturally declined. Articles in the journal are now contributed by a variety of readers and members, with the people at Selene mainly responsible for general drafting, lay-out, typing and so forth. Answering of enquiries, letters and general correspondence is handled by the secretaries and the printing of the magazine is now carried out by a commercial company, the duplicator at Selene no longer being required. All in all, the centre of activity of the Commune Movement during the period 1969–70 moved from a hill farm in Wales to the chaos of the BIT office among the slums of Notting Hill. The contrast in the physical surroundings is indicative of the contrasts and heterogeneity of the members of the Commune Movement. It is now time to take a look at some of the projects in which these members have been involved.

The commune scene in Britain: an overview

During the period leading up to and during the Second World War, Britain saw the spread of mainly rural experiments in communal living, generally founded by anarcho-pacifists of the Christian and Tolstoyan variety. In 1942 a publication by what was then called the Community Service Committee contained contributions from over fifty individuals and groups, giving the addresses of over thirty community experiments. Since that time most of the experiments recorded in that book have ceased to exist for one reason or another.[10]

It is only in recent years that community projects have begun to reappear in any significant number. Thus in August 1970 a *Directory of Communes* was published by the Commune Movement to coincide with the Festival of Communes held at the Roundhouse in London. The *Directory* contained about fifty separate entries concerned with the British commune scene. Although it would be true to say that of these fifty, a number of them were concerned with 'communes in the head', experiments still in the planning stage, it does give one some idea of the number of communes in existence in Britain today.[11] In presenting an overview of the nature and variety of the intentional communities in Britain, I shall be drawing upon the information contained in the *Directory*, and also upon my personal observations of those communes which I visited during the course of my research.

If one wanted to construct a classificatory framework of communes, one might choose from a variety of criteria to use as a basis for distinguishing the different types—whether the communes are rural or urban in situation, the length of time each commune has been in existence, the degree to which the members share the various activities of life such as work and income earning, play and creative activity, or beds and sexual activity. The variable that one chooses is largely determined by the nature and purpose of the classification that is to be constructed. As a major concern of this study of communes and their members was with attempting to explain and understand why certain types of people felt the need to live their daily lives in a communal setting, the classification of communes to be presented below is based on the communards' definitions of the goal or purpose of their particular experiment.

Most members of communes have some conception of the experiment of which they constitute a part as having some sort of purpose or goal—hence the term 'intentional community'. It is on the basis of the different intentions underlying different experiments that a fruitful distinction can be made between different types of communes. It is possible in this way to construct a basic six-fold typology: (1) self-actualizing communes, (2) communes for mutual support, (3) activist communes, (4) practical communes, (5) therapeutic communes, (6i) ascetic religious communes, and (6ii) mystic communes.

1 *Self-actualizing communes* By this type I intend to refer to those experiments that tend to be seen by their members as contributing towards the creation of a new social order by providing, within the community, that environment in which the individual members feel most free to find themselves, to develop their individual skills and creative potential to the utmost through the exercise of individual freedom.

100

2   *Communes for mutual support*   By this type I intend to refer to communes which are seen by their members primarily in terms of providing a setting of mutual support, a feeling of brotherhood, and a sense of mental, emotional and physical security for themselves. In other words, while they might well view their particular experiment as part of a wider movement for social change, the primary purpose of their commune is seen in terms of providing a haven of mutual reinforcement and understanding for themselves.

3   *Activist communes*   It is possible to distinguish those community experiments that are orientated primarily towards social change, but whose members seek to achieve this aim primarily by means of direct social involvement and political action in the wider community, and not solely by the mere fact of their living in a commune, although this latter aspect is generally seen as an integral part of their political philosophy. Such experiments I have termed 'activist communes'.

4   *Practical communes*   By 'practical communes' I intend to refer to those communes for whose members the prime goal is an economic or practical, materialist one. For them, one of the main attractions of communal living might be such things as the fact that it is a lot cheaper to buy groceries in bulk and to share housing costs than when one is living in an isolated, one-family dwelling. Such communes tend to be viewed by their members in terms of other practical advantages which they present, such as the convenience of having other people around to baby-sit for you, to look after your children and home while you are out at work, and so on.

5   *Therapeutic communes*   By this type I intend to refer to those communes that are seen by their members as having the prime purpose of therapy, aimed primarily at creating that social, physical and possibly spiritual environment within which particular types of people who are conventionally labelled as sick or deviant by certain sections of society can be cared for, encouraged to care for themselves, and generally helped to get better, in the sense of being able to live what is typically viewed as a more meaningful and rewarding kind of life.

6   *Religious communes*   There are those communes whose goal is defined by their members primarily in religious terms. For such people the goal of the commune is generally seen as that of fulfilling some purpose or other which they feel to be in accordance with their religious beliefs. Within this category one can make the distinction based on the different types of religious belief system,

101

between ascetic and mystic religious communes. The ascetic venture is generally guided by a belief in a transcendent God and the desire to do His work on earth by attempting to resolve the conflict between the ways of the world and the ways of God by bringing the world into closer accordance with the latter. The mystic venture is generally guided by a belief in an immanent divine power and the desire to attain oneness with it. Such ventures are generally less concerned with changing the world in accordance with the dictates of 'God up there', at least by relatively conventional means of practical action in the world, but are more concerned with the development of their members' spiritual consciousness and mystic awareness.

Before I go on to use this framework to examine some contemporary intentional communites, it should be pointed out that, although the typology is based on the actor's definition of the situation (i.e. on how the communards themselves define the goal of the commune), it inevitably distorts through simplification a very complex set of phenomena. In this sense I have created a set of ideal-type categories into which actual concrete examples of community experiments can be slotted with greater or less ease, although no one concrete example reveals a perfect fit with one of the above types. We shall return to this problem below.[12] Suffice it to state at this stage that the typology has been constructed as a heuristic device for introducing some degree of selectivity and order into the examination of contemporary commune ventures, and in order to make some meaningful distinctions between different types of communes.

Self-actualizing communes

To use that most hackneyed of underground expressions, the members of the self-actualizing communes are largely concerned with 'doing their own thing'. In suggesting that the communes briefly examined below can profitably be considered as examples of such a type, I am relying mainly on evidence obtained through conversations and interviews with members and through an examination of the articles and declarations of intent published by them. Common to all of them is the desire to drop out of conventional society and so to escape the constraints and personal 'hang-ups' associated with life in straight society in order to remould their lives with the aim of attaining true personal freedom through self-awareness and self-development.

1 *The Rochester Arts Commune*

The following account of a venture which appears to be typical of the self-actualizing type of commune is taken from the *Directory of Communes*. (N.B. By the summer of 1972 this commune had gone out of existence.)[13]

Well it all started about six months ago now. One of us had stayed for a short while in a Yorkshire Commune and came back with new views on life and with hopes of building a commune in Rochester.

We had been friends for quite a while before this but after deciding to start the commune, the work we had to undertake brought us much closer together and soon we became quite a happy family. The commune soon became our ideal aim in life style and as we visited other communes we started building new views on exactly what the commune was to be.

We started our propaganda, spreading news about the commune, trying to make connections with other commune groups, and trying to get help—slowly things begin to take shape. We wrote articles for *Communes* mag and *Gandalf's Garden* and beggingly wrote to as many hip millionaires as possible—the result was a lot of fun, but not much money.

We are now miscalled 'the Rochester Arts Commune' by a lot of people, because of the covers and the posters and also probably because most of us are, or have been, Art students—but we never intended the commune to be specifically concerned with the arts. However, because of our artistic background, it seems likely that a bias will probably swing that way.

Professionally we are trained in a wide variety of things including dress designing, tailoring, three dimensional working, illustrating, photography and of course fine arts. We intend to use all of these things to make a living but not by confining ourselves, rather by learning and using each other's skills. We will sell our own paintings and drawings and maybe do some portrait work too; we also hope to print more posters and also decorative letter paper and envelopes etc. Then we want to design, make and sell clothes, maybe even printing and dyeing our own materials; we also have plans for doing graphics and photography for the underground mags; one day we may get a potter's wheel and kiln too.

Our main aim, we all agree, is to get as far away from the plastic society as possible. To slow down into a large farmhouse somewhere in the woods, meadows and rivers of the countryside, where we can remould our lives and live uninhibited by the hustles of straight life. We will also then use the commune as a country retreat for those who badly need to get out of town.

We want to be as self-sufficient as possible, growing our own food, cooking our own bread and maybe even one day keeping our own milk cows and chickens.

The commune itself is not of a Religionist or Political background in the same way as Gandalfs Garden or Rada Krishna temple, but still we do hold the same ideas of God, life and death and we are loosely involved in the use of group meditation and chanting. But at the moment our beliefs play a bigger part in our individual lives than in the commune's life style.

Politically we remain left, very left—our own ideals in lifestyle 'communist' whilst our world-view is anarchist-cum-Yippy. We put any decision to be made to group-discussion, and the decision has to be unanimously liked before any actions are made.

2   A commune in Norfolk

In Norfolk about twenty miles from Norwich and forty-five miles from Cambridge a commune has been in existence since early 1970 which I visited that summer. The membership had originally consisted of four young people who had been friends together in London, their ages ranging from twenty-one to seventeen. Two of them had dropped out of university courses—one of them leaving an English literature course after one year and the other leaving a sociology course after a similar period. They had been discussing the idea of forming a commune together the previous summer, and had eventually found a suitable site in Norfolk.

The building itself was originally a farmhouse, built around 1680, which had been divided into three cottages, with kitchens and sculleries built on the back. With the building went about one-third of an acre of garden and a similar size plot of rough land with outbuildings and sheds. The house itself consisted of some twenty-two small rooms, but when I visited it the members were living in the one cottage that had electricity and a water tap, while they busied themselves renovating the rest of the property, tending the small vegetable garden and looking after their twenty-odd hens. The purchase of the property had been made possible through an inheritance of a couple of thousand pounds by one of the members. They had spent £850 on buying the property, they expected to spend about £700 on renovating it, and they had spent £300 on tools, food and living expenses from the first few weeks, legal fees, removal expenses from London and paying off overdrafts.

Although the commune originally consisted of only four members, these numbers were increased up to about a dozen on many weekends when friends came up from London to stay. However, as with most communes, the situation as regards numbers was in fairly frequent flux. Two of the original members left, and the remaining couple were joined by another young couple—an ex-graduate and his American girl-friend. In the five months up to August 1970, one of the members estimated that they had had up to fifty people staying with them at one time or another. They estimated that they would eventually expand to about eight or ten permanent members, with room for visitors. They had no rules about who could or could not join them, but felt very strongly that anyone who did join would probably have to be first of all a friend and second a communard. That is, they placed a far greater importance on personal compatibility than on political ideology or social philosophy. In practice this meant that they expected people who considered joining them to visit in the first instance, then spend some time with them, and then commit themselves to living there by mutual agreement.

An indication of the overall goal or intention behind the commune was given in a short article written by one of their members in June 1970.[14]

> We want to develop this place not simply as a retreat for
> people all of the same age and type, but a place where people
> of all ages and outlooks can come and live our way of life with
> us. Also we would like to feel part of the local community and
> have them see what we are doing and accept us.

What did the way of life there consist of? They did not have any fixed system of work such as might involve such arrangements as labour credits and so forth. It was left up to the individual to work as and when he wanted, and at what he wanted to do. In the early days of the experiment most of the work consisted of renovating the buildings, tending the vegetable garden, and looking after the chickens. One of the members operated a silk-screen printing process, others of them spent time writing, whilst they also anticipated setting up a sort of arts and crafts workshop for the people of the local community. They had also opened a small shop in the vicinity for the sale of their goods and the produce of other local people. However, little income was obtained from such sources, and most of the members earned their income through casual labour around the district, whether as farm labourers or as general painters and decorators. In addition one of the girls had a part-time job as a waitress at a local hotel.

The members hoped that as the commune became established they would become less reliant on casual labour outside the commune, and base their economy increasingly on growing their own food, making pottery, clothes, posters, leatherwork and other crafts. The commune had a joint bank account and anything earned by anyone or donated went into this account. With the numbers at four they drew out of the bank approximately twelve pounds a week which paid for their day-to-day living expenses and from which was also taken a pound a week pocket money per person for them to buy tobacco, beer and so forth. Items that involved a larger expenditure such as car tax, tools and so on were paid for directly out of the bank account. Food was bought in bulk to save expense and their standard of living was necessarily frugal.

As with so many other communes of this type there was almost a complete absence of rules and formal regulations. Decision-making was usually arrived at by general agreement. They had no fixed rules about private and communal property. The house and car were treated as communal property, as was the money, but the members tended to keep their own clothes and some of their books as private personal possessions. This lack of any formal organization was something that characterized most of the communes where the emphasis was on the creation of that environment within which the members would be most free to develop and fulfil what they felt to be their essential selves. This feeling was expressed in the article referred to above where the communard wrote: 'We will develop our ideas as we go along, and meet the situation as it arises and settle matters between ourselves as people, rather than having some blueprint to which we must rigidly stick.'[15]

3 *Old Rectory Farm*

About twenty miles from the Norfolk commune there existed another commune, housed in a large building that was once a rectory and consisting of about nine bedrooms with a total of about twenty rooms. The big old house was surrounded by about four and a half acres of land. The majority of this was uncultivated when I visited the group, the remainder being devoted to vegetable gardens and chicken runs. The house was held in trust by the founder of the group, and while there had been groups of people living there for some time, it was only comparatively recently that they began to think of themselves as a commune. Originally, the founder member of the group, a novelist, had invited people to join her in the country mainly to share the costs of running such a large house. Since then the group has evolved from an unintentional community to one with some sort of collective purpose behind it. However, this collective goal was one of individual development and fulfilment more than anything else. Thus they have written of themselves:

We have no formal aims or policy. We don't consider ourselves part of any movement, including the commune one. We think that the way to heal this society is by healing ourselves. By trying to live full and satisfying lives we automatically work some change on the people we meet.

As with many communes, the intention behind the experiment was one of both individual change and societal change, the latter through the former, to which priority is given.

As with many communes, this particular venture received a stream of visitors throughout the year. However, it had a nucleus of some seven or eight adults of all ages. Including the four children, the ages of the members ranged from forty down to two years. All the adult members were artists of one sort or another—painters, writers, sculptors and so forth. Their individual incomes were obtained through their creative work and also through casual labour and occasional jobs. This income was supplemented in one or two cases by unemployment and supplementary benefits. They were virtually self-sufficient with regard to vegetables. Each person was expected to contribute £2·50 a week as payment for food, and a further contribution of a similar amount was made towards the payment of rates, electricity bills and so forth.

All adult members were expected to share the household chores and the required jobs around the house and garden, without any distinction as regards sex. Decision-making was through a general process of very open group discussion. It was through the maintenance of such openness with each other that the members felt that they managed to avoid the usual emotional problems that accompany group living.

Again, there were no formal rules or regulations about procedures for selecting members or about property ownership within the commune. Most of the members appeared to keep most of their personal possessions private, income was not fully pooled, and the house itself was the property of the founder of the group who was holding it in trust for one of her sons.[16]

4   *A London commune*

Typical of many small groups of drop-outs to be found in any of the cities of Britain, living together in a flat or house, was the commune I visited in the spring of 1970. About seven young people, all aged between eighteen and twenty-three years, were living in the top flat of a condemned building in Notting Hill. They were all from the provinces originally and had been attracted to London from what had appeared a dull, boring and meaningless existence in their home areas.

They had come together almost accidentally, as sharers of cheap and convenient living accommodation, and had never considered themselves as constituting a commune until people started defining them as such. This labelling in turn started them thinking about what being a commune implied. The only intention behind their group living, as they described it to me, was that of 'doing their own thing'. However, they also explained that the communal living was an important aspect for them in so far as they had established a sort of brotherhood amongst themselves. They felt that it was an important aspect of living as a group that 'no one was above or below you'. They were all equal, working together and living together and helping each other. They also felt that they were performing an important function in so far as they were one of the best-known 'crash pads' on BIT's lists. This meant that, while they were inevitably flooded out from time to time with temporary visitors who had a habit of stealing their clothing and records and other possessions, they were at the same time in a position to help those newly arrived in London with no roof over their head to find their feet. Thus while I was round there talking with them, a young Scottish girl arrived who, they explained, had come there one evening, having been given their address by BIT, with no money, no friends, and no roof over her head. She had stayed with them for a few weeks until she had found her feet, and was working as a receptionist at the time I met her. The communards told me her story with the kind of pride that I imagine social workers display after having dealt with a successful case.

This girl had come to the commune that evening, in fact, to buy some LSD from one of the members. Two of the communards made money dealing in drugs, apart from taking part-time and temporary jobs painting and decorating. The income that they each received was through a variety of channels. One of them had a job as a gardener, a favourite job of many London hippies, as anyone who walks round Kew Gardens or Regent's Park would be able to discover for himself. One or two of them had savings off which they were living, while another earned money through writing. Another, the specialist of the group, so called because he was a specialist at so many things, turned his hand to photography, candle-making, cooking and occasional paid employment of the casual labouring variety.

In many ways this group was the least communal of all those that I visited. They did not eat communally regularly, neither did they pool their incomes. Neither did they have any long-term plans for the community. In fact the house was due to be demolished in a few weeks' time. They all had vague plans for the immediate future. Four of them, two couples, hoped to go down to Cornwall and start a small business there, possibly a small boarding-house venture. They had money which they had saved and also some money from an inheritance. The two 'dealers' planned to go down to the south coast for the summer to earn money 'pushing', with the vague long-term plan of eventually buying a place in the country where they could concentrate on creative work such as designing and making clothes, candle-making and so on. Neither of them could conceive of the possibility of ever going back to a conventional job in straight society. From their point of view it was far better to be your own boss with a little money than work under someone else's authority for a lot of money. It had been their experience that, although they were frequently short of money for daily living expenses, it always seemed to turn up when it was needed from some source or other.

What rules the group had for the running of the commune were minimal and unwritten. The nearest thing that approached a rule was concerned with that perennial problem of group living—the problem of personal privacy. Thus it was an unwritten rule in the house that if anyone wanted to be on their own in their own room for any purpose, then they would go round the house telling people or put a notice on their door to that effect, and then no one would disturb them.

While one gained the distinct impression when visiting certain communes that the members had made what they felt to be a life-long commitment to the communal way of life, with regard to the members of this group one departed with a rather different impression. For them the commune appeared to represent a significant but temporary staging-post on their life's journey. It was an important experience for two main reasons. First, it provided them with a free and open environment within which they could experiment with their lives at that period in their lives which is socially recognized as being a period of role experimentation. The difference between the members of this group of young people and the majority of their contemporaries was that the roles and social identities with which they were experimenting were not those of bank clerk, devoted husband and father, and so on. Such identities held no real attraction for them, as their attitude towards taking a full-time job revealed. They were experimenting with deviant life styles such as drop-out, drug-pusher, artist, craftsman and so forth. Two of them, in fact, described to me how both of them had a number of habits in the past such as heroin, 'speed' and so on. They had tried out these drugs just as they had experimented with alcohol and LSD. The commune provided them with an environment in which they could experiment with their lives in such manners. Secondly, the commune acted as an important support for them during this period of their lives, not only in the sense of providing them with the physical space for them to 'seek their selves' but also in the sense that they themselves recognized, in providing a sense of brotherhood, a feeling that each one of them could rely upon the other in times of need. In many ways they were fortunate to possess this kind of security at such a period in their lives. If youth is that period when the individual tries out a range of new cultural, sexual and occupational models of himself, then very few of modern youth will have experienced the range of models that some of the members of this London commune will have experienced by the time they emerge from this particular age span.

5 *Eel Pie Island Commune*

Dear Andrew: I think you'll have to take a chance on me being in and just arrive here one day. . . . there's no room and unlimited room here . . . I mean the health department have stipulated 16 maximum and yet there are 40 of us. You must come soon and understand what it's like here, because it's meaningless for me to try to explain anything by letter. . . .

Such was my invitation to Eel Pie Island Hotel where, in 1970, there evolved a commune which towards the end of its life held up to seventy young people. The hotel is a three-storey building sited on a small island-in the Thames at Twickenham. In the 1950s and 1960s it had been the venue of some of London's top jazz musicians and had been the springboard for the Rolling Stones. Although the building that the commune occupied had once been a hotel, the impression it conveyed to me on my first visit was something of a cross between an old derelict warehouse and a workhouse. As one explored within the building, one was confronted with long bare corridors, with what had once been the hotel bedrooms on either side. The floors of these bedrooms were covered with mattresses and sleeping bags. Their doors were decorated with posters, painted symbols, words such as Love and Peace, the first names of the occupants, poems and so on, most of the poems and symbols making fairly direct references to 'tripping' and psychedelic experiences.

The origins of the commune in the first instance were quite unintentional. A group of friends were living in Richmond, a few miles from Twickenham. Some of them had lived together as a group during the summer of 1969 on a farm in Cumberland. One of the men took on the task of renovating and decorating the place with a view to developing some sort of 'arts laboratory', and as there was ample living space in the empty hotel with its nineteen bedrooms, kitchens and bars, he decided to stay there. He invited some of the others to join him. For them it was in the first instance a good cheap place to stay. From the small nucleus word spread that there was a place to live on the island, and others just came along and moved in.

The people living there in the early months of 1970 never consciously thought of themselves as constituting a commune. In this respect they were like the people at Old Rectory Farm. Like them, also, they first began to think of themselves as a commune when people began labelling them as such. The first specific instance of this was when one of the early members received a letter addressed to the 'Eel Pie Island Hotel Commune'. This label spread throughout the underground press, and along BIT's information channels. The result was that more people joined the group at the hotel, and numbers grew. However, while the members in turn began to think of themselves as a commune, they refused to type themselves as being any particular sort of commune with any particular goal or collective purpose. It was constantly stressed when one talked with the people there that each person in the commune was an individual on his own particular journey. At regular intervals during conversations with members of the commune, they would point out that what they were telling me of life in the commune was only their personal viewpoint, and I would have to talk with everyone to obtain a full picture.

There were, in fact, some recognizable types living in the commune. There were a few political types there, who defined themselves as anarchists and talked of guerrilla-type tactics in the local urban community; there were a few 'junkies' living there; and there were the teenage-runaways and others for whom the hotel meant little more than a roof above their heads, where one had easy access to drugs and all the other things that seem to make life worth living at a certain stage in life. However, the majority of members appeared to me to be involved in a journey of self-exploration and experimentation. They would have agreed with the people at Old Rectory Farm that the most important thing was to heal oneself, and to attempt to live the most full and satisfying of lives. This was made possible on the island because the members were to an extent free from the constraints of the conventional world. The process of developing self-awareness was aided within the commune, many felt, by the living out of one's life in the intimate company of others who were understanding and concerned and the establishment of honest relationships within the group. Such a development ensured that any member who was attempting to play at a particular type of role, who was trying to present his self in a particular manner which was not really him, would soon have his game spoilt by the others in the group. By such painful experiences, it was felt, true self-awareness could be developed. In addition, many of the commune members had been aided in their own process of self-discovery through the chemical means of drugs. At the same time, while many of them had had a long and varied experience with different types of drugs, it was noticeable that they spent at least part of their time reading the

111

works of such mystics as Ouspensky and Gurdjieff. 'Tripping' had provided them with experiences which they then sought to examine and enter into more deeply through the work of such mystics. It was among such people that one found the community tradition that has always been associated with certain types of mystic belief systems reasserting itself.

If the Eel Pie Island Commune had a central ethic, it was that individuals should be free to follow their own path, to develop and experiment in their own way, without any hindrance from anyone else. In true Zen manner, they would refuse to define the nature of their community, as by the very act of definition one would delimit the phenomenon and restrict the possibilities open for development that they felt to be there. This refusal to structure the community was revealed in their almost complete lack of formal rules or procedures. In the early days before the hotel was filled to the absolute limit, people did not 'join' the commune, they simply moved in. After about a week of occupation, someone would take it upon themselves to go and ask them for a contribution towards the rent. The property was rented, and in *ad hoc* fashion someone had decided in the early days that it would be a good idea if they had a rent book and the rent was collected regularly, so he took it upon himself to collect contributions towards payment of the rent each time it became due. Likewise, someone decided that it would be nice if they had electricity in the hotel, so he took it upon himself to collect the money necessary to pay for the supply to be switched on and to collect contributions towards payment of the bills. They had no rules about the minimum rate of contribution by individual members towards these funds, people just gave what they felt that they could afford. Some gave nothing, those that were working paid more. Again, they had no rules or duty rosters for the performance of household chores. Someone would decide that the corridors needed sweeping or painting, and would set about doing it, others would join in and help. Similarly, people had thought that it would be nice if there was a communal meal during the day, so some people had just got together and prepared huge meals for anyone who was around and cared to eat.

Such *ad hoc* arrangements with such a large and heterogeneous group of people obviously led to problems. Thus one of the reasons that the experiment in communal living on Eel Pie Island came to an end in 1971 was the fact that many of those who had taken it upon themselves to collect money for the rent, electricity bills and so on, left and no one else took their place, with the result that debts eventually mounted up to unmanageable levels. The commune had no formal rules about sharing property and incomes, but in a group with such large numbers and with a population that was almost constantly in a state of flux, it would have been extremely difficult to have kept one's personal possessions private for long. In fact, theft was a great problem for the people at Eel Pie. Another problem was in deciding on the policy to be adopted towards the large numbers of people who kept on arriving at the hotel searching for a place to stay. A short item in the *Arts Lab Newsletter* of March 1970 referred to both these problems:

> Somebody is stealing from them—a total of £200 has gone from different rooms, 200 records, record-player, clothes, tools, and also letters are opened and parcels haven't arrived.
>
> A guy at the Commune has adopted the role of fascist housekeeper. There's a big bar downstairs and he takes it upon himself to throw out dossers he doesn't like. He's got some strange system for selecting them. The problem with people crashing is that some people in the commune approve of it and some don't. There's only one person who does anything about it and that's this guy. Though somebody has written on the wall: 'it's a crime to throw people out at night in the middle of winter'.

It was this 'open door' policy which constituted another major factor behind the death of the commune. During the summer of 1970 a large group of communards went to a pop festival at Bath for the weekend. When they returned they found that about thirty new people had moved in. By this time, small groups of people had already left the commune to go travelling round Europe for the summer.[17] The influx of such a large number of new members created a division within the commune as a whole. The older members had evolved a certain kind of group consciousness and shared feeling about the nature of the commune and what they were trying to achieve there which was not shared by the new members. Given that the commune was at that time fairly evenly divided with regard to the numbers of the two camps, it would not have been physically possible for the long-term members to eject the new-comers, even if they had wanted to. What resulted was that the commitment of the older members to the commune on the island was reduced and they began to leave to form new ventures and explore new paths.

However, although there were no rules about sharing resources even when the commune was an on-going venture, it was noticeable that the richer members of the commune always seemed to be helping the poorer ones out. One thing that struck me very strongly on one of my first visits was the almost ritualistic manner with which communards who were eating in the café in Twickenham that they

113

frequented, would offer whatever it was they were eating or drinking, whether it was beans on toast or a cup of tea, to all the others present to share with them. It was the same with cigarettes and 'joints'. With regard to income, many of the members worked at jobs in the locality, particularly at the bakery on the island which appeared to depend on the commune members for a major proportion of its labour force. A few of the members obtained money from the sale of their creative work, whether this was writing, cartoon drawing or whatever. Some of them earned money through 'pushing' drugs. Others were in receipt of unemployment or supplementary benefits. Some did not work at all, neither did they receive state assistance, but survived through obtaining food from local stores and from money lent or given to them by other members of the commune. One or two of the members had begun to plant a few vegetable seeds in the garden of the hotel, but apart from this no effort was made to make the commune self-sufficient. Given the numbers and the small amount of land, this would have been an impossibility in any case.

Although I have considered the Eel Pie Island Commune as an example of the self-actualizing type of commune, it is important to emphasize that many of the members did not see the commune purely in terms of transforming their own lives, they also viewed the experiment as an attempt to transform the nature of social life in general. Thus one of the members went to great lengths to emphasize to me that they did not see themselves as dropping out of society into a rural commune. Rather, they were seeking to live out their lives in front of the people of Twickenham with the aim of changing society through their personal exemplary actions. By the very fact of living their lives in the way they did, they hoped to 'turn others on' to this alternative life-style. In addition, the commune was important to many members from the point of view of it providing them with a sense of brotherhood and mutual support. This aspect was exemplified for me by the enthusiasm with which they described an event that took place there one Sunday. A couple who lived in the commune and who earned money through pushing drugs had made some profit out of their transactions. They decided to spend this extra money on providing a communal 'acid-trip' for everyone in the commune. Thus one Sunday morning forty Eel Pie Islanders 'dropped acid' together and for at least a week after this event, while I was visiting the commune, members were telling me what a marvellous experience it had been from the point of view of developing the community spirit. In fact, many of the members of the commune viewed these three aspects of the community life as inseparable—the transformation of the self within an environment of mutual support and concern, with the further goal of transforming the nature of social life in general. In the next section, attention will be turned to a consideration of those communes where the primary emphasis was on the brotherhood aspect of communal life.

Communes for mutual support

1 *Selene Community*

Reference has already been made to the Selene Community and the role of its members in the growth and development of the Commune Movement. The energies that they have invested in the promotion of this movement is an indication of their concern with helping to create a new social order—the alternative society.[18] At the same time, their actual venture into communal living, Selene, appears as an interesting example of a commune which is seen by its members primarily as a haven of mutual support, as providing that emotional and psychological security that had proved difficult for them to find as members of conventional society. Thus one of the members remarked to me in conversation as follows:

> My interest in community living is really part of a search for true friendship, acceptance and rewarding relationships with others. I always felt the odd one out in normal life. In the outside world such relationships are only found within families, and you cannot get in on such arrangements unless you happen to be a member of the family.

Another of the members explained their attraction towards communal living at one stage during my stay with them in terms of their hope that they would be able to avoid making decisions, that the commune would make all the decisions for them. This person saw his involvement in the community very much in terms of his search for a mother-substitute. He explained his involvement with pagan religion in similar terms, the worship of the Mother God and so on. On another occasion this member explained how he saw the main personal advantages of living in a commune:

> I see a community primarily as providing validation for myself in particular, and others, by having around me people with the same ideas as me. Then, if I want to go out and dig, they will as well. Security comes next—emotional—if someone dies and you are a monogamous couple, it's disaster. If you are twelve it's not so bad.

However, while the members of Selene certainly saw their venture in these sorts of terms, they would also have agreed with some of the viewpoints expressed by members of those communes that I have labelled as 'self-actualizing'. Thus, one of the members explained their original motive for joining a commune in the following terms: 'What I wanted really was an environment in which I could live all the time what one professed to believe in.'

Originally the commune came into being as a social entity in November 1965 in Wheathampstead, and consisted of the present three members. Whilst their pagan, pantheistic beliefs were strong at this time, the vegan ethic that they then shared was of great importance in bringing them together as a community. The vegan ethic has now gone. In 1967, however, before this took place, the group of three left suburbia for Wales, where they had bought twenty acres of wet, boggy land and a caravan in which to live. There they were joined for some time by additional members, but due to personality clashes none of these remained permanently. In October 1968 the house in Wheathampstead was finally sold, as was the land and the caravan and the resulting capital, supplemented by some money from an inheritance and a gratuity, was invested in the purchase of the farm which at present holds the group.

This fifty-four-acre Welsh hill farm is situated some ten miles from Llanbedr in the middle of one of the most beautiful rural areas in Wales. The farmhouse itself is very old and built of stone, although for a long period during its occupation by the group one of the stone walls in the kitchen had been replaced by a sheet of polythene. Although the main room in the farmhouse is dominated by a magnificent stone fireplace which one of the members constructed, the house appeared to be in need of extensive renovation and alteration, during the period of my visits. The members of the community had made little effort to farm the land, apart from earning small amounts of money through keeping ponies on 'tack' during the winter months. At one stage they were given three hens, but these died. The majority of their time was devoted to the production of the journal, *Communes*, and to coping with visitors and dealing with their voluminous correspondence. Their annual income of £900 was obtained mainly through pensions, sickness benefits, and savings. Basic expenses for the running of the house, food, electricity bills and so on amounted to about £750 a year, while a further £200 was absorbed by renovating and improving the house. All income was shared. The members hoped to develop the income-earning potential of the farm in future years.[19]

There would appear to be three major themes in the ethos of the community. The first is their aim of building Selene into a fully integrated community of like-minded people. However, they were quite definite about the type of person they want to attract to the community. The strict demands they made of any potential recruit distinguished Selene as a commune for mutual support from those self-actualizing communes where virtually no criteria are laid down

116

for potential new members. This strict setting down of rules about the type of person desired would seem to indicate not only a lack of desire to accept those types that do not conform to the image of themselves held by the members of such communes, but also a desire to preserve their home and their settled order and the resulting sense of security experienced by the members. Thus the members of Selene have written:[20]

> We are interested only in sensitive people—introverts—as we find extroverts too exhausting and they find us too dull, and we find communication with people of low intelligence laborious and unrewarding while they find us complicated. And we want to live with people who share our love of nature, our interest in the cult of the mother and the old pagan religion, and find value and meaning in the great all-embracing sentiment of pantheism. These are our soul-mates and the people with whom we would feel completely committed in our community, and anything less than complete commitment would be a poor alternative.

In addition, the commune was particular about visitors, especially those who were extroverts and heavy smokers. Visitors were charged a small sum of which the major part was contributed to the Federation Fund of the Commune Movement. Rules for joining Selene were fairly clear also. The prospective member must first of all spend a few weeks at the community, at the end of which period he might be offered a year's trial membership. At the end of this year the membership would decide by a two-thirds agreement whether to offer full membership. After this, if the recruit had the necessary economic means (at least £4 a week) his assets would be gradually merged with those of the community and he would become a full member. Unfortunately for the members of the community, by 1970 no one had joined them on a permanent basis, despite their relatively long life compared with the life of other communes.

A second major element in their ethos is their belief in a system of group marriage as being preferable to the conventional institution of the nuclear family. Their reasons for this belief emphasized strongly the support they believed such an arrangement provided for the individual. In their own words:[21]

> The monogomous family in its traditional isolation is the greatest barrier to all social reform as well as, ultimately, the instrument of the most devastating form of grief known to man and we urge its abolition. . . . Human beings die; our community does not. Grief will inevitably strike the person whose love is narrow unless they die before their loved one and leave their

117

erstwhile companion to mourn their departing. We have no wish to harbour the spectre of grief in our midst and we see our affective bonds permeating the community and protected by the living instead of horribly truncated and buried with the dead.

In our community there will be no orphans, for they are everybody's children; there can be none destitute and lonely in old age for they are everybody's relatives and they can have both the company of each other and the younger members' stimulation. There will be no widows or widowers. No child will be subject to the petty whims of a particular parent and no one will seek to exploit another. . . . Our ideal is a relationship which is based on trust, understanding and empathy, and which deepens naturally with the passage of time, simultaneously encompassing others who share our feelings, thoughts and ideals. In community we will recover a unity of purpose which will lay the stark figure of loneliness which is stalking our barren civilization.

In the third element of the Selene ethos, the belief in the old pagan religion, there can be found a similar emphasis on the need for mutual support and self-validation, and the desire to join with others and seek to overcome that sense of personal isolation and aloneness that can accompany the life of the individual. In addition, there are to be found those traditional elements of the mystic belief system— the belief in the immanence of the divine and the belief in the possibility of becoming one with this power. There is also the recognition of the importance of the ecstatic experience when one steps outside the taken-for-granted routines of society and the everyday view of the world. In the case of the members of Selene, this state of ecstasy was to be attained through ritualistic means rather than through the chemical means of drugs, but the aims are similar—although here again the love of the members of the commune for ritual can be viewed in Durkheimian terms as reflecting a need to reinforce their faith and sense of community. All these elements are to be found in the following extensive quotation from their writings.[22]

Our pagan, pantheistic sentiment is elusive and exceedingly difficult to relate, but we'll try to convey the feeling in allegory. We see man on the bleak, windswept edge of the world of samsara, having confronted the concrete images and walked past them; to find that they are made of cardboard. . . . In the distance—towards the centre—people are still happy . . . still looking only on the faces of objects—never into their being. Their orbits are closed, confined within their own rational limits. But on the edge, the world is dark and cheerless, and no longer self-validating, and the very concreteness of the world is the basis of its remoteness, estrangement, unreality. But through the mists wafting on the forest border, the other-world of faery beckons, bewitching, confounding reason, threatening madness, a delirious satisfying, infinitely validating madness which in the material . . . world is like the light of an extinguished candle. . . . Faery calls but withers before an answer, hidden in the mists of birth, ever immanent, but never grasped, the great mother, compassionate, an intense and lovable experience in ecstatic union, in devotion, in communion deep in the greenwood. . . . There's a compelling call to scream with the wind—or laugh with him—or sigh as he sweeps over the heath; to stand naked under the infinite canopy of the dark sky and speak to the moon goddess in silent contemplation until her being fills one's whole consciousness and the mind is annihilated to leave a void or, from the other side, the awful joy of bewitchment, the madness and excitement, and profound peace of entry into Faery. And here is Pan . . . A creator—the lord of the forest. There's an urge to dissolve, to embrace the trees, to absorb their being and be absorbed by them, to feel the earth beneath bare feet, the very body of the mother—the great womb in which all her children still have their roots; and an urge to be with other people, real people who speak to her who we do not name, others who have found the chink in the veil and find a peace in Faery, who communicate not in words, but in songs and gestures, and address not each other in isolation, but the goddess in union, people who find peace and fulfilment in that enchanted place where life is death and death is life. . . .

This is our greatest wish, our endeavour, and our idiom of expression. To join together in ritual, to still the ego in mantra, to stir the old rhythms by the circular dance and charge the stones with magic, to invoke Pan and the madness of wild excitement and all the force and life of wild nature, and to sink then into the arms of the goddess, to feed from her breast, to accept the whole universe from her, and give her in return— oneself.

Thus the people at Selene hope eventually to become a commune made up of like-minded people who share with them their feelings for the old pagan religion and 'the language of the moon'. This hope was far from attaining fulfilment by late 1971, but attention will now be turned to a consideration of a commune made up of a group of like-minded deviants which can also be viewed as a commune for mutual support.

2 *The Trans-Sex Trip*

Reference has been made to the role of communes in helping members of a cognitive minority to maintain their deviant belief system. Communes can be seen as performing a similar type of role for various types of deviants, by providing them with an environment of mutual support. Thus there existed in London a community consisting of trans-sexuals who, it would appear, had been attracted towards the communal style of life, in part at least, by the fact that they shared certain problems in common with which the institution of the commune assisted them in coping. This commune constitutes a particularly clear example of members of a deviant sub-culture coming together to form a commune.

A brief excursion into the field of the sociology of deviance will help to throw some light on the types of processes involved in leading up to such developments. One can put forward a very crude model of the career of the deviant, involving six major stages. (1) An individual lives in a group where certain qualities and acts are viewed as abnormal or deviant. For instance, the wearing of facial make-up and female attire by a male on occasions other than at fancy dress dances or similar events is viewed as odd. (2) The individual is believed to exhibit certain deviant qualities or acts. For instance, the individual is seen to be wearing female clothes and adopting feminine types of behaviour by certain 'moral entrepreneurs'. (3) The individual gets defined as a deviant. In this case he would probably get labelled as some sort of sexual pervert. (4) The individual's actions may come to the notice of one of the official agencies of social control, whether this be the police and the courts, or the psychiatrist and the mental hospital, and his case may be processed through one of the official channels of these agencies. (5) This social processing only serves to propel the individual further into organized deviant life and out of conventional life. For instance, our trans-sexual may be thrown into contact with other trans-sexuals in prison or in hospital, there establishing contacts which he maintains after his release. (6) The individual eventually comes to accept his label as a deviant. Thus, the trans-sexual, having been brought into contact with other trans-sexuals, will see himself reflected in the lives of others who are so labelled, and also find himself labelled by significant others as a trans-sexual, and so come to accept and define himself in this fashion, becoming a member of this sub-cultural group.

A sub-culture is likely to come into existence when a group of people discover that they suffer a common fate and face certain types of problems in common. Given their shared interests and problems, they are likely to interact with each other once they have made contact and discovered their common ground, either out of choice or because normal interaction with normal people has been found to be impossible or unattainable. Through such interaction a deviant sub-culture will evolve, presenting 'a common understanding and prescribed ways of thinking, feeling and acting when in the company of one's own deviant peers and when dealing with representatives of the conventional world'.[23]

However, they are faced with a common dilemma in so far as they seek to engage in the kinds of activities that their society labels as deviant, and yet at the same time pass as conventional citizens in the conventional world in order to avoid social punishment and, in the case of those deviants involved in 'crimes without victims', to earn their means of livelihood. One likely solution to this problem is the formation of a commune made up of members of the same deviant sub-group. Outside the commune they can seek to pass as ordinary citizens, within the commune they can pursue their deviant activities hidden, to some extent, from the gaze of moral entrepreneurs and the authorities. This would appear to be the solution adopted by the members of the 'Trans-Sex Trip'.

Here is Daphne's account of the commune:[24]

We used to be called the Chapel of Isis Commune, when it was more an idea than a fact. It consists now of four people living here, who are all trans-sexuals or nearly so.

Two of us (J and P) have jobs as males, one (M) now has a job as a woman, and I am general landlady, housewife, slave, general chaos-sorter and spare time—or spare hand— astrologer and yogi, etc.

Formally, two rooms are let (to M and P), but we share generally. Two of us (J and D) are here weekdays, as J works round the clock at weekends and writes history during the week.

We have a goggle box, which I now find rather a menace.

Visitors include T/S and S/C (Sex change) people, kinkies, astrologers, Commune Movement people . . . and some actually write first. . . . If they do not write people are likely not to get a lot of attention, and it is difficult to gauge the quality and character of their interest(s).

Politically we appear to be a heck of a mixture: one M.O.B./ C.M. type non-violent anarchist and theosophist gardener (little me), a fairly straight labourite (J), a rather conservative believer in armies and the Boss Man Answer (to Chairman Miaou) and a liberal minded Irish R.C.

A sex-change friend and a well known beautician brought M and P into the fold.

As changes occur, I hope they will be in the CM-

Gandalphian direction, while retaining something of the present trans sexual basis.

Activist communes

In labelling the following group of experiments as 'activist communes', I am seeking to locate their distinguishing characteristic which sets them apart from other communes to a certain degree in their orientation towards bringing about radical social change. They are largely seeking to bring about social change and create the alternative society not solely through the exemplary action of living as a commune and 'doing their own thing', but also through involving themselves in direct, radical political and social action in the local community, seeking to encourage local people to demand and obtain greater degrees of control over their personal lives and over the affairs of their own neighbourhood. Typically their aim is the encouragement of participatory democracy within local communities through encouraging local inhabitants to claim their right to decide and influence decisions that affect their own lives, rather than relying on the 'powers up there' such as central and local government to make the decisions for them.

1   A south London commune

When I visited this commune in the suburbs of south-east London six men and two women, including one married couple, were living together in a large detached house owned by a local hospital from which they held the lease. The house itself was situated on the edge of a quiet, middle-class, suburban residential area, near to a large working-class housing estate. The group had been together since the summer of 1969. With regard to their original aim and their activities the group appeared typical of the 'red base' type, urban, politically motivated commune that is common on the continent.[25] In fact, the original idea for forming the commune had developed after a number of the present members had visited the continent as friends in their days as students and spent some time in urban communes in Germany and Holland. The general idea of such 'red bases' is of a group of people living together as a group, demonstrating in their actual living a co-operative, socialist way of life to the members of the wider community. Many of these communes on the continent have, in fact, evolved through a group of politically motivated young people, usually libertarian socialists or anarchists, coming together in the first instance on social and political action projects, and then deciding to live together as a group in order to increase their impact as a group on the wider community, and at the same time live the kind of life now that they would wish others to adopt after the revolution.

This was the thinking behind the original establishment of the commune—to move into a suitable building, to establish a 'red base', and involve themselves as a group in local community action projects. They also hoped to exert an influence on the wider community through seeking to present through their communal mode of life an alternative to the competitive, acquisitive and exploitative mode of life which they saw as characterizing capitalist society. In both of these two original aims the group felt that they had been relatively unsuccessful. Thus they felt that their impact on the neighbourhood as a commune living a co-operative mode of life had been almost negligible. This they attributed partly to the fact that in the area in which they lived there were a number of small student hostels, with the result that many of the local people assumed that their house was a similar kind of institution and therefore nothing out of the ordinary. The occupants of the commune could easily be mistaken for students in terms of their general appearance. With regard to their aim of developing the commune as a community action centre for the neighbourhood, the commune members also felt that they had achieved only a limited level of success. This fact they also attributed partly to the nature of the neighbourhood in which they lived. Prior to the actual establishment of the commune, the members had planned to find a suitable house in a solidly working-class district, a depressed area where social problems were particularly acute and where there would thus be some fertile ground for them to work upon in terms of 'radicalizing' the local inhabitants. In actual fact they had experienced great difficulty in finding a suitable house in any area, and the one they eventually occupied was located in a predominantly middle-class residential area, where the inhabitants were quite capable of making their demands heard if they had a mind to do so, and where the local economic and social conditions were those of middle-class affluence rather than working-class deprivation. In other words, the communards had discovered that there was very little demand for a group such as theirs in the neighbourhood, and they had found it almost impossible to create the demand. They had thus turned their attentions more towards the working-class estates. Here again they had encountered problems—the main one stemming from their realization that it took a good length of time before a group intent on community action could come to be accepted by the local inhabitants as a group of people with the interests of the local people at heart, and not be viewed as 'a body of dangerous radicals and long haired students who know nothing about local conditions and are only interested in creating trouble and furthering their own political ends, and who will soon move on to another area anyway'.

As a consequence, the members of the commune had been involving themselves as individuals rather than as a group in a variety of local political activities, such as picketing local supermarkets where South African produce was sold, and lobbying the local Trade Union Council about unions with investments in South African firms, and so on. In addition, the house itself acted as the meeting-place for a variety of local radical and social reform groups. This involvement with radical politics had been one of the common bonds that had brought the communards together in their student days. Their other main shared interest in those days was their involvement with the Student Christian Movement. Two of the communards, in fact, worked as full-time officers for this organization while living at the commune. Two other members were curates. Another was a clinical psychologist with a London hospital, and another was a teacher. The odd man out, so to speak, was the member who was not a Christian, had not been to an institute of further education, and who worked as a gardener. He had become a member of the commune after having been involved in the occupation of 144 Piccadilly in the late summer of 1969 by a large group of mainly young people. He had answered an advertisement inviting a 'destitute hippie' to join the commune—he was the destitute hippie.[26]

The members pooled all their income. Out of this pool 10 per cent was used to finance their community/political activities. Private possessions were maintained, although certain items such as the record player were viewed as communal property. They shared an evening meal together each day, and in addition held a weekly meeting of all members of the commune at which problems were discussed, issues raised, and decisions collectively arrived at.[27]

2 A commune in north-west London

Similar to the commune in south London both with regard to its general orientation and the nature of its membership was a commune that I came across in north-west London. A brother and sister had inherited some money from a deceased relative. They did not know what to do with the money as their political beliefs and social consciences militated against their investing it in stocks and shares, which they felt would contribute towards the perpetuation of an economic and social system to which they were opposed. They eventually resolved this particular radical's dilemma by buying a house in the Finsbury area of London with the idea of forming a community of friends and like-minded people who together might create some form of a 'red base', community action centre for the surrounding community.

The commune eventually got off the ground in January 1970. By September of that year the commune consisted of nine people, made up of three couples, three individuals, one dog and six cats. Their age range was from twenty to twenty-seven years. Of the three female members of the commune, one worked as a teacher, another as a clerk and the third worked in the Civil Service social surveys department. Of the men, one worked as an articled clerk with a firm of solicitors that concentrated mainly on dealing with civil liberties issues; another worked as an organization and methods expert with a large London hospital, a third worked as a petrol pump attendant, while another of them worked as a full-time organizer for a Christian charity organization.

The internal organization and running of the commune was of a rather *ad hoc* nature. Decisions were mainly taken by the individuals concerned. Where the issue affected the community as a whole or involved a major item requiring joint expenditure, the decision was arrived at after a group discussion, which usually took place over the evening meal which they shared together. The preparation of the evening meal was performed on an *ad hoc* type of basis also. There was no official rota for the task—whoever was around during the early evening or whoever felt that it was his or her turn to do the honours acting as communal cook for the evening. With regard to finances, all those who earned an income were expected to contribute £3 a week towards the cost of food, and £3.50 a week towards the general costs of rates, electricity, gas and so on. People who were not earning were not expected to make a contribution. Large items of expenditure were met by an *ad hoc* contribution system. In general the commune had no formal rules except the usual precautionary one of prohibiting the possession of drugs on the premises, to guard against the possibility of being 'busted' by the police.

Of the members of the group, four had been friends together as students. Other members had joined the commune as friends and 'friends of friends' of individual members. The other major common denominator that the members of the group shared and which helps one to understand how they originally came together, was their political commitment and involvement—particularly in the Young Liberals. In this light it is interesting to note that at the Liberal Party Conference at Eastbourne in September 1970 there was a discussion on the broad strategy to be adopted by the party in the future. A split emerged between the old guard who maintained that the only road open to the Liberal Party was to continue to seek parliamentary strength through contesting as many seats as possible at general elections; and the activists, largely drawn from the ranks of the Young Liberals, who argued for a strategy based on community action, seeking to mobilize people to demand a greater control over their own environment and an increased voice in the making of those decisions that significantly affected them. It was the broad aim of this commune to implement this type of strategy.

The members of the commune were described to me by one of their number as 'radicals with no place to go'. This is a theme that will be dealt with at greater length in a later chapter.[28] Here I would just point to the fact that during the course of my research I encountered many young radicals who, having been initiated into radical politics through the Campaign for Nuclear Disarmament and the civil disobedience campaigns of the Committee of One Hundred, had come to define their political position as that of a libertarian socialist or anarchist. As such, they felt unable to identify themselves with many of the contemporary left-wing groups such as the International Socialists, the Socialist Labour League and so on, who were seen by them as old-fashioned, authoritarian, Leninist parties. Where to go? Whom to join? How to further the aim of achieving a libertarian socialist society?—these were the problems that have troubled and continue to trouble people of this political persuasion. The position that many of them have adopted in recent years, apart from giving up in despair, is that of involving themselves in direct community action projects of one sort or another. This involvement with ordinary people over issues of immediate and local concern to the inhabitants of a neighbourhood, with the emphasis continuously placed on 'grass roots' participatory democracy through tenants' control of their own estates and community services, has now replaced, for many anarchists and peace movement activists, the involvement in what they now tend to define as the rather meaningless jaunts through the city streets—the mass demonstration.

For such people it is meaningless to talk about the 'revolution' and at the same time confine one's activities to an occasional demonstration on some general issue or other. For them, if one is genuinely seeking to create a more just and more humane society characterized by the radical decentralization of power and decision-making, and if one believes that the means to attain this goal should be commensurate with the end, then one of the most obvious paths of action leads to an involvement with the affairs, public issues and personal troubles of the people around one. For people of this persuasion, not only must the 'revolution start with the life of the individual', it should also start with the individual's activities in the local community. For such people, the only defence against a centralizing and authoritarian regime is seen to be a politically aware and active public prepared and capable of standing up for their own rights.

This general perspective is not at all untypical of the opinions expressed to me by some of the members of the commune in north-west London. As with the South London Community, with whose members they had some slight contact, however, they felt that they had, by the late summer of 1970, achieved very little in terms of their aim of becoming a centre for community action. The reasons they provided to explain this were threefold. First, they had by that time only lived in the neighbourhood for seven months, which was too short a time for what they saw as a long-term project that needed to be prefaced by a lengthy period of getting to know the neighbourhood. Second, they had found that they needed to spend a great deal of time coping with the internal problems of the commune. They had experienced the usual quota of personality conflicts, personal 'hang-ups', differences of opinion and so forth. These had taken up a sizeable amount of their time and energy during the early months. Third, they had encountered the straightforward problem of finding sufficient time as individuals to devote to community affairs. It was pointed out to me by one of the members that most of them had quite time-consuming jobs, and in addition they were involved as individuals in other spheres of political and social action such as the National Council for Civil Liberties and the Young Liberals. Also, in the words of my informant, the members of the commune were all good 'demonstration fodder' who could be relied upon to turn out for demonstrations on issues about which they felt strongly, such as Vietnam and South Africa.

Despite these problems, the members of the commune felt that they would gain some success in time as, unlike the situation with the South London commune, they felt that the neighbourhood in which they were living faced a number of problems which could develop or be developed into issues of public concern. These problems centred largely around the inadequacy of the local community services such as education, health and housing. At the same time, a member expressed his fear that the commune would develop into a haven for social misfits, with the inevitable result that a disproportionate amount of the group's time would be spent coping with individuals' personal 'hang-ups' rather than with political and social action. In fact his fears for the future would appear to have been justified, although for rather different reasons. The latest information that I received about this particular commune was in a letter from one of the members, who informed me that the sister who had originally bought the house with her brother had left the commune and was demanding the return of her share of the original sum invested. As a result, this particular experiment in communal living was threatened by the possibility that the house would have to be sold. This is a problem not likely to be encountered by the group to be considered next, who do not own the property in which they are housed.

E*   127

3   *A community craft centre*

Reference was made above to radicals with no place to go and with no movement to join, and to how many peace movement activists have become involved in community action projects of one sort or another. Until a couple of years ago there was in existence a venture manned by ex-C.N.D. and Committee of One Hundred activists that sought to promote the values of non-violence, brotherly love, and concern for one's fellow man—this was called the Mobile Voluntary Work Team. The basic philosophy underlying this venture stemmed from the belief that mankind was threatened by nuclear and biological war, by conventional wars, and by an increasing tide of poverty and exploitation. Such a future was seen as arising out of the political and economic structures of the capitalist world, with their centralizing, competitive and destructive tendencies. To overcome these problems it was felt that the radical must work towards a society organized in fairly small economic and political units, in which work is done in response to need rather than greed, and where goods and services are provided free of charge in a spirit of love and mutual aid, rather than to obtain the greatest profit. Faced with this goal, the members of the Mobile Voluntary Work Team sought to involve themselves in a creative effort to develop such a way of life by attempting to live it out in their daily lives. They sought change through non-violent exemplary action, by seeking to create units of their alternative society, by seeking to live without money, and by providing services to those in need without demanding repayment of any kind. The group travelled the country offering themselves as a volunteer labour force, sustained largely by donations and by their efforts at obtaining free food and other necessary supplies from shopkeepers and inhabitants of the locality in which they happened to be based. Unfortunately this experiment came to an end, largely due to a decline in the number of voluntary recruits to the team and the disillusionment of the originator of the scheme with the possibility of creating a non-violent revolutionary force in Britain, and due to his feeling that there was an insufficient level of practical commitment among radical people to start a growing trend towards an alternative non-violent society.

However, one of the members of the team determined to continue with the attempt to create an alternative society by means of establishing a permanent craft centre to cater for the basic needs of an area, guided by the same ideas as had guided the mobile force. After touring the country speaking to schools, peace action groups, Quaker groups and so on, a corner shop in St Ann's, one of the poorer districts of Nottingham, was offered to them as a base for their craft centre. In their first newsletter, Jill Maguire and Mike Stroud, as originators of the experiment, wrote of their aims:

> We would like to stress it will not be an 'arty-crafty' centre but will serve to make some of the basic needs of daily living, and amongst our activities will be furniture-making and repairing, general woodwork, toy-making, weaving of rugs and matting, dress-making and pottery. Besides obtaining our food and keep as gift, we also hope to beg our raw materials and everything made will be given away to the people of the area. The Centre will also teach them the crafts so they can come and make things for their own use.

As such, the original aims of the St Ann's Community Craft Centre were very similar to those of a venture that was started in south-west Lancashire and which was inspired to some extent by the same ideas and the same people as those who promoted the Nottingham experiment. Some indication of the similarity between the two ventures is provided by the following extract taken from an early newsletter of the 'Formby Un-Tied Workshop':[29]

> We are at present converting a three storey barn on the Formby Hall estate to a craft centre which will be known as 'Formby Un-Tied Workshop'.
>
> Our aim is to establish a working example of an alternative to the present economic system. It seems clear that a system based on the profit motive and status-seeking of individuals can only result in cruel competition where gain is dependent upon the loss of others.
>
> We envisage an alternative based on love and mutual aid, in which work is carried out free of charge rather than to obtain the greatest profit. Products from the Workshop will also be free. We ask local farmers and shopkeepers in their turn to support us by gifts in kind, and local people to contribute to the needs of the centre by offering materials, time and money. We are cultivating a market garden to supplement our food supply.

Having obtained the use of a terraced house in which to live near the shop in St Ann's, the first members of the Nottingham Craft Centre moved in during the summer of 1970.[30] They were joined by others and, since that time, they have had a fairly steady complement of about half a dozen members. Due to a lack of available space for full-time workshops the original aims of the Centre have been somewhat modified. First contacts, apart from food contacts with local shopkeepers, were made by the group with the children of the neighbourhood. Offered the use of a church hall, they opened a play centre for the children to use. All the materials needed in the play centre for such activities as painting, drawing, sewing, and general letting off steam were begged. Through their involvement with the children, the members of the Centre established contacts with the parents. Through them they learned of many cases where landlords were refusing to carry out necessary repairs to tenants' houses, due largely to the fact that the area was due for redevelopment. As a result, another area of community involvement emerged for the members of the group. The free services they have provided in this field have ranged from putting in windows to sweeping chimneys, as well as general painting and decorating. In a number of cases the group provided the necessary paints and wallpaper, which they in turn had been given by local shopkeepers. The group's van also proved valuable in enabling them to provide a free removal service for those local inhabitants who were being rehoused to new housing schemes in other parts of Nottingham.

One service which the group has initiated, the old folks' lunch club, has proved particularly worth while. Run on an entirely voluntary basis, meals have been provided once a week for about thirty elderly people living in the St Ann's area. The food is supplied on a monthly rota basis by local shopkeepers and wholesalers, and is cooked by local people who also provide some of the food. The group also initiated a mothers' sewing group, using the seven sewing machines that they had acquired. At the same time, the members have been developing another institution—a 'swap shop' to which local people bring the things they no longer need, and where other people can find the things that they need. In addition to these activities, the members of the group have also involved themselves in the activities of other local groups and organizations, such as the local adventure playground group, the tenants' association, and so on. Looking to the future the group hope to develop their 'factory-workship' ideas further, if they can obtain suitable property, in order to promote what they define as an alternative economic and productive system. Through the establishment of weaving, sewing, woodworking, and other craft workshops, the group hope to develop a working model of an alternative system of producing goods to meet genuine needs rather than the need for profit, a system in which the worker retains his status as an artist and a craftsman, working to fulfil himself and to meet the needs of others rather than to earn financial reward in a repetitive and stultifying work task. Through living their own lives according to the values of mutual aid and brotherly love and concern for their fellow men, the group seek to work towards the creation of an alternative society, described to me by one of the members as

A society where we think first of our fellow man's needs and do not exploit him. And where an individual can grow and develop his full potential and not live a life based on fear of others. A society where love and co-operation with others are the prime qualities, and not the selfishness and power seeking of our present structure.

This is a goal that was shared by the members of an activist commune in Liverpool who have sought to pursue it by means of a co-operative work community and a living commune.

4 *Open Projects*

'Open Projects' was the name used by a group of people in Liverpool to refer to the variety of enterprises in which they were involved in pursuance of their aim of creating a free and egalitarian society. 'Open Design' is a co-operative work community in which about six of their number are involved making furniture by hand, according to the specific needs of the purchaser. 'Open Print' is a similar venture providing offset litho printing facilities. *Openings* is their third-arm, a magazine produced by members of Open Projects and their friends. A fourth experiment was begun with some of the members of the workshop joining together to live as a commune.

Open Design represented an attempt by seven friends who were frustrated and dissatisfied with their jobs and way of life to live a fulfilling life according to their beliefs and at the same time provide a sound economic basis for the development of a commune. Trained in a variety of professions, as artist, teacher, academic, salesman, architect, buyer and philosopher, the original members of the group sought to relate their skills to people's needs and desires by designing and making furniture at fair prices. In this way they hoped not only to achieve a worth-while and fulfilling life for themselves, but also provide a viable alternative to the world which they had rejected. One of their number has written of the principles upon which the work at Open Design was based:[31]

Every item we make is unique since it is made *by* an individual *for* an individual—and yet the price is usually lower than that of mass-produced furniture, even though the techniques of mass-production are supposedly aimed at cheapness and efficiency.

Although mass-production probably had noble intentions when it began, and although we recognise that there will always be a case for it in certain spheres, we believe that on the whole it has overtaken itself and has begun to manufacture the cart before the horse. OPEN DESIGN only makes furniture for people who have said they need it whereas furniture factories make a regular maximum turnover and then hope to sell it. What they save in the manufacture they have to spend in the selling. And it is an expenditure that constantly has to rise to cope with a weary public who need to be more and more vividly entertained by the next captivating image.

OPEN DESIGN is not an escape from the present system of furniture manufacture and retail, it is in fact a direct challenge to it: as long as there are people who need furniture and who come to us for that furniture, we shall go on making it for them with the same love and care that we apply at present and at the same reasonable cost. Expansion will not mean exchanging 24 Wapping for a factory and our intimate partnership for a staff of hundreds. Another OPEN DESIGN nucleus will arise, started by individuals who feel the same way about the present state of the world—No. 25 Wapping is the first example of this. There is no chance of a hierarchy becoming too rigid or a bureaucracy becoming too wild, for the basic systems of OPEN DESIGN rule out these elements from the beginning.

We all do everything: not chaotically, but according to careful systems that we have evolved. . . . There is therefore no boss, no manager, no foreman, no chief: neither is there a secretary, nor a telephonist, nor an accountant, nor a cleaner, nor a delivery-man, nor a salesman, nor a P.R. officer. One of our aims is to live in an atmosphere of 'total responsibility', to avoid the situation where people *become* their jobs and so feel justified in neglecting everything else—their world, their environment, their homes, even their loved ones become the responsibility of a host of other people . . . or rather a host of other 'jobs'. Since most jobs don't contain enough sparks of life to cope with the terrific energy and passion of the average human being, people have to 'become' their hobby, with the result that they don't even feel responsible for their own work.

In practice, each member of the work community spends a certain amount of time each week cleaning and maintaining the property and manning the office apart from making furniture. Each individual makes his own furniture for his own customer, and thus each member can decide on how much he wishes to earn over a certain period according to the number of items of furniture he chooses to make. The customer is charged a standard rate for the number of hours necessary to make the particular item, then the cost of materials and purchase tax is added to the final sale price. The income obtained in this fashion is not pooled, but a certain amount is put towards improving and extending the workshop facilities. Originally the members had hoped to develop a novel system of arriving at the price at which an item was to be sold—this was to charge the purchaser his own hourly rate of pay multiplied by the number of hours that the item had taken to be made. Unfortunately at one time it appeared as if most of the potential purchasers were likely to be students—as such, the scheme was deemed unlikely to provide a sound economic basis for the venture and was abandoned.

Open Print is a venture run along similar lines by another member of the group who trained as a printer. One of the main services provided by this project has been the printing of *Openings* magazine. The editorial that appeared in the first edition of the magazine would appear to place the members of Open Projects and their friends involved in its production firmly in the anarcho-pacifist tradition.[32]

Violent revolution and party politics are both ineffective ways of achieving freedom, equality and co-operation. They fail because of the distinction they make between ends and means, between the present and the future. They also fail because they seek to impose from the top ideals which, by definition, cannot be imposed.

Violence may produce some change with great bloodshed. Politics may produce some change with great delay. Often the change is no more than a change of leaders or a re-shuffling of privileges. Neither method has ever produced a genuine social revolution.

What we propose is a third way in which the means and the end are morally indistinguishable, where change begins at the bottom and grows outwards . . . we aim to live out in the present, as far as possible, the future of freedom and co-operation. In practice this is what it means:

It means making our own decisions and not taking it easy while someone else decides for us.

It means respecting an environment in which other people (as well as animals and plants) have to live.

It means working freely, producing for a need instead of for an artificially created market.

It means consuming freely, buying what we want instead of what someone else wants us to buy.

It also means education. Real education, not soaking up facts but learning to think and do things for ourselves.

Creative revolution doesn't need votes or guns. It began to happen in India under Gandhi and it can happen anywhere. All it needs to begin is a few people who decide to make it happen.

The attempt of the members of the group 'to live out in the present, as far as possible, the future of freedom and co-operation' was furthered when one of their number was provided with a substantial sum of money by his parents sufficient for him to buy a house in Liverpool to accommodate those members of the workshop and their friends who wished to live together as a commune. The group also entertain plans for the development of a parallel rural commune with a free movement of personnel between the two, the rural commune being seen as complementing the work of the urban commune as a political/community action centre, providing food supplies and acting as a retreat for the city-dwellers. Whether or not this ambitious scheme will come to fruition is difficult to say, certainly the experience of some of the members of the urban commune would seem to throw some doubt on this. Although the urban commune had only been in existence for a few months by the summer of 1971, the members had experienced a large number of problems associated with their venture into communal living. These problems centred on the usual personality conflicts, differing attitudes towards the goal and purpose of the commune, differences of opinion about living arrangements and the emergence of power relationships within the commune that are frequently encountered in such experiments in living. However, they had affected certain members of the commune sufficiently strongly for them to feel doubtful about its continued existence. At the same time, no one entertained any doubts about the future growth and evolution of their experiment in developing a co-operative work community. Perhaps their feelings about the living commune were due to the high level of their expectations about the rewards and potential achievements to be derived from such arrangements, and their sense of relative disillusionment when such benefits as they expected failed to occur. In turning in the next section to a consideration of some examples of practical communes, the members of such communes are more unlikely to encounter this problem. This is due to the fact that their expectations are typically restricted to the economic and material rewards and advantages of one sort or another to be derived from communal living, and such people do not normally base their experiments on such a coherent political philosophy as the members of Open Projects have done.

Practical communes

1 *Syrinx Co-operative Housing Association*

An example of that type of commune where the primary purpose has tended to be viewed in terms of the advantages of sharing housing costs and other economic burdens that can fall heavily on the shoulders of the individual is that of the Syrinx Co-operative Housing Association. One of the members of this group expressed how they saw the personal advantages of living with a group of others in terms of the fact that none of them would have been able to afford to live in the kind of house in which they lived as a group in north London without sharing the costs in some manner. As individuals they would have had to live in poor quality bedsitters and flats in undesirable areas of London. This was the main personal advantage of living in this way—the quality of accommodation that it afforded. The following account of this particular practical commune is taken from the standard letter that they send to any applicant.

> The Syrinx Co-operative Housing Association, registered in 1964 . . . is a non-profit making organisation, whose aim is to house its members.

> Our first modest venture . . . (a house in North London), consists of 4 large rooms, 4 small rooms, shared lounge, kitchens and bathrooms. The rents are fixed by the residents themselves at the Annual General Meeting. The house is situated in a quiet cul-de-sac and has a fair sized back garden, with lawn and trees.

> A returnable investment is required from each resident, the standard investment for a large room being £100, and for a small room £50. The standard investment carries with it the standard rent. A sliding scale of increases in rent has been calculated to assist those who cannot afford the entire standard investment.

> This amounts to about 12½p per week on £50 below standard investment. An incentive scheme also exists for those who wish to invest more and amounts to an interest rate of 6% tax free.

> The affairs of the Association are dealt with by the Committee of Management, which is elected from the residents of the Association and other professional people interested in us. Day to day matters of the household come under the care of the House Committee which meets when necessary.

Rooms are let either furnished or unfurnished. Each room has been assessed as a percentage of the whole house. A budget for the coming year is agreed at the A.G.M. and the rent of each room is then the percentage of the total budget.

(At present we have no vacancies and a long waiting list.)

Besides members' required investment in Share Stock, we also have Loan Stock facilities available to members and non-members alike, at an interest rate of 1 % above the Bank Rate or 6½ % whichever is higher.

Our aim is to bring together a group of people who have tastes and temperaments sufficiently in common to benefit from a degree of sharing some aspects of living and organising our affairs.

To even the most casual of observers, a number of differences and contrasts emerge when one compares a practical commune such as Syrinx with most other types of communes. First, with regard to membership—the typical membership of a practical commune is generally composed of middle-class, middle-aged professional-type people who read the *New Statesman*, vote Labour, and are active in local pressure groups to promote or defend certain specific issues of local concern. Second, with regard to recruitment of new members, one generally finds with practical communes that the prospective member is required to pass through a fairly formal set of procedures in order to become accepted as a member. Third, one very often finds that the number and range of official rules and regulations are much greater in practical communes than in many other types of commune. Certainly, at the Syrinx house in North London one discovered rules about smoking cigarettes in the house, about using the television, the electricity, about the presence of children in the house and so on.

2 *Postlip Hall*

These contrasts are apparent also to the members of practical communes, as expressed in a letter to *Communes* by one of the members of Postlip Hall, an Elizabethan manor house near Winchcombe, which is owned by the Postlip Housing Association Limited. The member wrote:[33]

I ought to say that we instinctively shy away from calling ourselves a community, being altogether too bourgeois for most of your members, and for their commitment to ideals. We are inclined to feel that the practical demands of this kind of project militate very strongly against an approach of pure idealism: too much traffic with the 'straight' world is needed, and this demands a good many compromises and accommodations.

However, at the same time as emphasizing the practical basis of their venture, the members of such experiments are also likely to emphasize that they are not entirely practical and materialistic in their orientation. Very frequently they have been attracted to such types of living arrangements not solely by the economies of bulk buying, but also out of a feeling of dissatisfaction with the conventional pattern of family life, with the nuclear family living an isolated life in its own separate dwelling. Thus, one of the members of the Postlip Housing Association has written of their experiment:[34]

Postlip is four largish families + one part time family + one bachelor, all rolled into a splendid guddle in a vast Elizabethan house in Gloucestershire. We are presently communal, but don't plan to stay that way in any but the loosest sense . . . we are a loose gestalt of powerful individualists who chance at this point to be moving in roughly the same direction, and who like travelling together. Spin-offs are partly practical, like bulk-buying for hungry kids-cats-passing Irishmen, a shared second car (that word 'second' marks us off, doesn't it?), and a fantastically mind-stretching environment for—in our terms—buttons; and partly the feeling that little boxes are not for living. . . . Maybe it's diversity: the chance to buck a chain-saw in the morning, de-shit an old and recalcitrant boiler and plant bulbs in the afternoon, pick apples in the late p.m.; and read poetry aloud in the evening around the fire, with beer and people and talk.

Though that's not all of it, either. . . . Postlip is a deliberate attempt to construct an improvement on little boxes for us and for the children.

The idea of forming a community which led to the birth of Postlip started when two families living a few miles apart in Gloucestershire decided it would be cheaper to buy groceries in bulk. The community has been established as a housing association. Each family becomes a co-owner of the property by investing money in the Association which then leases them a house at a nominal rent. All this provides a set of rules for joining and leaving the experiment, but the original members did find great difficulty in selecting those people whom they wished to join them—they saw a hundred people before they chose the last family.[35] Two artists, a novelist, an architect, a civil engineer, a psychologist and a flight lieutenant make up some of the members of the Association.

137

The members of such ventures as Postlip typically find themselves in a somewhat peculiar position. On the one hand they pursue straight occupations in the conventional world, but are dissatisfied with the living arrangements and family life they see as typical of that world. They feel a great deal of sympathy with the aims and aspirations of the younger, more idealistic members of the Commune Movement, but at the same time feel themselves to be somewhat apart from them in that they are generally more affluent, older, and more bourgeois or conventional in their general attitudes towards life than what they imagine to be the typical Commune Movement member. This was expressed very succinctly by one of the members of Postlip:[36]

we are very much on the fringe of the Commune Movement. For one thing, without being unkind or snotty, we have rather more money and are consequently able to go more deeply into debt to create this fairly square but ambitious construct. For another, we're not mystical, nor do we have a unifying and deeply felt principle; not that we're sceptical, just that our directions are quite other. You might say that we are poised between the entirely straight world, much of which we dislike and reject; and the total commitment to communality which most of your members feel. This could be a very uneasy and uncomfortable position, but we don't find it so. We have retained enough of our middle-class approaches to want private houses within the gestalt of Postlip; but discarded enough of them to want Postlip, and to work to make it happen.

At the same time it is possible to discover signs of a growing sense of affinity between such cognitive deviants who belong to an older generation and the communards of the modern younger generation. Thus in conversation with a member of a large commune in Kew organized as a housing association and consisting of about a hundred members, in the early spring of 1971, I asked him why he was prepared to discuss the life of his community with me in a far more open manner than he had been prepared to do when we had last met in the summer of 1970. He explained that the members had felt that there was a growing general awareness amongst people in general of the limitations of the nuclear family set-up, of the problems of loneliness and anxiety associated with life in modern society, · and a growing desire to search for alternatives on the part of ordinary people. On consideration, therefore, they had decided that they ought to try and do something to help these people by making themselves more open. They felt that there were certain limitations about the alternatives offered by the drop-outs of the younger generation, and believed that, for many people, an alternative such as they had to offer was more worth while. To this end, they had purchased a fourth house next door to the three they already occupied where people whom they encountered who were searching for some sort of alternative mode of life and living could stay, to act as a sort of half-way house where people could get to know the long-term members of the commune and yet feel that they were on their own ground and able to evolve their own style of living.

In developing the scope of their activities in this way, the members of the commune at Kew might be seen as moving in some small way towards becoming a therapeutic commune: a commune orientated towards providing care and support for particular types of individuals conventionally labelled sick or deviant in some way by certain sectors of society. In the next section attention will be turned towards a consideration of those experiments in communal living in Britain that are orientated primarily to this purpose.

Therapeutic communes

In this section, three therapeutic communes will be considered. The first two, Kingsley Hall and the Cambridge Cyrene Community, are (was, in the case of Kingsley Hall) experiments in the libertarian treatment of those designated mentally ill by society; the third, the Camphill-Rudolf Steiner Schools near Aberdeen are communities of children, teachers, doctors and therapists founded in 1939 where children with mental, emotional, and physical disturbances are admitted. In so far as the work at the Camphill Schools is based on the body of knowledge known as anthroposophy, which involves a whole way of thinking and looking at the world, and also involves knowledge not only of the material world but also of the non-material worlds, then these experiments in communal living provide a natural link with the next chapter, when attention will be turned towards a consideration of those communes that have been directed and guided by what their members feel to be their duty as believers in particular systems of religious knowledge.

1 *Kingsley Hall*

Kingsley Hall, during its existence from June 1965 until May 1970 when the lease held by the Philadelphia Association on the property ran out, represented an attempt by certain psychiatrists including David Cooper and R. D. Laing to develop an alternative method of treatment for schizophrenics within the context of a libertarian community of people. During its life it shared certain characteristics with the Cambridge Cyrene Community. First, no distinction was made between staff and patients amongst the people who lived there. Second, there was no obvious locus of institutional power. Decisions that affected everyone living in the commune were made collectively, otherwise the individual enjoyed complete freedom. Third, just as there was a determination not to type people as 'patient' and 'staff', as 'normal' or 'abnormal', the object of the commune was defined in terms rather different from those employed by the more traditional institutions designated with the task of making the 'abnormal' into 'normal' social actors. Rather than seeking to mould the individual into some pre-defined state of normality, the objective of Kingsley Hall was to provide a supportive environment for individuals to live out their 'madness', to work through the experience of the 'breakdown' and so attain that stage where they could start reconstructing their selves. The nature of this key idea in the founding of Kingsley Hall is expressed in the following passage:[37]

No age in the history of humanity has perhaps so lost touch with this natural healing process that implicates some of the people whom we label schizophrenic. No age has so devalued it, no age has imposed such prohibitions and deterrences against it, as our own. Instead of the mental hospital, a sort of re-servicing factory for human breakdowns, we need a place where people who have travelled further, and consequently, may be more lost than psychiatrists and other sane people, can find their way further into inner space and time, and back again. Instead of the degradation ceremonial of psychiatric examination, diagnosis and prognostication, we need, for those who are ready for it (in psychiatric terminology often those who are about to go into a schizophrenic breakdown), an initiation ceremonial, through which the person will be guided with full social encouragement and sanction into inner space and time. Psychiatrically, this would appear as ex-patients helping future patients to go mad.

The characteristics of Kingsley Hall and those which are shared by the Cambridge Cyrene Community become more readily understandable if one considers the processes at work in mental hospitals, to which institutions such therapeutic communes are frequently established as counter-institutions. Just as in society there exists a set of rules, often unarticulated, about what constitutes the correct and normal behaviour appropriate to certain situations, there also exist certain rules about what types of behaviour are bad, criminal, idiotic, or just plain crazy. Similarly, there exist certain culturally derived and socially sustained stereotypes which explain the significance of an individual revealing signs that, for instance, he hears voices when others around him do not, or when he sees certain things as real when he should see them as unreal, and so on. Such a person is typically defined as being mentally ill and as such in need of treatment. He is placed in the care of a psychiatrist whose appointed task is to make the person normal again, to re-socialize him. This is typically attempted within mental hospitals by a variety of processes and techniques, all of which are aimed at obtaining the patient's acceptance of the rules of the conventional world as defined by the staff. These processes all involve attempts to control the patient, to regulate his behaviour and to govern his thoughts and attitudes. Goffman, in particular, has examined in some detail the nature of some of these processes; the nature of the degradation ceremonies and other attempts to destroy the inmate's conception of himself, and the way the ward system and other control mechanisms are used to gain the patient's acceptance of the staff's definition of himself, their definition of the nature of his mental illness and the treatment required, and their definition of the nature of the changes in the attitudes and behaviour necessary for him to display before he will be allowed to leave the hospital as a normal healthy individual.[38] As such, the work of the traditional mental hospital is based on the assumption that there is something wrong inside the individual who displays crazy behaviour, that the problem lies within the individual and it is there that it must be tackled. This is an assumption that was not shared by the founders of the Philadelphia Association. One of them has written on this matter:[39]

Our studies have led to the view that in many cases, what is the matter is not an 'illness' in one person, but that something is the matter with a social process. This means that we have changed our view not only of the what of what is the matter but also of the where of what is the matter. The 'what' is not an 'illness', and the 'where' is not only, if at all, inside the brain or chemistry of one person. There is a complex disorder of a social field, which includes the chemistry of the people in it.

Only recently have sociologists, psychiatrists, anthropologists, and other social scientists come to the view that 'schizophrenia' has to do with communication. . . .

We have begun to understand that we cannot explain away experience but have rather to comprehend it. Research into the families of people called schizophrenic makes this clear. We see how people are driven into a corner in their human environments by contradictory wishes, demands and expectations flung at them, without awareness, by other people around them, and by themselves.

When driven far and forcibly enough into this corner, all
anyone can do is 'go up the wall'. . . .

To explore the contradictions in communication that at
times may lead any of us to act, or to be seen, as mad, we
needed a community with a flexible structure, where people did
not have to be forced into such roles as doctor, social worker,
nurse or patient.

In 1964 one of the founders of the Philadelphia Association
established a household of four people, three of whom were schizophrenics from a mental hospital. The experience obtained in that
setting confirmed their views that schizophrenia could be understood better in a libertarian household where all formal roles were
de-structured and done away with than in a mental hospital. Then,
in June 1965, the trustees of Kingsley Hall leased this long-established
East London Community Centre to the Association. Between that
date and 31 August 1969 113 people were accommodated there.
During this period the Philadelphia Association also created two
other smaller communities with similar aims to the Kingsley Hall
experiment. In each household the people living there made what
rules there were to govern their life together. Such rules as there
were did not oblige any member to work or earn money. Everyone
paid what money they could afford into a communal fund which was
used to pay for food, heating, electricity, repairs and maintenance of
the building. The individual member was provided with the opportunity to enjoy the fullest freedom. No one was forced to get up or
go to bed at any particular time, time of eating was an individual
matter. As there were no staff, no patients, and no institutional
procedures, no one person was in charge of another. Each individual
was allowed the freedom to follow his own path of self-discovery.
One of the members has paid tribute to this aspect of the experiment:[40]

Those who live here see 'Kingsley-hall' each in his own way . . .
in common to all who live here . . . is a bafflement or refusal as
to fulfilment of 'identity' . . . the problem is for each to discover some inner need—and to find a way to trust it. . . . It is
in honour of this, that Kingsley Hall is a place, simply where
some may encounter selves long forgotten or distorted.

Unfortunately, the Association's lease of Kingsley Hall expired in
May 1970 and the experiment came to an end. Since that time they
have been appealing for funds and practical support in order to buy
a house in London and a house in the country where the work
started at Kingsley Hall can be continued, and in order to promote
the spread and development of the ideas that led to the founding of

the original venture. Perhaps it is worth recording that of the 188 people who lived in the households established by the Association between 1965 and 1970, no one who had not been in a mental hospital before they joined went to one during or after their period of residence.

2 Cambridge Cyrene Community

Much of the thinking that characterized the experiments promoted by the Philadelphia Association, particularly with regard to the harm inflicted by the individual within total institutions such as mental hospitals, also preceded the development of the Simon Community Trust, from which has evolved a number of Cyrenian and Simon Communities throughout the country. Typical of these is the Cambridge Cyrene Community, which consists of a group of people living and working together in two houses in the centre of Cambridge with the aim of helping members of the Cambridge vagrant population who are suffering from mental and personality disorders. As with Kingsley Hall the community is run more along the lines of a household without any division of members into staff and patients than as a hostel or clinic with their formally defined roles and hierarchical power structures. The tasks and responsibilities involved in running the community are shared by all the members. Likewise, the object of the community is not to normalize the vagrants in order for them to return to society. One of their members has written of this aspect of the community:[41]

> In this way we believe the individual can recover his dignity and the security and friendship he needs, enabling him, if he desires, to return to society at large. However, our object is not to 'cure' people and return them to a 'normal life'. Society has rejected them and they society—We offer them an alternative in which to live.

As such, the community is based on that simple axiom that if you treat an individual as a unique human being worthy of love and respect, he in turn is likely to develop a sense of his own worth and dignity. On the other hand, if you treat an individual with contempt and as unworthy of respect, it is highly probable that the individual in turn will begin to consider himself as unworthy of respect, which in turn will only provide the necessary proof to justify the original view of him held by others and so the cycle develops. In sociological terms this can be expressed in the language of Cooley: to a large extent an individual's identity is a configuration of self-images or self-conceptions which originate in social processes. The individual's sense of his own identity will be largely dependent upon the various

143

reflected images of himself that he observes in the way other people treat him as an individual. Thus, the ideal of the community is not so much to work for the vagrants, but rather to work with them by sharing a common way of life, helping by understanding and experiencing their problems and treating them as individuals worthy of respect, and not as social inadequates in need of care and attention.

The community at Cambridge is fairly typical of most other ventures that have evolved out of the Simon Community Trust in so far as the community workers are mixed in age and sex but are predominantly under thirty years of age. Decisions are made collectively at weekly house meetings, where general issues and interpersonal problems are also raised and discussed. The workers are usually temporary, spending a few months of the year at the community, for which they receive the same sum per week as would an individual in receipt of supplementary benefits. Generally they have little or no formal training. They are frequently student volunteers, or people who intend to become students in the near future. The Cambridge Cyrene Community was only founded in 1969. As such it stands in great contrast with the Camphill–Rudolf Steiner Schools that have been in existence since 1939.

3   The Camphill–Rudolf Steiner Schools

The Camphill School near Aberdeen is a therapeutic community caring for boys and girls with mental, emotional and physical disturbances. There are about 200 children living there, with about 130 staff of whom about 55 are permanent workers. The work at Camphill is based on that body of knowledge of the physical and spiritual worlds developed by Rudolf Steiner and known as Anthroposophy. The Camphill movement itself originated as an idea in the mind of the late Dr Karl Konig who, in 1938 in Austria, developed the idea of a centre for handicapped children, having had some previous experience of similar institutions run according to the methods of Steiner. When Austria was overrun by the Germans in 1938 Dr Konig and a small circle of young friends who had gathered around him moved to Scotland. It was from this beginning that the movement grew.

It would be beyond the scope of this present work to attempt to summarize the tenets of the Anthroposophical belief system. Steiner himself viewed it not so much as a philosophical system or as a collection of theories, but as a way of thinking, as a 'path of knowledge, to lead the spiritual in the human being to the spiritual in the universe'.[42] He emphasized that his teachings were not derived from any ancient tradition, but were rather the objective reports of his independent spiritual investigations. As such he stressed that his statements about spiritual worlds, reincarnation, life before birth and after death should not be accepted as faith, but rather be used by the individual as material to help his own search for truth through study, meditation and spiritual effort. In similar fashion Steiner viewed his body of knowledge as leading not to remote mysticism, but as being applicable to the most practical human affairs—medicine, agriculture, science, the arts, and education. At Camphill, Steiner's contribution to the theories of medicine and education are put into practice.

What distinguishes Camphill from other residential schools and homes which care for the handicapped child? Dr Konig wrote of the 'three essentials' that distinguished Camphill as a therapeutic community from others. The first essential is the belief that the child is more than his physical appearance. The belief that[43]

> In his appearance he is merely the outer shell of an infinite and eternal spiritual being. . . . We are convinced that every human being has his individual existence not only here on earth between birth and death, but . . . was a spiritual entity before he was born, and . . . will continue to live after he has passed through the gate of death. Thus, any kind of mental and physical handicap is not acquired by change or misfortune. It has a definite meaning for the individual and is meant to change his life.

Thus the workers at Camphill approach the individual child in the belief that he possesses this spiritual core, this eternal, imperishable 'I'. As such[44]

> He is our brother and our sister. . . . We do not deal with the *handicapped* child; we deal with the *child* who is handicapped. . . . The nucleus of the being, the inmost kernel of his existence is not only infinite; it is divine. It is part of the divinity to which it will return and from whence it came and will come again. His crippled and distorted life is but one way back to the Father. . . . This is the first essential.

Whereas the first essential is concerned with the teacher's orientation to the child, the second essential concerns the teacher's orientation towards himself and his work as a teacher. As followers of Rudolf Steiner, the workers at Camphill believe that man is endowed with an inner force which has creative possibilities. A power which can move mountains. It is this inner spiritual power of creativity which they see as fading away in our modern technological society and which they view as one of the fundamentals of remedial education. To develop this inner power is the daily task of the teacher. If he does this, then it is believed that spiritual sources are opened up and intuition will guide his work. Thus, each morning the teacher, either through prayer, meditation, concentration or some other mental exercise, turns to this fountainhead of existence to sustain, develop and replenish his spiritual courage.

When Christ's disciples asked him, after he had successfully cast out the evil spirit that tormented the young man who suffered from falling sickness how they too could develop the power to heal in such a way when all their efforts had failed, He replied, 'This kind can come forth by nothing, but by prayer and fasting' (Mark 9: 29). The workers at Camphill seek to practise this by meditation, prayer or other mental exercise, but also by 'fasting'. They interpret this metaphorically, rather than literally however.[45]

> 'To cast out spirits' means to create a surrounding congenial to a handicapped child . . . an environment of loving peace and peaceful love . . . without noise and hurry, without restlessness and quarrel. And 'to fast' means to forgo the various temptations which today's life offers us: television, radio, drink, chatter, gossip and the many things that make life so difficult and unbearable. This type of existence is the greatest enemy of the handicapped child.

In fact, none of the houses in Camphill has a television, and the radio is used only occasionally, when the children are not around.

The third essential is based on the awareness that the human being is largely dependent on his environment and under the influence of his fellow men. The community with fellow men is seen as the essential womb and support of men. However, this womb is seen to possess several layers: from the mother's womb to the family to the village or local community through to the largest community—mankind as a whole. Every infant has to adjust himself in making the transition from one environment to the other in his passage through life. However, if the child fails to receive sufficient love, support and care when making this necessary adjustment, then he may be handicapped for the remainder of his life. The people at Camphill believe that many handicapped children suffer from this maladjustment. Hence they believe that it is one of the most important conditions for any kind of remedial education to provide an adequate social womb, to provide the child with a sense of community. This is the basis for their work with mentally afflicted people. This goal helps one to understand several aspects of the internal living arrangements within the community. For instance, no worker receives a wage at Camphill.

> We are convinced that we could not do our work in the same manner if we were employees and received a salary. . . . Wages

(not money) create a barrier between the one who receives and
the one who pays. To give and to take is a matter of mutual
human relationship; the true relationship goes as soon as
wages intervene.

Thus, finance is a community affair at Camphill. The school receives no grants from the state, in order to preserve its autonomy.
The income of the school is derived from the fees of £1,000 per
thirty-nine week year for each child. Ninety per cent of the children
at Camphill are maintained by local education authority grants. The
community also receives donations.

While the economic sphere of the community is characterized by
the sense of brotherhood that is maintained when no one receives
a wage, the value of equality is sought after in the sphere of individual
members' rights. Decisions affecting the budget of the community,
the building programme and so forth are decided by the various
committees, and the arrangements are such that each member's
voice can be heard when such decisions are arrived at. Moreover,
attempts are made to allow each individual member to do the kind
of work within the community for which he feels best suited and for
which he feels destined. At the same time, the people at Camphill are
aware of the individual's need for personal privacy, to be alone on
occasions either by himself or with his own family. Thus, each
worker has his own private living accommodation, whether this be a
cottage in the grounds or a private bedroom in one of the houses.

Thus the third essential of Camphill is the social order which they
have sought to create there. All three are seen as constituting one
way of creating those social conditions necessary for the 'healing
Spirit' to work towards the attainment of what they see as the
ultimate goal of remedial education: 'the renewal of the soul by the
living breath of the Spirit'.[46] Apart from the three essentials, the
workers at Camphill rely on three main techniques to assist the
handicapped child: education, therapy, and the use of medicines.
The educational system at the community consists of ten classes,
with one nursery class for pre-school children and an eleventh class
for young trainees between the ages of sixteen and eighteen. The
form of education is similar to that followed in Rudolf Steiner
schools in general. The main subjects are all taught in block periods
of three to four weeks for the first couple of hours of each day. The
class teacher, having taken on Class I at the age of six, goes up
through the school with it, teaching the main lessons and getting to
know the children very well. The establishment of trustful relationships between the teachers and the children is further facilitated by
the division of the community into fourteen living units, where the
children live together with their 'house parents' as family groups. A

147

balance is sought between the practical, artistic and intellectual elements throughout the whole education.

Due to the fact that the children who are referred to Camphill by the child psychiatrists and the child guidance clinics are usually the most serious cases, of the children who enter Camphill only about 20 per cent are able to leave at the age of sixteen to pursue their lives independently, without any further care or attention. About 60 per cent of the children who leave there are capable of working in 'sheltered workshops' such as the Newton Dee Village Community founded in 1960 and sited adjacent to Camphill. The remainder of the children require special care and attention for the rest of their lives after leaving the community.

The people at Camphill would probably be very quick to deny that Anthroposophy was a religion with Steiner as its prophet. However, from the sociologists' point of view Anthroposophy does constitute a body of knowledge which presents the believer with a way of looking at the material and non-material worlds, and as such can be seen as acting as a sacred canopy for its adherents. In fact the belief system, with its emphasis on the divine inner core that is within each and every individual, the belief in reincarnation and karma, can be viewed as akin to the mystic religions of the Orient, although in 1912 Steiner had broken away from the Theosophical Society due to his belief in the unique importance of Christ in human evolution. This ran counter to some of the ideas of the leading Theosophists of that time who looked towards the East for their spiritual knowledge. Many people have thus come to view Steiner as an Initiate of the West who offered a Christianized spiritual knowledge to the modern world. To the extent that the experiment at Camphill represents an attempt to put into practice the work of Steiner, it can be said to constitute a religious commune. On the other hand, to the extent that the work there is primarily orientated to the care of handicapped children, with the work of Steiner merely providing a useful source of guidance and advice with which to pursue this aim, then Camphill can be labelled a therapeutic commune. Some of the workers no doubt hold to one or the other definitions of the situation, but the majority view Camphill as both a therapeutic and a religious commune—the two aspects being seen as inextricably linked. As such, Camphill provides a link with the communes to be considered in the next chapter—those communes which are defined by their members primarily in terms of fulfilling some purpose or other which they feel to be in accordance with their religious beliefs.

6 Religious communes in Britain

At a time when church-affiliated religiosity is in decline, it appears that interest in religion is abundant. The fact that in the West religion can no longer be equated simply with the Church has many implications for the study of religion and of society in general. Since the mid-1960s there has been a significant re-orientation of the sociology of religion brought about by the dissatisfaction of certain authors with the state of the discipline at that time, and a felt need for their subject to take cognizance of the emergence of non-institutionalized religion.[1]

A major target of such criticism was the nature of the empirical research into Christian institutions and the characteristics of their members. Such research, it was argued, lent itself to the mechanical application of positivist research techniques and, moreover, it avoided questions that went beyond the immediate pragmatic concerns of the employer. Bellah in particular has argued that traditional forms of the sociology of religion are inappropriate in understanding the new forms of religion. He has argued that the complexity and flexibility in emergent systems of religious symbols requires a new theoretical position and a new set of research interests. He has argued for a meta-theoretical position of symbolic realism which involves treating religious symbols as 'real'. He has suggested that[2]

> To concentrate on the church in a discussion of the modern
> religious situation is already misleading, for it is precisely the
> characteristic of the new situation that the great problem
> of religion as I have defined it, the symbolization of
> man's relation to the ultimate conditions of his existence, is no
> longer the monoploy of any groups explicitly labelled religious.

It is in this light that the following examination of some of the contemporary communes in Britain may be viewed as a contribution to the re-orientation of the sociology of religion at the research level—the study of churchless religion. Primarily, however, this chapter seeks to present an examination of those communes and their members in Britain which appear as the present day carriers of the religious traditions of communal living examined in Chapter 2.

Communes based on mystic belief systems

Findhorn Community, Centre of Light[3]

Many communities have been inspired by religious beliefs and a determination to live a life in accordance with such precepts and injunctions. History shows that those communities that have been the most successful in terms of longevity of life have had as their basis a shared religious belief and purpose. In Britain there are a number of religiously-inspired communes, many seeing their function in terms of social action orientated towards their wider environment, action based on their religious convictions about how social life should be ordered. Of a somewhat different order is the commune at Findhorn in the north-east of Scotland. For the people of Findhorn their task is directed not so much by a set of principles outlined in a book written centuries ago, as by the direct guidance of God conveyed directly to the members. Thus one of the founder members of the Centre has written: 'I must make it clear that this is a spiritual community, not a social one, in which the whole operation is under God's guidance and direction.'[4]

In May 1969 the community published a brief statement of its beliefs and history:[5]

> The community at Findhorn consists of a group of people
> pioneering a new way of living. There are no blueprints;
> we seek and follow God's guidance which comes in different
> ways. . . . My wife Eileen hears the still small voice within
> and receives detailed guidance which we have followed with
> astonishing results. . . . We are living a way of life which
> is undenominational and therefore cannot be labelled. . . .
> Our aim is to bring down the Kingdom of Heaven on earth and
> therefore everything must be as near perfect as possible,
> perfect to meet the need for which it is sought. To do this
> we have had to go ahead and do the seemingly impossible. . . .
> Each of us has come along a different spiritual path and
> people of all religions are welcome at Findhorn, for this is a
> totally new conception of living. We are pioneering a new
> way for the New Age which is gradually unfolding and will
> require a new type of man.

In 1962 the Caddy family and Dorothy Maclean had settled at a caravan park at Findhorn in order to seek a new form of life. Caddy failed to find employment in the area despite genuine efforts to do so. He started to work on a garden at the caravan site:[6]

> Then started the expansion, step by step, under God's guidance.
> We had to learn the laws of manifestation, for each one of
> us had given up all and were now entirely dependent
> upon God's limitless supply to meet our needs. As we became
> aware of a need, together we would ask that the need be met.
> We learnt that our united thought and our act of asking
> were both important to manifest our needs, and we gave
> thanks immediately knowing in complete faith that they
> would be manifested.

In this manner the community has acquired numerous caravans, bungalows, a communtiy centre and sanctuary.

Findhorn, then, is defined by its members as a community pioneering a new way of life into the New Age of Aquarius. Its membership is composed of people who have travelled along different spiritual paths and from different social backgrounds. The members consist of young and old, short-haired and long-haired, hippies and 'straights'. The recent history of the community mirrors in many respects the development of certain contemporary mystical cults. Until 1968–9 the membership was largely composed of middle-aged, middle-class people. In recent years, however, they have been joined by increasing numbers of young drop-outs. The reasons for this development can to some extent be seen as due to the overlap that exists between certain aspects of the Findhorn belief system and that of the drug culture, in which drug sensations are defined in pantheistic terms. The goals of drug-taking have been frequently phrased in terms of 'expanding the consciousness', a term which is frequently used by the members at Findhorn. Moreover, many 'heads' give pride of place to the development of one's inner psychic state with the implicit, and occasionally explicit, devaluation of active involvement with the material world. Again, the sense of deep, personal relationship with fellow trippers that develops among drug-users is mirrored in the sense of community and group consciousness that is to be found at Findhorn. Finally, many drug-users have had, through the use of drugs, experiences which they have defined as 'mystical', through which their interest in mystic religion has been aroused. Many young people go to Findhorn to pursue this interest.

The conception of the divine held by the members of the community is far more akin to the mystic tradition of the Orient than the ascetic tradition of the Occident. 'God' is a term used because it is simpler than referring to the Universal Mind, Infinite Truth or the Universal Energy Source. 'God' is a word used to refer to a Universal Presence, an energy force which is acting throughout the world on all planes of existence, and which is within us and without. 'The Being "outside" is the Being "within". There is only that which is and has always been.'[7] It is through this 'Living Force' that is immanent in all things that the essential oneness of all things is to be found. 'I AM always there like the breath that keeps your body alive. Become aware of ME all the time. I AM the Living Force within your being. I AM life.'[8] Unlike certain mystical traditions which develop a distinction between the mass of believers and the elect holders of the esoteric truths, Findhorn specifically rejects a[9]

spiritual elite. The answers lie within each and everyone.
You need no teacher, no guru. All you need is an expansion of consciousness so that you can accept these truths. They are there for all mankind to accept when mankind is ready to do so.

Thus, there is no mandate within the belief system for any type of organization or for any particular method of spiritual development. It is recognized that each individual must find his own path.[10]

Try to understand there are hundreds and hundreds of different paths but they all lead to the same goal. That is why every soul must learn to do its own seeking and never try to follow someone else's path unless it is inspired to do so from deep within.

This injunction to 'do one's own thing' would seem to go some way towards avoiding the traditional sectarian problem of being in the world but not of it. However, it is recognized that the things of the spirit must be placed before all else. Eileen Caddy, whose spiritual name is Elixer, received the following message couched in biblical terms:[11]

First things have to be put first in every soul for it to find true satisfaction in this life. You cannot serve Me and mammon, the choice lies before every soul. He who has much in the way of the world's goods will not find it easy, for all that has to be given second place and at times has to be given up completely.

However, although the things of the spirit are to be placed before all else, this does not mean that one's actions in this world are irrelevant. Repeatedly in the messages received by Elixer there is the emphasis on the importance of individual exemplary action in this world. As one member commented, 'It is not much use talking about faith if you do not demonstrate what faith really means to you by living it.' The New Age is seen as being built upon the foundation of Love. This Tolstoyan emphasis on the need for one's actions in this world to be characterized by the spirit of purest love is accompanied by a similar emphasis on the power of non-violence, with the injunction to 'Resist not evil but overcome evil with good.'[12] Linked with this is the stress on the need to look for the best in everything, to 'dwell on the things of the Light and ignore anything of the dark'. The people at Findhorn believe that if attention is paid to the 'voice within', then everything will fall into place. At the same time, however, the good things of life are not expected to fall from the holds of Royal Air Force bombers from Lossiemouth. The right attitude towards life and towards people is seen as being of vital importance. It is the 'power of positive thinking' that will make a significant contribution to the coming of the New Age. Hence one should not dwell on past mistakes when one hears the voice within, for 'there is a silver lining to every cloud, no matter how dark it may appear at the time. Therefore look for the silver lining and never rest content until you have found it.'[13] As one would expect from a belief system with such a strong mystic element, greater faith is held in the individual's intuition than in his intellect alone. However, while Weber's characterization of the mystic's relationship with the divine as being that of a vessel rather than an instrument is typical of the attitude of the members at Findhorn, one also finds an emphasis on the need for self-discipline. This seems more akin to the ascetic tradition. In addition one finds recurring references to the fact that the people at Findhorn are in fact the instruments of the divine, the hands and the feet of God, placed on earth to fulfil His great plan.

The Findhorn belief system contains distinct adventist notions. The purpose of Findhorn as a centre of light is none other than that of bringing down the kingdom of heaven to earth by means of exemplary action. The function of Findhorn is to demonstrate in practice the workings of the divine laws so that those who are ready to learn can see and recognize. This adventism is expressed in terms similar to Zoroastrian terminology. Findhorn is viewed as a centre from where the forces of light will emanate to counteract the forces of darkness (i.e. materialism) throughout the world. More specifically, the tasks of Findhorn are seen as two-fold. One is that of demonstrating to the drop-outs of the younger generation who have rejected the materialism and the restraints of straight society a positive way of moving towards the Age of Aquarius. The other is to demonstrate to the world how to work harmoniously with the inhabitants of the 'Elemental World': the Devas and the nature spirits.

Although Findhorn is sited on a sandy and wind-swept part of the Morayshire coastline, its gardens produce a range of vegetables for their vegetarian diet. The results revealed in the two-acre garden are explained by the harmonious co-operation between the beings of the three kingdoms or planes of existence: 'Man', the 'Devas', and 'the nature spirits'. 'Man', the organizer and practical creator of the garden, is represented by Peter Caddy. He is not a sensitive, and is unable to contact directly the other realms of existence inhabited by the Devas and nature spirits. 'The Devas are the Angelic Beings who wield the archetypal forces. There is one of these for every species of the plant kingdom and in addition there are Devas of sound, colour, wind, etc.' Dorothy Maclean, whose spiritual name is Divine, is able to communicate with these architects of the plant kingdom, to hear them as the voice within during meditation, and to consult about the garden and the growth of plants.

Just as the Devas provide the blueprint for the plant world, so the nature spirits are seen as carrying out the actual work. These nature spirits, under the leadership of Pan, the god of nature, communicate with the people at Findhorn through a sensitive known at the community as Roc. It is to Roc that Pan has manifested himself at Edinburgh, Iona, Findhorn and other places and has made clear the necessary task at Findhorn, which is to show to Man that he must work in co-operation with the nature spirits and the Devas if the earth is not to be turned into a polluted and ruined desert as a result of ecological disaster. To quote Sir George Trevelyan:[14]

> The world of nature spirits is sick of the way man is treating the life forces. They [the devas and elementals] are working with God's law in plant growth. Man is continually violating it. There is a real likelihood that they may even turn their back on man whom they sometimes consider to be a parasite on earth. This could mean a withdrawal of life force from the plant forms, with obviously devastating results.
>
> Yet their wish is to work in co-operation with man who has been given a divine task of tending the earth. For generations man has ignored them and even denied their existence. Now a group of men consciously invite them to their garden. . . . The delight in the deva world is apparently great. At last men have begun to wake up. Since the spiritual world is all one, a great living unity, the news shoots around instantly and the devas throng in with joy to help.
>
> They are literally demonstrating that the desert can blossom as the rose. They also show the astonishing pace at which this can be brought about. If this can be done so quickly at Findhorn, it can be done in the Sahara. If enough

men could really begin to use this co-operation consciously,
food could be grown in quantity on the most infertile areas.
There is virtually no limit if 'factor X' can be brought
into play on top of our organic methods.

If God's hand is at work in the garden, then it is also to be seen
manifesting itself in other ways—particularly in the laws of manifestation. Whilst those who wish to join the community permanently
are required to provide their own living accommodation and pay
their share of the rent, rates, electricity and so on, many of the
items that have required the expenditure of relatively large amounts
of capital such as the community centre and the sanctuary have been
funded by voluntary donations from friends of the community. While
these people are thanked for their generosity, the real thanks are
given to God who is viewed as having used these people as His
agents to fulfil the need which the people at Findhorn had made
known to Him. Briefly stated, the laws are seen as working in the
following manner. Peter Caddy or one of the other members will
have a sudden idea or hunch that something is needed for the
community. This will be interpreted as the voice of God. Eileen
Caddy (Elixer) will then be asked for a 'reading' on the matter, to
confirm it. This ability of Eileen to contact God as the ultimate
source of all authority for advice on almost any matter means that
one of the major practical problems of communal life—decision
making—has been dealt with at Findhorn without to date causing
dissent. Eileen usually receives confirmation that it is God's will that
they go ahead and obtain the desired item. The community members
then feel utterly confident that their need will be satisfied, and proceed
to make arrangements to obtain whatever is desired, whether they
have any money available for such a purpose or not. They believe
that where one has sufficient faith in God, then He will go before
and prepare the way. On a sufficient number of occasions to cause
one to challenge standard explanations of coincidence and chance,
Findhorn has in the past been provided with well-timed gifts of
money, to pay for items obtained or with people with the necessary
skills to complete particular jobs in hand.[15]

It is interesting to speculate on the consequences for the world-
view of the people at Findhorn if their needs failed to be met by
means of the laws of manifestation. Bearing in mind Festinger's
theory of cognitive dissonance, one might expect that it would take
more than a few isolated failures to shake their faith.[16] The only
instance of such a failure which has come to my attention was
when a caravan that seemed as if it was to be manifested in answer
to the request being made known, having been promised by the
potential donor, failed to be delivered. This apparent failure on the

laws of manifestation was explained as being due to the failure on the part of the potential recipient to give thanks to God for the answering of her need. Other possible explanations that would be available if such an instance were to happen again would include the fact that the exact nature of the need has to be specified before it can be met. One could always claim that an individual had not provided sufficiently detailed instructions for the need to be met.

Reference has been made to the fact that many of the problems traditionally associated with communal living are avoided at Findhorn due to the ability of Eileen to receive direct messages from God, on the basis of which major decisions are made. There are, however, a number of sensitives at Findhorn, and again it is interesting to speculate as to the possible consequences of two sensitives receiving conflicting 'readings'. To my knowledge, however, this has never happened. The day-to-day running and organization of the community is very much in the hands of Peter Caddy who tends to allot daily tasks among the members, deals with the bulk of the correspondence, and escorts the visitors around the community. By virtue of his position as the founder of the Centre, his status as the husband of Eileen, and his undoubted organizational ability and personal charm, Peter's authority is rarely challenged. When a dispute does occur between members of the community, then it is the diplomacy of Peter which is frequently called upon to restore the calm.[17]

Given the nature of the Findhorn belief system, with the emphasis on the direct relationship between the individual and the divine presence and the recognition that there is no one spiritual path to be pursued, one would not expect to find there any intricate system of ritual. The nearest approximation to ritual at Findhorn is the rhythm to their day with their communal mid-day and evening meals in the community centre, and the periods of meditation and prayer in the morning and evening in the sanctuary. They also carry out their own wedding and christening ceremonies at the community. At the morning sessions in the sanctuary Elixer's message from the Light received during the previous night is read out, along with other messages that have been received by the different members of the community. It is at this morning session that the assembled attempt, not so much to pray together as to channel Light and Love to those with whom they have spiritual links in different parts of the world.

In the light of their stated aim of bringing down the kingdom of heaven to earth and their rejection of any esoteric knowledge that is capable of being understood only by an élite group, it might be expected that the members of Findhorn would be actively involved in seeking the conversion of the masses. In fact, they make efforts to shield the exact nature of their experiment from the eyes of the inhabitants of their immediate neighbourhood. They feel that any attempts to proselytize in that area would be wasted. It is their belief that all who are led to seek the light will be led to Findhorn at some stage or another. Hence they refuse to involve themselves in any active attempt to convert the non-believer. This is a characteristic of other groups sharing similar types of beliefs, such as the Anthroposophists at Camphill who make no attempt to convert others to their way of thinking—each must find his own way and one should not interfere with another individual's karma. This attitude was expressed in a message received by Elixer:[18]

This is but the beginning of tremendous happenings. It will have a chain reaction and nothing will be able to stop it. . . . Never try to justify Me or what I have said. Let each soul seek within and find the true interpretation of My prophecies. If he accepts them, well and good, but if he rejects them, let him go. Never try to convince any soul. This is something each individual will have to seek and find within, without any outer signs to convince him. He will simply know what is the truth and in that knowledge he will find perfect freedom and peace of heart and mind.

In keeping with this type of injunction, the activities of the members at Findhorn concerned with spreading the Light are confined to sending their literature on request and receiving visitors. They do not invite people to visit them, neither do they ask for financial contributions for their literature or for their hospitality, but leave it to the conscience of the recipient and visitor. However, while the community never actually invites anyone to visit or join them, they appear to have no formal membership criteria. This 'open door' policy was expressed in a message received in which Elixer was told:[19]

You are living and creating something here which the many long for, but do not know how to achieve, and they will want to know more and see more, so again I say to you be ready for anything. You will find seemingly very unlikely people will become really interested in all you are doing. Let them all come, see that they take part in what is going on, for only by taking part can they really find out. This is an action group living a life, not one that spends its time talking and doing nothing.

In practice this policy of open-armed love is tempered by a strong dose of wisdom in that those who do join the life at Findhorn are expected to contribute to that life in some practical way or another, to provide their own accommodation and to contribute to the work and running expenses of the Centre.

However, Findhorn is characterized by a wide variety of types of members. There one finds archetypal middle-aged, middle-class people and married couples, older members, young professional couples who are visiting, and an assortment of young people who appear as typical members of the spiritual wing of the underground and who, when I was there, were forced to be somewhat less than open in some of their habits for fear of upsetting the other members of the community, most of whom did not even smoke cigarettes. Thus one of the most vigorous helpers in the kitchen was an eighty-two-year-old lady from San Diego, California who had written to Peter Caddy in the summer of 1969 to inform him that the Lord had instructed her to go to Findhorn. Despite Peter's efforts to dissuade her from making the trip, she persisted and arrived at Findhorn in the September of that year. Another elderly lady whom I came across at the community had, like many of the older members, first heard of Findhorn through their involvement in the Universal Foundation. This organization is a body that sees its function as 'providing co-ordinated information in a universal setting, about the emergent New Age, and the founding of the Universal Kingdom of Love on earth, in all its manifest forms'.[20] The members of this organization are all concerned with the mystic's quest of 'the restoration of man's direct link with Divine Love, Wisdom and Power'. The headquarters of the Foundation is now sited at Findhorn. The relationship between the Universal Foundation and Findhorn has been outlined by one of the Presidents of the Foundation:[21]

> The Universal Foundation is rather a principle than an organisation and seen as that which lies behind the establishment generally and universally of what Findhorn demonstrates in particular and locally, spreading outwards from a specific centre, under divine guidance. . . . The Universal Foundation needs Findhorn as a prime example of what it signifies universally in terms of the manifestation of God's Kingdom on Earth.

Among the younger members who were living there during my stay, there was R. He had worked as a research officer/technician at one of the Scottish Universities, then spent some time working with mental patients, and had held a number of temporary jobs of various sorts. He explained to me how, as a child, he had always been interested in myths and magic, and in later life he had become interested in parapsychic phenomena and such things as extra-sensory perception. Towards the end of 1967 he had first met Roc at his flat in Edinburgh. He heard of Findhorn and began to feel that his life was beginning to take on some direction for the first time. He visited Findhorn and decided to stay. While remaining firmly involved in the mystical side of the community activities, for R one of the most important things that he had found during his stay was the opportunity provided for the individual to develop his potentialities to the utmost. He had found that work at the community was organized on a day-to-day basis. He was involved in a variety of types of work, thus he never got bored or lost interest in what he was doing. In this attitude, R was displaying an orientation towards communal living typical of the members of what were termed in the last chapter 'self-actualizing communes'. Thus he also emphasized the importance, for him, of living in close proximity with other aware people, and how this breaks down all the artificial masks that we use and construct as defence mechanisms in the conventional social world, and so enables the individual to discover his real self. R's plans for the future involved schemes for travelling to the East, 'just to see what I see, to discover and to learn'. He was particularly interested in visiting Indonesia to study the Subud belief system, to which he was attracted due to its emphasis on the equality of all seekers after truth, its emphasis on joy and the spreading of the glory of God and Light in everything that one does.

A few months after my stay at Findhorn there was a Subud conference in London and B, whom I had met at Findhorn, spent the weekend in our flat. He had arrived in London for the weekend with nowhere to stay, had been meditating at Gandalf's Garden when the 'voice within' told him to come round to our flat. B was then aged twenty-one and was unmarried. He had lived for most of his life in a coastal resort where his parents owned a small hotel, and where he had worked as a gardener and as a salesman, among other things. He had only been at Findhorn for a short while prior to my visit, but he struck me as typical in many ways of those young people I met during the course of my research who had rejected the materialism of the contemporary culture and who spent their time moving around the country from one place and group to the next, searching for enlightenment, self-knowledge, or maybe for a home. B had a wide experience of various types of drugs. He had been arrested and fined on a drug possession charge in his home town. He said he had not had a happy childhood and had felt himself to be socially inadequate, unable to relate to people who led conventional jobs. He had suffered a nervous breakdown when he had tried to live a straight life.

K was only slightly older than B but was far more conventional in his dress and appearance. He and his wife were both teachers, but were regular visitors to Findhorn. Brought up in a Quaker household, he had decided by the time he went to university that the way of the Quakers was not his way. He spent most of his time at university reading books on mysticism, the occult and parapsychology. This interest he explained in terms of his feeling at that time that there must be more to life than all the materialism that he saw around him. He was on a search for truth. When teaching in Scotland, he had travelled up to Findhorn to talk with Peter and Eileen Caddy two or three times a week. Eventually he had gone to live at Findhorn for a year, until he awoke one morning and felt that the time had come for him to leave, his work there had been done. His 'inner voice' had spoken, and so he just packed and left that same morning, believing that one must act immediately upon the urgings of the inner voice. Since that time K had been a regular visitor at the community.

In contrast to K, D was unmarried and in his late thirties. An American who had been involved in the film business and the London underground scene prior to his move to Findhorn, he had made the journey north because his stars had indicated that he should leave London. He had originally ignored his reading, but everything began to go wrong for him in London. The person who was running the financial side of the film in which he was involved absconded with the funds, he found it difficult to get a flat, and when he succeeded he was flooded out by the numbers of people who used his flat as a place to stay. Finally, he was not getting enough time for solitude in London for meditation and to work on the songs and the plays he hoped to write. The lesson he felt that he had learnt from these experiences was not to fight one's stars, but to go with them. One of his hopes for the future (his stars said that he should stay at Findhorn for a year) was to establish a commune where people could go and spend their time following their horoscopes in order to discover what they were, what they should be and so on. D earned a small amount of money at Findhorn by doing the horoscopes of visitors and members of the community. Apart from his interest in astrology, D made constant use of the *I Ching*, as did many of the younger members of the Findhorn Community and other communes. He was also interested in the writings of Krishnamurti, an interest also shared by a number of the other members. Like them, D had also had a wide experience of various forms of drug use.

By June 1971 the membership of the community consisted of about forty-five adults and ten children. Permanent members live in their individual caravans or bungalows, while visitors live more communally by sharing those caravans specially reserved for their use. The basic group of members is greatly augmented during spring and summer by ever-increasing waves of visitors. In 1969 the community received about six hundred visitors, and this figure must have increased since that time. Judged in terms of longevity of life and size of membership, Findhorn must be viewed as one of the most successful of the contemporary British communes. The members there would explain this by the fact that it is built upon a solid spiritual base and not upon the sand of mere material interest. The heterogeneity of its membership also sets it apart from other ventures in communal living. However, the aim of working towards the creation of the New Age, the belief in a Universal Presence, and other aspects of the Findhorn belief system are not unique. They are shared by individuals and groups involved in other commune ventures, such as the Centre Nucleus.[22]

Centre Nucleus: a New Age community

The Centre Nucleus consists of a group of people who have come together as a west London resident community, which was founded in 1966. The members have written of their purpose as a group:[23]

We have gathered together in a bond of Spirit, Truth and Love, to write in daily living the Constitution of the Universe. By meditation, reflection and perseverance, we struggle to master 'self' and reach the all-seeing, all-knowing Centre within, from whence comes the vision, inspiration and government of New Age planetary Man.

Like the people at Findhorn, then, the members of Centre Nucleus see themselves as working towards the creation of a New Age. Like the people at Findhorn, also, they tend to reject the modern age for its overwhelming emphasis on materialist values. The present society in the West, they feel, is characterized by too great a stress on the attainment of material prosperity. The effort invested by individuals in the struggle to obtain ever more material wealth, they argue, has been so great that the medium involved, the human mind, has been forgotten. The subordination of the human mind to the prime goal of material advancement has resulted in its breaking down under the strain, into states of neurosis, schizophrenia, ulcers and so on. This is causing man to lose his sense of true values and the realization of his true nature. Thus the problem that faces man in the modern technological society—the re-assertion of the primacy of human values over those instruments of production which were originally intended to serve these values. The need is to combine the qualities of the people of the Orient with those of the people of the Occident, to strike a balance between the deep-thinking Easterner and the swift-acting Westerner.

The members of Centre Nucleus believe that the answers to the problem lie within man himself. The future of mankind is seen as depending upon each individual discovering his self and setting into motion his own 'God-Force', and making his commitment to unite with other bearers of this God-Force in order to remould the world according to the divine will. The key to unlock the door to these inner powers within the individual is the practice of deep meditation. The technique of deep meditation will enable man 'to make a one-million-year leap in the stage of his evolution',[24] as it is claimed. Furthermore, this opportunity for self-development is available to all who accept the seven basic axioms of Centre's belief system, these being seen as the seven steps through which mankind will better the world.

The people at Centre Nucleus share not only their adventist notions with the members of Findhorn, but also share a similar conception of the nature of the divine. Just as at Findhorn reference is made to a 'Universal Energy Source' or 'Universal Presence' that is immanent in all things, at Centre Nucleus reference is made to a 'Master Intelligence of the Universe' which operates at the centre of all things. Individual and group minds are viewed as extensions of this Master Intelligence. However, it is possible for the individual to 'tune in' to this Master Intelligence by surrendering his own ego. By giving up his own personal 'I', the individual can become one with the absolute 'I'. This is the essential process by which the ultimate fulfilment of mankind is to be attained. The way for the individual to attain this state is by practising deep meditation. Once the individual has attained this state of 'cosmic consciousness' he becomes a 'nuclear personality', at one with the cosmic 'I' and capable of ascertaining the correct course for mankind as mapped out by the divine will. He also becomes 'capable of utilizing normally unavailable cosmic energies in the performance of feats usually considered to be superhuman'.[25] It is argued that once a sufficient number of men have attained this status of 'nuclear personality' they will be able to unite and draw upon these energies to so restructure the world that 'man's evolution will miraculously leap to its next plateau'.[26]

In order to understand how the venture in communal living at Centre Nucleus fits into this overall scheme, some background knowledge of the history of the community is necessary. In 1962 a fellowship was founded by Christopher Hills known as the Commission for Research into the Creative Faculties of Man. The Commission, which has a membership of some 4,000, is dedicated to[27]

the advancement of the type of communication necessary
to hasten the inevitable marriage between the ever-merging
realms of Science and Spirituality, it is actively engaged in the

discovery and collection of empirical evidence to support the teachings of Yoga and the validity of the existence of spiritual and psychic phenomena.

As part of this work, the Commission has attempted to create a network of freely co-operating groups and individuals who, together, would work towards the goal of a new world order upon a variety of creative projects, each project being seen as part of one major spiritual plan. The name given to this project was 'Centre'. As part of this overall project, a New Age Centre was founded in London in 1966—Centre Nucleus. The goal of this venture was seen as that of acting as a prototype of a group of people working together as a freely formed community towards the conscious evolution of a society based upon universal love. It is anticipated that similar ventures will be founded throughout the world, so that eventually there will be established a great network of 'spiritual universities' where a new way of life will be evolved through the conscious development of the human personality and its powers.

The philosophy of social change adhered to by the members of Centre Nucleus is one that rejects the use of violence, and emphasizes the power of love, non-violence and exemplary action. In this one finds a direct parallel with the belief system of Findhorn. Thus:[28]

> To convince mankind once and for all that there is a better alternative to conflict-by-war, we must now discover, orchestrate and perform the Divine Music, so that all the bugles and drums and flagwaving will seem absurd by comparison.
>
> If we can create a single valid community . . . then children will run away from school to join it, soldiers will desert their regiments to serve it, artists will sacrifice everything but their art to contribute to it, businessmen will topple their money gods to worship it, and the entire world will be at war—but this time with all of humanity on the same side—against poverty, famine, disease, hate, fear.

The headquarters of the Commission for Research into the Creative Faculties of Man is a six-storey building in West London —Centre House. The top three floors of this building house the community. The average age of the members is about twenty-four. There is a mixture of the sexes and social types among the membership. There is no formal body of rules about decision-making and so on within the community. There is a reliance on self-discipline rather than structured discipline. Important decisions affecting the Centre are taken in group meditations, which are normally held daily in the morning and evening. Although the members have come from a variety of social backgrounds, they share a common orientation towards the commune as an environment within which the self can be transformed. In this light, the venture at Centre House could be viewed as somewhat akin to the self-actualizing type of commune. However, it can be distinguished from those communes of this type considered in the last chapter by virtue of the fact that it is seen by its members in terms of an overall cosmic plan. At the same time, the means of meditation, group living and group encounter sessions employed by the members of Centre Nucleus to obtain consciousness of self are similar to the techniques used by members of other communes to develop self-awareness and enlightenment. However, whereas drugs are frequently used by such people as part of their quest for truth, the members of Centre Nucleus reject such chemical means of expanding the consciousness. One of the members has described the community:[29]

> We are here at Centre to fulfil our inner aspirations by a
> process of evolution, which brings out our intuitive virtue,
> opens our beings to the deep and manifold significance of the
> Universe, and, ultimately, moulds us into the supreme
> prototypes and incipient ambassadors of the New Age.

Another has made specific reference to the cosmic intelligence. 'Centre is living in harmony with the plan of the cosmic intelligence (God) and manifesting divine love in resonance with others of the same aim.'[30]

In Chapter 2 reference was made to the key characteristics of mystic belief systems, including such features as the belief in the immanence of the divine, the possibility of the individual establishing a direct relationship with God or the divine, and the possibility of the individual attaining the status of a divine vessel. These features can be seen to be present in the belief systems of both Findhorn and Centre Nucleus. Both involve a belief in a universal energy force which is acting throughout the world on all planes of existence, which is within us and without. Both involve a belief that it is possible for the individual to become attuned to this cosmic force, to become one with the divine. Both communities see themselves as working towards the creation of a New Age through the implementation of a Divine plan, utilizing spiritual forces and the more conventional means of non-violence and exemplary action to attain this end.[31] As such, both experiments can profitably be viewed as modern-day examples of the implementation of a mystic belief system through the practice of communal living.[32] In the next section attention will be turned to a consideration of some contemporary religious communes that fall more easily into the ascetic tradition of religious thought and experiment.

Communes based on ascetic belief systems

The Kingsway Community

> We intend to create a society, moved and sustained by the
> example of Christ, in which we deal with each other as brothers
> and sisters.[33]

This is the aim and purpose of a community housed in West London
which can be viewed as belonging to the ascetic religious tradition of
community building. In Chapter 2 it was pointed out that the
distinctive characteristics of the ascetic religious belief system
included the belief in a transcendent, omnipotent God, the status of
the individual as an instrument of God's will, and the injunction to
the believer to seek to resolve the tension between the ways of the
world and the ways of God through active agency in the world to
bring it into accordance with the religious ethic. In the following
full presentation of the statement of purpose of the Kingsway
Community some of these aspects can be located:

> The natural ability of man to live through co-operation with
> others has, in each one of us, become injured and become
> invalid, and this because of a condition of fear in a society
> run on a 'competitive' basis as our society is.
>
> We do not wish to adapt to this society, to accept that
> condition.
>
> Rather, we intend to create a society, moved and sustained
> by the example of Christ, in which we deal with each other as
> brothers and sisters. We do not want our actions to be
> variations in a manner of bargainings: we will give attention
> to others not because it is to our personal advantage, not
> because we will get something out of it, but simply as we have
> life in us.
>
> As brothers and sisters we recognise that it is our
> Father's will—it is in the nature of earth—for all our needs
> to be covered. Therefore we repudiate the mere financial
> structure of society, and we work to give food and shelter and
> fellowship, as rights, to our neighbours in need. And, working
> together in the service of Christ we are serviceable one to
> another, and bold to heal and recreate society.

Here are the hallmarks of the ascetic religious tradition, particularly the urge to bring the world into conformity with the will of
God through active agency in the world. How does it appear in
practice?

The community had its origins with David Horne and his wife
some five years ago. He had come up from North Devon to study

at the Royal College of Art in London. In many ways it was London itself that set David along the path towards community. As he expressed it to me, before coming up to London he had read Aldous Huxley's *Brave New World* and thought that things might well appear to be moving in such a direction, but when he arrived in London he found that this anti-utopia was already a reality there. A Christian who believed that it was not enough to be a 'Christian for five minutes a day', but that one must live one's whole life according to Christian precepts, he saw how pointless and ineffective it was being the good Samaritan and giving the beggar the shilling he asked for, and then walking off leaving him in exactly the same situation, except that he now had a shilling in his pocket. The Christian must open his door to his neighbour, he must consider others' needs as his own, see that the welfare of his neighbour is his own welfare. So he opened his door to the social inadequates, the dossers, and the lonely. His wife and he obtained two adjacent flats in west London in which they were joined by up to about half a dozen others. Numbers grew so that in 1969 they took over the lease of a large house with a garden in west London.

The basic idea behind the community was to create a Christian community, an extended family, to care for those in need, the oppressed, and the sick. Technically, it was hoped that this would be achieved through the establishment of a nucleus of about seven Christians, committed to the ideal of a Christian community, who would then be able to form the hard core of the extended family. David Horne has expressed it as follows:[34]

> It is achieved [the community], technically, by establishing an extended family. At least two couples and several friends take up the rooms suitable to their separate needs in a house; then there are at least three women to share the workaday life, and there is sufficient income. Everyone puts into the kitty such money as they can. Any money surplus to the week's spending is given to the Church: the Church owns the house, and administers money wherever it is called for, and connects ailing households with the strong. This group of people living together, having security only in fellowship, are sufficiently resourceful as to provide for their neighbours— whoever is in need. Some who are homeless will complete the family group, which will keep an open door, a common table, and a dormitory, so that others may have their basic needs supplied until the next community house is opened. Every community will differ according to its members and its locality, but together they will be a recreated society.

When I visited it, the house held about thirty-six people, of which about seven viewed themselves as Christians. The house had held up to fifty people on some occasions, the number of temporary visitors depending to some extent on the weather conditions and whether it was warm enough to sleep outside or not. Apart from David, his wife and two young children, and a number of others who could be said to form the stable core of the house, the other members were made up of drug addicts, alcoholics, people just out of prison with no place to go, and people who had just been led there because they had no roof over their heads and no friends to lean on.[35] From talking to people at the community, one could construct an ideal typical story of how people came to start living at the house. Arriving in London from Ireland or the provinces, either a drug addict, in trouble with the police, just out of prison, or some other form of social misfit, without money, food and homeless, eventually hearing about the existence of the house and the possibility of getting a roof over one's head there and also something to eat—so they arrive and many of them have stayed. When I visited the community one of the members estimated that there were probably six to eight drug addicts in the house, a couple of alcoholics, and the bulk of the others were people who had come to the house having left home and arrived in London with no money, food or job, and been directed there by knowledgeable members of the less fashionable underground of the London scene, or occasionally a social worker or priest.

Only about ten of the members of the community at that time held full-time jobs, others were receiving supplementary benefits, others received pensions and sickness benefits, others took part-time jobs as and when they needed the money. Each member of the house was expected to contribute a certain sum of money up to about £5 per week into the kitty to pay for rent, rates, food and so on. At the house meeting which I attended, however, we were informed that only ten of the twenty-seven members of the community who were expected to make some financial contribution towards the running of the house had, in fact, paid anything over the previous week. People were beginning to discuss what sanctions might be used, if any at all, on offenders. Apart from this expectation about financial contributions, the house had few other rules of any sort. Such rules as there were had been made by the meeting of the house assembled after the communal lunch every Sunday. One such rule was that all drugs were locked up in the safe, the key to which was kept by a reliable and respected member of the house, and who would provide the addicts with their required 'junk' when asked. Otherwise, if he found any drugs of any sort about the house, he destroyed them. Although this policy had led to violent arguments, most of the members saw the dangers of leaving dangerous drugs

167

within the reach of children. Otherwise, daily tasks such as washing up, preparing the communal meal and so on were organized on an *ad hoc* basis, although some members were trying to arrange some sort of rota system on my last visit.

David had worked as an art teacher in a local comprehensive school, but he resigned that post due to pressure of work in the community, and was supported by the community. His time was spent on administrative matters, stopping fights, acting as an amateur social worker on behalf of some of the members of the group with regard to finding them jobs, accommodation, suitable doctors, visiting people in clinics and hospitals, and generally lending a sympathetic ear to people and providing a roof over their heads. However, the community was far more than a progressive social work agency run by some religiously motivated people on communal lines. For some of the people living in the house, the community was nothing more than a cheap and agreeable place in which to live while they searched for a place of their own. Others, however, who were not necessarily Christian but agreed with David's aims and the ethos of the house, spoke very strongly about the house as a community, with each person living for the others, helping each other, and seeking to live their life in co-operation with others, his brothers, rather than in competition with and fear of them.

It was among this group of people, that the future plans of the community were discussed. Their idea at present is to move out of London to a farm in the countryside, away from any main urban centre, and there to live a life more in keeping with the Christian principles that inspired the foundation of the community. Apart from making it more possible for addicts who are trying to break their habit to succeed by going away from their old urban haunts out in the country, there is the urge to get back to nature, and to develop as a self-sufficient community in which everyone will contribute through work and income. 'For those who would serve Him the community farm will be a seminary. For those who are destroying themselves in the city it will offer life renewed.'[36] In January 1971 seventeen members of the urban community were anticipating a move to a farm on Exmoor, but they missed their chance due to the time they spent trying to raise the necessary capital of £9,000. In order to finance their venture, the people at Kingsway were seeking financial aid from various sources. The Nuffield Foundation provided them with a grant of £250 for their household purse and a similar sum for them to establish and equip the small workshop they were running at the community. The community has a tenuous relationship with the Methodist Church, and promises of help and assistance have come from these quarters, particularly from the West London Mission with which Lord Soper is associated.

Indeed, David Horne had been promised a house purchased by Lord Soper and the West London Mission if he could gather around him a 'Christian hardcore' that would ensure that the community was run according to Christian principles. However, by the summer of 1971 David had been unable to convince them that the group deserved this kind of support. Talking of the members of the Methodist Church and of the West London Mission in particular, David has written:[37]

> They understand efficiently run hostels; they will not
> appreciate shabby, sub-culture homes such as ours. They
> preach the Christ with filthy hands, but they prefer to deal
> with the immaculate Christ. We have not yet proved to them
> that this community 'works', and we are not likely to.

Social workers with expert knowledge of the intricacies of the state welfare system have also been approached for advice on fund raising. Finally, individuals have been appealed to for financial aid.

If they succeed in raising the finance necessary to form the rural commune, then it is anticipated that it will be characterized by a body of ritual and a set of principles that will ensure its continued existence in the service of Christ. Thus it is anticipated that each day at the rural commune will be characterized by three ritualistic activities: morning breakfast preceded by prayers, the evening meal, and the end-of-the-day prayers.[38] During the week general meetings will be held to discuss the community affairs, seminars will be held on 'Reality and Revolution', and there will also be a weekly meeting for prayer and meditation. The two major rules of the proposed rural community include the rule about prescribed drugs being administered from the safe. The other involves a commitment on the part of each member to give all his personal wealth and earnings to the household purse, whether the earnings are obtained from the sale of produce or the sale of labour power. The economy of the proposed commune will thus be based on the axiom of 'from each according to his ability, to each according to his need'. It is anticipated that any surplus money in the community purse will be given to the Church. By such means it is intended to create within the community relationships of brotherly love and concern, and ultimately to recreate society, according to their interpretation of the will of God. Such a goal and purpose is shared by other religious communes in Britain, in particular by the members of The Grail Community.

The Grail Community

The Grail Community is an all-female community in Pinner, Middlesex.

There are about eighteen members living there in a large house, which four of them run as a conference centre. Each of the members is involved in some individual area of activity. One lectures on catechetics, another is a family group organizer, another works on a community development programme, two more are training as social workers, while another member looks after the large garden. Other members are involved in writing, teaching, and the promotion of monthly concerts which attract up to eighty people regularly. Their activities as a group include publishing books, records, discussion material and a regular bulletin called *In Touch*.

All the members belong to the Roman Catholic Church, and as Catholics share a similar purpose and ethos. This has been described by one of their number.[39]

This purpose follows the broad lines traced by the Dutch
Jesuit priest who began it all in the 1920's. . . . 'The purpose
of the Catholic Church is to build mankind into a community,
a brotherhood based on loving relationships between God
and man, and man and man. As such the Church exists equally
and simultaneously for its own members and for the wider
community of man. The same could be said of the Grail, the
specifice purpose of which is to forward the purpose of the
Church as outlined above, through living as a community
and sharing this experience with others, through working to
foster community in different ways in the churches and
through working directly with people both inside and
outside the Church.'

Here, in this passage, one can make comparison with the ethos of the Kingsway Community. Particularly with regard to the attempt to resolve the tension between the ways of the world and the ways of God through active agency in the world, particularly through trying to live the godly life in the here and now, seeking to change the world primarily through exemplary action.

Within the community major decisions are arrived at by the members of the group as a whole in discussion. A weekly house meeting is held when ideas are raised, advice sought, problems aired, and the past events of the week discussed in general. There are a number of elected posts within the community, including that of president. One of the members also acts as treasurer. All money earned by the members is pooled. Each member receives a small allowance for personal use, but anyone requiring any extra money for some purpose or other must discuss it with either the president, the treasurer, or the community as a whole. The members eat communally on most occasions. As far as ritual within the community goes Mass is held once a week in the house. In addition most members normally go to Mass at their local church daily, while before supper each day those of the members who are at home go to the chapel to pray together. The important part played by such ritual in the lives of the individual members and in the life of the community has been expressed by one of the members: 'Once a week there is Mass in the house. It is truly a celebration and a strong authentic expression of our communal life and worship. As a result we all want to be there for it.'[40]

The procedure to be followed by those intending to join the community follows the lines that are typical of those adhered to by other communities. It consists of an initial period during which the prospective member and the community get to know each other, the one deciding if she wants to stay, the group deciding whether they want her to stay or not. This initial period is followed by a longer period during which the prospective member begins to integrate herself increasingly into the life of the community, and begins to choose the particular area of work with which she would like to be associated. At the end of this stage, if and when she thinks she is ready and this opinion is shared by the community as a whole, then she becomes a full member. 'She reaffirms the intention of her baptism into Christianity and undertakes, to the best of her ability and with God's help, to live according to the ways of this community.'[41]

Conclusion

In examining some of those communities in Britain that have been moved and directed largely by the religious convictions of their founders, certain similarities and contrasts between what have been termed the mystic and ascetic communities can be seen. All four of them look forward to the establishment of a new age and a new social order characterized by the brotherhood of man. They all see themselves as working towards the attainment of this end at least partly by their own exemplary action, by living out their lives as a community of brothers and sisters according to those values of love and care for their fellow living beings which they hope to see implemented on a world-wide scale in the future. At the same time, all four of the communities considered placed great stress on the importance of prayer or meditation as a means of communion with God or the divine, seeing their own actions in this world as being guided and sustained to a greater or lesser degree by this supernatural power.

On the other hand, however, the communities reveal a number of important differences. The most obvious contrast lies in the differences between their respective belief systems. Both Findhorn and

Centre Nucleus share a belief in a Universal Power which operates on all levels of existence and which can be located in all things and in all men. Kingsway and the Grail, on the other hand, view this divine power, God, as to some extent separated from the material world, as a transcendent being rather than an immanent force. In particular the paganistic elements in the Findhorn belief system, such as the belief in Pan as the god of nature, lie in direct contrast with the Christian belief system adhered to by the members of Kingsway and the Grail. Furthermore, whereas the members of Findhorn and Centre Nucleus believe that it is possible to communicate directly with the divine, and to receive specific advice and guidance on particular issues from this source, the members of Kingsway and the Grail are directed less, if at all, by direct communication and more by the example of the life of Christ upon which they seek to base their actions. In similar fashion, the members of Findhorn and Centre Nucleus place a far greater emphasis in their belief systems upon the direct intervention of the divine power in the affairs of the material world and in bringing about the new age to which they look forward than do the members of the Kingsway and the Grail communities. The latter place a much greater emphasis on the importance of the direct intervention in the affairs of the world of men inspired by the Christian ideal in bringing about the social and spiritual changes necessary for establishing the community of God and man, and man and man. Thus, whereas the work of the members of Kingsway and the Grail is concerned not only with spreading the word but also with intervening directly in the affairs of the world in various observable ways, Findhorn and Centre Nucleus are more concerned with developing as 'New Age Centres' from which the forces of light, for change and the creation of the new age, will emanate. Thus, while the |members of the latter two communities define their task in terms of demonstrating in practice the workings of the cosmic forces to which they are attuned, so that those others who are ready to learn can see and recognize their existence and so further the Cosmic Plan in their own fields of activity, the members of the Grail and Kingsway communities are equally concerned with direct intervention on the social scene through, in the case of Kingsway, setting up home and keeping an open door and offering the fellowship of Christ to all who come, and, in the case of the Grail, 'working to foster community in different ways in the churches and through working directly with people both inside and outside the Church'.

The following account of a Christian community in London appeared in the *Directory of Communes*. It illustrates the importance attached by members of ascetic communities to direct action on the social scene around them.[42]

The community is based and run on Christian ideals and principles, all members being committed Christians, though not necessarily part of the institutional Church. Each member has a single or shares a double-bed-sitting room but otherwise rooms are communal. The group eats together in the evening and meets together at the beginning and end of each day for prayer and discussion. A monthly meeting is held to discuss any serious matters and to make any decisions concerning the community as a whole. . . . Using the community as a base, members have attempted in various ways to serve some of the social needs of the local neighbourhood. This has involved running children's playgroups, old people's clubs, youth clubs, also pioneering a remedial reading scheme for teenagers falling behind on school work. Ad hoc things such as work-camps involving decorating or repairing old people's flats and organising collections for charities have also happened here. And there is some involvement in local politics—usually giving support to other bodies who are attempting to improve the social conditions of people in the neighbourhood.

Although the communities examined in this chapter have been treated separately from those considered in the previous chapter, due to the fact that their members share a common commitment to live a life together that is inspired and guided by their religious convictions and an unwillingness to compromise these convictions in the practice of their daily lives, it would be wrong to consider them as being of a completely different genus from the other experiments considered. The involvement of the members of the ascetic religious communities in social action shows them to share in great measure the orientation of the members of the activist communes considered above. In fact, in many of those communes labelled 'activist' I encountered during the course of my research members who proclaimed adherence to the Christian faith. In one of them two of the members were curates of the Church of England, in another one of them was a lay preacher in the Methodist Church. In practice, then, there might appear to be little to distinguish certain activist communes from those communes that can be considered as belonging to the ascetic tradition of community building. The differences lie mainly in the greater emphasis of the latter on such things as the shared ritual of group prayer and meditation, their frequent demand for prospective members to fulfil certain criteria pertaining to religious faith, and in the members' own definition of the nature of their commune—as a venture inspired primarily either by their political or their religious convictions, by their beliefs as Christians or by their beliefs as 'political animals', in so far as they find it

173

possible to distinguish between these aspects of their personal identity.

In similar fashion, the belief held by members of mystic communes in the importance of the individual's expansion of his consciousness and the development of his powers of awareness reveals a close affinity with the beliefs and attitudes held by the members of the self-actualizing communes, particularly those who have had some experience with the use of hallucinogenic drugs. However, this link is more than an ideological one. Many of the younger members of the Findhorn Community had spent some time as members of other communal ventures where the emphasis had been upon the development of the individual's latent creative powers prior to joining the Centre of Light at Findhorn. Likewise, many of the members of self-actualizing communes whom I encountered during the course of my research had visited the experiment in the north-east of Scotland and had been impressed and influenced by what they saw there. Thus when I asked one member of a commune in Norfolk whether he had been influenced by anybody in particular in deciding to join a community, he denied that there had been any particular figure or model that had acted as a source of inspiration but that he had 'learnt a certain amount from Peter Caddy at Findhorn'. It could also be pointed out that the pagan belief system adhered to by the members of the Selene Community reveals strong similarities with the animistic elements in the Findhorn belief system. Once again, the distinction made between the various types of community venture had been based on the members' own definition of the purpose and goal of their own experiment. Thus it is possible to distinguish between those communes where the only goal upon which all the members are agreed is that of promoting social change through the personal quest for truth and the self-transformation of the individual members through the development of their creative potential, although individual members, as individuals, may well define their purpose in terms of some grand spiritual or cosmic plan,[43] and those communes such as Findhorn and Centre Nucleus where all the members are agreed upon the nature of the venture's goal, defining it in terms of their relationship with some 'God-force' or Universal Presence and the re-shaping of the world according to the will of this divine power.

However, while it is possible to make these distinctions between various types of communities using those categories and definitions of the situation employed by the members themselves, I would emphasize again that it is the similarities between such ventures rather than the differences that are most noteworthy. Almost without exception, the community ventures that have been considered have been inspired by a rejection on the part of their members of certain aspects, if not all, of contemporary life and society, and represent their attempts to move towards an alternative style of life and the creation of an alternative society, a new social order. In the next chapter attention will be turned towards an examination of some of the types of individuals that have become involved in this quest.

7 The paths to community

Introduction

If one spends any time visiting communes, then a number of points strike the observer. Perhaps the first thing is the fact that communitarians are not of a single distinctive type—their motives for joining a community vary, the kinds of lives they led prior to joining differ, as do their hopes and aspirations.

At the same time as one is struck by the heterogeneity of the communitarians, one also becomes aware that many of them do, in fact, share a number of characteristics, the most frequent of which is a rejection of the way of life that is generally accepted and taken for granted by the vast majority of the population. This rejection frequently involves not only a reaction against the routines of modern urban life but also a rejection of the kinds of standards that guide the everyday activities of the common man in the everyday social world. One of the areas of study with which I concerned myself during my research was centred around such questions as 'Who are the communitarians? What causes certain types of people to reject the conventional world and seek an alternative mode of existence? How are certain individuals led to choose the way of community?' In this chapter an attempt will be made to provide some answers to these sorts of questions. It is hoped that, through an examination of certain characteristics of the communitarians, some understanding might be obtained of this unique type of social action.

By social action I intend to designate human conduct as an ongoing process which is devised by the actor in advance, that is, which is based on a preconceived project. Taking as the point of departure Weber's postulate of the subjective interpretation of meaning, I am concerned with the understanding of social action as the meaning which the actor bestows upon his action, i.e. the meaning his action has for him.[1] In so doing, the main concern is with the question of how the actor defines his situation within the social world. In viewing action in this way, as motivated behaviour, I am drawing largely from the work of Alfred Schutz.[2]

Schutz distinguished between two different types of motives. Motives which involve ends to be achieved, goals sought for, are termed 'in order to' motives; motives which are explained by reference to the actor's background, environment or psychic disposition are termed 'because' motives. The two types of motives possess different time structures. The future tense dominates 'in order to' motives, the past dominates 'because' motives. As I project and plan my action now, I am aware of my 'in order to' motives, for it is precisely these motives which spur my action. The 'because' motives, however, which could explain certain aspects of my actions, remain rather more obscure and marginal to my awareness. For instance, I enter the café *in order to* buy myself a meal, but I am planning to buy a meal and to eat it *because* I have not eaten anything all day and because I am hungry.

The crucial difference between these two categories of motives is the one of time-perspective. If questioned about my purpose or intention with regard to entering the café, I can answer that I plan to eat a meal, and if asked why I plan to eat a meal I can refer to the past and point out that I am hungry because I have not eaten all day, i.e. I am conscious of certain experiences/non-experiences during the time period prior to forming a plan of action which 'explains' this project. However, I might possibly be the victim of some disease or other which causes me to use up energy at a faster rate than the majority of people, a fact of which I am unaware, but which is known to you, the observer, and which constitutes an important part of any causal explanation of my behaviour. Thus, a satisfactory explanation of any individual's pattern of social action would seem to require an enquiry into these three areas: (1) the actor's own definition of his project or goal-to-be-achieved; (2) the actor's own definition of his past experiences and states of being which have led him to the formation of his particular project; and (3) those 'objective' factors which the scientific observer hypothesizes as being of significance in any causal explanation of the actor's choice of plan of action, but which are not necessarily seen as significant by the actual actor concerned. In other words, in order to gain an adequate understanding and explanation of an individual actor's pattern of meaningful behaviour, the observer has to concern himself with (1) the actor's consciously held 'in order to' motives (2) the actor's consciously held 'because' motives, and (3) objective factors underlying these motives.[3]

An article in the magazine *Modern Utopian* referred to the variety of consciously held motives adhered to by the members of a single commune:[4]

> There were people who thought of themselves as being primarily communitarians, or primarily farmers and back-to-the soil revolutionaries, or primarily political revolutionaries (anarchists) or tao-archists for whom farming and community was just an integral part of the totality, or just plain hermits who wanted to live in the wood.

However, just as there exists a whole variety of typical, consciously-held motives that spur different individuals into establishing or joining communes, so one frequently encounters a variety of consciously-held motives guiding the action of a single person. Witness Joseph Burtt who was a founder member of the Whiteway commune in early twentieth-century Britain:[5]

> it is very hard to say if it was the horror of industrial cities or the degradation or shame in my participation in an evil system of the workers, that gave me a passionate desire to escape to some spot where I and my friends could settle and cultivate land.

Faced with this complexity of empirical reality, the sociologist's technique is frequently that suggested by Weber, the construction of ideal-types.[6]

> An ideal type is formed by the one-sided accentuation of one or more points of view and by the synthesis of a great many diffuse, discrete, more or less present and occasionally absent concrete individual phenomena, which are arranged according to those one-sidedly emphasised viewpoints into a unified analytical construct.

Thus one of the first problems that faced me before going out into the field was the felt need to attempt to create ideal-type communitarians, characterized by typical motives, and typical actions aimed at the attainment of typical ends, as a heuristic means of getting to grips with the subject (and measuring real-life communitarians against this yardstick).

This was the strategy adopted above in order to distinguish between different types of community ventures. There a basic typology was used, and if the purpose of this chapter was to attempt a full coverage of all the different types of individuals involved in some way or another in every type of community project, then a similar framework could be utilized. However, my original concern in embarking upon a study of communes and their members in Britain was with examining this movement as one involved in the creation of a new social order, an alternative society. One of my particular interests was with those members who were seeking, through communal living, to transform completely the nature of individual life in all spheres of activity, and who were seeking to create for themselves a style of life completely alternative to that pursued by conventional folk in conventional society. As a result, my interest in those communitarians whose orientation and interest in community experiments was less than this, in so far as they did not seek such a wide-ranging transformation of their individual life-style through communal living, was limited. Thus my interest in those commune members who were primarily interested in communes from the point of view of the practical economic and material advantages to be obtained through such a life was marginal. Peripheral to my major area of interest, also, were those people working in therapeutic communities who viewed their involvement in such experiments primarily in 'social work' terms, as contributing to the provision of a caring and supportive environment for particular groups of people suffering from what are conventionally labelled as physical and mental disorders. This is not to say that I was not concerned with members of practical and therapeutic communes *per se*. In so far as members of such communes viewed the experiment and their own activities within it not solely in terms of either its economic or remedial function, but primarily in terms of contributing towards a radical transformation of their individual lives, and social life in general, then their self-identification as individuals working towards the creation of a new way of life caused me to consider them as such. As a result of these self-imposed restraints on the area of my research, the framework to be presented below reflects that adopted in the preceding chapters in a truncated form.

On the basis of my early encounters with people living in communes or making active attempts to form one, an initial typology of communards or communitarians, on the basis of their consciously-held 'in order to' motives, suggested itself as a potentially fruitful working basis for the study of the processes by which individuals came to be members of a commune. It appeared that one type of communard embraced those who were concerned with bringing about radical change in society through direct involvement in political and social affairs particularly at the local community level, and who viewed the commune as an important base for such activities. Such people generally live in an urban commune of the activist type. This type could be distinguished from those who placed little or no emphasis on bringing about social change through such direct action measures, but sought to promote this end primarily by the creation of a commune as a means of creating that kind of environment within which they themselves, as individuals, would be

179

happiest, and which in turn would act as an example for other people to follow in reshaping their own lives and so reshaping society. Within this broad group of communards, however, a further distinction emerged, a distinction based on the different personal goals which they sought as individual members of community experiments. The freedom-seekers were those who were seeking through the means of community to create that social world for themselves that would provide them with sufficient personal freedom to follow their own pursuits unhindered by the constraints of the straight world, as a means of discovering their true self and actualizing their felt potentialities as creative human beings. On the other hand, the security-seekers were seeking to create within a commune that social world from which they might obtain that sense of belongingness and the accompanying sense of emotional and psychological security that they felt they were unable to obtain as members of the outside world. Both these latter types were estranged from conventional society and were seeking to create an alternative society, but for different reasons. The one was searching for an escape from the constraints of the conventional world, the other was seeking to escape from what they experienced as the anomic conditions of the modern world where, far from suffering under social constraints of various kinds, man is left alone, without true friendship or support. The freedom-seeking type of communitarian was generally to be found within the self-actualizing type of commune, the security-seeker within those communes characterized in the preceding chapters as being primarily orientated towards the provision of mutual support for their members. Mystic and ascetic communes in general revealed a membership consisting of all three types of communitarian, but with a predominance of freedom-seekers in the former, and activists and security-seekers in the latter.

I began my research with these three basic ideal-types in mind.[7] However, I would re-emphasize at this point that ideal-types are analytical constructs. The activist, freedom-seeker, and security-seeker are not necessarily to be found in all their purity anywhere in the empirical world. I attempted to use this strategy merely as a heuristic device. The types were intended to act as general guidelines directing my enquiries during the research process.

Thus it should be pointed out that the majority of communitarians, if asked about their motives for seeking to join or to found a commune, would probably refer at some point or other to all the three 'in order to' motives that underlie the three ideal types referred to above. They would refer to their desire to change the world, their desire for the freedom to follow their own path or 'do their own thing', and also refer to the importance of the sense of brotherhood and friendship to be found within a commune. The problem that faces the researcher in cases such as this is to discover whether one of the motives carries more salience with the individual than any of the others. The communitarians' response to this type of enquiry would probably be, 'All these things are important to me—don't ask me to separate them, I can't.'

At this point it would appear that the researcher has gone about as far as he can go. However, the great advantage of any form of participant observation is that one is not dealing with the respondents at a single point in time and space. Participant observation enables the researcher to keep the respondent within his observational field over a period of time and in different situations. Thus the participant observer frequently finds that he receives different replies to similar questions depending on when and where he asks them. For instance, one might ask an individual about his motives for joining a particular commune at an early stage in the interaction. One would be highly likely to receive some sort of 'official' reply to the query such as one might read in a formal statement of intent published by the commune members as a whole. Later on during the period of the observer's participation in the life of the commune, that same individual communard might well inform the researcher that what he really hopes to achieve through living in a commune is such-and-such a thing, not necessarily the same goal as that embraced by the commune members as a whole. Through participant observation one can form an overall impression of the respondent, of where his prime interests lie, of how his actions fit his articulated statements, and so on. There is, of course, a major drawback with this kind of research, however. The reader is forced to rely almost entirely on the subjective judgments formed by the observer in the process of his interaction with the observed. This problem is not unique to participant observation techniques, however, and what is obviously needed to counter it is replication of the research.

The freedom-seekers

The majority of people I met in communes could be termed, according to their 'in order to' motives, as freedom-seekers. For them, the great attraction about communal life was the opportunity it gave them to live in an environment where they could enjoy the freedom *from* the constraints of the conventional world, and the freedom *to* literally 'do their own thing'. For them, the main magnet was the opportunity to discover themselves, to develop their creative capabilities, and to establish what they considered to be real and genuine relationships with others, as well as with themselves. This is not to say that this was their sole motive, rather that it was their main one. Through transforming their own lives they sought to present

181

to others an example for them to follow in re-creating their lives and society in general.

However, within this broad group, when one began to consider individual life-histories, it appeared that individuals fell quite naturally into three sub-groups. The main criteria in this classification were age and previous political involvement. A distinction emerged between those aged over twenty-five who revealed a past history of involvement in radical politics and social movements, and those of a similar age range with a history of little or no involvement in such activities. A third group emerged, constituted by those aged under twenty-five with a very low manifest interest in conventional politics and radical political movements and an even lower degree of involvement in protest politics. These three sub-types I labelled the 'privatized radicals', the 'artists' and the 'trippers', respectively.

The trippers

Alan   What do we hope to achieve? To create that environment
       where all that is possible can become possible. We
       hope to develop into a centre for artists of all sorts
       to do work, to encourage people in the area who
       otherwise would not have had the chance to develop
       their artistic abilities.

Phil   Well, first of all there is the interpersonal thing—to develop
       honest and truthful relationships with others, with
       none of the lying and putting on fronts of straight
       society—this would result in genuine awareness. You
       can take criticism from friends. Also, I like the
       country, I want to grow my own things and watch them
       grow. Also, very important is the freedom thing—the
       fact of creating your own environment within which
       everything you do will be out of choice.

John   If you live in a flat it is easy to set up walls, to set
       up your illusions and be happy with them. What is
       important about Eel Pie is that living together with
       others, particularly with people who are very aware of
       people's illusions and games—your illusions are
       continually being shattered. You can be happy in a flat—
       the whole of society is geared to perpetuating the
       illusion—and having your illusions shattered is a very
       painful process—but it is a very limited sort of happiness,
       and finding out who you are, the real you, becoming
       real, is the only thing in life. This is the important thing.

Alan was the spokesman for a small group of young people who formed a commune in the country in early 1970; Phil was another twenty-year-old living in west London who was, when I met him, waiting to hear whether his group had been successful in their bid to buy a small property in East Anglia for the purpose of forming a commune; John was of a similar age and was living at the Eel Pie Island Hotel when I met him, although his plans were to move in the very near future to a smaller commune in south-west London prior to moving to the country to form a community.

Although all three were at a different stage in the commune way, they were all representative of the large number of young people I met who were largely from middle-class backgrounds, well-educated, and who to some extent epitomized the drop-outs of the modern young generation.

John had attended boarding school until he was sixteen, where he had spent his time 'defying all the petty rules that they had there, which was an education in itself really'. From there he went to a sixth-form college, a technical college and then to art college for a one-year pre-diploma course. However, he failed to complete this course, dropping out as he 'saw through the game they were all playing'—they were required to spend their time on what John described to me as 'smooth, abstract, trendy painting', which was not what he wanted to do. Since that time he had held a variety of jobs, mainly as a self-employed furniture maker and interior decorator. When I met him at Eel Pie, his income was derived from occasional decorating jobs and from some money he had received through the sale of a jeep which he had once owned.

Prior to moving into the hotel on the island, John had been living in a flat in west London. He knew some of the people who started living on the island, however, and for him 'it seemed a good place to stay', and so he moved in. However, Eel Pie was far more than a good place to stay. It was an important staging-post on his journey the aim of which was, as he expressed it to me,

> to try and give up the ego and just live and be. This is the
> important thing, and when we have all got there, then everyone
> we meet should be influenced. The material things and so
> on are not important—the important thing is to be real
> and live.

For John meaningful social change could only be brought about through personal change and inter-personal influence through exemplary living. Asked about his interest in political issues and political involvement he responded:

> I've never really been involved in political issues and that kind

G

of thing. I used to go on C.N.D. marches and demos,
but I wasn't serious about it—it was just part of a desire to be
different. Nowadays I am not concerned with politics—
that game is just an ego thing for politicians. The problem
is me and my ego. One gets above it all and sees the root
problem in the ego.

Joe, a fellow member, revealed a similar involvement with the
problem of self-discovery and personal identity. Asked about what
he considered the commune had to offer, he replied:

O.K., there are material problems but there are other more
important problems such as 'Who am I? What am I here for?'
It is amazing how many people you would think were thick
who do ask these questions, especially the young, but then
they give up or become satisfied with cars and things.

Expressed in his own words, Joe's personal philosophy appeared to
be: 'Each individual's life should be a search for fulfilment, you
don't necessarily know what it is, but you will know when you
arrive. When you have arrived, then you start again and create a
new reality.' Just as Joe's search for self-fulfilment mirrored John's
search to become 'real', their personal backgrounds revealed
certain basic similarities. Joe had also been to boarding school and
had been a rebel against the rules and regulations of the institution.
The rebellion had not been one of principled objection to certain
aspects of the school's regime however. Rather, the reason he was
suspended at the age of thirteen was that he wrote a 'pornographic
novel'.[8] He was born in Lincolnshire, the illegitimate son of a teacher.
His relationships with his mother had always been strained. John,
on the other hand, described his relationships with his parents as
'O.K., but they don't really understand where my head is at.' This
response was the type most frequently encountered. The relationship
between parent and child was not so much one of direct conflict as
one that involved a breakdown in understanding and a lack of
communication.

Joe was eventually expelled from his school for his persistence in
going into town for drinks, despite having been 'gated'. By this
time however, he had taken his examinations and he went to
university to study zoology. After a year, however, he changed
subjects to study psychology. Joe explained the reasons behind this
change in terms of his declining interest in zoology. He was interested
in ecology but not in learning the names of blood vessels. He wanted
to study psychology in order to 'fit the image of a man with a wide
range of interests'.

It is interesting to note that, just as John explained his participation in C.N.D. demonstrations in terms of his desire to be 'different', i.e. as part of a solution to a felt identity problem, so Joe's choice of psychology as a field of study was explained in terms of a desire to present a particular image of himself. His description of his appearance when attending the few lectures that he did attend revealed a similar concern with appearances and impression-management. He described his appearance at lectures in terms of his shoulder-length hair, his long beard, being without shoes, wearing an earring, a crucifix hanging from his neck, and a chain from his waist. It was while at university that Joe began mixing with the 'beats' in the town and also began 'pushing' drugs around the university. In the end he failed to take his final university exami-nations. Due to his repeated failure of a first-year botany examina-tion he had been asked to leave the university but had continued to attend lectures, but his interest in psychology declined as he found that there were too many 'rat-men' involved in running the course.

This pattern of disillusionment with further education as one element in the process of dropping out mirrored John's experiences at art college, and was a pattern that I came across repeatedly in my contacts with the younger members of communes. Thus Ann, a girl in her early twenties with a young child, had studied psychology at university like Joe, but had failed to complete the final examina-tions, having cracked up during the final examination period, and had refused to try to take them since.

Joe began 'pushing' while at university, and it was through this activity that he came to the notice of the police, his awareness of this being the main reason for him moving to London. In London he continued earning 'bread' by some small-scale 'dealing' and also took a job with a research institute in west London. He left this job to move to the hotel on Eel Pie island. There, like many other members of the community, he was working at a local bakery as an unskilled hand. He had a somewhat novel view of work. He did not find the work boring, claiming that 'it all depends on how you view it—if you are doing a job you may as well do it to the best of your ability.' He appreciated the pride that the Indians at the bakery took in their work. However, the main joy that Joe claimed he found in his work was not so much the pay at the end of the week, but the energy that he claimed was generated within him through mixing in a different environment with different people (i.e. different from the people at the commune). He argued that such was the stimula-tion he received through this, that the ideas kept buzzing around his head and the pay at the end of the week was like an added bonus.

This attitude towards work contrasted with that held by other members. One viewpoint that was perhaps typical of a certain school of thought was expressed to me by Tom in response to my

185

question about why he did not work, having seen him borrowing money from a fellow-communard:

> I can't get it together. Some of them maybe need bread—I like bread but I don't miss it.—Maybe I'll end up some day getting a job. I would rather use up my energy staying in bed. Others use and get their energy through working. Some don't see the machine, they see the fields—they can get up there, I can't. The routine would get me down.

Joe, however, despite his enjoyment of his work, claimed that if he found himself getting into a rut, then he would leave the job without a second thought. This was the pattern revealed through conversations and exchanges with trippers in other communes: an occupational history marked by the frequent changing of jobs, attempts at being self-employed as decorators and artists and so forth in preference to working for someone else, dealing as an occasional source of 'bread', and a refusal to consider the conventional nine-to-five routine, with the implied working towards the goal of security of old age, the subjection of one's individual autonomy to the will of another, and the willingness to submit to meaningless and boring routines.

Don's parents were middle class. His father was a university lecturer. Aged twenty-one he described his relations with them as one of 'restrained tolerance'. Don was living in a rural commune and his income of around £5–7 a week was derived from a variety of sources, including selling his own goods, supplementary benefits, and occasional donations from his parents and friends. Again he revealed the pattern of an unfinished education—in that he had attended a university for a business studies course, but had failed to complete it. Likewise, his past occupational history was similar to that displayed by John and Joe in that it consisted of 'selling hot-dogs for five days, selling dope for eight days'. For Don, the prime personal advantage that he felt was to be obtained through living in a community was the opportunity it provided for one to live a life true to one's own principles and wishes. The goal of the commune, which he considered to be a realistic one, was that of 'becoming self-sufficient, a happy and beautiful place to live, to be artistic and have a valuable output, and to help others to see the light.'

Living in the same commune as Don was Alan. Alan was from a middle-class background, although both his parents had died when he was young. Aged about twenty-one, he had attended a public school which he had enjoyed. He felt grateful to the school for the self-confidence that he felt it had instilled in him, although he disliked the motivation and ideology behind the process, the belief held by the students and staff that the future élite of society were being prepared to take on their inevitable role as leaders of men and industry. He had bought the property that housed the commune out of an inheritance that he received when he was twenty-one. His income was derived to a certain extent from being able to draw on what remained of this capital, occasional labour of about two days a week, and a few shillings from the sale of eggs. He anticipated the future income of the commune as stemming from the sale of eggs, the sale of posters and so forth produced on his silk-screen, the sale of home-made clothing and other forms of produce.

Alan revealed the same type of educational and occupational background as was revealed by other trippers. He had attended university for one year, specializing in sociology. He had enjoyed the experience, but when he had returned for the commencement of his second year he stayed for a week and then left, arguing that he could see the way it was all going, that he was being 'processed'. He dropped out. His occupational history since that time was one of irregular and occasional employment. Living in London, he held no regular job, but took odd jobs decorating, distributing leaflets and so on. He explained his reluctance to take on a regular job in terms of the fact there was nothing he wanted to do as a career, and his reluctance to 'get caught up in the system'. Alan had spent a year doing voluntary service overseas where he acquired most of his basic knowledge of construction work, which he was putting to good use in the renovation of the property that housed the commune.

As with other trippers Alan could be described as having an identity problem, but one which he did not feel as acutely as did John and Joe. 'I've never known what I wanted to be, although I've always known what I didn't want to do', he told me. It was while he was at university that he felt a need for an alternative, which necessarily implied having similar student-type people around. Involved to some extent with students politics, going on demonstrations and so on, Alan had become not only dissatisfied with university but also with this form of action. Hence the establishment of the community 'was a way out sort of personally and—kind of—not as a new tactic but as a way of trying to gain the same sort of ends in a more constructive way'. Whereas the seed of the commune idea had been sown in Don's mind after seeing communes in America, the seed had been sown with Alan in Africa. 'I suppose the seed of the idea started as a result of building and doing things in Africa. I felt that I wanted to go out there to do something but then felt why not start here in this country.'

Comment From these brief pen-portraits a picture emerges of the kinds of experiences that have led a growing number of young people to reject the conventional mode of existence and to seek to link their personal search for self-fulfilment and sense of meaningful personal identity with a search for an alternative mode of social existence. At a period in their life when most of their age contemporaries are in the process of making their choice as to their future career and life-pattern,[9] these young people have felt unable to make this choice on society's terms.

As an attempt to find a solution to this personal problem of identity, they have sought to discover what they believe to be their own, unique, individual identity within the context of communal living. They have dropped out of the educational process which they have viewed as preparing them for roles in society which they had no desire to occupy. Education for one of the trippers whom I encountered was 'a process, at the end of which you take your place as another computer programmer'. The most typical view of the conventional educational process and the qualifications obtainable through completing this process was that it had been a useless and irrelevent experience for the way of life that they had chosen to follow. They have felt unable to adopt any of the conventional occupational models available within society. Such roles could only be adopted, they argued, at the cost of personal autonomy and self-fulfilment. The meaningless routine that they saw as characterizing the daily round of work and home was, for many trippers, the most unbearable aspect of life in straight society. As one of them commented:

> It is this thing of getting up at 7 or 8 o'clock in a morning and toddling off to work and coming back in the evening, and just you and the wife sitting and watching t.v., and you do the same the next day and the next day. . . . God, I wouldn't like that.

Given this estrangement from the roles and social identities offered to the young person in modern society, many of the trippers have been at a real loss as to what they should seek to become. The result has been that many of them refuse to think about the future but concentrate on the present, upon 'being' rather than 'becoming'. This estrangement has led to a rejection of modern British society and a determination to find an alternative way of life which would enable them to mould their lives according to their own autonomous wishes, utilizing their felt creative potential to create a meaningful and rewarding life for themselves, within the framework of an intentional community.

If one seeks an answer to the question of why these young people have failed to find an attractive adult identity to take on as their own, when many young people seem to be able to manage the transit from youth to adulthood, and accept their social identity as their personal one, without resorting to dropping out, then I think one has to turn in the first instance to those 'dis-alienating' factors which can be seen as having led certain young people to the position from where they were able to conceive of alternative modes of individual existence and to the position in which they felt able to act upon these inner promptings.

For instance, the relatively affluent social origins of many of these young people can be seen as providing them with a view of the world in which the acquisition of material goods no longer appeared as the be all and end all of life, or as sufficient compensation in themselves for the kinds of deprivation involved in leading a life to which they felt no attraction. Many of them have tasted the fruits of materialism and have found something lacking.

Again, their largely middle-class social origins and level of formal educational attainment placed them in a position from which it appeared that the range of career models available to them required some degree of self-conscious choice on their part. A choice far wider than might appear to the working-class educational 'failure' from the secondary modern school who can conceive of no other future path for himself but a job as an unskilled labourer with a local firm, a fate which many take for granted. The extension of one's personal horizons and the related ability to reflect upon oneself, one's position in the scheme of things, one's actions and one's mode of existence in general, that comes through education must also be a factor that should enter into the thinking of anyone seeking an explanatory framework within which to place the action of this sector of dissident youth.

Many young people experience feeling of dissatisfaction with, and disaffection from, their personal mode of existence. There exists a certain conflict between their social identity and their own personal sense of identity. But, for a number of practical reasons they feel unable to act upon the inner promptings of their 'true self'. Perhaps they feel obliged to contribute towards the support of parents or family—which requires them, in turn, to hold on to a secure job. Undoubtedly many young people would be attracted to an alternative mode of existence if they did not feel that their prime obligations lay towards their wife, their children, or the payment of a mortgage. Many young people have undoubtedly felt forced to come to terms with society, and this is the crucial factor. One can point to the unmarried status of most of the young trippers, to the fact that few of them have any offspring to care for, and that their backgrounds frequently reflect some degree of affluence, which means they do not have to contribute towards the support of their parents. All this means that they do not have the same claims made on them as do the less free. They are somehow more free to follow their own inner urgings than is the uneducated, married labourer with a mortgage, and his parents living with him. If youth is that period in the life cycle when the individual is granted a degree of relative freedom to experiment with a range of cultural, sexual and occupational role models as a prelude to becoming a member of the adult world, then the trippers have seized the opportunity to experiment with deviant identities, given their disaffection from the conventional ones. They have drawn from models and exemplars outside the conventional range of available social identities adopted by large numbers of youth, for whom such identities are frequently considered natural and are taken for granted as the only available paths to be followed.

Of crucial importance in understanding how and why these young people have chosen to live the way they do is the personal experience that each one of them has had, already predisposed as they were to desert society as it is, which led them to the awareness that communal living constituted one possible answer to the personal problems they were experiencing. Thus Don encountered intentional communities for the first time and his interest was aroused, when he visited some communes in the U.S.A. John and Joe had both experienced a communal form of life that was led by their friends in their drug-centred existence and had been first introduced to the Eel Pie Island Commune by personal friends who were living there. With Alan, his first experience of communal living had been while working in Africa, and then he and a few friends had been on a camping holiday one summer on the continent and it was there that they realized what a rewarding experience it could be—living as a group. For other trippers the significant experience was a magazine article or a book which they read, which inspired their imagination and suggested the answer of communal living to their felt estrangement from conventional society and their personal identity problems. For others, the significant experience might have been some chance encounter with someone at a pop festival or at the offices of BIT. Each tripper has had some experience at one time or another which brought to his awareness that there were young people like him, with whom he could identify, who were living a new and rewarding style of life which appeared to offer him also the chance of leading an equally rewarding and fulfilling kind of life of the sort which he felt unable to lead within the confines of straight society.

On this point it appears relevant to mention the fact that although the majority of trippers had wide and varied experience of various types of drug use, and I have used the term 'tripper' as a convenient short-hand label for them, at the same time the drug experiences of these utopians were to some degree incidental to their choice of the communal way of life. Whilst most trippers viewed their experiences with the powerful hallucinogens like LSD as important in opening their eyes to the world, I encountered only one respondent who claimed that 'acid' had the conversion effect upon him that many people claim for it. For the majority, however, 'acid' was a step on the way to communal living, an experience which they valued for itself and for the insight derived, but which was by no means the sole factor that caused them to drop out. The majority were well on the way to 'tuning in' and dropping out before they 'turned on'.

The artists

Whereas Alan, John, Joe and the other trippers were very much of the modern young generation, another group of communards impressed me very much as belonging more to the 'angry young man' generation of the 1950s.[10] While the experiences and backgrounds of the individual trippers are interesting in themselves, their real significance lies in their being representative of a particular social group in society—that rapidly expanding group of dissenting young who, dissatisfied with life in conventional society, are seeking to establish a meaningful alternative for themselves and others. However, during the course of my research I came across a number of communards who expressed their 'in order to' motives in similar terms to those used by the trippers but who, on account of their personal backgrounds, characteristics, age, and typical experiences, could not be grouped together with the Timothy Learyites. One such group I labelled the artists. Although this group was personified, for me, in the membership of one or two communes in particular, again I would make the point that their real significance lies in their being representative of a particular social group in society. The nature of this group will, I hope, become clear. The nature of the 'in order to' motives that were held by this type of communard can be discerned in the following quotations:

Joan   The important element, which is something that I think we are all pretty much agreed upon, is that we are all trying to live the most honest, the straightest of lives in relation to ourselves, and to each other, and to the people outside; although we realise that we have to earn a living.

Terry   I see communes as an environment where one can establish authentic relationships with others, where people can become authentic themselves—where their defences could be demolished and you can get at the real 'you'. Once we leave our off defences we establish the 'I-Thou' relationship that Martin Buber

has written about—you become one with the other
person, you are no longer separate, you form a union.
I also want to escape the constraints of the system,
of employment and clocks, and to gain the freedom
to write and to paint.

Expressed in these terms, the projects of the artists are almost identical to those of the trippers, if stated in somewhat different language. The first statement was from the founder of a commune in Norfolk, the second from a conversation I had with a lecturer in liberal studies who, that same day, had handed in his resignation in order to 'escape the constraints of the system' and who was actively involved in trying to form a commune. Despite such similarities, however, the typical life pattern revealed by my encounters with artists revealed important differences between them and the trippers.

Perhaps the most obvious difference lay in the factor of age. Whereas the age-range of the trippers was seventeen to twenty-seven the age range of the artists was thirty to forty. Again, while the majority of trippers were unmarried, the typical artist was either married or had been married at some stage, and was either divorced or separated from his previous partner. In fact, what appeared as one of the significant factors in the recruitment of such people to the community form of life, was the experience of the failure and breakdown of nuclear family life. For the typical artist the commune was not just an environment within which one could discover oneself or attain freedom, but was also important as a replacement for the nuclear family. This was felt particularly strongly by the women, one describing the nuclear family to me as 'a repressive and horrible institution that makes you realize how cruel two people can be to each other'. Thus, out of about a dozen communards that I considered fitted easily into this category of artist, four were either separated or divorced; two were legally married to each other but each had a lover with relationships between all four apparently quite open and friendly; another two were married and living together; whilst another two were not married but were living together and were expecting a child. Another two were unmarried and unattached.

Just as many of the trippers sought an income from the sale of their creative work, and supplemented this from a variety of sources, ranging from occasional work of a conventional nature to begging in the streets and shops; the typical artist obtained some income from the sale of his work. The differences lay in the degree to which they were forced to supplement this income with money from other sources. Thus, one informant was a successful playwright who could expect to receive up to £1,000 for a play. Another was a moderately successful novelist whose income was largely derived from royalties and publisher's advances. The sale of paintings and sculpture was the major source of income of another two. Others, and I am thinking particularly of a short-story writer and two poets, were forced to supplement their income by relying on occasional seasonal labour, supplementary benefits, and unemployment benefit.

While the artists, typically, tended to think of themselves primarily as artists, a number of them revealed an occupational history characterized by the holding of a variety of jobs, usually of a short-term nature. Such jobs ranged from being a night watchman at Kensington Palace Gardens to running an arts laboratory, from working on the railway to 'living in the woods', from working on building sites to working in hospitals. In this respect the occupational careers of certain artists mirrored very closely the occupational history of the typical tripper.

One of the general rule-of-thumb guides that I tended to rely on in 'typing' respondents and informants was whether or not certain key themes occurred naturally in the conversation without any conscious forcing on my part. What one found with many trippers and with the artists was that the themes of revolution, political action, and radical social change rarely occupied the stage of conversation for any great period of time. Reference has been made to the apoliticism of the trippers. A similar point might be made about the typical artist. At the communes in Norfolk on which most of these observations are based, it was noticeable to me that the themes of revolution and the alternative society rarely raised their head in conversation. At one commune, only when I noticed a copy of the anarchist monthly journal *Anarchy* on the mantelpiece and asked the commune members present whether they were anarchists or not did the issue of their political affiliations and their self-identification as political animals occur. What transpired was that, while the typical artist was more interested in current affairs than the typical tripper, in so far as the reading of newspapers was a regular pastime, the level of past political involvement revealed was rather limited. The degree to which one can generalize about the typical artist is obviously extremely limited, given the small size of my sample. However, the actual population of artists is rather small. Thus although the typical artist was an apolitical animal who revealed little interest in parliamentry politics and little past involvement in conventional or protest politics, I did find that one or two of them had been politically active in either the Labour Party, the Communist Party, or C.N.D. If forced, the typical artist would probably define himself as an anarchist. More likely, however, would be the complete rejection of a label of any kind. Thus the particular commune of artists on which much of this analysis is based proclaimed their aim as follows:

We have no formal aim or policy. We don't consider ourselves
part of any movement, including the commune one. We
think that the way to heal this society is by healing ourselves.
By trying to live full and satisfying lives we automatically
work some change on the people we meet.

The account of the origins of this particular commune has been
given elsewhere in this work.[11] Most of the members had found
their way there as friends of friends. They had visited the group for
a holiday or to get away from London, found that it was a stimulating place to live and work, and so stayed. However, if one wants
to understand what had brought such people to choose the community way of life, two factors seem especially significant. The first is
the fact that the typical artist can earn his living anywhere, he is not
tied to a particular geographical location because of the need to
perform a regular, nine-to-five job. This obviously allows the typical
artist a far wider range of personal freedom and mobility than can
be enjoyed by many who are employed in a more mundane occupation. Secondly, the typical artist is free from that other great tie—
the family. The break-up of their nuclear family life had severed a
tie which keeps more people than is perhaps fully realized 'in the
system'. Given the resulting availability of the typical artist for
dropping out, then one can readily understand the attractions of a
commune, with the promise of artistic stimulation, the free time
that results from the sharing of household chores, the economic
benefits that accrue through sharing costs and growing one's own
produce, the company and fellowship of talented artists, and,
perhaps most important of all, the possibility of being oneself in an
environment free from the normal constraints associated with life
in conventional society.

The privatized radicals

The third and final type of freedom-seeking communitarian I
labelled the 'privatized radical'. The typical life-history revealed by
such actors was one characterized by a high degree of political
involvement, either in conventional party politics or in protest
politics. Their 'in order to' motives that led them to the commune
idea are readily understandable in terms of their disillusionment
with conventional politics of any sort as a means of social change.
A disillusionment accompanied by a determination to do something
about their own lives, even if they might not be able to change the
lives of others directly through political means. For the privatized
radical, the creation of a commune was typically seen as an attempt
to construct a new social world on a small scale, a world within

which the individual might live a full, fruitful and rewarding life, and a world which it was hoped would act as a model for others to judge their own world by, that would sensitize others to the possibilities inherent in the human condition.

The backgrounds of the privatized radicals differed from those of the trippers and artists in terms of the youth, experience with drugs, and apoliticism of the former; and in terms of the apoliticism of the latter. However, the 'in order to' motives of the typical privatized radical were frequently couched in similar terms to those of the other freedom-seeking types. Thus Brian, an ex-Committee of One Hundred activist, expressed his interest in communes in the following terms:

> I want to live in a commune, in the country, and grow things
> and be happy. I want to discover myself. I don't know who ,
> I am yet. I've been carrying myself around for 30 years and
> I don't know what I am. I want to create the environment
> that I can discover myself in, and others themselves, and me
> them and them me—a meaningful, creative, peaceful, happy,
> dignified life instead of the crappy, pressure-ridden life we've
> got now. . . . I have seen these old guys who have spent their
> lives in the Labour Party and the SPGB and its tragic. I want to
> do something for me my wife and kids and a nice life and
> nice people. Its valid too and an unlimited amount of people
> can do it too.

Paul, when asked about the goal of his projected commune, replied, 'No goal—I just hope to enjoy life and influence society a little.' Answered in slightly different terms:

> I am interested in a style of living with others where work and
> play and home life are more integrated—where I have more
> control over my own destiny and help to ensure that my
> children (and others) grow up in a healthy environment.

On the basis of these articulated motives there is apparently little to distinguish this type from the other types dealt with above. Most communitarians explained their projects in terms of contributing towards the creation of a new social order, and in terms of enriching and developing their own personal selves. It was when one turned to a consideration of the different paths leading up to community that the distinctions emerged.

As mentioned above, one of the major factors that led me to treat the privatized radicals as a type was the degree to which they revealed a past involvement in conventional political action of all kinds. While sharing with the trippers and the artists a felt estrangement from the prevailing social order and the modes of personal existence that they felt one was required to lead within this social order, they had actively sought to change this order by conventional means of party and protest politics. It was their disillusionment with the effectiveness of such means that led them to concentrate on creating their own private utopia in the here-and-now, as a step towards building the hoped-for revolution on a society-wide scale in the future. This personal venture was at the same time seen as a significant act from the point of view of change at the societal level, given their belief that meaningful social change could only be brought about through changes at the intra- and inter-personal levels. Thus, while the sources of their original estrangement from the existing social order and their conception of the ideal society might be very similar to the original sources of estrangement and the ideals of other communards, the path followed by the privatized radicals in their recruitment to the commune movement differed significantly from the paths followed by others.

Thus, the typical privatized radical would appear to have been actively involved in what might be termed libertarian politics for many years prior to involvement with the commune movement. This commitment appeared, typically, to have taken the form of an extremely active involvement in the British peace movement of the 1950s and 1960s. Thus both Brian and Paul had been members of the Campaign for Nuclear Disarmament and had participated in many of the Aldermaston marches,[12] but had taken their commitment further than most by their active involvement in the direct-action civil disobedience campaigns of the Committee of One Hundred and the Direct Action Committee. It is interesting to note that both Brian and Paul, when asked how they first came to the idea of communes, referred to their experiences during the days of their involvement with the direct action campaigns. Thus Paul first became interested in communes when he was active with the Committee of One Hundred in London and was sharing a flat with other activists. They talked a lot in those days about communes as 'the best way to live'. Brian explained to me how he was

> picketing an atomic weapons factory at Aldermaston in 1958
> and I met a bloke who was going to a commune in Wales.
> I suppose I didn't have very much to do next so I went with
> him because it sounded a good thing to do. I was unemployed at
> the time. I had been picketing for three months—it was a
> full time picket. I stayed at the commune for two years.

In fact, what strikes the observer is how natural the progression seems for the privatized radical from involvement in conventional party politics and the protest politics of demonstrations, pickets, and civil disobedience, to the politics of the commune. Evidence of their disillusionment with conventional politics is provided by the following remark made during conversation with one privatized radical. In response to promptings about whether he would consider voting for a political party at the next general election, he claimed, 'No, I would not vote. The parties are not going to change society. Voting has no relation to the true distribution of power in society and serves to generate the illusion of democracy.'

He went on to outline his own political career:

I am not a member of a political party at the moment. I have been a member of the Labour Party, S.L.L., S.P.G.B., and the anarchists—all left-wing things. I left smaller groups like S.P.G.B. and anarchists because I thought the majority of them had chips on their shoulders and weren't doing anything actively—they were sitting around talking about revolution but doing nothing. I decided if you wanted to do something you had to join a major party and work from within. This was before 1964. I threw everything into the Labour Party—I was a delegate, secretary of the local party. . . . I left about a year ago (1968) through disillusionment with the party and with party politics as well. There is a complete lack of understanding of the needs of the people. Once a person becomes a professional politician he loses contact with people completely. The idea of socialism died overnight when Labour got in. . . . I think mass civil disobedience is the only way you can influence governments now.

In response to questions about demonstrations, many replied to the effect that they considered demonstrations to be an 'establishment tactic, a sort of pressure valve for the government', which informed them of which issues were in the public mind and which merely allowed the participants to let off steam and then go home for another few months until their frustration worked up enough pressure to explode, when another demonstration would be held and the pressure released. As one respondent put it:

Demonstrations? Well I went on many of the C.N.D. and Committee of 100 demonstrations, I was arrested at one of the air bases and spent four days in solitary confinement because I refused to give my name and address as was agreed beforehand. That was a shattering experience. We've gone beyond demonstrations. I don't think meaningful change can come through conventional political means and I would include

197

demonstrations in that category. . . . Demonstrations can be good fun. They are mostly a waste of time.

Given this disillusionment with the traditional forms of radical action aimed at changing the world, the personal problem faced by the individual is 'where to go from here?' One typical solution adopted by the younger libertarians has been that of forming activist communes in the urban centres, from which base they seek to continue their direct action techniques. Others, the privatized radicals, who are generally older and have lost some of the millenarian zeal and the belief that the revolution is just around the corner that characterizes younger radicals, are placed in a more difficult position. They no longer believe that the revolution is imminent, but at the same time they are too estranged from conventional society and life to feel at home there. The problem for them has become the personal one of discovering how to lead a happy and rewarding life at the same time as retaining their commitment to such values as love, co-operation and non-violence. The answer that many of them have arrived at involves forming a commune, usually a rural one, where they can create for themselves a rewarding and fulfilling kind of life at the same time as retaining their radical purity. Within these communes they hope to create that style of life which they would like the whole of society to adopt in the future, and see their attempt to create a micro-scale model of this society as an important revolutionary act in so far as such experiments are seen as acting as models for other dissenters to adopt.

While it is relatively easy to trace the journey of the privatized radical once he has stepped on to the radical path, it is rather more difficult to explain why he took to this path in the first place, and to discover the origins of his radical commitment.

How does the typical privatized radical define the source of his radicalism? As might be expected, the origins differ from individual to individual. However, from conversation there appeared to emerge two typical paths of commitment. For some, their estrangement from the prevailing order stemmed from a gradual awareness of the horrors of war in general and of the use of nuclear weapons in particular, and a determination to try to counter these things—a determination which led them to join C.N.D. and similar organizations which appeared at that time (the 1950s) to be the only means available for influencing the course of events.[13] Thus Brian described to me how he 'gradually became aware of what was going on with the atomic and hydrogen bombs. It seemed so awful. One had to try and do something about it. It seemed very important to try to have some influence on events.' A similar revulsion against the acts of men in this world developed gradually with Martin. He described how, when he was away from school between the ages of three and fourteen due to his suffering from tuberculosis, his mother taught him to read.

> I read everything I could lay my hands on, all day and everyday, and through that my political views formed. I read history and political works. I became aware of the world and events. I was interested in war and read about it and through this I realised the brutality of war. I was interested in what caused them and read more about other wars. I felt they were bad things.

And later:

> The atom bomb horrified me. It made a great impression. The Suez invasion also. There was no justification, it was completely wrong. The Korean War was very wrong also. I had no sympathy with our troops. These things directed me to the peace movement very much.

For such people the commitment came first and the formal membership of an organization followed. For others, however, the membership of the organization preceded the growth of commitment to the cause of the movement. For them the initial project of joining the movement was for reasons other than changing the world. For them the movement appeared to be fun at one level, and at another appeared to offer them a sense of personal identity. Thus Paul told of how

> C.N.D. was a big thing at school and so I would have nothing to do with it. Then I saw the 1962 Aldermaston March on television and it seemed such a marvellous happening, fun-wise, that I was sold. . . . I went along to meetings at Uxbridge . . . took part in demonstrations and so on, was arrested, and by 1964 was very active with the Committee of 100 in London. . . . I left when the internal differences appeared to be becoming more important than the struggle.

The source of the typical privatized radical's estrangement from society is a moral revulsion against the horrors of the actions of men in this world, and the felt need to try and do something about it. They are estranged but not alienated. For them, radicalism is not so much a conscious response to experienced material and economic deprivation, or a response to felt threats to their status and prestige, but rather is a natural response to a perceived gap between the ways of the world as they are and how they ought to be. But this perceived discrepancy between the 'is' and the 'ought' is concerned not only

199

with the distribution of goods and prestige in society, but with the normative standards that appear to guide behaviour in the world. Their radicalism has typically stemmed not so much from a feeling of relative deprivation concerning their personal lot in life, as from a feeling of disgust with the rules of the game of life itself. Their major concerns typically revolve not so much around the bread-and-butter issues of trade-union politics, but with the quality of social life and personal relationships as a whole. If they had been born in the late 1940s or 1950s they might well have joined the freedom-seekers of the hippie movement. Born as they were in the 1930s and early 1940s, they joined the 'peace-niks' of C.N.D. and Aldermaston, only to join forces with the hippie generation in the 1970s through the commune movement.[14]

The security-seekers

Robert Nisbet has written of the fact that[15]

> Ours . . . is an age, on the testimony of much writing, of amorphous, distracted multitudes and of solitary, inward-turning individuals. . . . Whether in the novel, the morality play, or in the sociological treatise, what we are given to contemplate is, typically, an age of uncertainty, disintegration, and spiritual aloneness.

It is indeed true that many writers have commented on modern man's loss of community in large-scale, industrialized, urbanized societies. Modern society has been characterized by many of these writers as a mass society, one made up of an atomized mass of isolated individuals.[16] In presenting their analyses they have generally drawn upon the work of Durkheim. Durkheim viewed the human actor as essentially in need of limits and discipline. He viewed man as a being with almost limitless desires. As such, man was in need of control and discipline in order to restrain these desires and enable him to obtain peace of mind and to maintain social life without its collapsing into the 'war of all against all'. Society alone could play this moderating role. He argued that the discipline necessary for the maintenance of an ordered social life was provided by the normative standards of behaviour that guided man's actions in the various roles that they played. However, Durkheim argued that the rapid economic and industrial growth that characterized industrial society had occurred without a corresponding growth in the forces that regulate social behaviour in that society. The result of this was that man was left morally and socially isolated. The old order disappeared and no new order to replace the old emerged due to the speed of economic and industrial change. It was this analysis of the anomic social conditions that accompanied rapid economic and industrial change that Durkheim utilized in his examination of the various types of suicide, particularly 'anomic' suicide.[17]

Recent writers have adopted this framework of analysis, suggesting that without the reassurance provided by clearly articulated standards and guidelines of action to be followed, then in such anomic situations men frequently become involved in the search for new forms of community and new standards that will direct and guide their actions and control their passions. Frequently this search for new forms of community takes the form of involvement in radical social movements. Kornhauser, in his analysis of the politics of mass society, has continued along this line of argument.[18] He has argued, following Durkheim, that as society becomes atomized, characterized by the weakness or absence of secondary social groups that act as intermediaries between the individual and the central loci of decision-making in society, individuals become unattached, with the result that they become susceptible to ideologies which deal with issues in rigid and absolutist terms, and become eager participants in extremist movements that appear to offer them a new sense of purpose in life and a source of brotherhood and companionship.[19] Kornhauser's thesis has, however, been attacked on a number of points by many writers.[20] The evidence from empirical research would also seem to indicate its inadequacy as an explanation of the participation of all members of all extremist or radical social movements.[21] At the same time, there would appear to be no reason why the thesis propounded by such writers as Kornhauser should not provide an adequate explanation of one of the sources of support for radical movements. Most movements involve a variety of individuals who join for a variety of reasons, and many would appear to seek through their participation not only the promotion of the goals of the movement but also a sense of brotherhood and community through serving a cause.

In pursuing this line of enquiry, in seeking to discover whether communitarians in general were attracted to the idea of communal living by the promise of a sense of brotherhood and companionship which they felt unable to obtain in conventional society, I discovered in fact that the Kornhauser thesis was of only limited utility in throwing light on the sources of recruitment to communes. On the one hand, many communitarians would admit, if asked, that one of the attractions of communal living for them was the belief in the possibility of experiencing a quality of social relationship with other people that they felt unable to obtain in straight society. Thus, as one twenty-two-year-old informed me, 'There is something about being with people you can trust, you don't have to hide from them or lie to them. They don't hide things from you.' This 'something', for most communitarians, however, is not the sense of belonging to some sort of social womb which provides one with a sense of one's own worth through the creation of a haven of mutual support and reinforcement. It is, rather, the open and honest quality of the relationships typically encountered in certain types of communes which, far from providing the individual with a support on which he can rely, assured of his identity and his place in the scheme of things, gives rise to a completely different situation. Far from providing validation for the individual's own sense of self as a member of a coherent and like-minded group of people, such relationships create an environment within which the individual's sense of self is constantly being questioned by companions who are eager to point out to the individual the false masks and games that he is seeking to present and to play in their company. This experience, many communitarians feel, is essential if they are ever to discover their real self and their true identity. As one commune member remarked:

> What is important about Eel Pie is that living with others—
> particularly with people who are very aware of people's
> illusions and games—your illusions are continually being
> shattered. . . and having your illusions shattered is very
> painful, but . . . finding out who you are, the real you,
> becoming real, is the only thing in life.

For such people, the brotherhood they seek within a commune, while important in itself, does not constitute their prime aim, but is largely important in so far as it enables them to reach their ultimate goal—that of self-discovery. This type of orientation is very different from that displayed by the commune member who informed me, 'I think I am motivated around a mother-deprivation. So I want to live in a commune where people will look after me.'

For people such as this respondent, the prime attraction of communal living is the sense of group identity, of 'belonging', which they feel is to be obtained through such a form of life. For them, the commune is frequently viewed as a social womb, a protective and encompassing environment within which they can feel secure and at home. That this security-seeking type of communard is recognized as such by other commune members is evidenced by the following extracts taken from the correspondence columns of *Communes*.

> We are afraid that people who expect a community to be like a
> family just to look after them . . . would undermine the morale
> of the rest, especially when the latter were faced with physical
> (and seemingly more immediate and tangible) problems[22] . . .
> we are choosey about new members after lots of bad experience
> with 'beautiful people' who expect a community to be a

family (mums and dads, brothers and sisters, just to look after them).[23]

During the course of my research, I encountered members of communes who tended to adhere to this view of the community as a family. Generally speaking, one can distinguish between two types of security-seeking communitarians. The first type have typically experienced a personal life history of self-defined social isolation, having suffered from personal problems of various kinds that have made normal, easy interaction with others extremely difficult. Such people are naturally available for recruitment to social movements which appear to offer them a supportive environment within which they can establish the types of relationships with others that they have failed to establish in conventional society. The second type consists of those individuals whose normal world has suffered some major discontinuity, such as the breakdown of their marriage. With their familiar world shattered, such people are readily available for recruitment to those communes which appear to offer them a substitute home, a new world to replace that which they have lost.

One example of the first type of security-seeking communitarian would be the members of the commune known as the Trans-Sex Trip. The process by which sexual and other types of deviants can be led to join or form a commune was examined above.[24] There is little need to expand on that account here. It is sufficient to re-emphasize the point that when a deviant becomes labelled as such by his fellow men, then this label becomes what can be termed a master status trait, the dominant characteristic of the individual as far as his fellow actors on the social scene are concerned. His fellow men tend to base their interaction with the individual largely on their assessment of him as a deviant member of society, tending to ignore the other aspects of his character and social identity which could be considered normal. As a consequence, the deviant frequently finds it virtually impossible to interact with others as a normal human being in so far as other people deny him the opportunity once they become aware of the deviant label which he carries. While he is denied the possibility of normal social interaction, the deviant is placed in the situation of being to some extent a social isolate. Given that most people have a need to receive some affirmation through interaction with their fellow men of their worth as human beings, and given that this opportunity is frequently denied those considered deviant by their fellow men, then the solutions open to such people are mainly twofold.

The choice the deviant makes will largely depend upon the nature of his deviance. He can seek to destroy his deviant identity and public knowledge of it by seeking to begin his life anew with a

203

fresh identity in new surroundings where people are unaware of the deviant label that has been attached to him by the people in his previous surroundings. However, this solution is only a realistic and desirable one for those who wish to forgo their deviant behaviour and who feel that they are able to do so. If, on the other hand, the individual has no wish to refrain from that behaviour which caused him to be labelled a deviant originally, and moreover, feels unable to abstain from such behaviour, then this solution is neither realistic nor desirable. The second possible solution is for the individual to seek to become attached to a sub-cultural group where he can interact in a relaxed fashion and receive from a body of like-minded individuals affirmation of his worth as a human being, and so transcend the social isolation that can be suffered by the deviant within the dominant cultural group. One particular form of the sub-cultural group is the commune. Communes such as the Trans-Sex Trip offer a home and a supportive environment for particular types of deviants, sexual deviants in this particular case. Other types of deviants such as the drug addict can, however, be encountered living in a commune. Of course the degree to which a drug addict, or an alcohol-addict for that matter, is forced in this way to rely upon a sub-cultural group, depends on a whole variety of factors which affect his ability to maintain his habit at the same time as presenting the appearance of a normal social actor. However, during the course of my research I encountered a limited number of heroin addicts for whom the commune in which they lived was important not only as a place where they could 'fix' and where people could care for them if they became ill, but also as a place where they were treated as human beings and were accepted as important members of the group. To the extent that all commune members are cognitive deviants, in so far as their view of the world is radically different from the views held by the majority of their peers, then it is possible to argue, as was done above in Chapter 2, that one of the attractions of communal life for all commune members is that it presents a kind of shield against the attacks of others on the validity of their particular vision of the world; it represents one way in which the challenges of the cognitive antagonists can be countered and one's commitment to the deviant body of knowledge be strengthened and developed in the company of compatible others.

Furthermore, one does not need to be a sexual deviant or a drug addict to experience social isolation and seek security and support from a community. During the course of my research I encountered a number of commune members who had acquired neither of these social identities, but who were attracted to the idea of communal living for similar reasons. Generally speaking, such people had suffered from various types of psychological and personal problems throughout their life which had made them incapable of enjoying full and normal social relationships with other members of society. Such problems as extreme introversion, acute shyness, or one of the many forms of schizophrenia, had made it impossible for these people to establish close and lasting friendships with others. As a consequence of their inability to operate on the social scene, they have typically come to view themselves in similar terms to those in which they have been viewed by others—as strange, odd and different. As a result they have typically suffered feelings of great loneliness, of being the odd man out, and of somehow being excluded from the everyday world of normal people. They have felt themselves to be 'marginal men'. For such people communes offer the opportunity to establish the type of relationships with others that they have found impossible to attain as members of conventional society. Within a commune they generally hope to find an environment characterized by feelings of love, trust and care where they can find that sense of security and emotional support that has been denied them outside.

Typical of such an orientation was that displayed by Mick, who had felt socially isolated even as a child. His father had served in the Army and after that had worked shifts, with the result that the son's contact with him had been minimal. His relationship with his mother had never been a close one—'I wouldn't mind if I never saw her again' was his verdict. According to Mick she had not only displayed a habit of opening whatever mail he received, but had also discouraged his friends from calling at the house, with the result that he had enjoyed few social contacts of his own age throughout his childhood. One of the saddest experiences of his life had been when, one day, he discovered that he could no longer bring himself to join in the games of the other children—he did not know then why he could not, all he knew was that he felt unable to play with them any more. His brothers and sisters had all been younger than he and, he felt, less intelligent, and so he had never established close contact with them. Having brothers and sisters had meant little more to Mick than 'having four lots of toys to play with and to clear up rather than one set'.

After completing his education, he was employed as a research worker in a laboratory. Here his fear of social contact caused him a great deal of anguish. For instance, he would delay going to the stores to obtain the materials necessary for him to continue with his experiments for periods of up to three days because he lacked the courage to face interaction with the storekeeper. His feeling of social inadequacy was reflected in his attitude towards work. Whereas the majority of communards placed a prime importance on personal autonomy in work, according to Mick the less say he had in the making of decisions affecting his work the better. He was happiest at work when he was told what to do and then left alone to get on with it. Looking back on his time at the research laboratory where he spent thirteen years, Mick felt that his fellow workers had viewed him as odd and different, and he had never established any close friendship with any of them. In fact, he went so far as to claim, 'I don't think I have ever had any close friends.' Thus when he had lived in the south of England he had never had any friends in the neighbourhood in which he lived. The reason, he suggested, was, 'I can only cope with people in certain situations, when I get lots of validation. They have got to have a fair range of values the same as mine.' Thus the social contacts that Mick had established in his life had always been based on some shared interest. As he remarked to me, 'I haven't any friends just because they are people. They are always people who share some common interest.' The root of his problem, of his inability to establish close social relationships with others, Mick felt, was his schizophrenia. For him, this condition was particularly problematic in that he felt a great need and desire to establish close contacts with other people but, at the same time, he was frightened of relating to them. As he expressed it to me, 'I like to have people around but if I am in the presence of lots of people, then I am frightened of them.' His interest in communes and communal living stemmed, he felt, from his search for a mother-substitute. 'I think I am motivated around a mother-substitute,' he argued, 'so I want to live in a commune where people will look after me.' His marriage to a woman several years older than himself and his interest in the old pagan religion with its emphasis on the White Goddess, the mother-figure, also appeared to Mick to provide evidence for this claim.

However, Mick was not solely motivated by his search for a mother-substitute and an environment within which people would look after him and relieve him of the burden of personal decision-making. He also looked forward to the creation of an alternative society. Although his involvement in conventional politics had been limited to one spell of canvassing for the Labour Party, he still retained some faith in the parliamentary system of politics as a means of social change, although he was very disillusioned with the two major parties. To some extent his limited involvement in party politics and in the politics of protest reflected his low sense of political efficacy, feeling as he did that there was little that the individual could do to bring about social change on account of the fact that 'there are fifty million people out there'. This feeling contrasted strongly with that held by the majority of communitarians who believed that through living an exemplary life the individual could exert a significant impact on people and society in general.

However, Mick shared with these other communitarians a determination to live his life according to his convictions, without compromising his beliefs in the practice of living. It was this determination that to some extent explained his eventual involvement in the commune movement. Thus from his early childhood he had shown an interest in the occult, and when he was older he began to attend theosophical meetings. He explained:

it was mainly about astral planes and how good it was out there, and I thought it's a bit strange these people going to these meetings every week and then they go back and live exactly as they did before. If they were really the people they said they were they would do something about it. So what I wanted really was an environment in which I could live all the time what one professed to believe in.

Thus it was his vegetarian beliefs and his determination to practise these beliefs that led indirectly to his involvement in community experiments. His first interest had been aroused when he thought, 'wouldn't it be nice if there was a society of communities all over the place where vegetarians could go and not worry about what they were eating'. Again, it was Mick's resignation from his research post due to the fact that the laboratory were using animals in their experiments that freed him to some extent from the 'system' and enabled him to embark on his community project.

Sue was another commune member whose path to community had been one of loneliness and isolation in society, leading to her search for 'a group of people around you with whom you are involved'. For her, the most unbearable aspect of society had been 'all fragmentation, with people split up into their tiny home groups'. Throughout her life Sue, an only child, had suffered from acute shyness. Thus as a child at school she had few close friends. Due to her shyness she did not mix with her peers to any great extent. This lack of close friends continued after childhood. 'All my friends are now in the Commune Movement. Before I don't think I really had any.'

After reading some of the writings of R.D. Laing, Sue had come to define herself as being schizoid. This condition, she felt, explained her past inability to retain a job for any great length of time. Thus:

I had quite a few jobs, seven permanent ones and lots of temporary jobs in offices. I got fed up with some jobs but the main reason I left them was—well, being schizoid—one of the symptoms is that after a bit you feel that people get to know you, and you think they think you are not much good. So I used to move on somewhere else where I wasn't known.

207

At the same time, however, Sue's interest in communal living was not solely attributable to her experience of social isolation and her desire for companionship and a caring and supportive environment. A person does not wake up one day and say, 'The answer to my problem of loneliness is for me to join a commune—I shall do that at once.' Rather, one must first of all be aware of the existence of communes and have some knowledge of them, and secondly one must become aware that such institutions offer certain attractions which appear to provide a possible solution to one's problems. Thus Sue had been interested in the idea and practice of communal living for some time prior to joining. She described the origin of her interest. 'I was a Christian at one time and I was interested in Tolstoy, and that first interested me in community.' Later, Sue came into contact with a group of people, some of whom appeared to suffer from the same types of problems as she herself did and who identified themselves in similar terms. They decided to move out into the country to form a commune. Sue went with them. However, it should be pointed out again that she did not view her venture in communal living solely as a personal solution to her private problems. She also viewed it as an important contribution towards the creation of a new social order, one which would combine the anarchist's emphasis on individual freedom with the communist's emphasis on the social responsibility of the individual, based upon a federation of communes.

The second type of security-seeking communitarian included those commune-members and potential members who have experienced a major upset or change in their normal everyday pattern of life. Such a discontinuity has shattered their previously taken-for-granted world of work and family activities, and has rendered them available for recruitment to those communes which appear to offer them an opportunity to immerse themselves in a new world, to reconstruct a meaningful life for themselves and so overcome the loss of the old one.

It is difficult to make any further generalization about this type of communitarian. The type of discontinuity experienced can be as varied as the dimensions of life. Thus, some of the commune members with whom I came into contact had suffered a sudden nervous breakdown, others had experienced the death or desertion of their spouse, others had suffered the pains of trying to return to society after serving a prison sentence, while others had suffered unemployment or retirement. The processes by which such people have come to join a commune are almost as varied. However, it is possible to distinguish two typical paths. Some of them revealed a past history of radical thought and commitment, and were thus familiar with the ideals and practice of community, and who were made aware of the existence of commune ventures which they could join by their friends and contacts within such radical circles. The second type of path typically started with the flight from the remains of the person's old life, frequently to London, then to an encounter with someone who was aware of the existence of communes and also aware that such communes might provide the type of security for which the fugitive was seeking, and so finally to membership of a commune. The key personage in such an encounter might be anybody from an actual commune member, a priest, a social worker, an official of the Commune Movement, or merely with someone familiar with the commune movement in general and with certain commune projects in particular.

Typical to some extent of those who have followed the first path was the lady who wrote to me, describing herself as '68 years of age, healthy, capable, strong, with nothing to do, having been nursing all my life. I lack social contacts.' For this respondent the main goal of a commune was defined as 'happiness for lonely people' and 'freedom for children'. In similar fashion, the major aspect of life in conventional society which she viewed as intolerable was the inability to communicate with other people. Throughout her life she had been involved in the nursing profession. However, she had combined this with an interest and involvement in radical politics. Her parents had both been pacifists and very active in the socialist movement of the late nineteenth and early twentieth centuries. She herself had been a member of the Labour Party until she was expelled for attending a proscribed conference. She rejoined the Co-operative Party. She took an active interest in political and current affairs in general, having written to the press on a variety of issues some twenty times. As a pacifist who defined her politics as 'left of left', she had participated on a number of peace movement demonstrations such as the Aldermaston marches.

A humanist who held strong convictions on a number of issues, she found herself, in retirement, as she wrote, 'healthy, capable, strong, with nothing to do' and lacking social contacts. This lack of social contacts was, in a way, nothing new to her. She wrote of her experience as a nurse. 'In the nursing profession one gets very little social life, particularly in my day. One was always aware of being odd man out, I still do.' However, this problem became all the more acute with her retirement, finding herself a widow with time on her hands and her children grown up. She had first become interested in the idea of communal living when, as a health visitor, she had come across many lonely people, and had wondered in those days why such people should not live together and so overcome their loneliness. She became involved in an actual community project through reading a letter in the humanist journal *Freethinker*, which described a scheme for establishing a commune and invited interested parties to join. Sad to say, this particular scheme, at the time of writing, had suffered a number of setbacks due to potential members dropping out at the last minute when everything was ready for the group to occupy a suitable house.

Typical of the security-seeking communard who followed the second type of path to communal living was Ray, a Scotsman who had worked as a plumber in Glasgow and had been married there. One day his wife left him. He set off for London and spent some time living there. Then he learned of the existence of the commune at Eel Pie Island from one of the workers in the office at BIT, and he moved out to Middlesex to join the group there. Although a fully qualified plumber, Ray had left all his tools in Scotland, possibly because they reminded him of his previous life, and earned money through dealing in drugs. During the period when the commune was being used increasingly as a place to spend the night by large numbers of 'dossers', Ray took a leading part in their eviction, whereas many of the commune members would have preferred them to stay. One of his fellow members explained Ray's action in terms of his view of the commune as a support upon which he relied, a new home and a new world for him, and as such something which he was willing to defend against what he saw as potential threats to the stability and existence of his new surroundings.

A similar career was revealed by the member of another commune who told me of how he lost his job in the north of England and that same day set off to hitch-hike to London. This move was facilitated by the fact that he was unmarried and the fact that he found living with his parents both difficult and disagreeable. He had arrived in London late at night with very little money and no friends. He had spent some time around Piccadilly Circus, sleeping in the subways during the day and spending his nights in the small night clubs to be found in that area of London. During this time he was living mainly off 'pep' pills, and his health was suffering. Eventually he learnt of a commune in west London where he could obtain a roof over his head for a night's sleep. He had gone there, slept for nearly twenty-four hours, and had stayed. The prime characteristic of the commune which he valued above all others was, he informed me, the way in which everyone cared for everyone else, looked after each other, and took a genuine interest in the problems and concerns of each individual member.

For such people the prime attraction of a commune is the fact that it appears to represent a roof over their heads and a secure base upon which they can rely as they attempt to reconstruct their lives. Typically they reveal a background devoid of any political interest, radical commitment or activity. However, once they have become a member of a commune where they find themselves in constant interaction with people whose view of the world and of themselves, whose ideals and aspirations, are vastly different from those that were held by their acquaintances from their previous life, then such people frequently change not only their own conception of themselves but also begin to identify very strongly with their new companions, and begin to share their hopes for the creation of an alternative society. Typically, from feeling an outsider to the underground movement with which they identify the members of communes, they come to view themselves as fully-fledged members of this counter-cultural movement, and begin to take on the styles of this movement such as pertain to dress and language. They also begin to identify with the broad aims of this general social movement, and begin to define their membership of a commune in terms of working towards the creation of a new social order. As such, this career contrasts with that which is generally displayed by those communards who have been attracted to the idea and practice of communal living in the first instance by their radical commitment and their desire for social change. It is to this type of communitarian, the activist, that attention will now be turned.

The activists

The activist, as the label would seem to indicate, is that type of commune member typically to be found in the urban, activist communes of the type examined above.[25] In seeking to understand the original sources of the typical activist's radical commitment, a number of theories are available to be utilized. Basically one can distinguish between two types of theories of radicalism—class theories and status theories.[26] A theory of the first type generally seeks to explain an individual's radical commitment and action in terms of the actor's rational pursuit of his own personal and group material interests.

Thus it might be thought that those who ranked lowest on all dimensions relevant to the prestige stratification system of society, the underdogs, would be likely to find their way to becoming a member of a commune, particularly if that commune promised the abolition of all distinctions between man and man, and sought to create a society based upon the brotherhood of man. Such a venture would enable the deprived individual to overcome his lowly position as an under-paid, under-educated, badly-housed member of society. The argument against this type of reasoning is, of course, that those who rank low on all the salient dimensions of a society's stratification system are generally more likely to be alienated in the sense of viewing their lot in society as natural, inevitable, and something about which little can be done. Thus, although the poverty-stricken members of society are likely to be estranged from society, they are unlikely to involve themselves in radical social and political action aimed at changing the total structure of society due to the fact that they lack many of the intellectual, financial, and practical resources necessary to perform adequately as a radical political actor. To the extent that such people become involved in political action, then such action is more likely to be of the trade-unionist variety, the term Lenin used to depict that political action which sought to improve the conditions of the working class within the framework of the existing institutional arrangements of society, rather than of the revolutionary variety that seeks a radical transformation of the society as a whole.[27]

An example of a 'status theory' approach to the analysis of radicalism is that provided by such writers as Lenski and Galtung.[28] They suggest that it is fruitful to view a person's political and social attitudes and actions as a function of his relative positions on various dimensions—such as occupation, income, and education—which are considered salient in the ranking of actors according to prestige in society. Lenski's hypothesis is that individuals whose differences of status display a low degree of crystallization or congruence, in the sense that they occupy a high rank on certain dimensions and low ranks on others, will be more likely to endorse radical critiques of society than those whose status differences are roughly congruent, whose ranks are equilibrated in Galtung's terminology. Lenski provides some statistical evidence to support his hypothesis, but his explanation of why this should be so is extremely vague. He refers to the individual with a poorly crystallized status as a particular type of marginal man who is subjected with some frequency to social experiences of an unpleasant or frustrating nature, which leads the individual to react to this strain in some way against the social order which produces such experiences. The proposition appears to be that individuals find stressful a comparison of situations in which they are treated differently according to differently evaluated ranks. Inconsistent ranks or incongruences of status produce strain, and strain can lead to a reaction on the part of the individual against the social order. Unfortunately it is never made clear by Lenski whether or not the relationship between status inconsistency and a particular form of behaviour is independent of the individual's perception of that inconsistency.

Galtung introduces into his argument the related notion of reference groups and relative deprivation, suggesting that many forms of aggression arise from an individual perceiving the discrepancy between the way he is treated when his 'top dog' status is emphasized and when his 'underdog' status on another dimension of the society's stratification system is emphasized. He argues that the destabilizing effect of this discrepency in the relative positions occupied by the individual on different dimensions will produce a mobility pressure, the individual will seek to equilibrate all his rank position upwards. However, it can be argued that if there are no channels of upward mobility open for the individual, then rectification is likely to be sought by other means. One possible reaction could be in the form of radical political activism, aimed at bringing about a change in the structure of society in general and of the actor's structural position in particular. It is further possible to argue that if an actor has tried all the conventional channels of upward mobility and has tried the more conventional means of transforming the social order, then it is possible that failure could lead to withdrawal from the conventional social world in order to establish at a micro-level that kind of social system where status and stratification systems do not exist, where all are equal and are treated as brothers. Such a project could conceivably lead to attempts to form or join a commune.

Galtung's theory shares similar limitations as that of Lenski. Both are based on the assumption that it is possible to identify objectively the number of dimensions in the stratification system of any given society. It is also assumed that any particular dimension has a fixed number of ranks, and that each dimension has the same number of ranks as every other dimension. Without making these assumptions then, they would be unable to define and measure the various degrees of status crystallization or rank disequilibrium. In fact, such assumptions are unjustified, the number of dimensions in the stratification system of a society and the number of ranks or equivalence classes upon any one dimension are empirical issues. As Doreian and Stockman have convincingly argued:[29]

> it is impossible to establish in advance the number of ranks on all dimensions. Furthermore, although there may well be a sense in which particular ranks on dimensions are held to be consistent, we cannot assume that each dimension has the same number of ranks.

Unless the researcher can take into consideration the actor's definition of which dimensions constitute the key components of the stratification system of his social world, and unless the researcher can take into consideration the degree to which the individual considers the criteria by which prestige is allocated in society as significant for himself personally, then he is forced to rely on a number of *a priori* assumptions about such matters which are not necessarily valid. Moreover, as long as the researcher does not restrict his definitions of the number of dimensions and the number of ranks within dimensions to those which the actors themselves

213

define as existing, then it is always perfectly possible for the researcher to explain an individual's radicalism by reference to an objective correlation between the actor's behaviour and his relative position on one dimension compared to his position on others. All the researcher has to do is to create new and additional dimensions for the stratifying of individuals in society, and sooner or later he is bound to discover some evidence of status inconsistency or rank disequilibrium according to his criteria.

A further limitation of both the class and status theories of radicalism is that they can be seen as displaying a built-in bias to the extent that they imply that, whatever the public claims of the radical about the sources of his radicalism, the real motivation stems mainly from his self-interest *vis-à-vis* his position in society. Neither of these theoretical approaches would appear to allow for the fact that the individual might be genuinely incensed by what he views as man's inhumanity to man, and so becomes a committed radical through altruistic motives, through a genuine desire to create a world deemed more fitting for human beings in general to live in.

Despite the apparent limitations of these theoretical approaches, my search to understand why certain people were led to form or join communes in general and activist communes in particular was to some extent guided by them. I found them of limited use. The middle-class social origins of the majority of communards, their relatively high level of educational attainment, and, where relevant, their once relatively high income-earning ability and potential, constituted evidence contrary to what one would have expected from the absolute deprivation-class theory of radicalism. The majority of communards have, in fact, rejected those materialistic goals that constitute the driving force of many working-class political activists. Whatever the origins of their radical belief system and commitment, it is not to be located in feelings of absolute deprivation as society's underdogs. For the majority of communards, this is a position of which they have no direct experience and frequently little knowledge.

The utility of the status theory of Lenski, Galtung and others is rather more difficult to assess. On the one hand, the majority of commune members are young, their average age being around the early twenties. This, it might be argued, involves disequilibrium to the extent that such young people are well educated. The reasoning would be that such people rank high on the dimension of education but low on the age-related dimensions of power and influence. As such, they experience relative deprivation to the extent that they feel deprived of the opportunity to occupy a status of power and influence for which their educational qualifications equip them, but which their age prevents them from occupying. Certainly the facts would appear to uphold this type of thesis. The majority of commune members are young, from middle-class social origins, well educated, but earning low incomes, living in poor-quality housing and pursuing occupations that carry little or no prestige. In fact many are unemployed. However, when one goes behind the facts one discovers an important feature for which the theory fails to prepare the researcher—this is the fact that the majority of communards have consciously chosen to occupy their low status on such dimensions as occupation and income. Such dimensions are not recognized by the typical communard as significant. The relevance of one's position on such dimensions for the life of the individual is denied.

This rejection of the stratification system of modern society and the values upon which it is based is, however, not rejection by those who have been denied access to the higher rungs of this system. Rather, it is more frequently a rejection by those who have had a first taste of the fruits of such a system and found them wanting. Thus a number of commune members have held jobs that were potentially rewarding in financial terms, but have given them up in order to seek out what they view as a more meaningful and intrinsically rewarding form of life. Typical of this experience was that of a member of an activist commune who had worked as a buyer for a large firm for fifteen months before giving it up to join a commune. He described his job as 'buying soap wrappers and similar high grade rubbish. I worked for fifteen months earning £1470 a year, it was insane.' Again, many commune members have dropped out of higher education due to their disillusionment with the educational system, which they tended to view as being orientated solely towards preparing them for some preordained slot in an occupational system which they also rejected. One of the questions which I asked many commune members was whether they ever wished that they possessed higher educational qualifications. Going through my notes almost randomly, here are some of the replies that I received to this query from members of an activist commune.

X. No, I place little value on 'pieces of paper'.
Y. No, I consider them irrelevant.
Z. No, they are useless in my chosen way of life.

One source of youthful radicalism, it has been suggested by certain writers, lies in the rebellion of the young against parental authority, which has become generalized into a rejection of the way of life personified by the parents. This thesis, however, failed to throw any light upon the sources of the activists' radical commitment. As pointed out above, the typical relationship between commune member and parents was revealed to be one of misunderstanding and inability to communicate rather than enmity and conflict.[30]

Another approach which seeks to explain an individual's radicalism by reference to his socialization experiences suggests that the radical is highly likely to have been exposed to radical perspectives by parents who held such views of the world and transmitted them to their offspring during the socialization period. This thesis appears only to be relevant for an understanding of the sources of a limited number of commune members' radicalism. Thus, of sixteen activists from whom I obtained information on their relationships with their parents, eight claimed to get on well or very well with them; five claimed to be on friendly terms with their parents since they had left home; while three claimed that their relationships were merely polite, superficial or average. Of the eight who claimed to have good relationships with their parents, all but one of them claimed that their parents were sympathetic to their attitudes and actions. Of the parents of these seven, five were described as Labour or Liberal Party supporters, the remainder were described as 'mildly conservative'. The other member who got on well with his parents described them as politically apathetic and unable to understand why their child was doing things he did. Of the five commune members who described their relationships as friendly since they had left home, the parents of two of them were Labour or Liberal Party supporters whose attitude was described as sympathetic. The parents of another member were described as politically apathetic and their attitude towards their child's actions and attitudes as 'passing interest, but secretly wishing me into a straight job'. The parents of the other two were described as Conservative Party supporters whose attitudes were described as 'disbelief, and occasional horror', and 'they accept that I can do what I like now, but my father is still not pleased when I do things my way. We agree to differ, though I am still not completely straight with my dad.' The parents of the three members who described their relationships as merely polite or superficial were all Conservative Party supporters, whose attitudes towards the life led by their offspring was described variously as 'disagreement', 'you'll grow up soon', and 'difficulty in understanding but no real interference'.

Despite the obvious limitations of this type of data, taken as it is from such a restricted sample (although, in fairness it should be pointed out that the relevant population is very small in Britain), it is sufficient to indicate the dangers of attempting to adopt a single theoretical approach to explain all forms of radicalism. No doubt the radicalism of certain individuals stems from their position in the social structure, from their feelings of absolute or relative deprivation or position of rank disequilibrium, whilst the radicalism of others undoubtedly stems from their personal rebellion against parental authority, and for others stems from their internalization of the radical ideas of their parents. However, no one theory can explain the origins of each individual's radical attitudes and actions. Thus, with regard to the impact of family background on commune members and their belief systems, the parents of a few of them had encouraged them, it was claimed, in their quest for an alternative style of life and their desire to create an alternative society. On the other hand, the parents of others had sought to discourage them, viewed their activities with horror and disbelief and, as was the case with a few isolated instances, relationships were such that the member had no desire to see his parents again as long as he lived. Again, the data indicate the variety of political backgrounds from which the commune members came.

Although the nature of the phenomena and the data make generalizations about the sources of communards' commitment to radical belief systems and modes of action extremely suspect, one can make generalizations about the career of the typical activist commune member, of how he has come to identify himself as a radical and of the path he has followed to become a member of a commune. For a person to identify himself as a radical, he must develop attitudes about the social world and life in that world sufficiently distinct from the views held by his contemporaries for both them and he, himself, to view him as a cognitive deviant, as different. The nature of this difference in world views must be such that he comes to be typed as a radical by others and also by himself. Whatever the origin of his deviant world view, the individual labelled a radical is then faced with a number of choices and projects of action. He can seek to maintain his radical attitudes, but refrain from implementing them through involvement in various forms of radical political and social action. He can choose to remain a curdled idealist or become a committed activist, seeking to involve himself in a variety of activities aimed at bringing about social change. For the radical who chooses the activist path, a further possible choice confronts him with regard to the type of activity to be pursued. He can choose to involve himself in radical parliamentary politics, trade-union activity and so on, he can also choose to pursue his goals through joining a commune. For the individual to actually join a commune he must be aware of the existence of such phenomena, he must come to believe that such a way of life might help him further his own aims, he must somehow establish contact with either an existing commune or with people who are seeking to form one, he must define his own life situation as sufficiently free for him to radically alter his everyday way of life, and he must gain admission to a commune. This career can be illustrated diagrammatically (p. 218).

This type of career can be traced in the life histories of activist commune members. Before going on to consider a number of specific cases in detail, a number of general points can be made. First of all, whatever the origins of the typical activist's self-definition as a cognitive deviant and radical, this had usually been the result of a long and gradual process during which the individual had come to feel increasingly different and apart from the majority of his contemporaries rather than from some conversion experience as some

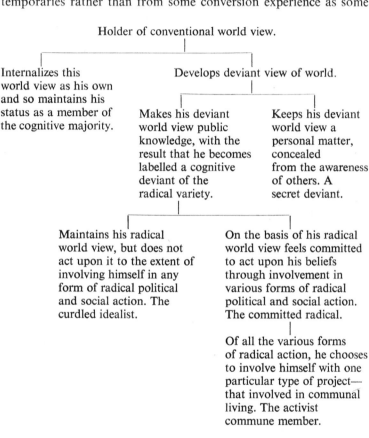

Holder of conventional world view.

Internalizes this world view as his own and so maintains his status as a member of the cognitive majority.

Develops deviant view of world.

Makes his deviant world view public knowledge, with the result that he becomes labelled a cognitive deviant of the radical variety.

Keeps his deviant world view a personal matter, concealed from the awareness of others. A secret deviant.

Maintains his radical world view, but does not act upon it to the extent of involving himself in any form of radical political and social action. The curdled idealist.

On the basis of his radical world view feels committed to act upon his beliefs through involvement in various forms of radical political and social action. The committed radical.

Of all the various forms of radical action, he chooses to involve himself with one particular type of project—that involved in communal living. The activist commune member.

modern-day St Paul on the road to Damascus. As one respondent replied to my query of whether there had been a particular moment in his life when he had felt that he would be unhappy leading what most people would call a conventional social life, 'No, not really. I thought I would like to achieve different aims in life very young.' Other factors can be mentioned which appear to be significant for an attempt to understand the career of the activist in general. Whatever the relationships of activists with their parents, typically they have faced only limited parental opposition throughout their lives to their pursuance of their own lines of action. To that extent they have been reared in a libertarian kind of family environment which has been conducive to the development of their commitment to act out their beliefs in the real world rather than confine them to the world of ideas in deference to the wishes of parents and significant others. Furthermore, the unmarried status of the typical activist has, to some extent, meant that he has been freer to follow his own radical inclinations than he might have been with a wife and family to care for.[31] Furthermore, the typical activist reveals a greater likelihood of having completed further educational courses than of having dropped out as did many of the 'trippers'. Thus of sixteen activists, half had completed a university course, five had completed an art college course, and four had completed their full-time education after taking their advanced G.C.E. at secondary school. As was remarked above,[32] the exposure to full-time education at any advanced level is highly likely to stimulate the student's critical judgment and rational scepticism. The student is thus more highly sensitized to any apparent breach between the articulated central values and abstract ideals of society such as fairness, respect for the individual and justice, and what they perceive as reality. This fact has to some extent been reflected in the amount of student unrest that has characterized university life in recent years. The involvement of students in such activities has not only had a radicalizing effect on many, but also accustomed many students to an activist role, a commitment to further their beliefs through active involvement in student politics and other forms of radical action. Such has been the experience of many members of activist communes.

The fact that many activists have completed a course of further education also explains, to some extent, their choice of an urban commune through which to pursue their goals. Living in a city enables them to pursue careers for which their education has prepared them, careers which they would be forced to forfeit if they lived in a rural commune. Significantly, the choice of occupation made by such commune members reflects their rejection of the contemporary social order and their commitment to the creation of an alternative. Typically they follow such vocational careers as teacher, cleric, social worker, charity and voluntary service organizer— careers which are divorced as much as possible from what the typical activist would view as the exploitative nature of the production and distribution industries. A number of further points can be made about the choice of an urban, 'red base'-type commune as a form of radical action in itself and as a base for further forms of radical action orientated toward the local outside community. To a large extent, the form of action any radical involves himself in will depend upon his own self-definition as a political animal. If one

219

defines oneself as an anarchist, then one does not usually involve oneself in parliamentary politics as one might conceivably do if one described oneself as a Marxist-Leninist. The choice of an urban commune as a project of action to some extent reflects the political self-identification of the majority of activists as libertarian socialists or, in many cases, anarcho-pacifists. Typically, such a self-definition implies disbelief in the efficacy of parliamentary politics as a mechanism of social change and a rejection of all élitist political movements in general. It typically implies a belief in the need for people to control their own work and community environments, and a belief in the necessity and desirability of 'bottom up' forms of control rather than 'top down' varieties which involve the control of the mass by a small and privileged élite at the top of the hierarchy. Given such a set of beliefs, then the choice of an action project such as an urban commune aimed at the encouragement of ordinary people to exert their collective power to control their own work and community life in general as a counter-weight to the power of the central decision-makers 'up there' follows naturally.

The following examination of the paths to community pursued by some activist commune members will illustrate some of these points. Tom was in his mid-twenties and earning somewhere in the region of £1,000 per annum from the design and construction of hand-made furniture. Having studied at art college, he had worked as a teacher for a number of years prior to his move to furniture-making. Since he had left home he had got on quite well with his parents, although prior to his move they had had occasional disputes. His father was a clerk who tended to vote for the Liberal Party, and who was inclined to view his son's activities sympathetically but with some worry. Tom's personal political background was typical of that revealed by other activists. He defined himself as more or less a pacifist, identifying himself with such figures as Ghandi and William Morris as an anarchist believer in decentralization. There had never been a particular moment in his life when he had realized that he would be unhappy leading a conventional social existence, rather, he said, 'I became aware of this slowly at quite an early time in my life'.

His involvement in an urban commune reflected his political self-identification and also his disillusionment with conventional parliamentary and protest politics. Thus while he was interested in political affairs in general, he had never been a member of a political party, as he had 'always found actual parties too rigid'. He considered voting irrelevant, sympathizing with the view expressed by a fellow communard:

Suppose I vote: I 'choose' a man already elected for me by the local party. If he gets in (or even the other man) will he

represent (i) me? (ii) his constituency? (iii) his party? (iv)
himself? Sometimes (iii) and (iv), never me. How could he? He
doesn't know me. Even if he did, the machinery of politics
wouldn't let him.

Tom estimated that he had written to the press about once a year in
order to promote various issues. He considered that none of his
letters had ever had any effect. Apart from his attitudes to such
conventional means of political expression, he tended to view
demonstrations as a waste of time, although he had been involved
in a number of demonstrations on such issues as nuclear disarmament, the Vietnam War, and Women's Liberation. He had also been
a member of the Peace Pledge Union and the Campaign for Nuclear
Disarmament.

Tom's first interest in communes had developed 'slowly, through
some reading' and, as he phrased it, 'seeing the obvious'. This
contrasted with the source of his fellow members' first interest which
typically stemmed from some experience of living communally.
Thus one of his fellow communards described the origins of his
interest as 'Vaguely by being in a good hall of residence at University.
Consciously when I was in a communal flat with a theatre company
at the Edinburgh Festival.' Others described their first interest as
arising, variously, 'through friends who were keen on the idea',
'through meeting other commune members', and 'through friends
in a theatre group'.

Among the characteristics of straight society which Tom found
particularly intolerable were 'its violence', 'its lack of freedom',
'its mediocrity', 'its lack of standards' and 'its centralization'. These
are the kinds of attitudes typically held by the 'trippers', but in the
attitude towards the use of drugs displayed by activists such as Tom
a distinct contrast emerges. For Tom drugs were 'good to give to
armies but pretty useless in solving any of the real problems'. This
belief that drugs represented an escape from the problems of life and
the world rather than a positive solution to these problems was one
shared by other members of his commune. Thus another member
expressed his view that drugs were 'the same as nicotine and
alcohol—great if they are taken as a relaxation from or an aid to
constructive, positive living. But very sad and I would say dangerous
if they became a substitute, an escape from living.' Thus, activists
such as Tom did not look forward to the 'turning on' of the whole
world population through psychedelic drugs, but rather saw communes as contributing to the creation of a new social order 'by
seducing more and more people away from the technological
society'.

Whereas Tom described himself as a pacifist and anarchist, Carl described himself as a 'left wing socialist, drawing substantially but critically from Marx, based on Christian humanism'. He did not consider himself to be a pacifist. This difference in self-identification was reflected in certain other aspects of the attitudes and beliefs. Thus Carl had once been a member of the Fabian Society but had left, not because of any disillusionment with political parties in general, but because he disagreed with their policies. He felt that they were 'too acceptant of the established political institutions'. Then again, whereas Tom would not have voted on principle, Carl would vote for the Labour Party, feeling that it was better to have a Labour than a Conservative government. Also, Carl showed a greater willingness to participate in demonstrations involving violence than did Tom. Although, like Tom, Carl tended to view demonstrations as a means of change as being of limited value unless they were part of a variety of activities aimed at social change, he argued that they were '*one* form of showing that ordinary people do have power—but it must always be in the context of other organising work'.

Carl had been active in student politics at university where he studied philosophy and psychology prior to taking up his post as a clinical psychologist. It was while at university that the idea of living in a commune first occurred. 'A few friends who I met through the Political Commission of the Student Christian Movement while at college wanted to live out in a more permanent way the things we had been fighting for in the universities.' A practising Christian, Carl was very much concerned with living out his life according to those values and ideals in which he believed in a sectarian manner in so far as he sought to avoid compromising his beliefs. As he phrased it, 'My concern is that one should live out in one's own present style of life the values one is struggling to bring out in the society as a whole.' However, Carl combined this belief in the importance of exemplary action with a commitment to an active involvement in the affairs of the local community, although he had been forced to moderate his plans a little in the light of practical experience. Thus he described the goal of the commune in which he lived as being, from this point of view, not only that of

> providing a richer and more diverse living-place than a bed-sit or newly-wed's house, but that we would be a 'catalyst' for local community struggle. We are now more modest in our expectations. It is still a possibility but requires far more time and deliberate planning than we seem able to provide.

Just as Carl held a fairly definite idea of the goal of the commune, his decision to join in the formation of it had been a deliberate one as a conscious response to the problems that face the cognitive deviant, whether he be a sexual or a political deviant—the pressures to change one's mode of thinking and acting that stem from the cognitive majority. As Carl phrased it: 'The decision to join the commune was worked out over months and settled on the basis of a longstanding "dis-ease" with the ability to withstand on one's own the pressures to conform'. While Carl and his friends had decided to pursue their political and social aims through a commune project as an efficient means of promoting these ends, one can see that the commune idea was also attractive from a purely personal perspective, providing the cognitive deviant with moral support and sustenance, providing a 'richer and more diverse living place than a bed-sit', and so enabling one to avoid the fate one of Carl's co-members described as being 'submerged in the general suburban-semi mass'. For a number of Carl's fellow members the idea of a commune as one possible way of life was planted in their minds after some personal experience of living in West German socialist communes. One of those who had visited such experiments on the continent was Colin. Like Carl, he was in his mid-twenties but, unlike him, was married.

Whereas Carl's parents were Conservative Party supporters who tended to view their son's activities with some disapproval, Colin's father was a clergyman with whom he got on very well. His parents were Liberal Party supporters who fully approved of their son's involvement in an urban commune. Colin had studied theology at university and was an assistant curate in the Church of England. Identifying himself as a radical socialist, Colin revealed a personal history of involvement in university politics, demonstrations on such issues as Vietnam, South Africa, Rhodesia and so on. He had also on several occasions written letters to the press to promote various causes. He doubted whether such letters had ever any influence, and he tended to view demonstrations as being of limited utility also. 'They are now largely a waste of time but not when part of a more general strategy in order to make a specific point. Then they can still be worth while.' Despite this involvement in what might be termed protest politics, Colin had never been a member of a political party, the reason being that he 'never felt any party represented my socialist beliefs adequately'. Like Carl, however, he voted for the Labour Party. He had once been a member of the Campaign for Nuclear Disarmament and the Committee of One Hundred, but had left them as he ceased to consider them useful organizations. His self-identification as a revolutionary socialist and as a Christian was reflected in his view of those aspects of conventional society which were particularly unbearable or intolerable for him—he pointed to the capitalist economic system, but also to the consequences of this system on the values of society, seeing the

H*

emphasis on materialism and the selfishness of national policies as a natural consequence of the capitalist economic system. However, Colin had not developed his view due to some particularly painful experience of the world, rather he claimed, 'it has been my feeling for years'. His self-identification as a radical had been the result of a long and gradual process rather than some conversion experience. His commitment to life in an urban commune stemmed partly from his disillusionment with other means of change and also from his belief in the efficacy of a commune expressing 'a little more adequately a shared community that can act as an effective force on social issues' and so contribute to the beginnings of an 'alternative society, which he described as 'developing institutions that can undermine our present social institutions by a creative challenge and a radical critique leading to radical action for a new social order'. He shared the view of Carl and Tom that drugs had little contribution to make towards the attainment of this new social order.

Bittner has argued that radicals differ from other people, not so much with regard to the content of their beliefs and values, but rather in their uncompromising moral rectitude, based on a complete adherence to a few overriding principles which guide their conduct in all situations.[33] Radicals usually attach this single-minded emphasis to some principle that is already known and valued in society, albeit as one principle among many. What is radical is not the tenet itself, but the militant acceptance of its sovereign and unqualified supremacy, and the reaction that this entails against the perceived ambiguities of the heterogeneous standards of thought and behaviour that are traditionally sanctioned in society. Thus Carl referred to his concern with the need to live out in one's present style of life the values one was seeking to bring out in society as a whole. With another activist, Jane, it was the commitment to the values of freedom, love and co-operation that lay at the base of her radicalism, and it was the contrast she perceived between the values that guided the action of normal people in the world and the values to which she felt committed that led to her involvement in radical political and social action. Thus she was unable to point to any particular aspect of conventional social life which she found particularly intolerable, but rather pointed to the fact that 'the overall quality I can't understand is the exploitation of man over man which exists in all aspects of the system'. It was this perception of a gap between articulated belief and practice that had led her to reject the Christian faith in which she was once a believer. As she explained the reason for her leaving the Church, 'I couldn't understand the duality existing in what one believed and what one practised.' Whatever the source of Jane's overriding commitment to the values of freedom, love and brotherhood, the growth of this commitment had been a gradual one. Thus she claimed that there had never been a particular moment when she had realized that she would be unhappy leading what most people would consider to be a conventional life, rather there had been 'just a very gradual feeling that many things in society were "wrong" and inevitably that led on to my "opting out"'.

Prior to her opting out Jane, who was unmarried and in her early thirties, had attended grammar school and then art college. In reply to my query as to whether she ever wished she possessed higher educational qualifications, her answer was typical of the attitude displayed by many communards. 'No, qualifications seem very irrelevant to living, and only needed if one wants more power, status, money.' Following the completion of her full-time education, Jane had worked at a variety of jobs including nurse, analytical chemist, stewardess, au pair, dental nurse, travel agent, shop assistant, marionnette operator and hand-loom weaver. She defined her goal as a commune member in terms of 'finding ways to build an alternative structure of society, based on more humanistic values'. Despite her almost life-long involvement in radical activities of one kind or another, Jane's parents were politically apathetic and were not interested in political issues to any great extent. At the same time she got on very well with them, although she claimed that they found her life and ideas difficult to understand. However, they were by no means antagonistic towards their daughter's attitudes and actions. They could not understand why she had chosen the style of life she had done.

Whereas Carl and Colin described themselves as revolutionary socialists, Jane found it difficult to label herself in political terms. Although she was a member of an anarchist group, she placed greater emphasis on her belief in non-violence as the key to her political identification. Asked how she defined herself politically she replied, 'I don't know. I can't find a category to fit into. Non-violence, I guess, is my basic way of working.' This matter of self-definition as a political actor is important from the point of view of understanding the modes of action pursued by the individual. Thus, Carl and Colin as revolutionary socialists claimed that they would vote Labour and maintained that the reason they were not members of a political party was not so much their objection to political parties *per se*, but rather the fact that they had been unable to find a party that held sufficiently radical views for them to join. Tom, as an anarcho-pacifist, claimed that voting was a complete waste of time and explained his non-membership of a political party not in terms of party policies but in terms of their structure as parties—they were too rigid. Jane, as a believer in non-violence and as a member of anarchist groups, shared Tom's attitudes. Thus, asked if she had ever been a member of a political party, she replied, 'No, never. I did not consider it right for any group to impose certain ideas on to others and use people for their own ends.' Similarly, with regard to her attitude towards voting, she replied, 'I would not vote because, again, it means choosing to let others be the decision-makers. I feel decisions should come about at a grass-roots level.'

Jane's choice of an urban commune as a way of promoting the values of freedom, love and brotherhood can be understood in terms of her principled rejection of parliamentary means of change and her belief in the limited value of demonstrations as a source of change. Although she had participated in a number of peace movement demonstrations at such places as Holy Loch and Aldermaston, Jane held the view that demonstrations 'have a value of perhaps making a few folk aware, but I don't see them worthwhile as an end in themselves'. Her choice of an activist type commune can also be explained to some extent by her rejection of the use of drugs as a means of personal and societal transformation. With regard to the issue of drugs she shared the attitude typically displayed by the majority of activists: 'whilst I don't condemn it, I don't think it an answer to today's problems, or valuable in opening one's mind. I think awareness can grow from within, and should not need chemical reactions to bring it about.'

Someone might conceivably construct a grand theory about why people choose to join communes and which seeks to embrace all those who have ever lived in communes of one sort or another throughout history. What I have been trying to do in this chapter has been to illustrate the variety of communitarians in contemporary Britain. In so doing, I have attempted to touch upon the relative inadequacy of certain existing theories concerning radicalism, arguing that no one theory can satisfactorily explain the commitment of all types of communitarians to the ideal and practice of communal living. I have tried to reveal how different people join different types of communes with different ends in view, formed on the basis of different experiences. What communitarians do share in common is a felt estrangement from the existing social order, although the original sources of such estrangement can vary markedly from individual to individual, and a related utopian desire to transform the social world from what it appears to be to what they feel it ought to be. Moreover, while I have been unable to locate any single cause for their estrangement from the existing order and their initial taking up of the radical career of the utopian, it is possible to outline at a very general level the kinds of processes involved in their radical career which has led them to an active interest and involvement in the commune movement. In each of the case histories examined in this chapter, the individual has become available for recruitment to the commune movement as a consequence of his dissatisfaction with the status quo. Through some means or another they have become aware of the existence of communes. As a consequence of any of a variety of possible experiences and for a variety of reasons, they have come to believe that such a life style might be a better way of living than their more conventional form of existence. In addition, they have managed to define their own life situation as sufficiently free for them to feel able to break with what had been their previous life routines. Finally, and perhaps most crucially, they have managed through some means to establish contact with others whose views, ideas and so on have proved sufficiently compatible with theirs for them to consider the rewards of sharing significant areas of their life with them to outweigh the rewards to be derived from a straight existence. One of the rewards to be obtained from communal living for such people, whatever their prime motive for joining any particular venture, is that in living with others who share at least some basic ideas in common, one is better able to maintain and strengthen one's commitment to a radical or deviant world view in the face of the attacks from those who can be termed cognitive antagonists. It is to a consideration of this world view that attention is turned in the next chapter.

8 The world of the communitarians

In the previous chapter attention was turned towards a consideration of the different types of communitarians and the paths they had
followed which had led them to the idea and practice of communal
living. It was argued that in order to understand fully the actions of a
human actor in the world, one must try to understand what his
world looks like, the major features of his construction of reality.
This chapter is an attempt to construct a model of the world of the
communitarians.

Sense of identity

The world of the actor on the social scene is made up of many
interlocking and related spheres of interest, but one of the most
significant of spheres is the actor himself—his self. How do communitarians view themselves? If they possess a sense of identity,
what is its nature? How do they define themselves?

Perhaps the most common characteristic shared by communitarians with regard to this sort of question is a general reluctance to
label themselves in any way. This applied not only to themselves but
to their group as a whole. Thus a number of communes were
reluctant to call themselves by that name, because 'we might well
become what a commune is supposed to be, rather than what we
are'. Again and again the emphasis would be that 'we are not types
here, we are all individuals'. If pressed about what sort of individual
they were, then one rarely obtained a direct answer.

Some respondents were asked whether they thought that anyone
could ever really understand them. It was thought that if a person
felt that this was possible, he would be far more likely to understand
himself, have some sort of conception of the sort of individual he
was. The typical response to this query was 'No, because I don't

think I fully understood myself'. Some of the responses are given
below to illustrate this point.

> I don't know whether it is possible for one person because
> surely one person cannot have so much understanding that he
> can fully understand another because we are finding ourselves,
> realizing ourselves, all the time. No, because we can't know
> ourselves all at one time.

Or, again, 'Not really, because I don't fully understand myself at
the moment. I like to think that someone will fully understand me,
but at the moment I fluctuate between different points of view too
much.' Thus what emerged was that the typical communitarian
possessed no clear and straightforward conception of himself as an
actor on the social scene (who does?), but rather defined himself in
terms of an individual, somehow apart and separate from other
individuals, and too complex an organism to be understood by the
individual himself, let alone by others. This type of feeling can of
course lead to a strong sense of isolation, of being alone. This was
expressed by one respondent in reply to the question about whether
he thought anyone could ever fully understand him. 'I would like to
think that, man. I would really like to know somebody because I
don't think I ever have. . . . I have always been apart somehow.'

I was interested to discover what type of person or historical
figure was admired by the respondents. It was an attempt to discover what types of role models they held before themselves as
ideal types, and why they held the models they did. In other words,
very few of us could answer a direct question about 'Who are you?',
but most of us have our heroes, our gurus. It was thought that an
enquiry into this sphere of the consciousness of the communitarians
might reveal information about the type of person they would like
to be, if not necessarily about the type of person they felt themselves
to be. The names that emerged were those that one would have
expected, given the tradition of community that they have inherited.
From the trippers there emerged Buddha, Annie Besant, Krishnamurti, Gurdjieff, Alan Watts, Aldous Huxley and Timothy
Leary; from the 'red base' activists there emerged Marcuse, Guevara,
and Marx; and from the anarchist tradition there emerged Thoreau,
William Morris, Malatesta, Tolstoy and Gandhi.[1] Many trippers
felt that such 'pop' figures as Donovan and Dylan spoke for them
and expressed their feelings far more ably than they themselves
could.[2]

However, more often than not, there appeared to be no single
person or group of persons that the respondent could point to as a
mentor, guide, or significant other. Many felt that they had not been
influenced by anyone in particular, if anyone at all. What mattered

229

was that you were, and the person you had to answer to was your-self.

> When one goes into it, the person one wants approval from is
> oneself. We are not happy with ourselves if we are giving less
> than the best of ourselves. . . . It is coming to terms with our-
> selves, within ourselves, and to get approval from ourselves. . . .
> We are the harshest judges ourselves . . . you cannot get away
> from it that eventually it is yourself that you have to answer to.

Despite this, it is not surprising, given the mentors that were mentioned, that where a respondent could be persuaded to define himself politically, the typical self-definition was that of liber-tarian-anarchist.

> If I have to, I would call myself some sort of anarchist, but
> then a lot of anarchists would say I wasn't one. My ideas about
> authority, centralised government and so on are the criteria by
> which I judge myself an anarchist.

> Libertarian/anarchist—it means I don't put much faith in
> parliament, although I concede that they have done some
> things, but I also know that they have done a lot of nasty things.
> It is all a big con—capitalism, to grind us down.

> Libertarian/pacifist. I am opposed to politics on a mass scale.

In addition, some activists typed themselves as revolutionary socialists.[3] At the same time, many respondents refused to type themselves as political actors. This was, for some, because they felt unable to type themselves in any way. As one respondent informed me, 'I hate labelling. I find it very difficult to answer, not because I don't want to but because I don't know how to.' Others failed to type themselves as political actors because they felt such a contempt for politics as such that they felt unable to associate themselves with that sphere in any way. Thus one tripper, when asked how he would define himself in political terms, responded, 'I wouldn't. I disbelieve in politics. I think they are a lie.'

This type of attitude towards politics and life is typical of that held by members of the drug culture. However, it would appear that if someone does have an idea about what he would like to do with his life, the path he would really like to follow, then this could indicate that he has some idea about what sort of person he feels himself to be, or what he would like to be. Thus, I was concerned with enquiring into the nature of the life projects held by the com-munitarians. For many of the youthful trippers the future was unknowable and hence not worth thinking about. Life was to be led for the present moment. If one tried to plan for the future one would corrupt it. Others saw life as possessing meaning in so far as one helped to 'leave this world in a better fit state for our children to live in'. Others saw their life in very personal terms of 'doing good things because they are good in themselves such as painting and making things. This is probably what I will do to make bread.' Or, 'just to get down to something worth while for me and my family. A working, a human, a true commune.' For the more hedonistic amongst the trippers the aim of life was 'to have every experience and when you have had every experience there will be nothing left except death'.

On the other hand, for some their personal future was seen in terms of their increasing estrangement from conventional society:

> I think about the future in terms of my relationship with
> straight society. I am very aware that I am going further and
> further away from any chance that I'll be able to identify
> myself—even in part—with the everyday society. I suppose lots
> of others, young people, are feeling this way. One takes comfort
> in this thought and hopes that something will come from this—
> co-operation and a new way of life, a new society, an alterna-
> tive society.

In contrast with the kind of career-mindedness that appears to be so typical of man in modern society, where life seems programmed along a pre-ordained pattern of childhood, college, work, promotion, retirement and death, few of the communitarians interviewed could provide me with a map of their future life. The most typical response was couched in the general terms of fulfilling oneself through life, of discovering oneself, and thereby leaving the world a better place for ensuing generations, this being accompanied by a greater or lesser degree of reluctance to label themselves in any way as belonging to this or that category of social actor, other than that of individual.

Human nature

At the root of many philosophies of life or interpretations of the world, if one digs deep enough, one frequently discovers certain basic assumptions about human nature—whether man is naturally good, bad, creative, submissive, greedy, selfish, aggressive and so on. On the foundations of these often implicitly held assumptions is built a large part of the individual's world view, about the necessity and desirability of certain institutional structures such as modes of government, systems of reward and punishment, established pat- terns of social intercourse and so forth. For instance, if one believes that man is naturally aggressive, greedy, selfish and acquisitive, then a belief in the necessity of strong agencies of social control, firm political leadership, and intolerance of apparent deviance would seem to follow quite naturally. On the other hand, if one believes that man is naturally good, generous, co-operative, loving, creative and kind, then a belief in the value of individual autonomy, the evil of strong centralized government and repressive institutions in general would seem to follow quite as naturally. Anyone who has ever tried to argue, without success, the case for, say, British nuclear disarmament, or the case against corporal punishment or hanging, with someone of the opposite persuasion, will appreciate the point I am trying to make. Too often one realizes after many fruitless hours of argument that there exists no common ground on which one can argue. The basic assumptions about human nature, the purpose of life and so on which form the framework for the views held about specific issues are in conflict, and they are not generally susceptible to influence; for if one's basic assumptions are threatened, so is the remainder of one's interpretation of the world, one's ability to make sense of the world is placed in question.

It was therefore one of my self-imposed tasks to enquire into the feelings the communitarians held about human nature, in the belief that once one had got to these roots, much else would be more readily understandable.[4]

As might have been expected from libertarians and anarchists, the typical communitarian revealed a basic faith in humanity, in man's natural goodness and innate creative potential. On a number of occasions I was informed that every man was an artist. Others were rather less idealistic, but only marginally so.

> I have a basic faith in humanity. I believe people are basically good. They are often irrational—they have psychological and sexual hang-ups and bread hang-ups—but basically they are O.K. If you treat a person as he would like to be treated and in a genuine way, that's how it should be.

Others, however, were prepared to make generalizations at one level, but were prepared to recognize that, while some individuals might be good, others were evil. Thus, 'I think basically everyone is just a bit frightened. This is why it is important to communicate, because once you have overcome that you can get down to where somebody is good or evil.' Generally speaking, the younger the respondent, the more likely he was to believe that man was basically good. Older respondents tended to refrain from making such generalizations, and tended to be cynical of the idealism of the younger communitarians. The typical response from such people was, 'You can trust some people, there are others you can't. I don't like to generalize about human nature.'

At the same time, there was often revealed in discussion with such communitarians the nature of the painful clash between the ideal and reality that had caused them to water down their assumptions. Thus:

I feel that I would like to trust everyone, and feel that I should always give people the benefit of the doubt without having to consider whether I can trust them or not. But I am afraid bitter experience is teaching us that we must not trust people too readily because people have proved themselves very ready to take advantage of any openness we might have towards them . . . we are now a little more discerning in accepting people as readily as we have done in the past.

This contrast between the younger idealists and the slightly older realists was revealed in the admission procedures to different communes. At Eel Pie where the 'every man is an artist' view prevailed, anyone was admitted who could find a room—in fact no one was admitted as such. They just started to live there and join in the activities. This procedure contrasted very strongly with the detailed admission procedure demanded by other communes. For instance:[5]

Visit first for a few weeks to explore the scope of mutual fulfilment in each other's companionship and all the aspects of personality which can't be adequately covered by writing. After this, for our part, we would decide by a two thirds agreement whether to offer a year's trial membership. This would be a year of full participation, but without any commitment either way. At the end of the year, we would decide again by a two thirds agreement whether to offer full membership. After this, our assets and yours' would gradually over a period of four years be brought to a state of equality, and in everything else, our commitment would immediately become mutual and complete. Our decision on acceptance will be based entirely on consideration of economic feasibility and compatibility. You must be able to contribute at least £4 a week to the community's income, whether from investments, or from earnings outside the commune, or by increasing income from the farm by investment of capital and work. Our criteria of compatibility are a very radical mind, a fair degree of sensitivity or introversion, reasonable intelligence and sympathy with our ethos.

Thus, while it is once more difficult to generalize, the theme that emerges on this issue is that at root man is basically good, but has been estranged from his essential goodness by the society in which he lives.

Straight society: the grey world

The key to most forms of radical social action is felt estrangement from the prevailing social order on the part of the individual, and a determination to do something about it to bring reality into closer approximation with the ideal. The form of action chosen provides some indication of those particular aspects of the status quo from which the radical feels estranged. On this basis, one would expect those who are prepared to go to the lengths of dropping out of the conventional world in order to create an alternative to be estranged not merely from what they define as specific and limited abuses, but from the society as a whole, its values and institutional patterns in general. In like manner, one would expect those radicals who felt relatively deprived with regard to the unequal distribution of economic wealth and reward in society to concentrate their activities within the realms of the trade union and the 'conventional' revolutionary channels of the Communist Party and the left-wing socialist parties. One would not expect them to drop out and thereby almost inevitably deprive themselves of some of the standard fruits of the 'system'. In the light of this kind of reasoning it is interesting to note that, in response to questions about the nature of their felt estrangement from conventional society, virtually no communitarian mentioned such issues as the distribution of wealth and income in society. Their condemnation of society was more concerned with an attack on the values that they saw as underpinning all areas of life, and their personal 'hang-ups' were concerned with what they saw as the resulting quality of individual life in the grey world. The features of life that the communitarians viewed as particularly unbearable centred on such things as the competitive nature of conventional life, the rat-race, the isolation of individuals from each other, the meaninglessness of the routine of life, the lack of individual autonomy, the sense of powerlessness, the dehumanizing effects of trying to live a human life in a capitalistic and technological world.

Some communitarians included just about everything in their rejection of the conventional world: 'the emphasis on authority, punishment, morality, guilt, shame, efficiency, perverted sexuality, poverty, advertising, big business, capitalism, royalty, legality, etc., etc.' Others referred to the values that they saw as typifying the conventional social order and with which they felt no sympathy: 'pretentiousness, materialism, and lost values which even, to a degree, could have been lost for thousands of years'. For some, the meaningless routine of daily life was what struck them as the most unbearable aspect of life outside.

It is very difficult to pin down. It is this thing of getting up at

7–8 o'clock in a morning and toddling off to work and coming
back in the evening, and just you and the wife sitting and
watching t.v., and you do the same the next day and the next
day. . . . God I wouldn't like that.

For others, it was the competitive rat-race as they saw it. 'The whole
competitive bit—everyone is trying to get one up on everyone else.
People are anti-people. Most of them hate each other. They rush
about—it's just mad, it's insane.' And, again: 'I hate the rat-race, the
feeling that you have got to trample everyone else down in order to
get on. I don't think it is worth it. I would rather not get on if you
have got to do that.'

For others, life in the conventional world was just seen as a
pointless and meaningless exercise, a tragic waste of human potential
and ability.

It's all so bloody pointless. People largely spend their lives
doing a job they don't particularly enjoy. All the wives are at
work. The whole system stinks. They all live in these little
boxes. They have another little box on wheels for Sundays. They
are just not using their abilities. And there's the bloody t.v.—
that's another box. And the women go to bingo—I think I'm
going mad.

For others, while rejecting what they saw as the dominant values of
the society as a whole, they singled out specific features as being
particularly unbearable or intolerable. For instance, the way life
appeared to be ruled by the clock was particularly intolerable for
certain freedom-seekers.

It's the time thing. Get up at this time, go to work at this time
and so on. It's the 'when' you have to do your work rather than
work itself. Also there is the authority thing that you notice in
the cities—policemen all the time searching you . . . the attitudes, the status symbols, the ridiculous morality, all this
falseness and pretence. The whole load of values have got
screwed up.

Here, it was the felt powerlessness of the individual in the face of
inhuman and human agencies of control that struck the respondent
as being especially hateful. For others, particularly the security-
seekers, it was the isolation of the individual in a mass society,
combined with the powerlessness of the individual. 'It's all the
fragmentation, with people split up into their tiny home groups, with
most people working for some capitalist employer with not much
autonomy, and they can't make decisions about what they do with
their life.' And underlying most responses was the feeling that life in

the straight society was not a life fit for human consumption, but one fit only for machines which is what they saw it turning people into.

> Capitalism generally destroys the souls of people—turns them into machines, even though people themselves are not aware of this fate. At school they are conditioned to accept authority, they leave school and are conditioned to the fact that they have to find a job. They are conditioned to thinking that they must get married and settle down and buy a house, and once they have settled down and bought their house they are trapped for the rest of their lives. Capitalism has got another cog to its machine. Everyone seems to fall into this rut—I fell into it.

Man in society

If life in the straight society is so worthless, meaningless, inhuman and repressive, then one is naturally led to ask why people tolerate such conditions, or are they forced to tolerate them against their inclinations? The answers provided by the communitarians to this enquiry varied between those who emphasized the degree to which people in society were conditioned by such agencies as the mass media to accept the world as it is, and those who emphasized the role of the individual himself in conditioning himself to accept his lot in the world. For the typical commune member, man in society accepts society as it is because he is not aware of any alternative way that collective and individual life could be ordered. He is blinkered, only able to see what is, without being able to envisage anything that might be. For some, this lack of awareness was seen as a consequence of individuals' own actions. They have conditioned themselves. 'I think they have conditioned themselves more than they have been conditioned. They insulate themselves, their minds, and they chop off chunks of their minds and they lose some of their feelers.' Others saw this acceptance of the status quo as being a consequence of a conditioning process to which the individual is subjected:

> Brainwashing is important—the media of the straight press, t.v., and the pop business that keep people, they just recreate the same things without much change. . . . How many people get the chance to form their own opinions. They live largely on a diet of the *Daily Mirror*, *News of the World*, and the *People*, Radio 1 and Coronation Street—this is taking it at its worst.

Others rejected such a 'conspiracy' theory of the mass media, and just emphasized the fact that, while certain individuals might desire to opt out of or change their mode of life, they can conceive of no alternative, no relevant mode of action.

I don't know if people in straight society are reasonably content. If they are they are probably not being honest with themselves. I think in a lot of cases, like with the young, they do not see any way out. They cannot conceive of anything different. Maybe this is something we can do, give an example, show that there is one way out. . . . The mass media, advertising and consumption have a pretty good hold on people, so much that they have to work for the next week's wages rather than think.

Whether man is conditioned by outside agencies or whether he conditions himself to accept his lot in life, what does emerge is that, for the communitarians, most people are tied to the prevailing system not so much by the chains and coercive power of some ruling élite, but are rather willing victims who are enchained by their own lack of awareness. They are prisoners of their restricted mode of perceiving social reality and of their place in that reality. People play the game of life because it is the only game they know.

How then do the communitarians explain the fact that they themselves have managed to break out of the taken-for-granted view of the world? How have they managed to break the chains that tie people to the system? What makes them different from the majority of people?

What made the communitarians different from normal people, in their own eyes, was frequently a determination to live a life that was seen as being in accord with one's true self.

I try to be truthful. I believe in myself—I cannot live a lie. I cannot be someone I am not. I have got to be myself. I would like to think that I am real.

Others emphasized the fact that the only difference between themselves and others leading more conventional lives was that they 'want something more out of life than to work for someone else from nine to five and live in a little house and have to slog to exist'. For others the difference lay in their refusal to settle for less than their ideal. 'Many people have had the spark of life extinguished. Many settle for less than their ideal. I am one who is willing to take risks for the sake of my ideal.' Other communitarians saw the difference between themselves and the 'straights' as being more specific. For instance, 'One thing, being schizoid—it's so lousy out there that there is more to push one from behind. Another thing, we had more resources than others.' For others, the difference was due to the fact that their awareness had developed to a far greater degree than with others.

I don't know. Perhaps a lot of it has been mental illness—in a

237

way, that shook me up a lot. The fact that I've read a lot, and
started to look around me. . . . I began to read about the
American hippies and that—the whole principle of dropping
out—and I began to think 'if you can't beat them, drop out'.
This is my political thinking at the moment. Set up an alternative society. We cannot change capitalism as such by orthodox
means, by parliamentary elections, because we would only elect
another capitalist government. All you can do is drop out
completely and set up an alternative society and hope you can
make it sufficiently attractive to draw people away from
capitalism.

The ideal type drop-out one frequently tends to imagine is one
who has 'turned on, tuned in, and dropped out'. In fact, only a very
limited number of communitarians with whom I came into contact
talked of their drug experience as some sort of conversion experience which had, like a miracle, removed the blinkers from their
eyes and allowed the sun to shine in for the first time. More often
than not, where the communitarian had used drugs, the experience
had enabled them to 'see' far more clearly what they could already
perceive unaided. For the majority, the views they held and their
stance *vis-à-vis* straight society were natural. The problem was not
one of explaining why they viewed the world in a different light from
the rest of society, but more a question of why the rest of society
did not view the world in the way that they, the communitarians,
saw it. They were the sane ones, it was the rest of society who were
insane. How, then, do the drop-outs envisage a sane society?

The alternative society

For an individual to feel aggrieved with his lot in society, he must
possess some conception of what his lot in life ought to be. He must
perceive some gap between the 'is' and the 'ought'. Similarly, one
would expect those who have rejected and dropped out of the
existing social order to possess some conception of an alternative
social order, an ideal or utopia from which a critical stance towards
the status quo may be taken. What does the utopia of the communitarians look like? What is the nature of their alternative society?
   Anarchists and libertarians in general have traditionally refused
to concern themselves with mapping out blueprints of the future
society, in the belief that any detailed scheme drawn up in the 'now'
would merely recreate another repressive framework that would
determine the nature of the society to be created at some unspecified
time in the future under changed social conditions. Such an exercise
would involve a direct contradiction of the belief in the desirability

of the autonomy of the individual to shape and control his own life free from the dictates of any master, human or inhuman. Given the libertarian tradition that the present-day communitarians have inherited, some more consciously than others, it is not surprising that very few of them are prepared to provide anything like a blueprint of the alternative society that they hold as their goal. The nearest one gets to such a map is the federation of autonomous communes that is the articulated goal of the Commune Movement. As one ex-secretary of the movement expressed it to me:

> I do have a vision. A federation of communes, each one autonomous, as big as you like. Everyone doing just what they like, taking into account what others want. Trade between communes on the basis of need. Everybody caring about everybody else. So much interaction that if you damage anyone else you automatically damage yourself.

In this brief statement of aim, however, can be found the two key components of the alternative society as envisaged by the communitarians: the presence on the one hand of individual freedom and autonomy and, on the other, co-operation and mutual interdependence between individuals and groups. The values of individual freedom and co-operation between a brotherhood of men are the recurring themes in the utopian visions of the communitarians. This should come as no surprise, as we have already discussed how, in their critiques of the existing order, they make special reference to the lack of individual autonomy, the competitive nature of the rat-race life, and the social isolation of the individual in the mass society.

A look at some of the responses I obtained in reply to my probing about the nature of the image of the alternative society will serve to clarify the nature of these counter-values on which the new social order is to be based. First of all, the value of individual freedom: 'My aim is a society in which each individual can have the right and the space to exercise their creative autonomy.' From another respondent:

> Alternative society? I would define it as a society in which the alternative is always open. Present society is monolithic. I regard the alternative society as one where, if you don't like where you are, there are always a few choices available, and there aren't any barriers in between like forfeitable pensions or houses to sell. Freedom of choice is the prime criterion. Do what you like and it made easy to do what you like.

Other respondents emphasized their ideal of a society made up of individuals co-operating together, sharing and caring for each other.

239

For instance: 'To me the alternative society means people caring about one another and sharing. Straight society is all competing and thinking only about themselves.' Or, from someone with a similar ideal: 'My ideal is people working for each other and not for the slave money.' At the same time, these twin values were seen by many respondents as inextricably linked together, the attainment of one dependent on the attainment of the other. As one communitarian phrased it:

> If I used the words of the Bible, I am looking for the society in which the Brotherhood of Man is realized. It sounds very religious and idealistic, but I don't feel that there is anything short of that that can work. I can visualise various philosophies holding sway for a number of years, but the true society can only come about when man realises himself and realises other people in the true context. The Brotherhood of Man is the only society that I can visualise this working.

Traces of this Christian millennial tradition can be found in the response of another communitarian who, when asked of his ideal social order, referred to a rural, yet automated, arcadia consisting of self-sufficient communes, where man could regain his sanity:

> My vision? Blake's Jerusalem—'and did the Lamb of God walk on those green and pleasant hills'. Get away from the towns and cities and the false environment man has created on this planet. It is destroying mentally the human race . . . a federation of self-supporting communes . . . the profit motive removed so that people only produce things necessary for them. You could produce a car that would last a lifetime, the same with radios and t.v.'s. . . . Small communities producing just what they need. . . . Automation to reduce the drudgery of menial labour. I think anything is possible—the human mind is unlimited.

Other communitarians are even more millennial in their approach. 'You have visions so that you can see what is going to happen. But it is no use planning it because then you distort it, it is all happening. In about two years London is going to be the New Jerusalem.'

This apparent faith in the ability of man to shape the world to his wishes leads naturally enough to a consideration of how the communitarians propose to bridge the gap between the 'is' and the 'ought', between the present and the new social order, the straight and the alternative society. Before going on to consider this area of their world view, however, I think it is pertinent to enquire whether man, according to the communitarians, has a future to mould to his wishes or not.

The future of mankind

A number of writers have referred to the 'bomb culture' of the modern generation and the fact that much about the modern youth can be rendered intelligible when one takes into account the fact that many of them feel that man has no future and that life as we now know it on this planet is doomed to extinction.[7] One would expect it to be the case that, where a person anticipates the end of the world in the very near future, while he might well spend his remaining time on earth either preparing to meet his Maker or going on some marathon orgy, he would not entertain many long-term career-type plans concerning his life on earth. On the other hand, where a person feels that he can reasonably expect to live out a normal life span on earth, one would expect that person to be more concerned with mapping out his life project, planning his career through life. On this basis, one would expect the communitarians, who revealed an antipathy to future planning, to have revealed a certain amount of doubt as to whether man had much of a future on earth. In fact, what one does find is a certain degree of apparent contradiction in the views of the communitarians on this issue, a contradiction of which many of them were aware. On the one hand, many of them felt that man was heading along a suicidal path towards self-destruction, and at the same time they felt that man could avoid this end if he chose to do so. Most communitarians described themselves as being pessimistic about man's future survival on this planet if he continued along present paths, but at the same time their basic faith in humanity caused them to recognize the fact that this fate was not inevitable but could be avoided if man wished to avoid self-destruction.

Most of the respondents with whom I raised this issue saw ecological catastrophe as the major threat to man's existence. Pollution and overpopulation were the recurring themes. They appeared to many as a far greater threat than the possibility of nuclear warfare. Some of the responses to questions about whether people were optimistic or pessimistic about man's future survival will serve to illustrate some of these points.

One instance of the kinds of mixed feelings and emotions held by certain communitarians about the future is provided by the following quote from a young tripper living in a rural commune:

> I am optimistic about man's future but pessimistic about his
> survival. It is an emotional sort of thing. I am optimistic
> because there are incredible things happening and opening out—
> an explosion of world unity, of world youth. But on the other
> hand we could start a war within the next three weeks.

A slightly more fatalistic view of the future, yet one combined with a certain optimism about the personal future is instanced by the following response from an artist:

I am quite fatalistic about the more distant future. I feel somehow that we don't have very much time left to work out our ideas. I feel that so much of the power and destiny of the world is in the hands of people who will misuse and abuse their authority—so I just feel that the world will be destroyed before very long. We don't have much time left . . . but I don't feel too pessimistic when I think that it is up to us to do what we can with the time that's left . . . time is very short so we must get going and do what we feel within ourselves is the right way to live.

Or, again, a novel variation from a tripper:

I have a feeling that the Third World War is going to come. But I also feel that Phoenix is bound to rise from the ashes. At the same time, it wouldn't be a bad thing if it meant everyone fighting together, it would provide a sense of community and a strength of feeling.

I failed to find anyone else who was prepared to echo the feelings displayed in this last statement. The most common view of the future was of reluctant pessimism, the view that man was heading for disaster and that unfortunately there did not appear to be much to stop him polluting the atmosphere, overpopulating the surface of the planet and so on. 'I am a bit pessimistic. We seem to be messing it up. Pollution and overpopulation are the big problems.' Whereas many were a 'bit pessimistic', a number appeared to have virtually given up all hope concerning man's survival.[8] Here the crucial point appeared to be the recognition of the external threats to man such as nuclear weapons and pollution, coupled with a belief that man had proven himself incapable of living at peace and in co-operation with his neighbour. While the majority had a basic faith in humanity that helped to counter their pessimism about the future, for the most pessimistic this support was missing. For these people man is set upon the path to self-destruction and nothing is going to dislodge him from that path. For example, 'The future? Suicidal, frankly. This is not purely intuitive. . . . The realities of pollution, greed, the complete lack of co-ordination between people.' In similar vein:

If present trends continue the future is going to be disastrous, and I don't think anything is going to happen to change the trends: the isolation of people, the lack of concern or identification with the tragedies of Biafra, Vietnam, and the bomb.

And the ecological thing . . . and people not learning to live with one another.

Despite this almost universal pessimism, of which the last two respondents quoted were extreme illustrations, some of the communitarians were reasonably optimistic about the future. There was a feeling that man had learnt to live with the bomb, and that it was the bomb that represented the most immediate threat to man's survival. There was a recognition of the threats of ecological catastrophe and so on, but a feeling that man would come to his sense in time to avoid the threats from this area. One person who expressed this sort of view to me was, significantly, one who had arrived at the commune movement after a number of years' involvement with the peace movement, a privatized radical. His political development had been significantly influenced by the dropping of the atomic bombs on Hiroshima and Nagasaki. 'I am reasonably optimistic. . . . I don't feel that man will necessarily destroy himself. The bomb would have happened by now if it was going to, over the Berlin and Cuban crises. We have progressed a bit since 1945.' However, such optimism was rare. The most common interpretation of the future was one of pessimism when certain current trends were examined rationally, accompanied by a certain optimism when the communitarians' intuitive faith in humanity asserted itself. It might now be pertinent to enquire as to the extent to which communitarians viewed man as controlling the course of future events.

Man as an actor on the stage of history

It can be argued that, for a person to become a radical activist of any sort, rather than merely a curdled idealist, he must not only feel estranged from the existing order of things but must also see the possibility of influencing the future course of events and thereby see a close link between his own personal fate and the life of the wider collectivity in general. To use the language of an earlier chapter, the radical activist is generally one who is estranged from the existing social order and yet is not alienated, in the sense that he does not see life as being determined by impersonal forces beyond human control. On the basis of this kind of reasoning one would expect the communitarians as radicals to reject the view that the stage of history and social change is inhabited by forces beyond the control of the individual, and firmly believe that the individual, in concert with others, can significantly alter the course of future events. This, in fact, was the view most commonly held. It was stated most straightforwardly by the respondent who pointed out, 'I wouldn't be in the Commune Movement if I didn't think there was something I could

243

do to influence the course of future events'. For people such as this the issue was plain and simple: man makes his own history. Others recognized the fact that the individual alone can achieve little, but in concert with others the individual can alter the course of history.

For others, however, the issue was by no means as simple as this. While they recognized that man made his own history, they also recognized the essentially dialectical relationship that existed between man and society—a relationship which they found very difficult to express, as instanced by the following quotation.

> I think we are in control of events, and yet at the same time once we set things into motion certain things are bound to happen—and yet, at the same time they are not inevitable. It is very Buddhist this contradiction, which is very difficult to explain—like I feel that the way things are going world war is inevitable, but if we set about it now it can be averted.

This dialectical view of things was echoed by other respondents, particularly another 'ex-peacenik', veteran of the Aldermaston marches and sit-downs, a privatized radical.

> I feel we could alter the course of future events. For example, if all the people who had marched to Aldermaston had sat down outside the plant we could have got rid of the H-bomb, the same with Porton, Westminster and the whole government structure. If people want something enough they can—it just depends how badly they want it. But also I think there are powers that in effect are impersonal and uncontrollable—the international finance thing for instance. Wilson is meant to be in power, in effect he is under the control of the Swiss and the Americans. He is not controlling it and we are not and I don't know who is in charge.

Despite the obvious confusion felt by many individual communitarians on this issue, the most typical interpretation of the relationship between man and social change, naturally enough, was that men can alter the course of history and future events once they realize their potential and get together. Let us now look at how the communitarians propose to set about the business of social change.

The efficacy of conventional means of influence: the vote and the lobby

Given the range of people involved in the variety of experiments that together constitute the commune movement in Britain today, one would expect them to display a similar variety of orientations towards the different means of social change available. Despite this, one of the most significant shared orientations was that held concerning the utility of the conventional means of political articulation: the vote and the lobby. Almost without exception, one found a dismissal of parliamentary politics as either irrelevant, immoral, or just simply ineffective. The prevalence of this attitude among certain types of communitarians has been dealt with in the previous chapter. Therefore it will be sufficient to summarize briefly the range of attitudes.

The most typical attitude held by the trippers was that voting in particular and politics in general were both totally irrelevant. The extreme version of this view was expressed to me by one occupant at Eel Pie Island. 'Politics? One gets literally above that sort of thing. The real us is the soul above. We are real when we close our eyes. One's body is merely a mask. One must try to overcome the ego and egoism—that is the goal.' The disillusionment of the typical artist was expressed particularly poignantly to me by one respondent.

No, I wouldn't become a member of a political party. It is a question of the sort of people one associates politicians and would-be politicians to be—they are looking for power for themselves, no matter how idealistic they are to begin with. The ideals collapse and they become part of a machine in order to maintain their position . . . we listen to the radio from time to time which we usually find very depressing. We find it increasingly depressing and listen less to the news of world events. Everything is so distorted and out of proportion. For instance, the Biafran War—there are arguments about who should and who should not give aid to a population that is starving, and the oil companies have a vested interest in the war. This sort of thing is so repugnant that one raises one's hands in resignation and says: 'if that's the way it's going to be, then there's nothing I can do to stop it.'

Amongst the privatized radicals one found a similar disillusionment and resignation, a resignation which was an almost direct contradiction to their stated belief that man could influence the course of events. However, the human actor who is logically consistent in his views and interpretations of the world is a rare being. The typical privatized radical's view was adequately expressed by one of the 'ex-peaceniks'.

I have never believed in the Labour Party. . . . I wouldn't vote. It would be a bit like choosing between Daz and Omo. There is very little difference between them. . . . I take less and less interest in current affairs as time goes on. I find it boring. I subscribe to *Freedom*, *Anarchy*, *Resurgence* and *Peace News* but it seems so unimportant. The same things keep happening. Like

245

everyone else I suppose, I get on with my own life and let them get on with it, except my life is supposed to be an alternative whereas other people might not think their's is.

Amongst the security-seeking communitarians, one found a similar disillusionment with parliamentary politics and a felt powerlessness when faced with the size and complexity of modern society. One sensed, however, that the disillusionment was more with the personnel of the particular parliamentary parties and their policies rather than with the parliamentary system as such.

I did canvass for Labour once but I wouldn't do it again. I would probably still vote for them, but there is only such a slight difference that I wouldn't go to too much effort. . . . I am only slightly interested in affairs because they seem so vast and one has so little control over them that it seems irrelevant getting interested in them—there are 50 million people out there. I was a member of Labour a couple of years ago . . . my membership ran out. In Wales there is not just Labour and Conservative, there is the Plaid as well. I don't know whether it is justified to be disillusioned with Labour because I don't know what they are up against. I am disillusioned insofar as they have not brought about a socialist state.

With regard to the activist communitarians, those involved in urban projects for the purpose of exercising a direct and revolutionary impact on the wider local community, there emerged a distinction in attitudes towards parliamentary politics and the use of the vote as a means of influence. The distinction occurred between those who tended to identify themselves as anarcho-pacifists and those who saw themselves as revolutionary socialists rather than revolutionary anarchists. The anarchists tended to place more emphasis on change through exemplary action than did the revolutionary socialists, and tended to reject the vote as a means of influence far more readily. As one respondent expressed it, 'Voting has no relation to the true distribution of power in society, and merely serves to generate the illusions of democracy'.

This respondent laughed at the mention of the issue of voting, whereas a group of revolutionary socialists in an urban commune took the issue far more seriously, explaining to me how most of them had voted in the 1970 election for their local Labour Party candidate, although, they explained, it was not because they thought anything would come of it. They voted more to keep the Conservatives out than to promote the Labour Party. The typical attitude of such communitarians would be one of, 'I would vote Labour. I don't imagine it achieves much but it is better than doing nothing.'

Thus the picture that emerged was one of extreme disillusionment with parliamentary politics, and even where communitarians considered voting, it was for the negative reasons of trying to keep the Conservative Party out of office rather than for the positive reasons of trying to promote the cause of the Labour Party. It is worth while pointing out that, while many of the younger trippers have never involved themselves with political action, many of the older communitarians have been political animals in the past. Their disillusionment with parliamentary politics has grown over the years, and especially with the perceived failure of the 1964–70 Labour government to implement any radical policies. It was this disillusionment, coupled with the specific issue of the war in Vietnam, that gave rise to the mass demonstrations in the 1960s throughout the world against the American war in South-east Asia. It was felt at that time by many participants on the marches and demonstrations that such methods were the only means available to the people to express their opinions and influence the decision-makers. How do the communitarians tend to see demonstrations as a means of interest articulation and social change?

Demonstrations as a means of change and influence

A typical response that I received to my questions about attitudes towards demonstrations was, 'Yes, they have a part to play, but only a very limited one. In some ways they can be counter-productive. It depends on the sort of demonstration'. For some, demonstrations were 'the only way left to radicals to express their views', a view echoed by another respondent who felt that 'they do express a viewpoint, but rarely seem to have much effect'. For other communitarians, the importance of demonstrations lay not so much in the influence they exerted upon decision-makers as in the influence they had on the actual participants themselves. 'At least they bring together people who feel the same way. It strengthens you. You are not alone.'

For those typically involved in the urban activist communes the utility of demonstrations was seen as limited to those concerned with local and specific issues. There was the feeling that

the casual wander around London does not achieve anything, neither does a confrontation with the police when they will always have superior forces and manage to make it appear as if the demonstrators are the aggressors. We still go on demonstrations but these are more local and more specific.

This view was echoed by those who viewed demonstrations as safety valves for the Establishment rather than as important means of

I

radical political action. 'I don't think they achieve very much, I think they are just a safety valve for the Establishment. They can show how "democratic" they are by allowing people to go on demonstrations.'

For the majority of communitarians of all types, however, demonstrating, like voting, was seen as an irrelevant, fruitless and ineffectual pastime. To anticipate a later section of this chapter, they felt that the important sphere of radical action was not in a crowd marching through the city streets seeking to create a conflict situation with the police and thereby reveal the essentially repressive nature of the state and its agents. For them, the important sphere of radical action takes place within one's own head and in one's relationships with others. This was a recurring theme throughout the commune movement in general, and was expressed to me on a number of occasions with specific reference to the issue of demonstrations. Some of these are presented below. Each one presents this common theme, although in different words.

Basically, I don't think you can achieve anything through party politics or demonstrations. You have to start with the kids in the family. This is where it ends up and where it must begin if you want to radically change society.

Personally, I've no time for demonstrating now. They are at this present time only fanning the flame of discontent. We should really be looking inwards towards our social relationships with each other.

I do not like demonstrations because when they are over people feel good not so much through what they have achieved, but because of the actual experience of demonstrating. And the demonstration is a conflict situation—who is to say who is right or wrong? Each must find his own truth, not force others to see one's point.

Revolutionary violence and non-violence

This notion that each must find his own truth is an approach to life and conflict typical of the pacifist believer in non-violence. The belief that no one possesses the sacred hold over the truth and hence one should not attempt to force others to see the world from one's own particular viewpoint, logically implies a rejection of the use of coercion in general and violence in particular as a means of attaining one's end. Given this orientation, one would expect the communitarians to be attracted to the idea of non-violence as a revolutionary

248

means, to reject the use of violence as a means of radical social change, and to define themselves as pacifists. Certainly, the community experiments of previous ages have almost without exception been associated with strategies for non-violent radical change. Communes have traditionally been viewed by pacifists as the moral equivalent to war, as living witnesses of the nature of the non-violent and non-exploitative society to which the radical pacifist aspires.

Certainly, of the communitarians with whom I raised this issue, all but a few considered themselves to be pacifists, rejecting the use of violence as a means of revolutionary change. For many, this was an apparently simple and straightforward issue over which they had thought, come to their pacifist position, and were now firmly convinced of its essential correctness. Such respondents almost embraced the label of pacifist, for them being a pacifist was an important part of their identity as a radical actor on the social scene. Such people were not confined to any particular type of communitarian. Perhaps typical of this position was that expressed to me by one respondent who claimed:

> I am opposed to the use of violence against persons in any form. Yes, I would call myself a pacifist—I don't think I could inflict harm on others or use any type of physical force on any human being. I don't think good can ever come from the use of violent means.

For other communitarians, however, the issue was not so simple. A number were obviously intensely concerned with this issue and with the problem of trying to work out their own personal position. Typically, such people were the younger members of the commune movement especially the trippers whose ideas were still in the process of formation, and who were still searching for their true identity. For instance:

> A pacifist? In theory, yes. I believe very much in the need for peace, both on a world scale and on a personal one. But then I keep catching myself out in practice thinking very non-pacifist thoughts. I feel it would be very difficult to find the absolute pacifist position. At the moment this is the big thing, trying to find out what I am and where I stand with regard to pacifism.
>   Violence and social change? I used to think so but now I tend not to. You can achieve a goal through violent means but not satisfactorily, it can achieve what you want but if it is bred out of violence it will not be what it should be.

For others the issue was also a complex one over which they found it difficult to express their position. The main problem seemed to occur not so much over the issue of whether violence was good or bad. I met no one who was prepared to claim that the use of violence as a means was good in itself, in some Fanon-type analysis. The problem was that, while they were opposed to the use of violence for its own sake, when they looked at events in the 'Third World' of Africa, Asia and Latin America they felt forced to arrive at the conclusion that good can come from the use of violence. This problem was expressed to me particularly clearly by one respondent who had for many years considered himself to be a pacifist.

> I have given a great deal of thought to the question of violence as a means of change. At the interpersonal level, my own experience with my son, when violence brought the conflict between us out into the open, made me realise the therapeutic effect of violence at this level. As a means of social change, however, I am against it insofar as the end achieved by violence is never what you wanted to achieve in the first place. On the other hand, I have a great admiration for China and North Korea, and what would you do if you lived in Vietnam?

Another respondent, a privatized radical, was even more confused, particularly with regard to this issue of violence and the liberation movements of the Third World.

> I don't believe in non-violence, I might have done once. I am not sure. I don't know what the term means anymore. I am very mixed up. It is an awful thing but good can come from violent means—look at Cuba—it's a relative good but what did they have before?

In so far as such a position was typical of the confusion felt by a number of communitarians, it revealed a basic attraction to the pacifist's non-violent position, as held by the majority of individuals in the commune movement, but at the same time it revealed the painful realization that, on occasions, violence appeared to be a far more efficient means of attaining one's revolutionary goal than non-violence. It is true that by the generally accepted criteria, Castro's Cuba is a more humane and egalitarian society than was Batista's regime. This, of course, is the key problem that has traditionally faced radical pacifists—the problem of whether, to put it crudely, there are occasions when one's radicalism must be placed before one's pacifism. There is always the undoubted attraction of the apparent ease and speed with which the use of violence can attain its immediate and short-term radical goals. Apart from pointing to the tragedy of Vietnam, the pacifist reply to this is that[9]

All violence tends to be 'reactionary', whatever may be the

avowed objectives of those who employ it. While in the long run, the effects of violence can no doubt be counteracted in some measure, it always leaves scars: and such progress as is made in the direction of an egalitarian society is always achieved primarily despite violence and not because of it.

Let us look at the strategy envisaged by the communitarians as leading towards the alternative society.

Revolutionary change

Almost without exception members of communes saw social change as being brought about through the medium of individual and inter-personal change. The alternative society of the future must be lived by the individual in the 'here and now'. Through living an exemplary life characterized by the values of love and honesty, and the estab-lishment of genuine co-operative relationships with others, the individual makes his own revolution and influences others to make their own, so that eventually the entire social structure will be radically changed. As one respondent, a tripper, phrased it:

> You are changing society everyday as you live your life. . . .
> I used to have long debates with marxist friends about changing people or the system, and which came first. I used to think they were complementary but I now know that by living and acting the way I do I influence people, and if they in turn influence others, then it spreads.

Such a philosophy of change follows naturally from the belief shared by the majority of communitarians that man makes his own history, and that the majority of 'straights' are tied to the prevailing order of things not by the coercive force of the state, but by their own lack of awareness of any meaningful alternative to the present system. A view shared by many was expressed by one member: 'I don't see the proletariat rising up and throwing off their chains, because half the time they are very tightly holding the chains on.' The present social order is maintained by the fact that the majority of its members take it for granted as the natural order of things, and significant social change will not occur until the members of society start to question that which they have traditionally taken for granted. The important task, for the communitarians, thus becomes one of making people more aware, of expanding their consciousness, of getting them to question the nature of their individual lives and the society in which such lives are led. Moreover, given the liber-tarian nature of the communitarians and their belief that each one must find his own truth, such a task cannot be achieved through the

251

use of coercive means. Such a strategy would be self-defeating, in so far as it would merely involve the replacement of one alienating order by another. One cannot force people to be free. One cannot force people to reshape their own lives to fit their ideal. Rather, one must strive to get them to do it for themselves. The issue that many saw themselves as facing was expressed by one member in particular: 'People have got to be made conscious and take over their own lives. No one can make anyone's revolution for them, because if they don't want revolution it won't be a revolution for them.'

So the question for many has become one of how to get people to reshape their own lives. For them it was no use just preaching the word at people, and continuing to live a normal exploitative mode of existence within the capitalist system. One must live the new, non-exploitative, non-violent life now, so that one's life might be an example for others. An example which can act as a model by which others can re-examine their own lives and, if they find them wanting by comparison, set about reshaping them to a closer approximation to their ideal. This was the task that many communitarians saw themselves as facing:

> I would like to help change society, but I think you have to do it by example. I don't think you can tell someone how they should feel. You can condition them but you need the media which are usually controlled by the government. So I think you have to do it by example. I think a few hundred living in Haight–Ashbury for a few months—they changed the world by example because they were different.

Or, as another respondent phrased it:

> I don't think you can remould society by taking it en bloc. But one can do so, I think, by setting up lots of little examples. If they are good people will follow them, if not and they don't— well, they don't deserve to be followed.

It was with this issue of changing society through example that communes were typically seen as having a part to play in the creation of the new social order.

Communes and social change

Even those activists who viewed their commune primarily as a 'red base', as a centre for direct action campaigns aimed at the wider community, emphasized the fact that the commune itself was also an important revolutionary force as a model institution which would cause others to question existing institutional forms and so contribute to the growth of a new social order. For those not so involved in such direct action campaigns on the urban scene, the revolutionary potential of the commune lay in their ability to demonstrate to others an alternative and more satisfying mode of life than the straight life, so causing others to question the nature of their personal existence.

> By living a different way of life, we can make some people sit up and think 'maybe there is another way of life, maybe we ought to change our way of life'. For one thing they are not setting out to exert some sort of influence, they are not preaching. They have changed things for themselves and that is enough. If people want to follow, that is fair enough.

This attitude of getting on with the task of living your own life and of the counter-productive effects of active propagandizing was echoed by other respondents. For instance:

> Sure, I suppose it is an escape in a way, but it is an escape to something, to an alternative. Communes can help to change society if they grow enough and get schools and link-ups with each other—the federation thing. Also, they will have more influence if they do not try hard to influence people by going around shouting 'this is *the* way to live, look at us how marvellous we are'. They will just operate through example.

Communes were likened to 'the seeds of a new age' growing up amidst the dying old one. At the same time this task was not seen as an easy one.

> Communes can influence society and social change, but it is going to be difficult because it involves a rejection of all that people have been conditioned to thinking—about there being only one way to live, which is governed by education, career, and money. I think a lot of people are going to feel threatened by the fact that there is another way of life which doesn't involve all these things. I feel that there is going to be a lot of hostility due to fear because people can be successful without all the things we have been taught are necessary to live by.

It was realized by many that men were rigid beings who would not willingly change their mode of living and way of looking at the world. This task was viewed as particularly difficult because the present society was seen by the communitarians as such a greedy and materialistic one, and what the communes had to offer was not a materialistic heaven. The communitarians tended to see the important problems of life as those concerned with questions of individual identity and self-fulfilment and the quality of human relationships, rather than questions of the quantity of material goods possessed by the individual. As one tripper expressed it:

> O.K. there are material problems, but there are other more important problems such as 'Who am I? What am I here for?' It is amazing how many people you would think thick do ask these questions—especially the young—but then they give up or become satisfied with cars and so on. But there are lots of people who are dissatisfied with the constraints placed on life in straight society. There are plenty on the fringe of straight society and they come and visit us and talk to us.

Or, from another respondent a similar view:

> A federated system of communes throughout the world, each helping each other, can eventually show the rest of the society that the important things in life are human contacts and not material possessions. This is the thing that communes can offer. If they work, with the people in them not worrying about material things, they will make people think, 'Why are they so happy? Maybe there is something in it.' Remove the profit motive and show people that we can work because we love each other and not because we want to make individual profits, then we might start to hasten the destruction of capitalism a bit.

At the same time, communes were not seen as working for the new age on their own. Rather, they were seen as working within the framework of increasing numbers of people rejecting the standards and values of conventional society. It was in the fact that this rejection involved a movement against a whole way of life rather than merely against a specific economic or political system that the strength of the movement was seen.

> Communes are the one great hope, not on their own but accompanied by a growing rejection of society by increasing numbers of people. Large numbers completely rejecting society. Not changing it as it stands or reforming it, but completely rejecting the values that society stands on. The whole moral structure questioned like marriage and religion, and not just a question of capitalism versus socialism. You begin to realise that you cannot separate politics from these things, and they are all part of the same thing. Perhaps where political thinkers of the past have come unstuck is in that they have tried to separate economic policy from the moral structure of society. They have been concerned solely with economic and political issues. You need to completely revolutionise people's whole

way of thinking and way of life, and point out to them that what they consider as cherished values are in fact a load of rubbish.

'The whole moral structure questioned like marriage and religion.' In what ways do the communitarians question these props of the social structure? The next chapter will be concerned with a consideration of the role of the nuclear family in modern society and the possibility of the growth of an alternative institutional structure on the basis of the extended family relationships of the commune. In concluding this chapter, which has been concerned with an analysis of the views held by the communitarians of this world, attention will be turned to their other world—the supra-empirical reality depicted in their religious beliefs.

The religious world of the communitarians

What was initially surprising to me during the course of my research was how many communitarians did possess some conception of another world. Very few were prepared to describe themselves as completely without any religious belief-system. At the same time, very few were members of the institutionalized churches such as the Church of England or the Church of Rome. The attitude held by most members of communes towards church-going religion was one of disgust and revulsion with what they saw as the hypocrisy of most clerics and churchgoers, and the betrayal of the teachings of Christ through the compromises made by the churches with the world. From this standpoint they could be described as true sectarians. This attitude was expressed by one respondent in the following terms:

> My attitude towards organised Christianity is largely revulsion.
> I am not an atheist. I am very fluid about religion . . . if you
> ask me what part religion should play in the life of society—
> it depends what you mean by religion. If you mean formalised
> Christianity, people going to church and so on—this should
> have very little part to play in life. But if you mean real
> genuine Christianity, what Jesus was talking about—co-opera-
> tion, sharing, love, concern, being the Good Samaritan—
> essentially pacifism—that is a good thing.

The communitarians who did consider themselves to be members of the institutionalized Church tended to belong to those communities that were more specifically concerned with direct social and political action within the urban environment, if they were not involved in such ascetic communes as were described in Chapter 6. In fact two of the members of an urban activist commune were members of the clergy, while one of the members of a similar venture was a lay preacher of the Methodist Church. For such people, firmly located within the ascetic tradition of Western Christianity, one's religious convictions were not something that one merely talked about, but were something that one lived and implemented in action. For them Christianity should be implemented through social action. The Church was without meaning unless it was socially relevant. It was in this orientation that the major source of their commitment to the idea and practice of community lay.

Just as, for these communitarians, their religious beliefs fell quite naturally into the ascetic tradition of the West, for many more their beliefs fell equally naturally into the mystical tradition of the East. For the members of one community, this mysticism was expressed through an interest in the old religion of paganism, which basically involved a love for and feeling of oneness with nature. In one respondent's words:

> Sometimes one feels that the universe is fundamentally good and going in just about the right direction—that something is what it is because that is what it ought to be. When you get this—an overwhelming feeling—it is one aspect of mysticism, and this is what you can get through the old religion.

This love of nature and the feeling of being able to communicate with 'her' was, of course, most obviously manifested by the members of the Findhorn Community, but it was something which many communitarians shared, even the most irreligious. For instance, one privatized radical remarked:

> I am not religious at all in any conventional sense, although I do think of myself as a religious person. I detest anything to do with the ritual of religion. Thus, I lack sympathy with the Communauté de l'Arche where I spent ten days once.[10] However, I did find that a deeply religious experience—I am a heavy smoker but when I was there I never put my hand in my pockets for my cigarettes, it never entered my head. In fact smoking is not allowed there. I believe that man creates his own religions. I feel that there is no other purpose in life than what you make of it. My views are similar to the Buddhists but I am not a Buddhist, I dislike the ritual of regular meditation and so on . . . and yet I am religious in the sense of feeling a close link with Nature and a wonder at the sacredness of life. I feel guilty when I kill a wasp.

For others, particularly the young trippers, this mystical awareness of a universal force that links us all together as one was seen far more clearly. One respondent expressed this theme, which is common to all mystic religions:

> Religion is a very personal thing with me. I disbelieve in organised religion. I think it can be very fine and a beautiful thing. It means a lot to me—a relationship with a goodness, a life, which runs through everything, and which you feel and at times feel even more. There is no smallness, of 'I am less than the God I talk to', but a joy of living, of being alive and more important, of other people living . . . it is this general communication with something greater that gives you this feeling that we are all so very real and, deep down, we are all so very beautiful as well. It's just a matter of getting it together.

Or, a slightly more technical version:

> God, what we call God, is a sort of vibration. What crops up in every religion is simply the fabric of the universe—the vibrations of the atoms and the molecules, the vibrations of the universe. I have this idea that we reincarnate until we reach this very, very fine vibration which is—we become one with God—we are vibrating at the same level.

For some, this awareness that it is only on the material level that we are separate beings and that on a higher level we are all one has been obtained through the use of hallucinogenic drugs such as LSD. For such people, drugs were seen as having an important role to play in the birth of what they see as the New Age. However, there was also the recognition that drugs could become mere playthings, to be used every Saturday night as a substitute for alcohol. A not untypical view was that expressed to me as follows:

> I think drugs can be regarded as a means of instant awareness. Whilst this can work for some, I think it doesn't for a lot of others. Drugs are taking the place of educators, in the right sense—because people are educated away from themselves, and in such a way that they are not able to realise themselves; and there is no guidance from the church or the state into oneself and one's human relationships. Drugs, to the West, were inevitable. Because of the power structures of this country— the state and the church—because of the way that they are, it is also inevitable that there is going to be opposition to the use of drugs. Opposition based on fear, self interest, and lack of understanding. There is a place for drugs if people are taught how to use them . . . they can be an ennobling thing because they help people to realise themselves and gain awareness of the greater significance of life than that general pattern of life

that is followed in the West. . . . Drugs are very necessary in this society for a large number of people to be turned on.

In pursuing this aim of developing one's spiritual awareness a number of communitarians followed macrobiotic diets. While the majority of communitarians refrained from eating meat, either because of its price or because of their disgust at the thought of eating a once-living creature, others pursued, to my mind, the demanding regime of the macrobiotic diet. The purpose of this was, as one enthusiast informed me, 'to eat to fulfil one's needs not only in the physical sense but in the spiritual sense . . . food plays an important part in both one's spiritual and physical well-being'. This exercise in seeking to attain the correct spiritual balance through means of diet was not, however, viewed in the same light by all members of the commune movement. For some of the older members it was merely part of the fashion that had been taken up by the younger members of the underground. As one respondent phrased it:

No, we are not into the mystic scene. In fact, we tend to feel
a little cynical about the hippies and the 'beautiful people',
with their ying and yang and yoga and so on. We tend to think
of it as something of a fashion.

This is no doubt a view shared by many members of the straight society of the ideas and activities of the members of the commune movement. Indeed it was a view shared by those members of the commune movement for whom religion was merely a construct of man's imagination, a construct which inevitably reacted back upon man to deprive him of his essential autonomous and creative potential. However, the purpose of this chapter has not been to comment on the rightness or wrongness of such views, but rather to portray as faithfully as possible the social reality that the communitarians saw themselves as inhabiting.

9 Communes and the nuclear family

In Chapter 4 a distinction was drawn between the alienated majority of society's members who take the social world in which they live for granted, and the minority of utopians for whom the institutions of society appear as human constructs and, as such, amenable to radical social change. For many of the utopians among the members of the commune movement, one of the existing social institutions from which they feel estranged is that of the nuclear family. Indicative of this utopian mentality was an article in *Communes* which commenced with the statement:[1]

> The organisation of society into small family groups is not necessarily the best arrangement mankind can devise. The family as we know it is certainly not the best arrangement for some individuals. We should surely re-examine this institution in the light of modern knowledge, and ask whether society might do better to allow greater freedom in patterns of living.

For such people, their attempts to create an alternative style of life and a new social order involves, among other things, an attempt to create viable alternative institutional arrangements to replace the nuclear family. For some observers of the commune movement, this aim constitutes the key characteristic of real communes. Thus one correspondent wrote to *Communes* asking for information about the movement in Britain and specified quite clearly what she considered to be the most important characteristic of communes:[2]

> By commune I do, of course, mean more than just a collection of people living under the same roof for various financial and other practical advantages—I mean people who believe that the closed family way of life is outmoded and that a larger group is not only a practical way of living but offers a richer way of life.

In viewing the traditional nuclear family structure as one of the major bulwarks of the existing social order and therefore an institution in need of radical alteration, the communitarians share a common ground with many of the secular radicals and religious sectarians of the past. Among these one can mention not only such pioneers of community living as Robert Owen and John Humphrey Noyes, but also those arch-critics of such utopian schemes, Marx and Engels. Thus whereas Marx and Engels condemned Owen for what they viewed as his neglect of the class struggle, they praised him for his advocation of the abolition of the family. For Owen the institution of the family was a far more divisive force in society than class, serving to isolate men from each other, breeding loneliness and self-centredness. Thus he described the goal of the New Harmony experiment as being 'to change from the individual system to the social system; from single families with separate interests to communities of many families with one interest'.[3] The family was viewed by Owen not only as the main bastion of private property and the guardian of all those qualities of individualism and self-interest to which he was opposed, but also as an organ of tyranny by which the wife was subjected to and made the property of her husband, condemned to a life of petty drudgery and child-bearing. Thus he wrote:[4]

separate interests and individual family arrangements with private property are essential parts of the existing irrational system. They must be abandoned with the system. And instead thereof there must be scientific associations of men, women and children, in their usual proportions, from about 4 or 500 to about 2,000, arranged to be as one family.

Marx used the ideas of Owen and Fourier, another advocate of sexual reform amongst the utopian socialists, and incorporated them into his critique of bourgeois society. He attacked the institution of the bourgeois family, arguing that[5]

marriage, property, the family remain unattacked, in theory, because they are the practical basis on which the bourgeoisie has erected its domination, and because in their bourgeois form they are the conditions which make the bourgeois a bourgeois.
. . . This attitude of the bourgeois to the conditions of his existence acquires one of its universal forms in bourgeois morality. One cannot, in general, speak of the family 'as such'. Historically, the bourgeois gives the family the character of the bourgeois family, in which boredom and money are the binding link, and which also includes the bourgeois dissolution of the family, which does not prevent the family itself from always continuing to exist. Its dirty existence has its counterpart in the

holy concept of it in official phraseology and universal hypocrisy.

This view of marriage and the family as major supports of the bourgeois society and as repressive institutions to be abandoned in the New Age was one which united not only utopian and scientific socialists, but also Marxists and anarchists. Thus Bakunin wrote:[6]

As much as anyone else I am a partisan of the complete emancipation of women and their social equality with men . . . we want the abolition of family and marriage law, and of the ecclesiastic as well as the civil law, indissolubly bound up with the right of inheritance. . . . We are convinced that in abolishing religious, civil, and juridical marriage, we restore life, reality and morality to natural marriage based solely upon human respect and the freedom of two persons; a man and a woman to love each other. We are convinced that in recognising the freedom of either party to the marriage to part from the other whenever he or she wishes to, without having to ask anyone's permission for it—and likewise in denying the necessity of needing any permission to unite in marriage and rejecting in general the interference of any authority with that union, we make them more closely united to each other.

Despite the writings of such radicals, it has been left largely to the communitarians to seek to implement such critiques and proposals in the practice of living. For example, the experiments of the Perfectionists at Oneida in the United States involved a more radical departure from the conventional nuclear family style of life than possibly even Bakunin and Marx envisaged. John Humphrey Noyes, the founder of the Oneida Community, was born in 1811. He studied theology and began preaching in his home town of Putney in Vermont in 1834. He slowly gathered around him a small company of followers, and in 1846 this group of some forty members began their first experiment in communal living. In 1848, after some hostility from the public, they moved to Oneida in Madison County, New York. There they flourished and by February 1874 they numbered 283.[7] Nordhoff wrote of their membership at that time: 'there are among them lawyers, clergymen, merchants, physicians, teachers; but the greater part were New England farmers and mechanics. Former Congregationalists and Presbyterians, Episcopalians, Methodists and Baptists are among them—but not Catholics'.[8] For these people the Bible was to be interpreted literally. They believed that the second advent of Christ took place at the period of the destruction of Jerusalem and that[9]

the final kingdom of God then began in the heavens; that the

manifestation of that kingdom in the visible world is now
approaching; that its approach is ushering in the second and
final resurrection and judgement; that a Church on earth is now
rising to meet the approaching kingdom in the heavens, and to
become its duplicate and representative; that inspiration, or
open communication with God and the heavens, involving
perfect holiness, is the element of connection between the
Church on earth and the Church in the heavens, and the power
by which the kingdom of God is to be established and reign
in the world.

They adopted the name of Perfectionists because their basic doctrine was the immediate and total cessation from sin. Their aim was
to lead sinless lives. At the same time, they believed that the community of goods and people had been taught and commanded by
Christ. They believed that communism, extended beyond property
to include persons, was 'the social state of the resurrection', stating
that there was 'no intrinsic difference between property in persons
and property in things; and that the same spirit which abolished
exclusiveness in regard to money would abolish, if circumstances
allowed full scope to it, exclusiveness in regard to women and
children'.[10]

They abolished the institution of marriage and replaced it by a
practice which they termed 'complex marriage'. This meant that any
male or female members of the community could sleep and live
together as they wished. The 'exclusive and idolatrous attachment'
of two persons for each other was actively discouraged, such feelings
being viewed as selfish and sinful. In practice this did not mean that
life at Oneida was one long sexual spree or 'love-in'. Noyes was
particularly concerned, not only about the propensity for couples to
develop strong feelings of attachment for each other, but also to
emphasise that[11]

It is as important for the young now as it was for their fathers
then, that they should know that holiness of heart is what they
must have before they get liberty in love. They must put the
first thing first, as I did and as their parents did; they must be
'Perfectionists' before they are 'Communists'. . . . We have got
into the position of Communism, where without genuine
salvation from sin our passions will overwhelm us, and nothing
but confusion and misery can be expected.

Thus, the relationship of the sexes was placed under the guardianship
of the older members of the community. They taught the advisa-
bility of pairing people of different ages.[12] They ensured that no one
was forced to cohabit with another against their consent.

They also sought to control the production of children by a system of selective breeding that resembled an early form of eugenics. Thus Noyes wrote of their attempts[13]

> to produce the usual number of offspring to which people in the middle classes are able to afford judicious moral and spiritual care, with the advantage of a liberal education. In this attempt twenty four men and twenty women have been engaged, selected from among those who have most thoroughly practiced our social theory.

While members of communes in contemporary Britain have not, as far as I am aware, resorted to such techniques, they do share the view held by radicals of the past that the nuclear family is an important bulwark of the existing order. This was a view held particularly strongly by those female members of communes who placed at least some of their hopes for radical social change in the women's liberation movement.

Thus, when I asked one female member of an urban commune about the forces for change which she saw as contributing towards the creation of an alternative society, apart from communes, she replied, 'Women's liberation, I hope, if we can wake women up. Education—if we can really destroy that "brickwall".' Such people personify the links that have developed, and the felt affinity, between the members of the commune movement and the movement for women's liberation, finding their common ground largely in their search to develop an alternative society in general, and in their critiques of the role of the nuclear family in contemporary society in particular. To a certain extent this relationship between the commune and women's liberation movements can also be traced to the origins of the contemporary upsurge in their membership numbers. Both owe much of their recent growth to the spread of disillusionment with protest politics, especially in America, from where many of the models which guide the aspirations and actions of British communitarians and female emancipationists have come. Thus the commitment of many communitarians stems from a disillusionment with the politics of the demonstration and the picket line, and a felt need to pursue their revolutionary aims in what they consider to be more positive and constructive ways. Similarly, the recent growth in the women's liberation movement started in America when women radicals there began to realize that, while they were working for freedom for Blacks and Vietnamese, they themselves appeared to be victims of a very real kind of oppression—they were still treated as the cooks, dishwashers, coffee-makers, clerical assistants and sexual objects of the radical males. As this awareness grew, so did the movement for female emancipation.

263

In Chapter 4 an analysis was presented of the processes by which the social constructs of man, his language, roles and institutions, come to confront him as alien entities appearing to possess autonomous power, over which man appears to have little or no control. The consequences of these processes included, it was argued, the fact that the majority of people take the social world in which they live for granted. They view it as the natural order of things. Although such people were described as being alienated, they are frequently those members of society who feel most at home in the world. This feeling of being at home is due largely to their belief that life can hold no surprises, they know what they can expect from life and from other people and, moreover, they know who they are themselves, and other people know what they can expect from people like themselves. Thus, whereas the sociologist's knowledge of the social world is frequently couched in such terms as 'role', 'social system', 'social institution' and so on, the knowledge of the world held by the ordinary actor on the social scene largely consists of what Schutz has termed 'typifications'. The constituent parts of the ordinary actor's body of knowledge by means of which he makes sense of the world are, for Schutz,[14]

> elements of a network of typifications—typifications of human individuals, of their course-of-action patterns, of their motives and goals, or of the sociocultural products which originated in their actions. These types were formed in the main by others, his predecessors or contemporaries, as appropriate tools for coming to terms with things and men, accepted as such by the group into which he was born. But there are also self-typifications: man typifies to a certain extent his own situation within the social world and the various relations he has to his fellow-men and cultural objects.

The sum total of these typifications constitutes for the actor a frame of reference within which the physical and social worlds that surround him must be interpreted. The key characteristic of the utopian is that he does not feel at home in society and is able to see beyond the framework that constrains the world-views of the majority of his contemporaries. As has been pointed out, the aim of the communitarians is to break up this mental set, to increase people's awareness of the possibilities of creating alternative social worlds and identities. The general aim of the women's liberation movement is likewise to break down this framework, to attack the body of commonly accepted social knowledge in general, and the taken-for-granted definitions of the role of women in society in particular.

Thus, one of their spokeswomen has written:[15]

when I speak of female liberation I mean liberation from the myths that have enslaved and confined women in their own minds as well as in the minds of others; I don't mean liberation from men. Men and women are mutually oppressed by a culture and a heritage that mutilates the relationships possible between them.

One of the prime causes of the oppression of women in society, according to such people, continues to be the family, for it is primarily within the realm of the family that the place of women in society is defined and maintained.

The central problem is that this society has produced an image and a mythology of women that has deprived them of their humanity and creative role in society. For a variety of reasons, one of the central agents of this oppression has been the institution of the family. For one thing . . . the family seems, at present time, to be the primary *agent* of sexual repression in this society. For another, it is by defining women primarily within the family that this society has deprived her of her humanity and her creativity. If women are to liberate themselves, they must come squarely to grips with the reality of the family and the social forces that have produced it at this particular period in history.[16]

Thus, it is argued, if women are to transcend the image that defines them in their own minds as well as in the minds of men as inconsistent and emotionally unstable, child-like creatures whose place is in the home where they can fulfil themselves through child-bearing and child-rearing and looking after their man, then they must start the struggle with themselves, their own lives in the family. For[17]

Like woman herself, the family appears as a natural object, but it is actually a cultural creation. There is nothing inevitable about the form or role of the family any more than there is about the character or role of women. It is the function of ideology to present these given social types as aspects of Nature itself.

In the emphasis on the importance of the individual woman starting the revolution with her own head, and in the demand that people examine their own lives and their own personal day-to-day relationships, so increasing their awareness of the games people play and the roles people cast each other in, the women's liberation movement reveals a similar orientation towards revolutionary strategy as with those commune members who believe that only by freeing oneself from the mental sets of the existing social order can one attain that level of awareness of oneself and others as unique individuals that is seen as the pre-requisite for the creation of the brotherhood of man. These bonds between the two movements have become the firmer since members of the women's liberation movement, particularly in America, in their search to overcome the constraints that they view as being placed on the self-fulfilment of women by the institution of the nuclear family, have begun to experiment with alternative modes of living, explored through the means of communes.[18]

In what specific ways is the institution of the family seen as the main agent of female oppression? Juliet Mitchell has written of the family as being the linchpin in a causal chain that runs from maternity, the family, and absence from production and public life to sexual inequality.

It is argued that the myths associated with the family have been largely responsible for the cultural emphasis on male virility and female chastity. This has resulted, it is argued, in the situation where, within the family, men have been instilled with predatory attitudes, while women have been filled with deep sexual fear, accompanied by an equal degree of sexual ignorance. At the same time, this framework is viewed as defining the woman as a sexual object to be possessed by the virile male. Thus, the nuclear family is viewed as one of the prize agents in the repression of female sexuality.

In rather similar fashion, one of the prime advantages of the communal style of life over that of the nuclear family, as seen by certain commune members, was the fact that the emotional strain placed upon two people living constantly in each other's company, as in a nuclear family, is extreme and can lead to unhappiness, adultery and the breakdown of relationships. Within a commune, it was argued, no two adults need be forced constantly into each other's company, with a resultant lowering of emotional strain through the establishment of close and affectionate relationships with other adults. This close interaction with other adults, whether it involves sexual interaction or not, was typically seen as important for the self-development of the individuals involved and for the development of honest and genuine relationships between the commune members in general and the couple in particular. This point was emphasized by one respondent:

> The nuclear family is a repressive and horrible institution. It makes you realise how cruel two people can be to each other. . . . By conventional standards we had a happy marriage for years. But we realised that during this time, with all our conflicts and problems, one of us had to give way—eventually that person gets destroyed.

Also, where there are only two people, then misunderstandings can arise, you only get a restricted view of each other—in a commune there are others there to give an 'objective' account of their perceptions, clear the air, and so enable you to become more fully aware of each other as humans, clear up the misconceptions that develop through distorted perceptions.

Many of the commune members have had experience of the break-up of a marriage. This is particularly so with regard to the artists, and for such people the commune offers a further advantage over the conventional nuclear family style of life. Not only does communal living appear to ease the economic burden that can be incurred following such an event, but also there is the awareness that, whereas the family often breaks up over such occurrences, the commune can survive. This fact was mentioned by one respondent in particular who had experience of two unsuccessful marriages:

Of course there are personality clashes, but we are able to talk things out here. It's far better for my children too. I am not a very maternal person, and living like this means that they always have other sympathetic adults around. It has helped them, and myself, to adjust after the break-up with my last husband.

It is further argued that for the widowed, the elderly and the unattached in general, life in conventional society centred around the nuclear family system can be very lonely. Such people can find, within a community, companionship and worth-while tasks to pursue. This aspect of communal life appeals particularly to those people who have lost their spouse in the later years of their lives and who lack the company of children or age-peers. Such a person was the respondent referred to in Chapter 7. 'I am 68 years of age, healthy, capable, strong, with nothing to do, having been nursing all my life. I lack social contacts. In a commune I could be well occupied washing up, preparing vegetables, keeping chickens, growing tomatoes etc.'[19] However, this aspect of community life can also represent an important attraction for others who fear the prospect of growing old and lonely in contemporary society. Thus the members of Selene Community have written of the monogamous family as an instrument of devastating grief, for[20]

Human beings die; our community does not. Grief will inevitably strike the person whose love is narrow unless they die before their loved one and leave their erstwhile companion to mourn their departing. . . . In our community there will be no orphans, for they are everybody's children; there can be none destitute and lonely in old age for they are everybody's relatives and they can have both the company of each other and the younger members' stimulation. There will be no widows or widowers.

Some members of the commune movement, such as the members of Selene Community, are concerned to introduce the institution of group marriage within communities to replace the accepted mono-gamous marriage. The group marriage can be defined in similar terms to the nuclear family, except in terms of the numbers involved in sexual relationships with each other. Thus people practising group marriage are members of a social group characterized by common residence, economic co-operation and reproduction, having four or more members with at least two members of each sex, and based on deep affective bonds, genuine intimacy, and interpersonal commit-ment between all members. For the majority of communitarians whom I encountered, however, such proposals failed to arouse much enthusiasm. Such people preferred the commune as an extended family system made up of separate couples. They justified this view largely in terms of what they considered to be the best way to bring up children, believing that it was necessary for the children to feel secure in the knowledge of who their parents were and with whom they could establish the basic feelings of trust which such communi-tarians felt was essential for the development of the child. Thus one member informed me of his views on marriage:

> If by marriage you mean two people living together, that's fine. . . . I think the family unit as such, living in its 'semi' is a bad thing. . . . I don't really go in for the group marriage thing with everyone fucking everyone else because that just isn't a good way to bring up kids. I still think the couple as such is quite a nice unit. I am not really bothered about the legal thing.

Another respondent, married with two children, expressed a similar viewpoint. 'I am not terribly keen on the group marriage thing. I am fairly open-minded. I am not sure how it affects the kids. I feel that they need to know who their parents are.' However, to those who believe in the practice of group marriage, it merely represents an attempt to take the principles and ideals of communal living to their natural conclusion. Not only is it viewed as incorporating all the advantages that communal living holds over the nuclear family life, but also as presenting the possibility of cementing the bonds of fellowship within the commune by the development of the fullest and most intimate relationships between all the members. Moreover, its proponents have argued:[21]

> It is a fact that human beings sometimes fall in love with more than one person. For many, it may be a drive the satisfaction of

which is vital to their happiness, and therefore to the happiness of those closely associated with them. If such an occurrence gives rise to frustration and unhappiness on the one hand, and to jealousy, anger and mistrust on the other, what has been achieved? It might well be preferable to accept this new situation gladly. It is better to share someone's love than to have none of it. If all the persons are fond of one another, a new dimension of happiness may be added to their lives. If it is possible to love more than one person at once (children as well as husband, for example), then it would seem wrong to try to avoid doing so. This applies to either sex.

Whether the favourable view of group marriage is shared or not, there is fairly common agreement among commune members that the nuclear family system is not the only natural way of organizing social life, and that in its present enclosed and isolated form such a system only serves to separate people from each other rather than promote caring relationships between them. As such it represents a barrier to the attainment of their goal of the family of man.

'The family of man' has been one of the aims of utopians of many historical epochs, and the rearing of children capable of living a full life in such a social order has traditionally been one of the major concerns of such utopians, particularly those of a libertarian persuasion. Thus at Oneida the children who resulted from the arranged unions between community members were only left in the care of their mothers until they were weaned. They then became community property. They were deposited in a nursery under the care of special nurses. On reaching the age of three or four they were transferred to another nursery manned, like the first, by both male and female nurses.

Such a pattern of child-rearing was similar to that adopted by the members of the kibbutzim in the twentieth century.[22] In the typical kibbutz the institution of marriage has not been completely abolished, couples live together whose sexual union is socially sanctioned,[23] but the related institution of the family does not exist, if one defines this institution in Murdock's terms as 'a social group characterised by common residence, economic cooperation, and reproduction. It includes adults of both sexes, at least two of whom maintain a socially approved sexual relationship, and one or more children, own or adopted, of the sexually cohabiting adults.'[24] A kibbutz couple generally live in a bed-sitting room, while their children are reared in a communal children's dormitory. Although the children can visit their parents once a day, the majority of the time they spend eating, sleeping, and living in general, is spent in the special children's houses. Thus the kibbutz as a whole assumes the responsibility for the care and education of the children. They get their clothes from a communal store, and are cared for when ill by their nurses. These nurses and the teachers take on the responsibility for the socialization and education of the children as they advance according to their age through a succession of children's houses along with their age-peers.

In this way the kibbutz as a whole functions as if it were a family. Such practices follow naturally from the views held by the members of kibbutzim of their experiments in living as constituting steps towards their goal of social revolution. From their perspective, a major requirement necessary for the attainment of this goal is the rearing of children who will share the values of the movement, who will be accustomed to living according to the injunctions of the revolutionary creed, and who will be able to further the revolutionary cause initiated by the preceding generations.

In so far as the members of the contemporary commune movement share the revolutionary aims of the *chaverim*, seeking the creation of a social order characterized not so much by the fragmentation of its members into isolated nuclear family groups, as by the brotherhood of man as a whole, they too place a great deal of their faith for the future in their communally-raised children. As one respondent phrased it:

> I feel that society as it is, if one is considering the older
> generation, is probably beyond redemption, but I think all the
> time one must have a thought and an eye to the next generation,
> and this is where I think communes are of such importance
> and are a necessity, because it is the next generation who could
> make the communes. If we start them now and are successful,
> then the next generation will change society because this new
> way of living will be what is necessary for people to find
> themselves and to bear out all that they need to bear out in
> terms of relationships with other people and awareness of
> other people. So apart from the changing now which is
> essential, it is the thought for the future and the next
> generation which is of equal importance, if not more so.

Nuclear family life is typically viewed as a harmful environment within which to rear children by commune members. It is argued that[25]

> A major function of the family is to promote respect, obedience
> and conformity. In return it provides 'security' and indoctri-
> nates the children with the required responses. All this is
> damaging to the child if it restricts his free development as an
> individual. Creativity, always a kind of non-conformity, is now
> commonly suppressed in order that the child may fit into a

pre-conceived pattern. But it is possible to have safety
without servitude.

Infants in their helpless state need the care and devotion of a
mother. However, it is necessary for their development towards
maturity that they be weaned from this state as soon as possible.
Another basic need is association with other children of
roughly the same age. The traditional family usually fails in
this respect. The commune would provide a peer-group for
each child. . . . Each child has the security of his peer-group,
and the certainty of the presence of adults it can trust to look
after its welfare, without suffering from the emotional
disturbances or temporary aberrations of a particular parent. . . .
The diversity of interest and activities in the community
would tend to draw out latent abilities and keep the curiosity
of youth in operation. Growing up, the child need never be
without contemporaries to play with or adults to talk with: and
full participation in the democratic processes of the community
would ensure rapid linguistic and social development . . . it is
inevitable that the young should be affected by the environment
in which they grow up but it is our intention to substitute
questioning for blind acceptance, and participation for
obedience. In doing so we shall be conditioning the children for
freedom.

On this point, one of the scenes that remains in my mind of life in
one community in Britain was the sight of a group of adults trying
to complete the crossword in the *Guardian* and seriously consulting
two young boys aged eleven and thirteen as to the interpretation of
the clues and the possible answers. This scene symbolized, for me, the
relationships between the young and adults typically found within
communes, with the emphasis upon the creation of a non-coercive
environment within which the children can freely follow their own
paths of development and exploration.[26] At the same time, this
emphasis on the development of a free environment for the self-
development of the children often caused concern for the older
members of the communes, particularly over the problems of
discipline, where to draw the line, and how to reconcile one's wish
to allow the children to satisfy their curious natures in complete
freedom with the desire to protect the children from the dangers
that could be incurred in such exploration. Thus one informant
referred to the fact that he was 'worried about my six month old
child, as every time you warn it away from electric points and such
things then you are forcing it. I am very keen on the commune as a
free environment in which to bring up my kids.'

However, the nuclear family was typically viewed not only as a restrictive environment within which to rear children, but also as a restrictive framework from the point of view of the self-development of the parents in general, and the wife in particular. Thus many communitarians emphasize, in their critique of the nuclear family, the burden imposed upon women through child-rearing within such an institution. As one respondent phrased it:

> From the woman's point of view kids can be a real drag, although one loves them. They are particularly a drag when there are no other children to play with. In a commune there are other kids and other adults to share the burden.

For such people, one of the advantages offered by communal living was the possibility of being freed from what was felt to be the onerous duty of constantly looking after children. The responsibility could be shifted from the shoulders of the isolated monogamous couple, and particularly those of the wife, to the commune members as a whole. This was felt to be an attraction by most female members, but particularly by those women who had visions of a definite life project. For those women who had been to university or some other institute of higher education and whose career had been interrupted by childbirth, a life devoted to the kitchen sink appeared particularly burdensome and frustrating. A commune appeared to them as one possible solution, to what confronted them as an important problem.

Given these criticisms of conventional nuclear family life and the alleged advantages that communal living has to offer over such arrangements, one is justified in asking whether or not communes in contemporary Britain work with any more tangible success than did such experiments of the past as those inspired by Robert Owen, which were generally characterized by a relatively short life-span. How do communes work in practice?

Communes: problems and obstacles encountered on the path to and through communal living

In concluding his study of communities in the United States, Nordhoff listed what he considered to be the main attractions of communal life:[27]

> It provides a greater variety of employment for each individual, and thus increases the dexterity and broadens the faculties of men. It offers a wider range of wholesome enjoyments, and also greater restraints against debasing pleasures. It gives independence, and inculcates prudence and frugality. It demands self-sacrifice, and restrains selfishness and greed; and

thus increases the happiness which comes from the moral side of human nature. Finally, it relieves the individual's life from a great mass of carking cares, from the necessity of over-severe and exhausting toil, from the dread of misfortune or exposure in old age.

Despite such advantages, the history of community experiments has been one characterized largely by their failure to continue for any great length of time. Noyes, the founder of the Oneida Community, listed forty-seven such failures in his book *History of American Socialisms* and believed that, for a community to enjoy longevity of life, it must be based upon the firm commitment of the members to a religious belief system. Certainly the history of religious communities such as those of the Hutterites, Rappites, Shakers and Zoarites, would appear to support this thesis, as would the short periods of existence enjoyed by those communities that were inspired by the secular belief systems of such people as Owen and Fourier. This view is one that is shared by the members of certain religious communities in modern Britain. Thus one of the members of the Findhorn venture, which has been one of the most successful of experiments, judged by most standards, explained this success by reference to the fact that the Centre was guided by God and that the members shared a common spiritual base. He likened those experiments begun without such a shared religious commitment on the part of its members to 'houses built upon sand whose foundations get washed away at the first storm'. Certainly the problems encountered in communal living are such that, unless the members do share an overwhelming commitment to community life, such as can stem from a firmly held religious faith, then the collapse of the commune is highly probable. Whether or not the death of a commune automatically means that the venture has been a failure is another issue entirely, and one which will be considered below. In this section, however, attention will be turned to some of the many problems that appear to contribute towards the high death rate of such attempts to create alternative styles of life.

I think it can be asserted, certainly on the basis of my research, that only a small fraction of community ventures get beyond the embryo state of planning to their implementation in practical living. Many aspiring commune members have failed to confront the problems actually involved in communal living because the obstacles facing those who are seeking to initiate such experiments have defeated them. Such problems are mainly of a twofold nature. There are the economic problems involved in raising the capital necessary to finance the commune venture, and the related problem of finding suitable property of sufficient size and reasonable cost to house the experiment. The other range of obstacles centre mainly on the problems involved in gathering together a sufficient number of like-minded people to form the nucleus of the project.

Just as individual commune members have followed different paths to community, so have different communes followed different career patterns from the planning stage to that of practical implementation. Different career patterns involve different types of problems. Basically, one can distinguish between three ideal-type processes involved in becoming a commune. The first involves those projects made up of a group of people who have been brought together because they share a common view of the world, a shared political and social philosophy, and a shared desire to live in a commune. The second involves a group of people who do not consciously share any firmly articulated philosophy of life, but who are bound together by the common bonds of friendship, their friendship being based on the status of the members as individuals rather than as political believers. The third involves those people whose group identity is based on such bonds of friendship and also upon their common faith in a particular belief system. What is unique about the second group is that, usually, they have come together to live as a group purely on the grounds that they like each other's company and without any specific philosophy about communal living or about communes as such. They typically acquire the feeling that they constitute a commune after a process involving their being labelled as such by a variety of moral entrepreneurs. The application of the label of 'commune' to their group enterprise has typically caused such people to re-examine their life together in terms of the label.

Becker has written of the role of 'moral entrepreneurs' with regard to the processes by which certain acts become labelled as deviant. A similar perspective can be adopted with regard to understanding the process by which members of this second type of commune come to view themselves as constituting a commune. Becker has written:[28]

> Before any act can be viewed as deviant, and before any class
> of people can be labelled and treated as outsiders for committing
> the act, someone must have made the rule which defines the
> act as deviant. . . . Deviance is the product of enterprise in the
> largest sense; without the enterprise required to get rules made,
> the deviance which consists of breaking the rule could not exist.

This statement can be rephrased by substituting 'commune' for 'deviant act'. Thus it can be argued that, before any form of group living can be viewed as a commune, and before any group of people can be labelled and treated as commune members, someone must have made the rule which defines that particular style of life as constituting a commune. For the members of this second type of community experiment, the unintentional communards, their self-assigned identities as commune members has been a consequence of someone, a moral entrepreneur, applying such a label to them and this label being accepted by significant others and by the members of the group itself. Thus, the members of one group who had started their life together as an unintentional commune related the story of how they started living together as a group as a consequence of one of the members occupying a house which was too expensive to be run by a single person. Friends were invited to live in the house and share the cost. Other friends came for holidays, liked the place, and stayed. So the group grew. Then they started receiving letters addressed to 'X Commune'. Word spread around the British commune movement that there was a commune in existence at such and such a place, so they got more letters addressed to 'X Commune' and more and more visitors started arriving and enquiring about 'X Commune' of which they had heard.[29] A member of the group was invited to appear on the local television station to talk of their life together as a commune. So knowledge of the commune spread to the lay public. Eventually the secretary of the Commune Movement wrote to them enquiring about their life together as a group and as a commune for inclusion in the *Directory of Communes*. Thus, the group became officially labelled as a commune by the Commune Movement, while the members of the group vainly protested that they did not consider themselves to be members of any movement, including the Commune Movement. By the time I visited the group, they had come to accept the fact that they were stuck with the label of commune, and they had begun to accept it. Typically, once this stage has been reached, the members of the unintentional commune begin to think and talk together in a far more self-conscious manner about the nature of their life together as a commune. They no longer take their shared life for granted so much, and seek to work out in a very tentative manner some common philosophy by which they feel they would be able to identify themselves as a group.

For the members of such unintentional communes, the path to community has been characterized by a complete lack of obstacles, because from their point of view they have not followed any path. Their living together as a group has typically been brought about because they were all friends, and in response to the economic problems faced by one of their number. Therefore, in a paradoxical way, whereas the economic problems are frequently those that defeat the plans of many aspiring commune members and founders, in the case of the unintentional communards it has been the economic

275

problems which have contributed to their getting together as a communal group.

The economic problems are those which usually defeat the projects of those people who, together, constitute the nucleus of a potential commune by virtue of their friendship, and by the fact that these bonds are strengthened by a shared belief system and desire to live together as a commune. The problem of raising sufficient capital to start a commune venture is particularly acute for such people as they are generally young, and not usually the type to have placed money aside for such contingencies. Frequently they have failed to develop such habits, even if they might have wished to, by their reluctance to take up full-time, regular paid employment.[30] The bonds of friendship that unite the members of such groups have usually developed during their time together as students or children, or in some other group activity not directly related to communal living. The problems facing the members of such groups were described by a member of a group consisting of 'nine artists, potters, designers and land lovers'. Such groups do not face the problem of recruiting members for their venture, but rather the problem of raising the cash to finance the existing members.[31]

> We found a large farm-house and filled in an application for it.
> We were turned down. We are now collecting funds (our
> total joke bank account now stands at £2), money is a problem.
> Next week we will sell our bodies to the national health. We
> are collecting junk for a jumble sale but long-haired people
> don't have much jumble given to them, though friends have
> been over-generous to the jumble. We also have all the furniture
> we need and no house to put it in, nomadic and pennyless we
> may be but we will succed in our aim. Our dateline is July,
> we're in a hurry.

The members of this group had also tried writing off appealing letters to a number of 'hippie millionaires' without any success. In order to overcome this economic problem, the members of such groups normally have to give up their aim of purchasing property and be satisfied with renting a place. Otherwise they are forced to rely on loans from parents, inheritances, or to raise the amount of their combined savings to a level sufficient to acquire the desired type of property. The trouble with this latter course of action is that it takes time, and as time passes increasing numbers of the original group are likely to lose faith in the scheme and leave the group until eventually a hard-core of perhaps two or three people is left who are then faced with the problem of recruiting members as well as that of raising the necessary finance. In the face of such problems, the typical response of the few remaining hard-core members is to lose faith themselves in the viability of their original scheme and move out to the country as a small group or in family units to begin their new life, in rented property. However, as the level of the affluence of the members of such groups increases, so does the obstacle to the implementation of their schemes represented by the economic problem diminish. Thus the nucleus of the largest communal venture that I encountered during my research had originally come together as patients of the same psychotherapist. The stimulus for their experiment had come from one of their number who felt the challenge to prove that man could live at peace with his fellow men in the world without resorting to violence and war to resolve their conflicts. The original members all pursued sufficiently 'respectable' professions for them to tap the necessary sources of finance and legal knowledge which enabled them to form a housing association and commence their experiment. Their membership now consists of about a hundred adults and children and they have been in existence for about twenty years. They had recruited new members largely from the ranks of their friends and acquaintances.

In general one can state that, where a solution to the economic problem has been found by the members of those groups bound together by friendship and a shared world-view, then the commune project is likely to attain the stage of practical implementation. The same cannot be said about those people whose only common bond is a desire to live in a commune, and on which basis they have come together. The odds against such people attaining their collective aim are very high, for the initiators of such schemes face the economic problem and the problem of recruiting members.[32]

The personal columns of the underground newspapers and magazines usually contain a number of advertisements from people who are looking for a commune to join or from those who are looking for additional people to join them in their project. The correspondence columns of *Communes* are also full of letters such as the following:[33]

Can you tell me if there is a commune with these pursuits in England? Meditation and Self-realisation with musical and artistic leanings. Is there an 'island' anywhere for me? I am 26, single, can cook, type, farm (crops) and am quite practical with car maintenance etc. . . . I am in need of somewhere to uncurl and find myself. I want to be with artistic, musical people who KNOW and understand. . . . Please write and tell me if such a place exists.

A couple whom I got to know quite well during the course of my research had replied to one such letter in *Communes* which had invited people to join a small group in their plans to form a commune.

The saga of their attempts to form a community with these others provides some indication of their problems encountered by those groups who seek to form a commune on the basis of a shared desire of the potential members to live in a commune, without there existing any initial bonds of strong friendship between them.

The first problem was that the couple lived in Surrey, whereas the other members with whom they corresponded lived in the south-west of England. For a period of some months they communicated by letter. Eventually they all met for a weekend in Wales, the people from the south-west, the couple from the south-east, and a person who had come down from the Midlands with a view of joining them in their project. They discussed their plans about the types of property they would need, the areas in which they wanted to live, and how they would earn sufficient money to maintain themselves and so on. Unfortunately, the person from the Midlands dropped out of the scheme at this early stage, feeling somewhat apart from the others whom he viewed as impractical daydreamers. So the group was reduced to five adults and two children. They decided that they should all scan the newspapers in search of properties which might be suitable for the project. Here they encountered a major problem. They wanted a house of sufficient size to accommodate up to about a dozen commune members, with a large garden in which to grow vegetables (they were all vegetarians), and with outhouses suitable for conversion into workshops. They were also looking for property within reach of a sizeable urban centre where they could hope to find a market for their produce. They hoped to make and sell candles, leather goods and so on, and also earn some money through car repair work. What they discovered was that properties which met these requirements, mainly old hotels, were priced beyond the means of their collective purse. This economic problem was aggravated by the difficulties of communication caused by the geographical separation of the prospective members. For a period of about twelve months members of the group were travelling to and fro between the south-west and south-east of England. The longest period any of them spent in each other's company however was in the region of a weekend every two or three months, despite all the travel.

Realizing that it would be extremely difficult to buy a suitable place to house the group, the members started looking at property that could be rented. I accompanied some of them to a farm in Wales which they had been offered. During the long jouney there, they were enthusiastically discussing their plans and looking forward to their life together on this upland farm. Their disappointment was all the greater, therefore, when they arrived to discover that the description they had received from the owner was rather less than accurate. The farmhouse was in a terrible state of disrepair, and the picture that confronted them was one of squalor and filth. They decided that the property was not suitable. Once again their hopes had been dashed, and once again they had invested time and effort and money in a fruitless search for accommodation. Their life at this time largely consisted of hurriedly arranged excursions to view property, with their hopes high, only to have them destroyed when they realized that the property was either too expensive or unsuitable for them in some way or another. Such repeated experiences only served to weaken their resolve.

Eventually they decided that the only way they could hope to raise sufficient capital to buy a place which would suit their needs and provide them with security of tenure was for them to live together in a rented house in the south-east of England where they could all earn large incomes, save on living expenses through sharing, and pool their assets after a year and invest them in a suitable piece of property which would house the commune. The couple who lived in the south-east found a suitable house and arranged jobs for the two men from the south-west. Everything appeared to be going smoothly when the married couple from the south-west dropped out of the scheme. The reasons they gave were that they felt that they had not spent sufficient time with the other couple from Surrey to get to know them fully, hence their reluctance to give up their house and jobs in Devon to move to Surrey. Furthermore, as the parents of two children, they felt that the attitudes of the respective couples with regard to child-rearing practices would lead to conflict. Thus once more the hopes of the remaining members were destroyed, and the remaining complement of three was further reduced to two when the member who lived in Cornwall decided that he wanted to remain in the south-west to be with his girl friend who had not finished her full-time education and was unable to join the venture. Disillusioned, the couple from Surrey decided to move out of the town into the country on their own. They rented a cottage in Wales where they now live, surviving off the sale of hand-made candles, occasional part-time work, and supplementary benefits.

A similar experience was had by 'Michael' who advertised in a humanist magazine for people to join him in a community project. One of the respondent's to his invitation wrote to me of Michael's lack of success in promoting his plan:

I would like you to know that after 3 years, Michael's venture is so far a complete failure.
    When he has the people he has not the house, and when he has the house he has not the people, and never has he had

enough money. The only certain cash is his and my house,
together about £12,000.

We had one lovely house, and at the very last moment three
people fell out (both out of the project and with one another). In
fact, poor Michael has had a bad time and a lot of expense . . .
there does not seem much chance of me (or Michael) ever
forming a commune.

Thus, many ventures are defeated by the problems of raising sufficient capital and recruiting sufficiently committed members. The
people who are most likely to opt out of such schemes are those who
feel that they have most to lose by dropping out of the conventional
world, those who are married with children and a house (and who
fear the loss of their life savings in the collapse of a communal
venture). Frequently their felt 'responsibilities' to their children's
future and their fear of making the final commitment to a way of
life of which they know very little are such that they feel unable to
make the final step of joining a venture when they are faced with the
fact that the implementation of the idea into practice has become
imminent. Such people typically feel that they have far more to lose
through the possible failure of such an experiment than those young,
single commune members who do not have the responsibility of
providing for a family and children. Certainly it would appear that
it is far easier for a young, unattached individual to take up the
threads of his old life if the community experiment fails.

I wrote to Michael to ask him about the people who had opted
out of his project at the last minute, and his reply illustrates some of
the points made above.

The reasons for drop-out were never fully explained. In general,
I guess they felt that the place was too big, too expensive, and
therefore too risky for us to take on. When it came to the
crunch they apparently felt unable to move out of their suburban
semi, on which they had already paid about £1,000 in mortgage.

They were in a way a special group, yes; they included our
only 'threesome'—a married couple plus extra female. They
also had one young child, but they were not alone in this, so it
was not a deciding factor.

The wife had vacillated for a long time before declaring in
favour of the commune, and I think she may have had another
change of mind. There is always this danger with the women
of the middle generation, who seem particularly unstable when
faced with sharing projects. She probably changed her mind
back again later, but too late.

Finally, this group of four went to spend Xmas with some
new contacts in Brighton to see what they were like and

whether they might be okay for the commune. They had an absolutely horrific time, they say, and left early, shaken by the incident to the extent of doubting all our previous plans. This was of course foolish.

So the answer is that everyone starting a commune must know and trust all the others absolutely.

This belief in the need for all commune members to 'know and trust all the others absolutely' was a view shared by the founder of another commune which I visited, who wrote:[34]

The five of us were all friends before we started on this project, and we feel that it is important that anyone who joins a commune should be first of all a friend, and then a communard. This means in practice that anyone joining us would perhaps visit us, stay with us a bit, and then by mutual agreement commit themselves to living here.

However, while it is possible for prospective commune members to spend a sufficiently long trial period with the members of an existing commune on the communal premises for both sides to decide on their compatibility, this is difficult for those who are seeking to launch a completely new venture. Without spending a great deal of time in each other's company, in a variety of situations, then it is difficult to establish that degree of friendship and mutual trust necessary for the project to become successfully implemented in practice. As the letter quoted above indicated, however, attempts at short-term, trial periods of communal living can be sufficiently traumatic experiences for some as to cause them to drop out of the scheme altogether. It is this social problem of recruiting prospective commune members who will retain their commitment to the project through to its implementation in practice which, along with the economic problem of raising the necessary capital, defeats the plans of many utopian members of the commune movement. The projects of others are often defeated by the problems encountered in the actual practice of communal living, and it is to a consideration of some of these problems that attention will now be turned.

In the early chapters it was argued that the contemporary proponents of communal living are the bearers of a long utopian tradition. Some reference was also made in these chapters to the problems encountered by those involved in the practice of community, problems which contributed to the deaths of many of the early ventures. Just as many contemporary communitarians have been moved by ideals similar to those that inspired their predecessors, so many of them have had to confront the same types of problems that plagued the early pioneers. It is extremely difficult to point to a single cause of the collapse of any particular venture. It is easier to locate the final occasion of collapse, the immediate cause of failure such as economic insolvency. It is more difficult to isolate those factors which have contributed to the final death through economic insolvency. Thus many community experiments have failed through the collapse of their economic base, but frequently such a state of affairs has been brought about as a consequence of a number of factors which have contributed to the weakening of the resolve and commitment of the members to the principles upon which the experiment might originally have been founded. In fact, an examination of the history of community experiments reveals that economic causes of failure are very rare. The major causes of failure have traditionally been factional divisions and personal quarrels between members.

Whitney[35] estimated that the average life of a religious community was fifty years, that of a secular community only five years. The reason for this possibly lies not so much in the inherent sacredness of religiously inspired experiments as opposed to the profanity of the secular, but rather can be attributed to the fact that religious communities have managed to develop far more efficient systems of social control over their members than have secular communities. Thus religious communities have traditionally placed a far greater emphasis on faith rather than reason, stressing the importance of divine revelation and unquestioning obedience to the leader who has frequently been viewed as a prophet whose authority stems from spiritual rather than material planes of existence. From such suppositions an autocratic leadership pattern has typically evolved, such as characterized Katherine Tingley's rule over Point Loma. Secular communities, on the other hand, have typically been characterized by a belief in the reason of the individual and his right to criticize. As a result, secular experiments have usually been administered through democratic assemblies of their members. In such gatherings, with everyone free to express his own personal viewpoint, conflict inevitably arose. Thus, New Harmony had six constitutions in two and a half years, and was split by such issues as whether to have complete community of property or not and whether to allow the consumption of alcohol or not. Likewise, acceptance as a member of a religious group typically involved the subjection of the prospective member to a severe selection process where he was required to provide witness of his commitment, faith, and acceptance of the authority of the leader. Such members rarely caused dissension. Founders of secular communities typically believed in the immanent goodness of all men which only required the correct social and economic environment for it to be made manifest. As a result they usually pursued a more 'open door' policy with regard to membership than did the religious communities. The result was generally a commune characterized by an extreme heterogeneity of membership. Thus Haskell said of the members of the Kaweah Co-operative Commonwealth experiment which existed for a brief while at the beginning of this century in California: 'There were dress-reform cranks and phonetic spelling fanatics, word purists and vegetarians. It was a mad, mad world, and being so small its madness was the more visible.'[36] Such a social mixture inevitably led to dissent and internal conflict between the members. The propensity for secular communities to be split by dissensions has usually been heightened by the fact that a large proportion of the members of such communities have been attracted to such experiments as believers in individual freedom and liberty, ends which they have sought to attain through communal living. Such people, who have traditionally found the constraints of life in conventional society irksome, would be unlikely to accept without question the demands of the communal leaders. Thus life at the Whiteway Community was characterized by argument, conflict and dissension between the members who, as anarchists, refused to formulate any collective creed and refused to lay down conditions for membership, but allowed anyone to join them.

One other possible reason for the relative longevity of life displayed by many religious communities compared with the secular variety could lie in the fact that the members of the former have traditionally viewed their involvement in the communal experiment as a means to salvation. As a result, they have generally been more willing to undergo the rigorism of communal life as preparation for their ultimate goal. In contrast, the members of many anarchist and socialist communities have been searching for 'heaven on earth' in the here and now. When they have discovered that the actual practice of community living fell short of this yardstick, then dissatisfaction and disillusionment resulting in the break-up of the experiment frequently followed. Such was the fate of many of the experiments inspired by Fourier's ideas in the United States in the nineteenth century.

Whether a commune is inspired by religious or secular motives and systems of belief or not, if it is to survive for any length of time, then the problems which have defeated past experiments and which continue to trouble contemporary ventures must be overcome. Generally speaking, the problematic areas of communal life relate to the potential sources of conflict and dissension within the commune, and to the sources of conflict between the commune and the wider society in general and the state in particular.

Nordhoff argued that in order for a community to enjoy long life, the members[37]

should place *all* the power in the hands of their leader, and

> solemnly promise him unhesitating trust and obedience;
> specifying only that he should contract no debts, should attempt
> no new enterprise without unanimous consent, and should at
> all times open his purposes and his acts to the whole society.

However, the attempts of particular members of a community to assert their authority over the rest of the body can be an important source of conflict leading to the collapse of the venture. Thus the examples of Katherine Tingley at Point Loma and Robert Owen at New Harmony would seem to indicate that there is a strong likelihood for the founders of any communal venture to develop the belief that they themselves possess the sacred interpretation of the truth, and their attempts to impose their version of the truth on the rest of the membership can be an important source of dissent within the community. This was the problem that confronted the members of one community which I encountered during the course of my research, and was the reason why some of the members left. A house had been bought in a large city in the north of England and the owner invited his friends to join him in order to found a commune. His friends, mainly anarchists, joined him there, and for a short while life within the community was untroubled. After a while, however, differences of opinion emerged between the members over such issues as sexual arrangements within the house, whether the commune members were to devote themselves mainly to activist policies with regard to the local community or concentrate on the development of close and honest relationships between the members within the commune itself. One of the members described this issue as being concerned with whether the commune was to be inward or outward looking in its orientation. The founder of the commune wanted it to be an 'inward-looking' venture. In pursuance of this aim, he demanded that the members institute a practice of complete sexual freedom within the commune, a practice which one of the other members interpreted to me as being aimed mainly at satisfying the owner's desire to sleep with each woman in the house. The other members refused to agree with this demand. The owner then started using the fact that he owned the property as a means of coercing the others into agreement. It developed to the stage where he was leaving notices around the house containing threats as to what he would do if the others continued to refuse to comply with his requests. The final result was that the majority of the original members of the commune eventually left, because of the conflict over the particular issue of sleeping arrangements and also because of what they viewed as the owner's increasing tendency to view himself as the 'guru' of the commune, and his continued attempts to legislate over all areas of individual life within the commune.

This particular example illustrates a number of other sources of potential conflict within a community. One is the issue of sexual relationships between members. Noyes complained that among the accounts of the collapse of the American experiments[38]

Large departments of dangerous passion are entirely ignored. For instance, in all the memoirs of the Owen and Fourier Associations not a word is said on the 'Woman Question'. Among all the disagreements and complaints, not a hint occurs of any jealousies and quarrels about love matters. In fact women are rarely mentioned; and the terrible passions connected with distinction of sex, which the Shakers, Rappites, Oneidians, and all the rest of the religious Communities have had so much trouble with, and have taken so much pains to provide for or against, are absolutely left out of sight.

Although I obtained little direct knowledge of people leaving communes in contemporary Britain because of problems concerning the relationships between the sexes, there can be little doubt that this can be, and is, an important area of conflict. Thus one women wrote of her experiences of life in hippie communes in America:[39]

The talk of love is profuse but the quality of relationships is otherwise. The hip man like his straight counterpart is nothing more, nothing less, than a predator. His sexual experience is largely an act of conquest or rape and certainly nothing more than an expression of hostility. The idea of sexual liberation for the woman means she is not so much free to fuck but free to get fucked over.

Related to this issue is another potential source of conflict and disaffection of commune members. This concerns the conflict between the traditionally taken-for-granted definition of the role of the woman in the home as the cook and dish washer and the practice of living within a community that is seeking to institute full equality between the sexes with regard to work tasks within the group. This is something that can be felt particularly strongly by men, such as the male member of a commune in London who informed me that the biggest personal disadvantage of communal living was the time commitment to cooking and so on.

Very often, of course, it has been these issues concerned with practical living within the commune that have contributed to their collapse rather than issues of 'grand ideological principle'.[40] Thus things like people holding to different standards of cleanliness and hygiene can give rise to conflict within a community. Very often this conflict involves disputes between the sexes. Thus of seven responses I obtained from the members of one commune with regard to what they considered to be the greatest personal disadvantage of communal living, one male mentioned 'living in squalor', while the two female members of the commune emphasized this point. One remarked that the greatest disadvantage for her was 'sharing the kitchen and bathroom which others like kept untidy'. For the other female member the major disadvantage involved 'living in squalor, and sharing things like the washing machine and the sewing machine which tend to get bust'.

Another of the major problems of actually living in a commune is that of privacy, or rather the lack of privacy. That this has traditionally been a problem involved in community living is illustrated by the fact that Nordhoff remarked:[41]

Some things the communist must surrender; and the most precious of these is solitude. The man to whom at intervals the faces and voices of his kind become hateful, whose bitterest need it is to be sometimes alone—this man need not try communism.

This problem of the lack of personal privacy was mentioned by a number of respondents. Thus, for one member of a commune in the south of England, the major disadvantage of communal living was 'the lack of privacy within the community. There needs to be more "space" in every sense of the word.' The related problems of space and privacy were emphasized particularly strongly by the members of one activist community consisting of half a dozen people living in a terraced house. For them it was the occasionally felt lack of privacy allied with the continual demand on their time and energy made by the inhabitants of the local community that caused them particular stress. Thus one member informed me that the main disadvantage was the 'lack of privacy, and sometimes so much work, that one has little time to think'.

While continuous contact with fellow commune members was viewed by many as an important means of developing self-awareness, for others, particularly those activists who were more concerned with direct intervention in the affairs of the surrounding community than with self-discovery, such experiences were seen as causing personal stress and inter-personal friction. Few people have managed to develop the ability to love their fellow men as brothers all the time and in all situations. Even the most committed pacifist must feel, on occasions, conflict between the wish to follow the path of forgiveness, brotherly love and turning the other cheek and the temptation to follow the easier path of hatred and violence. For such people who do not live in a commune, however, it is possible for them to hide away from their fellow men for a while, to avoid those people who bring out the worst in them, and pursue other strategies which enable them to maintain their equanimity. For those who live in communes, however, the choice of strategies to be pursued is extremely limited. It is very difficult to avoid contact with someone whom you dislike when you share the same house together. This problem can appear to many commune members as insurmountable. Such a view was expressed by one respondent who informed me that 'A great tendency for close living produces tension of greater degrees than normal, and no way seems open to relieve them'. He was merely echoing the thoughts of Frances Wright who wrote, concerning the collapse of the Nashoba Community in America, 'That which produces in the world only common-place jealousies and every-day squabbles, is sufficient to destroy a community.'[42]

Many communes make use of a weekly gathering of all the members for them to air their grievances against members of the commune in particular and against the communal life as practised the previous week in general. These weekly encounter groups are, however, not a novel solution to the problem of personal conflict within a community. The Perfectionists at Oneida held regular meetings for criticism in which a member would be told, to his face, by the other people assembled, what their opinion was of him. The victim was expected to receive these criticisms in silence, accepting that they were given for his own benefit in a spirit of kindness and brotherly concern, rather than in any mood of vindictiveness. This is of course the theory behind the practice of 't-group' and 'encounter group' sessions: the belief that one's self-awareness can be enhanced through the criticisms of one's fellow men in a situation of complete trust and care.

Another problem encountered by members of communities which stems from the practice of group living and is related to the problem of privacy, is that of the sacrifice of individual freedom that certain people feel is required of them in communal living. When one's life is led in the close company of a group, then it follows that each individual's actions directly affect the lives of the other members of the group in some way or another. While this ecological fact is one that is viewed by many as important from the point of view of developing a true spirit of brotherly love and concern for one's fellow men, others can experience it as a particularly tyrannical restriction upon their individual autonomy. One does not necessarily need an autocratic leader for there to develop a totalitarian regime within a commune. The power of group opinion can be felt as equally dictatorial by some. Thus one respondent informed me that the major personal disadvantages of communal living arise 'when there isn't a balance between individual freedom and community'.

This general problem of individual autonomy versus community responsibility can also be made manifest over the specific issue of

K*   287 private property within a commune. Most communes that I visited in Britain during the course of my research had very few formal rules about sharing property and goods. Where they did, however, then one of the personal problems encountered by certain of their members was this conflict between the desire to conform to the socialistic principles of the community and the desire to retain ownership and control over what had previously been one's private property. Thus one member of an activist commune wrote of the major personal disadvantage which he experienced through living in a community: 'For one brought up on "individualised" possessions—the feeling that one is not a completely free agent in spending money for such things as buying an amplifier or seeing friends in Scotland.' Others, potential commune members, spoke of their fears of 'giving up a lot of personal possessions. I hate to think also that things we have had for a long time would be neglected by others, and that communal things would not be looked after by anybody.' It was largely on account of these problems of living in a commune associated with the question of individual autonomy and privacy versus community that Nordhoff recommended to prospective communitarians not to live in a 'unitary home', but that they should be numerous enough to form a village made up of separate dwellings.[43] This is exactly the strategy which certain members of the contemporary movement in Britain are seeking to adopt. Such a scheme was described in a letter to *Communes*:[44]

> I have been considering the idea of setting up a community for several years now and I feel that the time has come to put forward some definite proposals in the hope that these will lead to a positive response. . . . The type of community that I envisage is a small village of Libertarian/Pacifists close to or within a wider community which is still small enough to be a true community, say up to 50 of us. . . . This should be within 20 or so miles of a reasonably large city so that we are not cut off from cultural, political and social activities. Our group would in general work within our community supplying our own needs in most respects. . . . One main feature would be the possession of its own school which would take our children and some local children free and possibly some children of sympathisers as boarders at a price. The sort of economic activities that I envisage are a small holding or farm making use of what we consider to be the benefits of modern technology, and small workshops making clothing, furniture, pottery etc. on a semi-industrial scale. *Socially the community would provide complete freedom of personal action and privacy while offering communal facilities for common use.*

A similar scheme was outlined to me by a person who was a member of an existing commune housed in a unitary home and who had become dissatisfied with such an arrangement because of the problems outlined above. For such people who seek privacy and freedom of action at the same time as enjoying the benefits of communal living, such schemes of collective living appear extremely attractive.[45]

Of course, whilst such social problems are often the root causes of the collapse of commune ventures, economic problems can also lead to the same result. Thus, the death of the Eel Pie Island Commune was eventually brought about by rising debts and the inability of the members to pay their electricity bills and so on. This in turn was partly a result of the lack of any formal system of collecting finance within the commune and lack of any formal treasurer whose responsibility it was to pay the bills. Without such officers, it only required the departure of those few people who had taken such tasks upon themselves for the collection of contributions to pay for the electricity and water and rates and so on to be forgotten, with the result that the bills mounted up to a level where they were beyond the means of the members to pay. The departure of the original office holders could be traced to their growing dissatisfaction with life in the community and their declining sense of commitment to the project. This disillusionment could, in turn, be traced at least partly to the 'open-door' policy of admitting anyone who cared to join the community as a member. The result of this policy was that the hotel eventually housed an extremely heterogeneous assortment of social types. One of the early divisions within the community occurred over this open-door policy. Some of the members felt that the hotel was being turned into a doss-house and began evicting those whom they considered to be dossers. Others insisted on the right of such people to remain as commune members. As one of the members wrote:[46]

A guy at the Commune has adopted the role of fascist housekeeper. There's a big bar downstairs and he takes it upon himself to throw out dossers he doesn't like. He's got some strange system for selecting them. The problem with people crashing is that some people in the commune approve of it and some don't. There's only one person who does anything about it and that's this guy. Though somebody has written on the wall: 'its' a crime to throw people out at night in the middle of winter'.

Theft, which had been a problem of life in the Whiteway colony early in this century, was another problem encountered by the members of Eel Pie Island Commune, as it was with the members of other urban communes which I visited, where they frequently had 'crashers' sleeping overnight on the premises. Thus it was claimed with regard to the Eel Pie Island venture that 'Somebody is stealing from them—a total of £200 has gone from different rooms, 200 records, record-player, clothes, tools, and also letters are opened and parcels haven't arrived.' Additional problems confronted the members of another open commune:[47]

> There is no need, I know, to say that living and working in a community scene is far from easy. Here at 'Headsland' we have been trying since last summer to do one thing—live harmoniously with each other, and by virtue of having open house to all, spread our beliefs and air our views on Life and Society.
>
> To tell you of our present I have to tell you some of our past. Most of our mistakes stemmed from lack of communication and the failure to achieve realisation—spiritual development leads to harmony in everyday living—the sharing of all the chores and cooking should give as much pleasure as the evening and weekend times of relaxation. Love in the Giving!
>
> Simple things spelt our first and second disasters—people coming in their hordes (often 50 or 60 over a Friday or Saturday night) drained our meagre resources by eating all our week's food and drinking enough tea and coffee for an army; we ended up squabbling amongst ourselves. Because we never had time to discover ourselves or each other. Also, by keeping the doors open to all we attracted the attention of the police, with the obvious result of a 'bust'.
>
> We recovered from that but things never really got going again—lack of trust between the people living in the house and finally real animosity led to the second bust—brought about by one of our own who called the police on us.
>
> So now the remainder are trying to be Phoenix—we have the shadow of imprisonment hanging over our heads—but we also have our convictions, which give us strength to stand and fight for what we believe in, plus the love and support of so many beautiful people, including the landlord and his wife.

Finally, the open-door policy as practised at Eel Pie Island led eventually to the influx of what might be termed a second generation of communards, largely made up of teenagers, who did not share the views of the original members with regard to such issues as communal property and so on. I witnessed one occasion when one of the newer members sold a tent to a visitor. The tent had been acquired by the commune member when he had attended a pop festival with other members of the commune. He felt he had a right to sell it, as he viewed it as his personal property. Some of the original members who witnessed the transaction argued with him to no avail that the tent was in fact communal property, and as such not something that he could sell as an individual. Their arguments failed to impress the 'owner', and true to their belief in non-violence and the freedom of the individual, the others allowed him to complete his transaction, much to the embarrassment of the visitor who had unwittingly caused the dispute. Such experiences only served to convince the older members of the commune that the time had arrived for them to leave the venture in the hands of this second generation. Many of them left, and one of the final consequences of this was the death of the project through the inability of the remaining members to pay the outstanding debts.

The general problem of social control within a commune and in particular the problem of the appropriate attitude to adopt towards those members of the community who are considered lazy and scroungers has been another source of conflict and division between commune members. Thus the attempt of Captain O'Brien to expel slackers from the community at Orbiston in the absence of Abraham Combe, whose pacifist beliefs forbade him to use force, was an important source of conflict in the life of that particular experiment. The members of the Eel Pie Island Commune had to face this problem with regard to the question of the eviction of the dossers. In a way, this problem of the form of social control to be adopted only confronts those communities with a fairly large membership. For those characterized by a small membership, what certain members perceive as the laziness of others can lead to the collapse of the venture due to either of the two sides parting company. Such was the experience of one young couple who wrote:[48]

> We bought a very tatty cottage here in the Welsh
> mountains, towards the end of last year. We moved here with
> another couple and their young son. . . . The four of us, we
> hoped, with our children would form the basis of a community,
> which would grow. After a short time it became apparent that
> this wasn't altogether a good idea. It's easy to judge and blame
> people for not being what you expect them to be, and usually
> unfair, but to them community life seemed to be a nice idea
> and when hard work became involved it was easier to let
> someone else do it, and just sit back and talk. So we parted
> company.

Just as the problem of raising sufficient capital to finance a community venture is one that has defeated many schemes, the possibility that the capital raised might be withdrawn is one that can remain a threat to those communes which are largely financed by funds from a limited number of sources. Thus the marriage of one of the original members of the Whiteway Community who, as the provider of the bulk of the capital that initially financed the community, demanded half the income of the colony for the use of his wife and himself, caused severe problems for the remaining commune members. This risk to communal life that one of the original backers of the scheme will lose faith and leave, demanding the return of their original investment, is one that the members of an activist commune in London have had to face. One of their members wrote to me:

> Life may not continue here much longer in any case. Of the
> two people (brother and sister) who originally pooled their
> savings to buy the house, the sister has departed and now wants
> her share of the cash. So we may well have to sell the place.

The life at the colony at Orbiston was characterized by divisions over different interpretations of Owenite principles which eventually crystallized into a struggle between those in favour of full equality of all members and those in favour of a more realistic and worldlywise policy, involving different rates of reward for different classes of members. There was also conflict between the pacifist leader Combe and those who believed that something more than moral persuasion was required to run a community.

The history of many other community experiments, particularly those founded on some utopian socialist blueprint, reveals a similar incidence of disputes, conflicts, divisions and ultimate failures of experiments over matters concerning the true interpretation of the principles upon which the experiments were founded.

Surprisingly enough, I found little evidence of this sort of problem causing the break-up of any contemporary communes. The reasons for this are largely threefold. First, the majority of modern communities in Britain are characterized by a strong anarchistic bias which involves the rejection of any firm blue-print for social life and for communal life. Life in a community is characterized by the lack of any collective position or official line other than the belief that each member is an individual with a right to hold his own position on various issues, and with the right to 'do his own thing' so long as it does not impinge on the rights of other commune members.

Where this is the case, then there is little likelihood of the development of any clear polarization of forces within a group which could lead to clear splits within the membership on any one issue or principle. Conflicts are more likely to display a criss-cross pattern which acts against the formation of any basic division within the membership.

Second, many communities that were in existence during the course of my research had only come into existence after relatively long periods of planning on the part of their members. Most of the others had evolved rather unintentionally as communes. One of the results of both these processes was the development of a rather pragmatic attitude towards community life on the part of the majority of members. Thus many of the members of those communities that had only come into existence after a relatively long period of planning and preparation had moderated many of their ideals and principles during what to them had appeared to be a long arduous search for finance, property, members and so on. They had come to realize that if one wanted to live in a commune, then banks and building societies, bastions of the capitalist order though they might be, were frequently the only source of financial support. Similarly, many of them had become rather cynical of people with idealistic principles who would talk and talk about the moral superiority of communal living, but who never seemed to do anything to put their ideals into practice.[49]

Such people frequently came to share the views of the unintentional communitarians who argued that no body of principles or blueprint could enable one to cope with the day-to-day contingencies of communal living. The members of one such community in particular went to great lengths to impress upon me their disdain for those aspiring community members who were firmly committed to some detailed and preconceived plan about the true nature of communal living, only to leave the project after a while because life did not conform to their plan. Such people, they felt, would never make good 'commune fodder'.

A third reason for the rather pragmatic attitude that was typical of many commune members was the fact that most communities in Britain that I visited had not been in existence for any great length of time. One of the consequences of this was that few of them had much opportunity to develop ideological splits within their ranks. Another consequence was that they were still very much involved in the problems of day-to-day living in the commune, problems which left little time for the consideration of matters of grand principle. In addition, the majority of these communes were relatively small in number, few having more than a dozen members, and many of these members had been friends prior to joining the commune. The result was that most communes were characterized by a fairly general and broad, although unofficial, agreement on certain matters such as the nature of the collective goal of the commune and so on. The

293

unofficial selection procedure that many of these communes required prospective members to undergo also helped them to avoid ideological conflict between the members. On this point, in fact, it should be mentioned that very few communes in Britain that I encountered were in a position to accept new members. The properties which housed them were usually full to capacity.

Radical secular and religious groups that have sought to withdraw from the world have traditionally come into conflict with the rest of society in general, and the state in particular, over issues such as the relationship of the individual to the state in such matters as the taking of oaths, sending their children to state schools, the civil registration of marriage, compliance with health laws, and conscription and bearing arms in defence of the nation. It was this type of conflict with the wider society that was responsible for the migrations of the Hutterites from Moravia to Hungary, from Hungary to Russia, from Russia to the United States, and from the United States to Canada.

That few experiments in contemporary Britain have come into such conflict with society in this manner would appear to be a reflection of the degree to which the majority of commune members have been willing to accommodate to the ways of the world in order to pursue their communal form of life. It is also a reflection of the fact that there are not, as yet, sufficient a number of communes in Britain for the authorities to perceive them as a threat to the existing order. As a consequence, the major form of conflict between commune and society appears to take the form of police searches for drugs on commune premises.[50] A number of communes, in fact, seek to avoid this type of harassment by prohibiting the possession of drugs on the community property. The members of one commune I visited, however, used a variety of drugs within the community. When I asked them whether or not they were afraid of a police 'bust', they replied that the police knew drugs were to be found on the premises, but they were only really interested in apprehending the 'big pushers'. Despite this, those members who earned some money through dealing in drugs rarely kept their supply within the communal house, through fear of a police raid.

One of the traditional sources of conflict between commune members and the members of the wider society has been over their refusal to bear arms in the service of the state, the legitimacy of which institution having been frequently denied by the communitarians. While I came across a few commune members who had been conscientious objectors during the period when the British state practised conscription, the cessation of this practice has meant that one of the important sources of conflict between commune and state has been avoided by contemporary commune members.

Where an individual denies the state its claim to legitimacy, then one course of action that can be adopted by the radical who believes in the importance of social change through individual exemplary action is the refusal to pay taxes to the state. The majority of communitarians whom I encountered paid no income tax to the state, but the reason for this was the fact that few of them earned an income of a sufficiently high level to be taxed. In one or two cases this was seen as a political act by the individual, that is, the reason they kept their income below taxable level was so as to avoid paying towards the maintenance of a state whose legitimacy they denied. In the majority of cases, however, the low income level was a reflection of the commune member's unwillingness to take on regular, full-time employment. In fact, a number of communitarians obtained their main supply of financial support from the state in the form of supplementary benefits. While many refused to rely on such a source of funds, those who did justified their action in a variety of ways. Thus some would claim that they turned to the state only as a final resort, that they disliked doing it, and that in time they would become self-sufficient within the commune and they could cease drawing upon such sources of aid. Others justified their acceptance of state aid by claiming that society had been the cause of their past unhappy life, and therefore they were justified in taking the financial aid to which they were entitled as compensation. For the majority who drew upon state aid, however, the fact was not something of which they felt proud. Rather, their desire to live in a community and to pursue a particular form of life was stronger than their desire to retain their radical purity, and frequently the only source of financial support for those who wish to live in some rural area, before they become economically solvent through craft production and vegetable growing, is the state. Occasionally a commune member in receipt of state aid would inform me of what he considered to be the persecutory tactics of the local office of the Ministry of Social Security with regard to his attempts to obtain financial support, and I came across one case where the public health authorities had caused trouble for one commune, but apart from such reports and the cases of police searches for drugs, I encountered few instances of what communitarians considered to be overt conflict between the commune and the state.[51]

Apart from conflict between the state and a commune, the hostility of the people inhabiting the area surrounding a communal experiment has been a problem which has confronted many past ventures. Thus one of the earliest experiments in communal living in Britain, the attempt of the Diggers to create a co-operative colony, was frustrated by the inhabitants of the surrounding neighbourhood who, Winstanley wrote:[52]

set fire to six houses, and burned them down, and burned
likewise some of their household stuff, and wearing clothes,
throwing their beds, stools and household stuff, up and down
the Common, not pitying the cries of many little children, and
their frightened mothers, which are Parishioners born in the
Parish.

The Perfectionists of Oneida, the Theosophists of Point Loma, the
Shakers, and the members of such anarchist ventures as Whiteway,
also suffered at the hands of their neighbours. However, the problem
of the hostility of neighbours did not appear to be one encountered
by the majority of commune members in contemporary Britain.
Most of them suggested that their neighbours viewed them as rather
odd and strange, imagining the commune to be a house of drug-
crazed orgies and debauchery. However, during the course of my
research I did not come across any case of great and prolonged
hostility between commune members and their neighbours. This
was partly the result of the efforts generally made by commune
members to demonstrate to their neighbours that they were serious
in their attempts to create a new style of life and, in the rural areas,
to use their land in an economic manner. Commune members
typically appeared to be very concerned with establishing good
relations with their neighbours, and in most cases they appeared to
have succeeded.

Few people—if any—on the island object to their new
neighbours, the hippies. . . . 'They're a grand bunch of young
people. They don't cause any trouble and keep themselves to
themselves. They look a little odd in their strange clothes and
long hair but they're only young and they are not harming
anyone, are they?' said one matronly islander. . . . They have
become integrated into the life of Twickenham to the extent
where their presence in the street is no longer the subject of
gawping or sneering.[53]

Thus, in conclusion, it can be stated that the major problems that
confront communitarians in contemporary Britain are those associated with founding a commune, and the problems associated with
the tensions and stresses that result from a group of people living in
close proximity to each other.

If communitarians can overcome the problems associated with
raising capital to finance their venture and recruit a sufficient
number of suitable members to join them, then their project would
appear to be threatened more by internal conflict and division
between the members over issues like standards of cleanliness, the
behaviour of other members' children, and the alleged laziness of

certain members rather than over issues concerning the distribution of the community's resources, the interpretation of a belief system. It would appear to be the practical problems involved in group living that threaten the existence of most contemporary communes. The threats of ideological split and hostility from the state and the rest of society would not appear to be as great a problem for the modern-day experiments in communal living as they were for the pioneers of the past. It is the petty vexations rather than the grand issues of communal living that threaten community experiments.

Despite all the many dilemmas of communal living which have caused the collapse of so many ventures of the past and which continue to hinder the contemporary exponents of this life style, there is a great deal of truth in the point made in a review of Robert Owen's attempts to create a 'new moral world'. Harrison wrote:[54]

> Although the communitarian vision faded in the late 1840's and 1850's the desire for some personal and social equivalent of the new moral world remained. The most enduring aspects of a social movement are not always its institutions, but the mental attitudes which inspire it and which are in turn generated by it. . . . In many cases this is the real area in which change has been affected, rather than in legislation or the outward arrangement of society. The physical and intellectual experience which participation brings makes a lasting mark on the individuals concerned, even though they do not attain their original goals.

It is to a consideration of the potential contribution that contemporary communes can be seen as making towards the creation of a new social order in the modern industrial world that attention will now be turned in the concluding chapter.

10 Communes and social change

Throughout the preceding chapters a distinction has been drawn between the alienated and the unalienated members of society. It has been argued that for most members of contemporary society the social world which they inhabit is viewed as natural, as possessing a 'thing-like' quality of its own which appears to make social institutions unamenable to change through the actions of mere mortals. It has been argued that individuals can be defined as alienated to the degree to which they accept their own life and that of the society in which it is led as being controlled by impersonal forces beyond their control, and who thereby deny themselves any degree of world-creating and world-changing ability. Such alienated members of society were contrasted with the unalienated utopians: those who refuse to accept the world in which they live as natural, but perceive a gap between what is and what ought to be, and concern themselves with transforming their own lives, society, and its institutions into something more closely approaching their ideal.

What the alienated member of society takes for granted, the utopian puts in question, viewing the social institutions that channel social actions as human constructs that can be transformed by the actions of men in the world. Different types of utopians pursue different projects of action in order to change the world. The communitarians seek to transform the social order through the creation of alternative structures in the here-and-now. Through living exemplary lives within such counter-institutions, they seek to challenge the generally taken for-granted view of the world held by the alienated members of society, and thereby cause them to question those routines of everyday life which have traditionally been left unquestioned.

As such, the typical commune member falls into that radical

tradition defined by Buber as the utopian variety of non-Marxist socialist who[1]

> desires a means commensurate with his ends . . . believes . . . that we must create here and now the space *now* possible for the thing for which we are striving, so that it may come to fulfilment *then*; he does not believe in the post-revolutionary continuity. To put it more precisely: he believes in a continuity within which revolution is only the accomplishment, the setting free the extension of a reality that has already grown to its true possibilities.

Given that most utopians are concerned with the problem of man and society in general, and with the problem of creating those conditions deemed essential for man's happiness and full development in particular, how relevant is the formation of communes as a radical form of action aiming to transform the existing social order and create a new one—an alternative society?

In Chapter 3 an attempt was made to examine the nature of certain key problems faced by the individual living his life within the confines of modern industrial society. It was argued that, among such problems, that of personal identity was of particular importance. It was suggested that one of the consequences of recent social trends for the individual was an under-definition of identity that resulted in a reliance upon material goods as visible symbols of an individual's inner worth. It was argued that increasing numbers of people are responding to their life situation as small cogs in the big wheels of industry, community, and polity, by turning inwards and relying upon their private worlds of home and family for the reaffirmation of their sense of inner worth and dignity. The typical response of the individual to the problem of identity in modern society, it was argued, is a privatized one. It takes the form of an increasingly abstract and attenuated relationship to the larger social forces affecting jobs and community, and the focusing of one's attentions upon the personal strategy necessary to pilot oneself and one's family through the storm of life.

If the analysis presented in Chapter 3 has any validity, then it is arguable that any revolutionary strategy for radical social change in modern industrial societies such as Britain can no longer be based solely on the classical Marxist premise of the inevitable pauperization of the working class and the polarization of the classes with the development of the working class as a class for itself. The problem facing Marx was the social question, the question of the dehumanizing poverty experienced by the masses. He was convinced that the reason the French Revolution failed to found an order of freedom was that it failed to solve the social question. From this he concluded that freedom and poverty were incompatible. He sought to transform the social question into a political force through convincing the alienated masses that poverty was a political, not a natural, phenomenon; the result of violence and violation rather than scarcity. It was his belief that poverty would help to break their shackles of oppression because the poor had nothing to lose but their chains. Thus, while Marx always had as his ultimate goal the attainment of that social order where man should be free to develop whatever potential he might have, his theoretical and practical work was almost solely concerned in promoting the struggle to achieve a negative liberation for the masses, a freedom from oppression. Now it may be a truism to state that liberation and freedom are not the same, but Arendt in her book *On Revolution* has attempted to point out that 'liberation may be the condition of freedom but by no means leads automatically to it; that the notion of liberty implied in liberation can only be negative, and hence, that even the intention of liberation is not identical with the idea of freedom.'[2]

The major problem facing revolutionaries in modern industrial societies is not solely the social question of liberation of the masses from physical want and misery.[3] Of equal importance is the problem of freedom: the need for a development of the awareness on the part of the masses of their own potentialities and their power to transform every given state of existence into a condition for their own free self-realization. There is a paramount need to instil into individuals the positive desire for freedom to take control of their own lives and to realize themselves, rather than a purely negative desire for freedom from the absolute dictates of their bodily needs. However, it is at this point that the crunch comes—for even if modern man is reduced to something resembling a self-seeking cipher in some larger scheme, he is by no means an entirely unwilling slave. For the alienated members of society there appears to be only one game that can be played.

The members of society can be viewed as prisoners of a certain mode of perceiving social reality, and of their place in that reality. It is their acceptance and internalization of what is real, possible, practical, and obvious that makes the continuation of the system possible. While the state does have real direct coercive power through its control of the armed forces and the police, and while the state can be seen as the representative of the ruling classes in society, its real power rests on the acceptance of the prevailing system by the mass of people as the only way life and society can be ordered and run.[4] The real power lies in the fact that the values and the assumptions on which the system rests are never questioned by the mass of people. Thus people play the 'system's' game largely because it is the only one they know. The relentless drive of the experts for efficiency, order, and ever more extensive control, and the levelling down of all individuals so that they resemble predictable parts of some larger machine rather than self-determining beings, is accepted because the scientific and rational values and assumptions on which such activities are based are taken for granted by the mass of people as the only definition of reality that is plausible and available.[5]

Given this, then it can be argued that the social system can persist only as long as its members continue to take for granted without question the institutions, roles, and identities which constitute the system. It follows, therefore, that such human productions are fundamentally fragile. As Berger has argued, 'All socially constructed worlds are inherently precarious. Supported by human activity, they are constantly threatened by the human facts of self-interest and stupidity. The institutional programmes are sabotaged by individuals with conflicting interests.'[6] Thus, one can argue that the strategic problem facing those concerned with creating a new social order is one of influencing the consciousness of individuals so that they develop a felt need to create a richer and more personally rewarding style of life for themselves, and a willingness to forgo the rewards available to those who lead a conventional life style, and a determination to face whatever sanctions that might be aimed against those who deviate from conventional models.

Within this framework, the communitarians' non-recognition of the social norms, values and life styles that are treated as legitimate in the taken-for-granted routines of everyday life, and the production of counter-definitions, can be viewed as potentially revolutionary, in so far as by such actions, they cause people to question the taken-for-granted nature of their lives and to consider and develop alternative forms of individual, social and economic life.

To fulfil this potential, however, a number of criteria must be met. Among these, one might observe that the counter-definitions of reality, of values and norms, must have an audience that has ears with which to hear. Also, the counter-definitions being offered must be centrally situated: i.e. they must challenge the systems of values at the focal points of stress and tension. They must project a confrontation with the core organizing meanings and values of the society. In addition, they must offer forms of action and life-projects which embody alternative structures based on the counter-values and norms, and these must be visible to a sufficiently wide audience who perceive them as living examples of the counter-definitions of reality being implemented. Furthermore, it can be argued that such counter-institutions must appear to be meeting the basic material and physical needs of their members, thereby appearing as realistic alternatives to the actual function-performing institutions of the existing order.

301

With reference to the commune scene in Britain today then, communes can be viewed, and are viewed by their members, as attempts to create bases, areas of freedom and happiness to act as beacon lights for the new age. They are seen by their members as living examples of ways that life can be led and the self developed in productive harmony with others and one's environment and thus to act as a permanent challenge to the existing way of life and to the imagination of ordinary people.

To achieve any widespread influence, it can be argued that existing communes need many more additions to their ranks. The simple fact is that in Britain there are not many communes in existence, and many of these seem to be continually on the verge of collapse. Most have a small and limited membership and many are tucked away in isolated rural areas. Thus it can be argued that, while communes do represent alternative structures and life projects based on the counter-values, they are as yet too limited in number and size to have much influence on society in general and the ordinary man. This of course begs the question of whether or not it is going to be the ordinary man who is going to be responsible for heralding in the New Age, and this point will be returned to below. However, it should be pointed out that, despite all this, the communes and the people in them do offer living examples that challenge the visitor (they have literally thousands of visitors), and those who read of their activities through the general underground press and the more specialized magazines concerned solely with the coverage of community ventures. Such people are challenged not necessarily to go out to form an identical project, but rather to take hold of their lives and selves and start shaping them into something approaching their personal ideal.

Furthermore, there has recently been increasing coverage of various communes and alternative styles of individual and group life in the mass media aimed at popular public consumption. Such an increase in column space and broadcasting time could, of course, merely reflect the curiosity value attributed to such phenomena by journalists and programme editors. It may merely be an indication that the people who select the news for the public are just casting around for new freaks in the human zoo to titillate the imaginations of their public.[7] However, many of the articles and programmes that I have read and seen appeared, to me at least, as genuine and serious attempts to consider such experiments in living as what they professed to be—alternative modes of existence to be led by the individual and the group in modern society.

A significant threat to whatever potential for social change the commune movement might possess is inherent in this exposure to the mass public through the media. At the present time most communes in Britain have been in existence for a limited time. Many are still in the process of finding themselves, and are confronted by many of the problems referred to in the previous chapter. One of the consequences of publicity for such ventures could be that they become flooded by visitors, aspiring members, curious sight-seers and 'crashers' who would interfere with the attempts of the commune members to make their project viable. A further threat lies in the possibility that through the mass media defining commune ventures in a particular way, through portraying communes as this or that sort of experiment seeking to achieve this or that kind of aim, the commune members will seek to turn themselves and their experiment into what the mass media (and particularly the media of the underground) define it as. In so doing, there is the danger that the commune members will lose sight of whatever practical aims they might once have held and be content to bask in their reflected glory as the 'beautiful people'.

A second criterion that must be met if the alternative definitions offered by the communitarians are to fulfil whatever potential contribution towards the creation of a new order that they might have, it has been suggested, is that the counter-definitions of commonly accepted norms, values and definitions of the situation must be centrally situated in so far as they must challenge the dominant system of values at the central points of tension and stress. What are the focal points of strain within the value-structure of modern industrial society? It has been argued that, apart from the social problem of material want and deprivation, the major problem for increasing numbers of people is that of personal identity. It was suggested that a major potential source of tension in society stems from the lack of personal meaning and worth that men find in their work and daily routine.

In so far as the values and ideals of the communitarians can be seen, from one point of view, as reactions to these same sources of tension in society, it can be argued that the counter-culture of which their life styles are living examples possesses real potential for bringing about radical social change—a potential which is likely to increase as the social trends of urbanization, bureaucratization and centralization of power and decision-making, and the automation of the work process continue to develop, in so far as these processes constitute the source of the problems of life for increasingly wider sections of the population.

However, this is only one possible alternative. While it does not seem far-fetched to argue that in the future, if present trends continue, increasing numbers of people are going to look at the communitarians and their experiments in alternative living with envious eyes, it is also conceivable that the revolutionary potential of the communitarians' counter-definitions of reality could be negated by these same forces and processes. One could argue, that as present trends continue and men become ever smaller cogs in ever bigger wheels so the likelihood of their ever being able to conceive of the possibility of alternative styles of life will diminish correspondingly, the power of existing institutions and the difficulties involved in attempting to break out of these constraints increasing with the passage of time.

In turning to a consideration of the nature and revolutionary potential of these counter-definitions of reality, two major themes will be emphasized: the stress placed by communitarians and members of the underground upon individualism and the free development of the self, and the emphasis they place on togetherness and the creation of honest, creative human relationships within the context of the commune.

The stress laid upon cultivating the self and 'doing one's own thing' by the communitarians can be read as a rejection of the over-managed and routinized quality of life in conventional society. It represents an assertion of the claims of the individual self over the claims of society—a claim that the individual has the right to create his own life and that he can only hope to escape the constraints of society once he becomes aware of the extent to which he is a victim of the commonly accepted, taken-for-granted definitions of social reality.

The emphasis placed by the communitarians on 'togetherness' can be seen as an attempt to counterpose to the loneliness and competitive individuality of conventional urban and suburban life a new kind of communalism which is not restricted to the narrow confines of the nuclear family. This emphasis also goes some way towards explaining the interest revealed by many communitarians in Eastern philosophies and religions, characterized as they are by the notion that underlying the multiplicity of all life forms, there exists an all-embracing unity. The stress on the power of love and personal example can be understood in the context of the belief of many commune members in the spiritual and physical community between all things and of their sacred respect for all individuals.

Perhaps the real revolutionary potential of these attempts by the communitarians to present alternative definitions of reality lies in the very fact that they are displaying through their actions the possibility of alternatives to what many respondents considered as the nine-to-five business of daily life rather than just talking about such alternatives. For radical social change, through the agency of human actors, can only occur when, responding to felt strains and tensions within society, people begin collectively to question the prevailing social order and their own place in that order. For this to happen, they must not only be able to conceive of an alternative ideal ordering of life in society; people must first of all be able to envisage the realistic possibility of actually attaining personal and social change.

In other words, few people would suggest that communitarians are providing the sole answer to the problems of life in modern society. They are, however, pointing to the existence of these problems and displaying through their projects and life styles that alternative forms of individual and collective life are possible. There can be no single path to self-fulfilment. The path of community is only one possible way. But only when one understands the possibility of creating new and alternative forms of life can the prospect of choosing and pursuing one's own path arise.

It is here that I think the alleged revolutionary potential of the commune movement in particular, and of the underground in general, is crucially important. By offering alternative definitions of reality, by seeking to display that individuals can create for themselves a life where work has meaning, where companionship and individuality can be fruitfully combined, by seeking to live lives which form integral wholes and not fragmented sets of roles to be played at, the communitarians are seeking the subversion of conventional society from within by cutting away the moral cement that holds the existing system together. They are seeking to offer alternatives and working examples of the fact that man can create his own living environment.

The degree to which the communitarians are successful in this aim will obviously depend very much upon the extent to which they can meet the kinds of problems associated with communal living referred to in the previous chapter. These include the problems involved in reconciling individuality with communality, the basic problem of interpersonal relationships and compatibility, and the problems associated with economic survival. Although the history of contemporary communes could not be described by any stretch of the imagination as trouble-free, and even though many communes die, the fact that increasing numbers are being founded is evidence of the strength of the idea and the impact of the example set by the communitarians. In this context I think it is relevant to quote from an article by an American sociologist on the revolutionary potential of the hippies. He might well have been writing about the communitarians and the members of the underground in general. He has written:[8]

There is, as Max Weber would have put it, an elective affinity between prominent styles and themes in the hippie subculture and certain incipient problems of identity, work, and leisure that loom ominously as Western industrial society moves into an epoch of accelerated cybernation, staggering material abundance, and historically unprecedented mass opportunities for relative leisure and enrichment of the human personality. This is not to say that the latter are the hidden causes or tangible motivating forces of the former. Rather the point is that the hippies, in their collective, yet radical, break with the constraints of our present society, are—whether they know it or not (some clearly do intuit a connection)—already rehearsing *in vivo* a number of possible solutions to central life problems posed by the emerging society of the future.

Finally, is it possible to make any generalizations about the nature of the potential audience which might have the ears to hear and the eyes to see this rehearsal of 'possible solutions to central life problems posed by the emerging society of the future'?

Some light might possibly be thrown upon this question if it was rephrased and one asked which groups in society are particularly exposed to these problems. To the extent that the memory of the pre-World War II years of poverty still exists in the minds of many of the older generation, and to the extent that significant numbers of the working class and working-class youth still experience genuine material deprivation, one can argue that the important life problems for them still revolve around the social question of liberation from material want rather than the issue of personal freedom and self-fulfilment. For this reason one can hypothesize that it is largely upon certain sections of the middle classes, the young, and particularly the educated middle-class youth, that the message of the communitarians and of the members of the underground in general does, and will continue to, fall for the immediate future. However, I would argue that the size of this audience is likely to increase in future years as more people get together to create intentional communities, and as the memory of the poverty and deprivation of the pre-World War II years, which ties many people to the prevailing social order, becomes increasingly dim.

Increasingly, in the future, it appears to me, the problem of the quality of man's life in his work and in his daily routines is going to take on new significance in the minds of men. At the present time, however, it would appear that it is mainly amongst the educated young that such questions are being raised. The problems that increasing numbers in this group see themselves as facing include the apparent need to choose without adequate criteria between the many social roles that have been fragmented out of traditional society, the apparent need to work to earn a living rather than to fulfil oneself, and the apparent need to make sense out of the fractured roles and organizations that fail to provide a unified and meaningful sense of personal identity and purpose for the individual.

Given the fact that increasing numbers of educated youth are rejecting these demands and are searching for new patterns of life and living, then one can argue that the communitarians stand as one of the few available images or role-models towards which the young can grow without feeling the need to sacrifice themselves to such demands.

For the existing social order to be transformed through the creation of an alternative society it is necessary that eventually people *en masse*, and not just the young, become utopians through seeking to transcend their habitual patterns of action, their traditional ways of life, and their taken-for-granted expectations and ways of looking at the world. The growth and spread of such utopianism will be made more likely if the activities of the communitarians become more closely integrated than they are at present with the activities of other groups aiming at institutional and cultural change from the bottom up. Of special significance amongst these groups are the movements for workers' control and women's liberation, the movements for tenants' control, including the squatters, the welfare-client organizations such as the claimants' unions, and the 'free education' movements. The likelihood of close links developing between such movements and the commune movement could in turn depend very much upon the degree of co-operation and mutual aid that is established between the rural and the urban communes, for at the present time it is largely through the activities of the members of the urban communes that the personal contacts between the commune movement and these other movements are being made.

What is obviously necessary is for people in communes in particular and members of the underground in general to increase and expand their practical efforts to create viable alternative institutions to counter those institutions presently concerned with the processes of production and consumption in particular. That is, it will not be sufficient merely to talk about the alternative society and condemn the straight society and its members. The proponents of a new, non-coercive social and political order have got to take a leaf out of the communitarians' book and actually get down to the task of creating alternative institutions based on the values of co-operation, personal autonomy and participatory democracy which are sufficiently viable to seduce people away from their straight counterparts. One straightforward practical obstacle facing those seeking to create such counter-institutions at the present time is, of course, the lack of financial and material resources.

It is partly for this reason, but mainly because the kind of revolutionary process envisaged by those seeking the creation of an alternative society is one that takes place from the bottom up, as opposed to involving the seizure of central power, that the change brought about by the communitarians and the members of the underground is likely to be a slow, gradual, and cumulative process involving the steady expansion of the 'liberated zones' represented by the communes, the free schools, the experiments in the common ownership of industry and similar ventures.

A reading of the histories of past revolutions would appear to justify the argument that an age of freedom can never be attained by a revolutionary process that involves the forcible seizure of the central political power by a minority of the population. Another conclusion that can be drawn from such a study is that any attempt to establish such a non-exploitative order within the limited confines of the nation state is also doomed to failure. In so far as the kinds of developments that are taking place in Britain are also taking place throughout the North American and European continents, then it would appear that the commune movement within the context of the general underground movement has the potential of becoming one of the first genuine international movements for social change. The fact that the global ecological crisis is forcing people to question the role of trans-national capitalist enterprises and to start thinking of the social, political and economic systems of the world as a whole and not just of their own nation state and society, can only strengthen this process. The future of the movement to create an alternative society will depend very much upon its success in convincing the people of the world, and especially the people of the under-developed Third World, that the problems which they as utopians are seeking to confront at the present time are not unique to a particular nation state, but are those which all large-scale societies must eventually confront and seek to overcome if they are to avoid becoming poor imitations of the nations of the capitalist West and the state socialist East.

Whether or not the commune movement, along with the other social movements with which it shares basic orientations and goals, will ever fulfil their potential for making a significant contribution towards the creation of a non-exploitative social order must remain, in the final analysis, a matter of conjecture. One cannot make any decisive, predictive statement in the here and now about what is to be in the future. One cannot foresee at this time whether the alternative society which many communitarians believe to be appearing now will ever be realized on a society-wide and eventually a world-wide scale, or whether the statements and claims of the commune members will simply prove to have been empty rhetoric.

Ultimately, I believe, one's assessment of the revolutionary potential of any dissident group will depend upon one's basic value-position. Whether one believes that the modern-day communitarians are doomed to parasitic irrelevancy as a minority group living in their ghetto-like settlements, or whether one believes that they hold the key to a new and superior order of individual and social existence, will depend largely upon one's attitudes to the existing social order and the real nature of social change.

What one can claim with certainty, however, is that the creation of a society where we think of our fellow man's needs rather than exploit him, where an individual can grow and develop his full potential and not live in fear of others, a society where love and co-operation with others are the prime qualities and not the selfishness and power-seeking that appears to characterize the existing social order—the realization of such a society will never be achieved unless people actively and collectively seek to create such a world through transforming their personal lives and their relationships with others in the here and now, rather than just waiting for the revolution from above at some time in the distant future. This is the lesson that the communitarians have for those of us who share with them the belief in the desirability and attainability of such an age of freedom.

Notes

1 Introduction

1 Gene Sharp, *Exploring Non-violent Alternatives*, Boston, Porter Sargent, 1970, p. viii.
2 Quoted in Satish Kumar, *Non-violence or Non-existence*, London, Christian Action, 1969.
3 P. Berger, *The Precarious Vision*, New York, Doubleday, 1961, p. 10.
4 P. Berger, *The Social Reality of Religion*, London, Faber & Faber, 1969, p. 11.
5 P. Berger, *Invitation to Sociology*, Harmondsworth, Penguin, 1966, pp. 166–7.
6 A. Schutz, *Collected Papers, II: Studies in Social Theory*, ed. and introd. by A. Broderson, The Hague, Martinus Nijhoff, 1964, p. 231.
7 H. Blumer, 'Social movements', pp. 8–29, in B. McLaughlin (ed.), *Studies in Social Movements*, New York, Free Press, 1969, p. 8.
8 Ibid., p. 8.
9 R. V. Hines, *California's Utopian Colonies*, San Marino, Huntington Library, 1953, p. 5.
10 K. Mannheim, *Ideology and Utopia*, London, Kegan Paul, Trench, Trubner, 1936, p. 173.
11 Ibid., p. 176.
12 Richard Fairfield, *Communes USA, A Personal Tour*, Baltimore, Penguin, 1972, p. 3.
13 See T. Kelly, 'Communes in Japan', *Communes*, 31 February 1970, pp. 1–7.
14 See S. Engert, 'Living now for the time after the Revolution', in *Peace News*, 1740, 31 October 1969, p. 8.
15 See P. Van Mensch, 'Something on the Dutch commune scene', in *Communes*, 31, February 1970, pp. 10–11.
16 See M. Mader, *The Kibbutz—An Introduction*, London, World Zionist Organization, p. 2.
17 O. Klapp, *Collective Search for Identity*, New York, Holt, Rinehart & Winston, 1969, p. 63.
18 *Communes*, 37, March 1971, p. 21.

19 E. Goffman, 'The moral career of the mental patient', pp. 88–98, in E. Rubington and M. S. Weinberg, (eds), *Deviance: The Interactionist Perspective*, New York, Macmillan, 1968, p. 89.

20 For a similar approach adopted with regard to the processes by which an individual becomes a marihuana user, see H. S. Becker, *Outsiders*, London, Collier-Macmillan, 1966.

21 See Schutz, op. cit., pp. 11–19.

22 Ibid., p. 131.

23 See especially C. Nordhoff, *The Communistic Societies of the United States*, New York, Dover, 1966; J. H. Noyes, *History of American Socialisms*, New York, Dover, 1966; W. H. G. Armytage, *Heavens Below*, London, Routledge & Kegan Paul, 1961; C. H. Bishop, *All Things Common*, New York, Harper & Row, 1950.

24 It is interesting to note that in the urban activist communes where certain members claimed allegiance to such organizations as the International Socialists, such people did retain a fundamental belief in class conflict as the prime historical mover and at the same time accepted, albeit reluctantly, the necessity of resorting to violent means at some stage in the revolutionary struggle of the future.

2 The communitarian tradition

1 See Egon Bittner, 'Radicalism and the organisation of radical movements', pp. 928–40, *American Sociological Review*, vol. 28, 1963.

2 In distinguishing between religious and secular radicals I am merely trying to make an analytical distinction between those whose interpretation of the world and of the life situation of man in the world invokes a supernatural authority, those who relate the experiences of everyday life in the material world to another plane of reality; and those radicals whose interpretative schema bears no reference to any such ultimate level of reality, interpreting the world and the meaning of life in the world without any reference to any sacred realm or supra-empirical order of existence.

3 This analysis draws heavily upon the perspective presented in P. Berger, *A Rumour of Angels*, Harmondsworth, Penguin, 1971, especially Chapter 1.

4 Laura Ross, 'The Newhaven Commune, Edinburgh', in *Eclectics*, quarterly newsletter of the Student Christian Movement in Scotland, no. 1, mark 2, October 1971, p. 11. Emphasis added.

5 As one respondent expressed it, 'Sure, I suppose it is an escape in a way, but it is an escape to something, an alternative. Communes can help to change society if they grow enough.'

6 M. Mead, 'Communes: a challenge to all of us', *Redbook*, vol. 135, August 1970, pp. 50–1.

7 Quoted in G. Sabine, *The Works of Gerrard Winstanley*, New York, Cornell, 1941, p. 409.

8 This is a phrase used by Martin Buber in the foreword to his work, *Paths in Utopia*, London, Routledge & Kegan Paul, 1949.

9 The Himalayan Academy in California, U.S.A., requires its members, however, to take vows of celibacy and poverty and its residents are

L   311 considered to be in training for the priesthood. See Fairfield, op. cit., pp. 160–2. Similar sorts of vows are required of the members of the 'Radha Krishna Temple and Krishna Consciousness Society' in Britain.

10 For a personal account of life in this monastery, see Mark Hill, 'Samye-Ling', pp. 15–17, *Scottish International*, vol. 5, no. 1, January 1972.

11 See Chapter 6, 'Religious communes in Britain' below, for an examination of this community.

12 D. Horn, 'Kingsway', in *Catonsville Roadrunner*, no. 26, Summer 1971.

13 Ibid.

14 The world-rejecting ascetic as a religious type differs from the inner-directed ascetic type suggested by Weber. For the latter, the concentration of human action on activities leading to salvation is seen as requiring the participation of the individual within the world and its instituions, it being the responsibility of the individual as the elect instrument of God to bring the world into accord with God's will through such involvement. See Max Weber, *The Sociology of Religion*, London, Methuen, 1965, pp. 166–83.

15 N. Cohn, *The Pursuit of the Millennium*, London, Paladin, 1970, p. 253.

16 See V. Peters, *All Things Common*, University of Minnesota Press, 1965, p. 3.

17 While their principles include an injunction against litigation, one colony in Canada did decide to resort to legal defence over a dispute involving the people of the local area where the colony was situated. See J. Bennet, *Hutterian Brethren: The Agricultural Economy and Social Organisation of a Communal People*, Stanford University Press, 1967, p. 33.

18 See *The Community Voice*, no. 1, February 1970, published by the Kingsway Community.

19 B. Wilson, 'A typology of sects', pp. 361–83, in R. Robertson (ed.), *Sociology of Religion*, Harmondsworth, Penguin, 1969, p. 370.

20 This theme will be returned to in greater length below, see Chapter 6.

21 Quoted in Emmy Arnold, *Torches Together*, Woodcrest, Rifton, New York, Plough Publishing House, 1964, pp. 198–202.

22 See J. Whitworth, 'The Bruderhof in England: a chapter in the history of a utopian sect', pp. 84–101, in M. Hill (ed.), *A Sociological Yearbook of Religion in Britain*, London, Student Christian Movement Press, 1971. See also B. Zablocki, *The Joyful Community*, Baltimore, U.S.A., Penguin Books, 1971.

23 See Chapter 9, 'Communes and the nuclear family', for an extended discussion of this issue.

24 See Chapter 6 below.

25 John Pordage, 'Innocence appearing through the dark mists of pretended guilt', 1955. Quoted in Armytage, *Heavens Below*, p. 32.

26 J. Shawcross (ed.), *Coleridge's Biographia Literaria*, Oxford, 1907, p. 98. Quoted ibid., p. 38.

27 Quoted ibid., p. 239.

28 A. Huxley, *Brave New World Revisited*, London, Chatto & Windus, 1959, p. 159.
29 See A. Huxley, *The Doors of Perception*, London, Chatto & Windus, 1954. Also, see Huxley's introduction to *The Song of God: Bhagavad-Gita*, tr. Swami Prabhavananda and C. Isherwood, London, New English Library, 1951.
30 The Theosophists established a community at Point Loma in California in 1897 which remained in existence for over forty years. See R. Hines, *California's Utopian Colonies*, and also E. A. Greenwalt, *The Point Loma Community in California, 1897–1942*, Berkeley, University of California Press, 1955.
31 K. Marx and F. Engels, *Manifesto of the Communist Party*, Moscow, Foreign Languages Publishing House, p. 64.
32 See Engels's essay, 'Socialism: Utopian and Scientific', pp. 109–52, in L. S. Feuer (ed.), *Marx and Engels: Basic Writings on Politics and Philosophy*, London, Fontana, 1969.
33 M. Buber, *Paths in Utopia*, p.13.
34 Ibid.
35 This theme will be returned to below in Chapter 9.
36 Quoted in J. F. C. Harrison, *Robert Owen and the Owenites in Britain and America*, London, Routledge & Kegan Paul, 1969, p. 60.
37 *Communes*, 29, October 1969, p. 9.
38 Harrison, op. cit., p. 58.
39 Quoted in I. L. Horowitz (ed.), *The Anarchists*, New York, Bell, 1964, p. 575.
40 R. Sampson, *The Anarchist Basis of Pacifism*, London, Peace Pledge Union, 1970, p. 16.
41 G. Woodcock, *Anarchism*, Harmondsworth, Penguin, 1963, pp. 20–1.
42 For information concerning pacifist communities in Britain during the inter-war years, see *Community in a Changing World*, West Byfleet, Community Service Community, 1942; also see George Ineson's autobiography, *Community Journey*, London, Sheed & Ward, 1956.
43 Joseph Burtt, in his foreword to Nellie Shaw, *Whiteway: A Colony on the Cotswolds*, London, Daniels, 1935, p. 5.
44 In 1969 Lou Gottlieb, the legal owner of thirty acres upon which was founded the Morning Star Ranch, a commune in California, attempted to relinquish his legal title to the land and turn it over to a more universal figure—he deeded his land to God. However, as God was not recognized by the court to be a 'natural or artificial person', He could not legally own Gottlieb's property. See Fairfield, *Communes U.S.A.*, pp. 252–4.
45 Ibid., pp. 59–60.
46 Ibid.
47 See Chapter 9 below, for a discussion of the problems associated with communal living.
48 On a number of occasions when I first visited a commune during the course of my research, I would be informed that all of the members were 'individuals' by one of their number. I was frequently told that if I wanted to obtain a full picture of the group I would need to talk

with each individual member rather than rely upon the impressions of only one or two.

49 For instance, the following passage was written by one of the members of a small community in Gloucestershire: 'The centre has come into existence as a response to the problems created by modern life in the west, a way of life which is increasingly unsatisfactory and frustrating to all sorts of people and which seems to threaten the survival of man on this planet. It is not difficult to see that it is the individual who is the source of energy and life in society, that society has no violation or life apart from that of its individual members, that the ecological problems which now face us are created by individual acts from minute to minute all over the world. And it is not difficult to see that these same problems can only be solved in so far as the individual can change his modus vivendi so that he no longer contributes to their causes.' Peter Twilley, 'Membership of a Sarvodaya community', pp. 4–17, *Tat*, no. 1, January 1969, p. 5.

3 Man in society

1 *A Federal Society Based on the Free Commune*, a Commune Movement publication, p. 1 (emphasis added).
2 Ibid. (emphasis added).
3 M. Stein, *The Eclipse of Community*, New York, Harper & Row, 1964, pp. 283–4.
4 E. Fromm, *Fear of Freedom*, London, Routledge & Kegan Paul, 1942, p. 247.
5 H. Marcuse, *Reason and Revolution*, London, Routledge & Kegan Paul, 1968, p. 273.
6 Ibid., p. 289.
7 R. Nisbet, *Community and Power*, New York, Oxford University Press, 1962, p. viii.
8 Carlo Levi, *Christ Stopped at Eboli*, London, Landsborough Publications, 1959, p. 58.
9 Nisbet, op. cit., p. 15.
10 Fromm, op. cit., pp. 34–5.
11 It should be pointed out that Marx considered the state of alienation to be common to all members of capitalist society, bourgeoisie as well as the proletariat. Thus, in the *Holy Family* he wrote, 'The propertied class and the class of the proletariat represent the same human self-alienation. But the former feels comfortable and confirmed in this self-alienation, knowing that this alienation is its own power and possessing in it the semblance of a human existence. The latter feels itself ruined in this alienation and sees in it its impotence and the actuality of an inhuman existence.' Cited in D. McLellan, *The Thought of Karl Marx*, London, Macmillan, 1971, pp. 107–8.
12 The following analysis draws very heavily upon the work of Berger and Luckmann, see P. Berger and T. Luckmann, 'Social mobility and personal identity', *European Journal of Sociology*, vol. 5, 1964, pp. 331–43. See also, J. H. Goldethorpe *et al.*, *The Affluent Worker in the Class Structure*, Cambridge University Press, 1969.

13 R. Tawney, *Religion and the Rise of Capitalism*, London, Murray, 1926, p. 28.
14 A. MacIntyre, *Secularization and Moral Change*, London, Oxford University Press, 1967, p. 12.
15 Berger and Luckmann, op. cit., p. 336.
16 Ibid., p. 339.

4 Youth, the youth culture and the underground

1 O. Klapp, *Collective Search for Identity*.
2 Ibid., p. 63.
3 Ibid., p. 56.
4 See H. Blumer, 'Social movements'.
5 R. Neville, *Play Power*, London, Cape, 1970, p. 18.
6 See, for example, *Hapt*, July 1970: *Bitman*, nos 1, 2 and 3; *Arts Lab Newsletter*, March and April, 1970; *IT*, especially nos 65, 66, 68, 70 and 77; *Gandalf's Garden*, no. 34.
7 For example, the following advertisement appeared in *Peace News*, 1799, 18 December 1970: 'Commune Movement needs new London secretary. Ideal applicant would live in commune in Central London area, but anybody with time and energy and a telephone will do as long as he/she is prepared to help produce and distribute the magazine and deal with enquiries. No money in it.'
8 See Jock Young, *The Drug Takers*, London, MacGibbon & Kee, 1971, p. 126, for an attempt to contrast what he terms 'formal work values' with the 'subterranean values' of young drug-users.
9 Blumer, op. cit., p. 9.
10 B. M. Berger, 'Hippie morality', p. 153.
11 J. Berke (ed.), *Counter-Culture*, London, Owen, 1969, p. 22.
12 J. Nuttall, *Bomb Culture*, London, Paladin, 1970, p. 20.
13 F. Davis, 'Why all of us may be hippies someday', *Transaction*, vol. 5, no. 2, December 1967, pp. 14–15.
14 K. Keniston, *The Uncommitted*, New York, Harcourt, Brace & World, 1965, p. 271.
15 Norman Mailer, *The Naked and the Dead*, London, Panther, 1969, pp. 346–7.
16 R. Flacks, 'Social and cultural meanings of student revolt: some informal comparative observations', pp. 340–57, *Social Problems*, vol. 17, no. 3, Winter 1970, p. 348.
17 There are over eight million men and women aged between fifteen and twenty-four in Britain.
18 The rapid increase in fashion turnover has been attributed to other things apart from the increased problem of identity. See Klapp, *Collective Search for Identity*, p. 73. 'These extravagant styles reflect not only changing tastes but the fact that growing abundance in many countries makes it possible for more people to enter the fashion race and indulge their taste for novelties, including the vanity of wishing to be somebody else; psychological mobility (the ability and wish to imagine oneself in another's place) is stimulated by radio, movies, television, advertising, education, and the example of celebrities;

increasing leisure offers new opportunities for escapes and adventures of identity.'

19 Ibid., p. 102.
20 See E. Goffman, *Presentation of Self in Everday Life*, Harmondsworth, Penguin, 1971.
21 Davis, op. cit., p. 18.
22 P. Buckman, *The Limits of Protest*, London, Gollancz, 1970, pp. 221–2.
23 Neville, op. cit., p. 76.
24 This belief in sexual freedom was one propounded by Wilhelm Reich, who is frequently quoted by underground intellectuals in support of their claim that freedom from sexual inhibition constitutes an important step towards the creation of a free social order.
25 Allen Ginsberg, 'Consciousness and practical action', pp. 170–81, in Berke, op. cit., p. 174.
26 Schutz, *Collected Papers II*, p. 231.
27 Young, op. cit., p. 160.
28 W. James, *The Varieties of Religious Experience*, London, Longmans, 1952, p. 391.
29 Idem.
30 See, for example, Huxley (1954), *Doors of Perception*, and W. Braden, *The Private Sea: L.S.D. and the Search for God*, New York, Bantam, 1968.
31 L. Schneiderman, 'Psychological notes on the nature of mystical experience', pp. 91–100, *Journal for the Scientific Study of Religion*, vol. 6, no. 1, 1967, pp. 94–5.
32 In the *Directory of Communes* (1970) there were listed some fifty mystical/esoteric groups in London.
33 Letter to *Communes*, no. 29, October 1969, p. 29.
34 For a personal account of the techniques used at the Esalen Institute, see Rasa Gustaitis, *Turning On*, London, Weidenfeld & Nicolson, 1969.
35 See the account of Centre Nucleus in Chapter 6 below. The founder of this community, Christopher Hills, has co-authored a book on the subject of encounter groups. See C. Hills and R. B. Stone, *Conduct your own Awareness Sessions*, New York, Signet, 1970.
36 'Membership of a Sarvodaya Community', pp. 4–17, *Tat*, p. 4.
37 This theme will be returned to in Chapter 10, 'Communes and social change'.
38 Woodcock, *Anarchism*, p. 442.
39 Ibid., p. 450.
40 See especially G. Woodcock, 'Anarchism revisited', *Commentary*, August 1968; J. Newfield, *A Prophetic Minority*, New York, New American Library, 1966; G. Ostergaard, *Latter-Day Anarchism: The Politics of the American Beat Generation*, Ahmedabad, Harold Laski Institute of Political Science, 1964; T. Roszack, *The Making of a Counter Culture*, London, Faber & Faber, 1970; and M. Lerner, 'Anarchism and the American counter-culture', *Government and Opposition*, vol. 5, no. 4, Autumn 1970, pp. 430–55.

41 J. Beck, 'Paradise now', *International Times* (London), 12–25 July 1968.
42 Quoted by Lerner, op. cit., p. 435.
43 Dick Fairfield, editor of *Modern Utopian*, in a letter to WIN, 1 January 1969.
44 R. Elzey, 'Founding an anti-university', in Berke, op. cit., p. 232.
45 Nuttall, op. cit., pp. 198–9.
46 R. Bluer, 'Birmingham free you', *Peace News*, 1799, 18 December 1970.
47 Ibid., p. 6.
48 It is interesting to note that on the bookshelves of the majority of communes which I visited one would find a copy of A. S. Neill's book *Summerhill*. This fact is indicative of the interest taken by commune members in alternative educational systems in general, and in the work and example of Neill in particular. The son of one member of a commune with whom I spent some time was a student at Summerhill. See *Bitman*, 3, 1971, pp. 53–60, for a list of progressive/ alternative schools in Britain.
49 See, for example, Ann Link, 'A directory of alternative work', *Peace News*, 1824, 18 June 1971, p. 6.
50 Fifty-six claimants' unions were listed in *Peace News*, 1847, 26 November 1971, p. 9.

5 The commune movement in Britain

1 This practice was dropped, largely due to the increase in the number of new members.
2 There was founded at about this time in the mid-1960s a movement, 'Community Experiments Unlimited', by Emmanuel Petrakis. This eventually became the 'New Life Movement' whose members were committed to the goal of 'actively co-operating with each other to radically transform our sick world into happy, creative communities which assert life and love, and which are fulfilling for the individual'. From my experience this movement was little more than a list of correspondents possessed by Emmanuel Petrakis who always seemed to be asking for funds for some purpose or other. In early 1970 the 'New Life Movement' was merged with the Commune Movement.
3 T. Kelly, 'The need for urgency', *Ahimsa Communities*, no. 3, June 1965, p. 7.
4 It was at this time that the formal objectives of the Movement were changed from those of the Vegan Communities Movement to those of the present Commune Movement.
5 The issue of January 1971 was very small, as production got behind schedule and distribution was restricted by the strike of postal workers at that time. By February 1972 no issue of the journal had been distributed since March 1971. Production difficulties appear to have been at least partly responsible for this.
6 Inadequately described by Richard Neville as 'little more than a telephone surrounded by stoned optimists, all suffering, as someone

once said of an unfortunate actor, from delusions of adequacy'. R. Neville, *Play Power*, p. 50.

7 A letter to *Communes*, no. 29, October 1969, p. 34.

8 O. Thompson, 'Norfolk commune', pp. 9–10, *Communes*, no. 33, June 1970, p. 10.

9 See J. Harvey, 'Commune services report', pp. 26–7, *Communes*, no. 37, March 1971.

10 In fact a modified form of communal life is still led on the sites of two of the community ventures that originated in this pre-war period— the Whiteway and the Taena Communities. For an account of Whiteway, see N. Shaw, *Whiteway*. For an autobiographical account of life at the Taena Community, see Ineson, *Community Journey*.

11 In fact, the number of communes in existence is probably far higher than this. Not all communes would have contacted the Commune Movement with information about their existence, preferring to remain anonymous and so avoiding publicity and unwelcome visitors.

12 See Chapter 7, 'The paths to community'.

13 *Directory of Communes*, London, Commune Movement Publication, August 1970, pp. 14–15.

14 Thompson, loc. cit.

15 Ibid.

16 I have since heard that this commune has been disbanded, but I have been unable to confirm this.

17 I heard from one informant closely involved with the Eel Pie Island Commune that these journeys to Europe were defined by certain of the members as involving a process of 'spreading the word'. That is, they were to be compared to missionary expeditions, rather than holiday jaunts.

18 They have written of themselves, 'We are interested not only in developing as a community but in bringing about an alternative free society based on the autonomous commune.' See 'Selene Community' in *A Federal Society Based on the Free Commune*, a Commune Movement Publication.

19 These comments refer to the period 1968–70 when I was involved in field research.

20 Quoted from 'Selene Community' in *A Federal Society Based on the Free Commune*.

21 Ibid.

22 Ibid.

23 Rubington and Weinberg, *Deviance*, p. 203.

24 *Directory of Communes* (1970), pp. 25–6.

25 For an account of one such commune in Germany, see Engert, 'Living now for the time after the revolution'.

26 See C. Segal, '144 Piccadilly', *New Society*, 9 October 1969, for an account of the occupation.

27 For a personal account of the early life of this commune in South London see C. Ross, 'Equality of being', *Peace News*, 1855, 28 January 1972, p. 5. See also, 'Blackheath Commune', *Catonsville Roadrunner*, no. 26, 1971, pp. 9–10. By the summer of 1972 this commune had

ceased to exist. I have been unable to discover the cause of its death.

28 See Chapter 7, 'The paths to community'.
29 *Directory of Communes* (1970), p. 30.
30 See Jill Maguire, 'For ourselves alone or for social change?', *Peace News*, 1855, 28 January 1972, p. 3, for a personal account of life in the St Ann's Community Craft Centre.
31 Dave Craig and others, *Arts Labs Newsletter*, April 1970, pp. 44–6.
32 Editorial in *Openings*, no. 1, June/July 1970.
33 Letter to *Communes*, no. 35, December 1970, p. 19.
34 Sandy McMillan, 'Postlip Housing Association', *Communes*, no. 37, March 1971, p. 11.
35 See article in *New Society*, 3 September 1970, p. 403, on the Postlip Housing Association.
36 McMillan, op. cit., pp. 10–11.
37 R. D. Laing, *The Politics of Experience and the Bird of Paradise*, Harmondsworth, Penguin, 1967, p. 105.
38 See E. Goffman, *Asylums*, Harmondsworth, Penguin, 1968.
39 'Philadelphia Association', *Communes*, no. 34, September 1970, pp. 9–10.
40 Morton Schatzman, 'Madness and morals', pp. 288–313, in Berke, *Counter-Culture*, p. 313.
41 *Directory of Communes* (1970), p. 26.
42 Quoted in *Rudolph Steiner and the Modern Mind*, London, Anthroposophical Publishing Company. Unnumbered pamphlet.
43 Dr K. Konig, 'The three essentials of Camphill', pp. 143–54, *Cresset*, vol. 11, nos 3 and 4, Michaelmas 1965, p. 146.
44 Ibid., pp. 146–7.
45 Ibid., p. 149.
46 Ibid., p. 153.

6 Religious communes in Britain

1 See P. Berger and T. Luckmann, 'Sociology of religion and sociology of knowledge', pp. 412–27, *Sociology and Social Research*, vol. 47, 1963; P. Berger, *The Social Reality of Religion*; R. N. Bellah, 'Religious evolution', pp. 358–74, *American Sociological Review*, vol. 29, 1964.
2 Ibid., p. 372.
3 Much of the material used in this section can be found in A. Rigby and B. S. Turner, 'Findhorn Community, Centre of Light: A sociological study of new forms of religion', in M. Hill (ed.), *A Sociological Yearbook of Religion in Britain*, London, S.C.M.P., 1972, pp. 72–86.
4 Personal communication to the writer.
5 Peter Caddy, *The Findhorn Story*, Findhorn, Findhorn Trust, 1969.
6 Ibid.
7 David Spangler, *Limitless Love and Truth: Continued Revelation*, part 1, Findhorn, Findhorn Trust and the Universal Foundation, 1970, p. 9.
8 Elixer, *God Spoke to Me*, Findhorn, Findhorn Trust, January 1968, p. 12.

9 Ibid., p. 32.
10 *Findhorn News*, March 1969, p. 11.
11 Ibid., p. 12.
12 Elixer, op. cit., p. 18.
13 Ibid., p. 24.
14 *The Findhorn Garden*, Findhorn, Findhorn Trust, 1969, p. 5.
15 A recent example of the Laws of Manifestation in action was in December 1971 when the Centre purchased Findhorn House for a sum of over £10,000. This money was provided by a lady who had been left a large sum of money in her husband's will for her to spend as soon as possible after his death on 'God's work'.
16 L. Festinger *et al.*, *When Prophecy Fails*, New York, Harper & Row, 1964.
17 It would appear that reliance on the direction of Peter Caddy is declining since David Spangler has settled at Findhorn. See D. Black, 'Wholes within wholes', *Peace News*, 1855, 28 January 1972, p. 6.
18 Spangler, op. cit., p. 1.
19 *Findhorn News*, March 1969, p. 5.
20 *The Universal Link Concept*, p. 3, n.p., n.d.
21 *Findhorn News*, February 1970, p. 5.
22 By the summer of 1972 a number of significant changes had taken place at Findhorn since the time this chapter was written. The most obvious change has been in its expansion in size and in its range of activities. By July 1972 there were over a hundred members resident at Findhorn. In addition, commerical ventures in weaving, candle-making and pottery had also been embarked upon. The community was also far more concerned with communicating with the outside world by means of its theatre group, its musical and choral group, and through the taking over of the shop on the caravan site on which the centre is sited. In addition, they had started charging for their publications and had become a great deal more selective with regard to those whom they allowed to join as permanent members. They had also started charging fixed sums to guests who stayed with them.
23 From *An Introduction to Centre*, London, Centre Community, n.d.
24 Ibid., p. 2.
25 Ibid.
26 Ibid., p. 3.
27 Ibid., p. 4.
28 Ibid., p. 5.
29 Ibid., p. 6.
30 Ibid., pp. 6–7.
31 It is interesting to note that there are also personal contacts between the two ventures. The person who first provided me with the address of Centre Nucleus was closely associated with the experiment at Findhorn.
32 There are in Britain a variety of mystical groups whose members pursue communal life styles to varying degrees. The coverage presented in this chapter is not intended to be an exhaustive one. Reference perhaps ought to be made to a mystical group who pursue a communal form

of life but whose members participate in activities very different from those of the members of Findhorn and Centre Nucleus—the 'Radha Krishna Temple and Krishna Consciousness Society', described as 'A devotional commune who are seen in the streets in saffron robes and shaven heads chanting their Hare Krishna mantra. Vegetarian—also no drink, drugs, gambling or illicit sex', Nicholas Saunders, *Alternative London*, London, Nicholas Saunders, 1971, p. 102.

33 *Community Voice*, no. 1, February 1970.
34 Ibid., p. 5.
35 Overnight shelter has been provided for about 500 people a year.
36 David Horn, in January 1971 newsletter of Kingsway Community.
37 Private communication to the writer.
38 The use of the concept of ritual is based on Barth's general definition as 'sets of acts or aspects of acts which carry and communicate meanings in contexts vested with particular value'. See F. Barth, *Nomads of South Persia*, London, Allen & Unwin, 1964, p. 63
39 'The Grail Community', pp. 6–7, *Catonsville Roadrunner*, no. 26, 1971.
40 Ibid., p. 7.
41 Ibid.
42 Quoted in *Directory* (1970), p. 19.
43 Like the member of the Eel Pie Island Community who informed me that 'It's all happening—in about two years London is going to be the New Jerusalem'.

7 The paths to community

1 'In action is included all human behaviour in so far as the actor attaches a subjective meaning to it.' M. Weber, *The Theory of Social and Economic Organisation*, New York, Oxford University Press, 1947, p. 110.
2 See especially Schutz, *Collected Papers*, II, pp. 3–19.
3 Most action in everyday life appears a matter of habit that is not consciously deliberated upon. This does not mean that the actor cannot provide reasons for his actions if called upon to do so, given man's ability to examine his consciousness.
4 See *Modern Utopian*, vol. 2, no. 6, July-August 1968.
5 J. Burtt, in Shaw, *Whiteway*, p. 5.
6 Cited in J. Freund, *The Sociology of Max Weber*, London, Allen Lane, 1968, p. 60.
7 I was conscious of the dangers of commencing one's research with a set of pre-conceived little 'boxes', and spending the rest of one's research desperately trying to fill them up somehow, and in the process presenting an image of the world which failed to bear much resemblance to the real thing. The basic typology, from my point of view, acted as an important sensitizer during my enquiries. It provided me with some sense of direction during the research, and saved me from relying entirely on some osmotic process whereby all that I would need to know of the communitarians would pass from them to me by some mysterious medium without any prompting from me, somewhat like liquid absorbed indiscriminately by a sponge, to be squeezed out

later into some sort of meaningful pattern. At some stage in any research project, if the end result is to be anything more than a series of *ad hoc* observations, the data have got to be given a push of some sort in order for them to form any coherent structure and further one's understanding of the world. This exercise inevitably involves some simplification of the complex reality of the world; a simplification arrived at, if sociologists were honest with themselves and their audiences, by means of a greater or lesser degree of intentional or unintentional distortion through the selective inclusion or omission of evidence and subconscious repression.

The important point at issue appears to me to be the determination of the stage in the research at which one is going to create, however tentatively, one's little 'boxes'. On the basis of certain common-sense hypotheses formed early in the research, I decided to create my initial set of categories prior to any further field research, but with the express intention of constantly reminding myself to be prepared to serve a demolition order on them if they ever appeared to have ceased proving their worth.

8 He suggested to me that this was his way of trying to kill his mother at that age.

9 In sociological language, they are involved in the process of bringing to a close their enjoyment of the period of role moratorium (adolescence) and adopting one of the available role-models presented to them by society.

10 See K. Mannheim, 'The problem of generations', in *Essays on the Sociology of Knowledge*, London, Routledge & Kegan Paul, 1952, for an interesting examination of ideas about political generations.

11 See Chapter 5 above.

12 The Aldermaston marches, particularly 1958–60, had many communal characteristics of sharing, fellowship, and a spirit of co-operation. There were people eating, sleeping, and marching together for four days, often as groups.

13 See F. Parkin, *Middle Class Radicalism*, Manchester University Press, 1968, for an examination of the social bases of the British Campaign for Nuclear Disarmament.

14 See Mannheim, op. cit.

15 Nisbet, *Community and Power*, p. 19.

16 See, for instance, P. Selznick, *The Organisational Weapon*, Chicago, Free Press, 1960.

17 See E. Durkheim, *Suicide: A Study in Sociology*, Chicago, Free Press, 1951.

18 W. Kornhauser, *The Politics of Mass Society*, London, Routledge & Kegan Paul, 1960.

19 'Mass movements generally have the following characteristics: their objectives are remote and extreme; they favor activist modes of intervention in the social order; they mobilize uprooted and atomized sections of the population; they lack an internal structure of independent groups (such as regional or functional units with some freedom of action).' Ibid., p. 47.

20 See especially J. Gusfield, 'Mass society and extremist politics', *American Sociological Review*, vol. 27, 1962, pp. 19–30; M. Pinard, 'Mass society and political movements: a new formulation', in H. P. Dreitzel (ed.), *Recent Sociology*, no. 1, London, Collier-Macmillan, 1969, pp. 99–114.

21 See especially M. Rogin, *The Intellectuals and McCarthy*, Cambridge, Mass., M.I.T. Press, 1967. In my own research on members of the British peace movement I found little evidence to sustain Kornhauser's thesis. See A. Rigby, 'The British peace movement and its members', unpublished M.A. dissertation, University of Essex, 1968.

22 Letter to *Communes*, no. 33, June 1970, p. 17.

23 Letter to *Communes*, no. 32, April 1970, p. 14.

24 See Chapter 5 above.

25 See Chapter 5 above.

26 'In our usage class politics is political conflict over the allocation of material resources. Status politics is political conflict over the allocation of prestige. . . . Status movements are collective actions which attempt to raise or maintain the prestige of a group. . . . Class movements are oriented toward the "interests" of particular groups in the economic system of production and distribution.' J. Gusfield, *Symbolic Crusade: Status Politics and the American Temperance Movement*, Urbana, University of Illinois Press, 1966, pp. 18–20.

27 See V. I. Lenin, *What is to be done?* Moscow, Progress Publishers, 1964, especially pp. 51–93.

28 G. Lenski, 'Status crystallization: a non-vertical dimension of social status', *American Sociological Review*, vol. 19, 1954, pp. 405–13; J. Galtung, 'A structural theory of aggression', *Journal of Peace Research*, vol. 1, no. 4, 1964, pp. 36–54.

29 P. Doreian and N. Stockman, 'A critique of the multi-dimensional approach to stratification', pp. 47–65, *Sociological Review*, vol. 17, no. 1, March 1969, p. 52.

30 See Chapter 5 above.

31 It was noticeable that where a married couple were living together in an activist commune, they tended to share similar ideas, and tended to reinforce each other with regard to their radical commitment.

32 See Chapter 4 above.

33 Bittner, 'Radicalism and the organisation of radical movements'.

8 The world of the communitarians

1 One communitarian claimed, 'I haven't been influenced by many—Christ and Gandhi—I hope I could live a life similar to theirs, because they never seemed to harm anyone. This is the thing I am mainly concerned with.' The editorial statement of a magazine published by one communal group contained the following statement: 'Creative revolution doesn't need votes or guns. It began to happen in India under Gandhi and it can happen anywhere. All it needs to begin is a few people who decide to make it happen.'

2 One tripper remarked to me, 'certain records like Donovan—there is

so much in there that he can say better than us about where we are going.'

3 See Chapter 7 above.

4 The kinds of questions asked as introduction to this area of enquiry included: 'Some people say that most people can be trusted. Others say that you can't be too careful in your dealings with people. How do you feel about this?' 'Speaking generally, would you say that most people are more inclined to help others, or more inclined to look out for themselves?'

5 From the description of Selene Community contained in the Commune Movement publication, *A Federal Society Based on the Free Commune'*. See Chapter 5.

6 I have also been informed by other communitarians that Scotland is to be the New Jerusalem, others have told me it is to be Wales!

7 See, for example, Nuttall, *Bomb Culture*.

8 One respondent claimed, however, that man's survival was not the ultimate goal. 'I am always optimistic. I don't know whether man will survive or not. I don't see survival as the ultimate. There are so many creatures on this earth and man is just one of them. It doesn't much matter whether in a few million years man survives or not, provided something is surviving.'

9 M. Q. Sibley, *Revolution and Violence*, London, Peace News Reprint, March 1969, p. 4.

10 See *Catonsville Roadrunner*, no. 26, 1971, for an interview with Lanza Del Vasco, the founder of La Communauté de l'Arche.

9 Communes and the nuclear family

1 M. Hill, 'Patterns of living and loving', pp. 1–4, *Communes*, no. 33, June 1970, p. 1.

2 Letter to *Communes*, no. 30, December 1969, p. 16.

3 Quoted in Harrison, *Robert Owen*, p. 59.

4 Ibid., p. 60.

5 Quoted in J. Mitchell, 'Women: the longest revolution', pp. 11–37, *New Left Review*, vol. 40, November/December 1966, p. 13.

6 G. P. Maximoff (ed.), *The Political Philosophy of Bakunin*, Chicago, Free Press, 1953, p. 326.

7 See Nordhoff, *The Communistic Societies of the United States*, p. 262.

8 Ibid., pp. 263–4.

9 Ibid., pp. 268–9.

10 Noyes, *History of American Socialisms*, p. 265.

11 Nordhoff, op. cit., p. 275. Quoted from a 'Home Talk' by Noyes in *Circular*, 2 February 1874.

12 For similar recommendations but with regard to a different species, see A. Fraser, *Sheep Farming*, London, Crosby, Lockwood, 1965, pp. 33–4.

13 Nordhoff, op. cit., p. 276. Quoted from Noyes's 'Essay on Scientific Propagation'.

14 Schutz, *Collected Papers, II*, pp. 232–3.

15 Laurel Limpus, *Liberation of Women*, London, Agitprop, 1970, p. 1.
16 Ibid.
17 Mitchell, op. cit., p. 11.
18 *Woman*, vol. 2, no. 2, Winter 1971, a women's liberation journal, was largely devoted to an examination of some of the American experiments in communal living, and the position of women in such ventures.
19 See p. 209 above.
20 *A Federal Society Based on the Free Commune*, pp. 2–3.
21 Hill, op. cit., p. 3.
22 See M. Spiro, 'Is the family universal?', *American Anthropologist*, vol. 56, 1954, pp. 839–46.
23 But this union does not require the sanction of a marriage ceremony.
24 G. P. Murdock, *Social Structure*, New York, Macmillan, 1949, p. 1.
25 Hill, op. cit., p. 4.
26 One commune member has written: 'we are living towards the only way of life which will allow our children to grow and develop fully: one in which open, loving co-operation replaces fear and competition as the fundamental social principles'. David Horn, 'The Christian Family', *Community Voice*, no. 1, February 1970.
27 Nordhoff, op. cit., p. 406.
28 Becker, *Outsiders*, p. 162.
29 Typical of such enquiries was this letter in *Communes* that had been received by the members of one commune. It illustrates the important entrepreneurial role that can be played by the occupants of certain key positions with regard to the collection and dissemination of information (*Communes*, no. 29, October 1969, p. 31):

> We are a group of six people planning to establish a commune based on the common philosophical/religious bonds developing between us. It will be a self-supporting agricultural community, situated on an island off the west coast of Ireland . . . . We got your address, as being a successful commune, from BIT, and would appreciate any help, advice and survival information that you might care to give us.

30 A member of one group who were trying to get a commune venture off the ground wrote to me, 'Finances are our biggest problem, and this is maybe an aspect of our personalities . . . all very reluctant to go into regular jobs with little control of our own.'
31 'Rochester Commune', *Arts Lab Newsletter*, March 1970, pp. 5–6.
32 The following extracts from a letter written by a member of the Commune Movement who had attempted to form a commune and had confronted both these problems illustrate in some detail the nature of these obstacles (*Communes*, no. 32, April 1970, p. 16).

> Our community strivings over the past few months have come to little. We advertised quite widely . . . and also put a number of mimeographed sheets about, but response was small and those meetings which we were able to arrange were all unfruitful for one reason or another. Some were disastrous: one member of a unit—we saw mostly married couples—very keen, the other very

unkeen. Some were flat and somehow did not generate any impetus for further steps to be taken. Some were good, but there were other factors like difference in outlook, age, financial position, personal position, etc. which made further exploration impracticable. One nearly did come through and further arrangements were made, but the party in question eventually had second thoughts about the whole business and decided they were happy as they were for the present. . . . Then again, a lot of people just wanted to talk—it gave us the impression that 'communitying' is fast becoming a very fashionable therapeutic exercise—provided that actually setting up a community can be somehow indefinitely put off. . . . One last thing. Our own ethics . . . seem to hinge on the matter of setting up a community in a conventionally financed environment. I think this is one of the major stumbling blocks. So many more people would be available if no financial prerequisite were required. Needless to say, most of the people who have taken an alternative road have no money. A community in rented premises may be some sort of compromise answer. We are thinking along these lines—tentatively. It would at least allow something to get started, which seems very important at the moment.

33 Letter in *Communes*, no. 37, March 1971, p. 24. Of some thirty letters in this issue, fourteen of them were asking for information about communes to join, or were from members of existing communes inviting people to join them, or from people planning commune ventures and requesting others to join them in their quest.

34 O. Thompson, 'Norfolk Commune', *Communes*, no. 33, June 1970, p. 10.

35 N. J. Whitney, *Experiments in Community*, Wallingford, Pendle Hill Publications, 1966.

36 G. Haskell, 'Kaweah', *Out West*, vol. 17, September 1902.

37 Nordhoff, op. cit., pp. 411–12.

38 Noyes, op. cit., p. 652.

39 Vivian Estellachild, 'Hippie communes', in *Woman*, vol. 2, no. 2, Winter 1971.

40 I do not mean to imply that women's liberation is not a matter of grand principle. Rather, the grand principles involved in this movement are most frequently made manifest in the minutiae of domestic life.

41 Nordhoff, op. cit., p. 410

42 Quoted in Noyes, op. cit., p. 647.

43 Nordhoff, op. cit., p. 411.

44 Letter to *Communes*, no. 33, June 1970, p. 16. My emphasis.

45 Some insight into the restrictive nature of life that can be encountered by some individuals as members of communes can be obtained from a reading of E. Goffman's essay, 'On the characteristics of total institutions' in Goffman, *Asylums*, pp. 13–115.

46 *Arts Lab Newsletter*, March 1970, p. 5.

47 'Sidcup Commune', *Communes*, no. 33, June 1970, p. 10.

48 Personal communication. This experience would seem to mirror that of the members of the Sylvania Association, a short-lived Fourierist community in nineteenth-century America. Noyes quoted their testimony that 'Idle and greedy people find their way into such attempts and soon show forth their character by burdening others with too much labor, and, in times of scarcity, supplying themselves with more than their allowance of various necessities, instead of taking less.' Noyes, op. cit., pp. 648–9.

49 See letter cited in footnote 32 above.

50 See the account of the Sidcup Commune above, p. 290.

51 It was only after my period of field research had been completed that the 1971 Census forms were distributed to the population by the state. From correspondence with the members of a few communes since that time it would appear that, at least among members of what I have termed the activist communes, a large proportion refused to comply with the instructions requiring individuals to complete the forms. The apparent reluctance of the state to bring such dissenters to trial could be considered as a victory for those commune members and other members of society who sought by their refusal to say no to the dictates of the state. See *Peace News*, 1845, 12 November 1971.

52 Quoted in Armytage, *Heavens Below*, p. 23.

53 From an article on the Eel Pie Island Commune that appeared in the London newspaper, *Evening Standard*, 16 February 1970, concerning the attitude of the inhabitants of Twickenham towards the commune members.

54 Harrison, op. cit., p. 249.

10 Communes and social change

1 Buber, *Paths in Utopia*, p. 13.

2 H. Arendt, *On Revolution*, London, Faber & Faber, 1963, p. 22.

3 The fact that during 1972 the number of unemployed in Britain according to official statistics rose to the level of 1·5 million provides ample evidence that physical want and material deprivation remains one of the major social problems of British society.

4 For an excellent analysis of the state in capitalist societies such as Britain, see R. Miliband, *The State in Capitalist Society*, London, Weidenfeld & Nicolson, 1969.

5 This is emphasized particularly strongly by Roszack, *The Making of a Counter Culture*. See especially Chapter 7.

6 Berger *The Social Reality of Religion*, p. 29.

7 See, for instance, Jill Eckersley, 'The ones who get it together', *19*, June 1971, pp. 52–4.

8 Davis, 'Why all of us may be hippies someday', p. 12.

Bibliography

ABRAMS, P., 'Rites de passage: the conflict of generations in industrial society', *Journal of Contemporary History*, vol. 5, no. 1, 1970, pp. 175–90.

A Federal Society Based on the Free Commune, Commune Movement publication, n.p., n.d.

ALEXANDER, J., 'Sexual objects', *New Society*, 8 July 1971, pp. 49–50.

An Introduction to Centre, London, Centre Community, n.d.

ARENDT, H., *On Revolution*, London, Faber & Faber, 1963.

ARMYTAGE, W. H. G., *Heavens Below, Utopian Experiments in England 1560–1960*, London, Routledge & Kegan Paul, 1961.

ARNOLD, E., *Torches Together, The Beginning and Early Years of the Bruderhof Communities*, New York, Plough Publishing House, 1964.

Arts Lab Newsletter, 141 Westbourne Park Road, London, W.11.

BARTH, F., *Nomads of South Persia*, London, Allen & Unwin, 1964.

BECK, J., 'Paradise now', *International Times*, London, 12–25, July 1968.

BECKER, H. S., 'Problems of inference and proof in participant observation', *American Sociological Review*, vol. 23, December 1958, pp. 652–60.

BECKER, H. S., *Outsiders*, London, Collier-Macmillan, 1966.

BELLAH, R. N., 'Religious evolution', *American Sociological Review*, vol. 29, 1964, pp. 358–74.

BENNET, J., *Hutterian Brethren: The Agricultural Economy and Social Organisation of a Communal People*, Stanford University Press, 1967.

BERGER, B. M., 'Hippie morality—more old than new', *Transaction*, vol. 5, no. 2, December 1967, pp. 19–27.

BERGER, P., *The Precarious Vision*, New York, Doubleday, 1961.

BERGER, P., *Invitation to Sociology*, Harmondsworth, Penguin, 1966.

BERGER, P., *The Social Reality of Religion*, London, Faber & Faber, 1969.

BERGER, P., *A Rumour of Angels*, Harmondsworth, Penguin, 1971.

BERGER, P. and LUCKMANN, T., 'Sociology of religion and sociology of knowledge', *Sociology and Social Research*, vol. 47, 1963, pp. 412–27.

BERGER, P. and LUCKMANN, T., 'Social mobility and personal identity', *European Journal of Sociology*, vol. 5, 1964, pp. 331–43.

BERKE, J. (ed.), *Counter-Culture: The Creation of an Alternative Society*, London, Owen, 1969.

BESTOR, A. E., *Backwoods Utopias: The Sectarian and Owenite Phases of Communitarian Socialism in America: 1663–1829*, Philadelphia, University of Pennsylvania Press, 1950.

BISHOP, C. H., *All Things Common*, New York, Harper & Row, 1950.

BISHOP, M., 'The great Oneida love-in', *American Heritage*, 20 February 1969, pp. 14–17, 86–92.

Bitman, BIT, 141 Westbourne Park Road, London W.11.

BITTNER, E., 'Radicalism and the organisation of radical movements', *American Sociological Review*, vol. 28, 1963, pp. 928–40.

BLACK, D., 'Wholes within wholes', *Peace News*, 1855, 28 January 1972, p. 6.

'Blackheath Commune', *Catonsville Roadrunner*, no. 26, Summer 1971, pp. 9–10.

BLUER, R., 'Birmingham free you', *Peace News*, 1799, 18 December 1970.

BLUM, F. H., *Toward a Democratic Work Process*, New York, Harper, 1953.

BLUM, F. H., *Work and Community: the Scott Bader Commonwealth and the Quest for a New Social Order*, London, Routledge & Kegan Paul, 1968.

BLUMER, H., 'Social movements', in McLaughlin, B. (ed.), *Studies in Social Movements, a Social Psychological Perspective*, New York, Free Press, 1969, pp. 8–29.

BONDURANT, J. V., *Conquest of Violence*, New Jersey, Princeton University Press, 1958.

BRADEN, W., *The Private Sea: L.S.D. and the Search for God*, New York, Bantam, 1968.

BUBER, M., *Paths in Utopia*, London, Routledge & Kegan Paul, 1949.

BUCKMAN, P., *The Limits of Protest*, London, Gollancz, 1970.

CADDY, P., *The Findhorn Story*, Findhorn, Findhorn Trust, 1969.

CARTER, A., *The Political Theory of Anarchism*, London, Routledge & Kegan Paul, 1971.

Catonsville Roadrunner, 138 Mayall Rd., London, S.E. 24.

CICOUREL, A. V., *Method and Measurement in Sociology*, New York, Free Press, 1964.

COHN, N., *The Pursuit of the Millennium, Revolutionary millenarians and anarchists of the Middle Ages*, London, Paladin, 1970.

Commune Bulletin, Community Research Project, J. Plateaustrant 63, B-900, Ghent, Belgium.

Communes, Journal of the Commune Movement.

Community, 22a Dartmouth Row, London S.E.10.

Community in a Changing World, West Byfleet, Community Service Community, 1942.

Cormallen, P.O. Box 10065, Amsterdam, The Netherlands.

DAVIS, F., *On Youth Cultures: The Hippie Variant*, New York, General Learning Press, 1971.

DAVIS, F., 'Why all of us may be hippies someday', *Transaction*, vol. 5, no. 2, December 1967, pp. 10–18.

DENZIN, N. K., *The Research Act*, Chicago, Aldine, 1970.

Directory of Communes, Commune Movement, 1970.

DOREIAN, P. and STOCKMAN, N., 'A critique of the multi-dimensional approach to stratification', *Sociological Review*, vol. 17, no. 1, March 1969, pp. 47–65.

DUNBAR, R., *Female Liberation as a Basis for Social Revolution*, Boston, New England Free Press, n.d.

DURKHEIM, E., *Suicide: A Study in Sociology*, tr. G. Simpson, Chicago, The Free Press, 1951.

ECKERSLEY, J., 'The ones who get it together', *19*, June 1971, pp. 52–4.

'Eel Pie hippies put on a smile', *Evening Standard*, 16 February 1970.

EISENSTADT, S. N., *From Generation to Generation, Age Groups and Social Structure*, New York, Collier-Macmillan, 1956.

ELIXER, *God Spoke to Me*, Findhorn, Findhorn Trust, January 1968.

ENGERT, S., 'Living now for the time after the revolution', *Peace News*, 1740, 31 October 1969, p. 8.

ERIKSON, E. (ed.), *Youth: Change and Challenge*, New York, Basic Books, 1963.

ESTELLACHILD, V., 'Hippie communes', *Woman*, vol. 2, no. 2, Winter 1971.

FAIRFIELD, R., *Communes U.S.A., A Personal Tour*, Baltimore, Penguin, 1972.

FARQUHARSON, R., *Drop Out*, London, Blond, 1968.

FESTINGER, L. *et al.*, *When Prophecy Fails*, New York, Harper & Row, 1964.

FEUER, L. S. (ed.), *Marx and Engels: Basic Writings on Politics and Philosophy*, London, Fontana, 1969.

Findhorn Garden, Findhorn, Findhorn Trust, 1969.

FLACKS, R., 'Social and cultural meanings of student revolt: some informal comparative observations', *Social Problems*, vol. 17, no. 3, Winter 1970, pp. 340–57.

FLACKS, R., 'The new left and American politics after ten years', *Journal of Social Issues*, vol. 27, no. 1, 1971, pp. 21–34.

FRASER, A., *Sheep Farming*, London, Crosby, Lockwood, 1965.

Freedom, anarchist weekly, 84b Whitechapel High Street, London E.1.

FREUND, J., *The Sociology of Max Weber*, tr. M. Ilford, London, Allen Lane, The Penguin Press, 1968.

FRIEDENBERG, E. Z., 'Current patterns of generational conflict', *Journal of Social Issues*, vol. 25, no. 2, 1969, pp. 21–38.

FROMM, E., *Fear of Freedom*, London, Routledge & Kegan Paul, 1942.

GALTUNG, J., 'A structural theory of aggression', *Journal of Peace Research*, vol. 1, no. 4, 1964, pp. 36–54.

Gandalf's Garden, World's End, New King's Road, London, S.W.10.

GIDE, C., *Communist and Co-operative Colonies*, tr. E. F. Row, London, Harrap, 1930.

GILLIE, O. 'Richmond Fellows', *New Society*, 1 January 1970, pp. 5–6.

GLASER, B. G. and STRAUSS, A. L., *The Discovery of Grounded Theory: Strategies for Qualitative Research*, London, Weidenfeld & Nicolson, 1967.

GOFFMAN, E., *Asylums*, Harmondsworth, Penguin, 1968.

GOFFMAN, E., *Presentation of Self in Everyday Life*, Harmondsworth, Penguin, 1971.

GOLDETHORPE, J. H., LOCKWOOD, D., BECHHOFFER, F., PLATT, J., *The Affluent Worker in the Class Structure*, Cambridge University Press, 1969.

GOODMAN, P., *Growing Up Absurd*, London, Gollancz, 1961.

GOODMAN, P., *Utopian Essays and Critical Proposals*, New York, Vintage Books, 1964.

GORMAN, C., *Making Communes*, London, Whole Earth Tools, 1972.

'Grail Community, The', *Catonsville Roadrunner*, no. 26, Summer 1971.

GREENWALT, E. A., *The Point Loma Community in California, 1897–1942: a Theosophical Experiment*, University of California Publications in History, 48, Berkeley, California University Press, 1955.

GUSFIELD, J., 'Mass society and extremist politics', *American Sociological Review*, vol. 27, 1962, pp. 19–30.

GUSFIELD, J., *Symbolic Crusade: Status Politics and the American Temperance Movement*, Urbana, University of Illinois Press, 1966.

GUSTAITIS, R., *Turning On*, with an introduction by B. Inglis, London, Weidenfeld & Nicolson, 1969.

HALL, S., 'The hippies: an American moment', in NAGEL, J. (ed.), *Student Power*, London, Merlin Press, 1969, pp. 170–201.

HARRISON, J. F. C., *Robert Owen and the Owenites in Britain and America: The Quest for the New Moral World*, London, Routledge & Kegan Paul, 1969.

HARVEY, J., 'Commune Services report', *Communes*, no. 37, March 1971, pp. 26–7.

HEBERLE, R., *Social Movements: an introduction to Political Sociology*, New York, Appleton-Century-Crofts, 1951.

HEDGEPETH, W. and STOCK, D., *The Alternative, Communal Life in New America*, New York, Collier-Macmillan, 1970.

HILL, M., 'Patterns of living and loving', *Communes*, no. 33, June 1970, pp. 1–4.

HILL, M., 'Samye-Ling', *Scottish International*, vol. 5, no. 1, January 1972, pp. 15–17.

HILLS, C. and STONE, R. B., *Conduct Your Own Awareness Sessions*, New York, Signet, 1970.

HINES, R. V., *California's Utopian Colonies*, San Marino, Huntington Library, 1953.

'Hippies: an abortion of socialist understanding', *Socialist Standard*, vol. 65, no. 784, December 1969, pp. 179–81.

HIRSCH, S. J. and KENISTON, K., 'Psychosocial issues in talented college dropouts', *Psychiatry*, vol. 33, no. 1, February 1970, pp. 1–20.

HOLLOWAY, M., *Heavens on Earth*, London, Turnstile Press, 1957.

HORN, D. 'The Christian family', *Community Voice*, no. 1, February 1970.

HORN, D., 'Kingsway', *Catonsville Roadrunner*, no. 26, Summer 1971.

HOROWITZ, I. L. (ed.), *The Anarchists*, New York, Bell, 1964.

HUXLEY, A., *The Doors of Perception*, London, Chatto & Windus, 1954.

HUXLEY, A., *Brave New World Revisited*, London, Chatto & Windus, 1959.

INESON, G., *Community Journey*, London, Sheed & Ward, 1956.

INFIELD, H. F., *Co-operative Communities at Work*, London, Kegan Paul, Trench, Trubner, 1947.

331

INFIELD, H. F., *Utopia and Experiment, Essays in the Sociology of Co-operation*, New York, Praeger, 1955.

IT, 27 Endell Street, London W.C.2.

JACOBS, P. and LANDAU, S., *The New Radicals, a Report with Documents*, Harmondsworth, Penguin, 1967.

JAMES, A., 'Choose your neighbours', *Vanity Fair*, September 1971, pp. 52–5.

JAMES, W., *The Varieties of Religious Experience*, London, Longmans, 1952.

JUNKER, B. H., *Field Work: an introduction to the Social Sciences*, introduction by Everett C. Hughes, University of Chicago Press, 1960.

KEAY, D., 'Life in the house of the hippies', *Woman's Own*, 23 January 1971, pp. 12–19.

KELLY, T., 'The need for urgency', *Ahimsa Communities*, no. 3, June 1965, p. 7.

KELLY, T., 'Communes in Japan', *Communes*, no. 31, February 1970, pp. 1–7.

KENISTON, K., *The Uncommitted*, New York, Harcourt, Brace & World, 1965.

KENISTON, K., 'Heads and seekers: drugs on campus, counter-cultures, and American society', *American Scholar*, vol. 38, no. 3, Winter 1968, pp. 97–112.

KENISTON, K., *Young Radicals, Notes on Committed Youth*, New York, Harcourt, Brace & World, 1968.

KLAPP, O. E., *Collective Search for Identity*, New York, Holt, Rinehart & Winston, 1969.

KONIG, K., 'The three essentials of Camphill', *Cresset*, vol. 11, nos 3 and 4, Michaelmas 1965, pp. 143–54.

KORNHAUSER, W., *The Politics of Mass Society*, London, Routledge & Kegan Paul, 1960.

KRIMERMAN, L. I. and PERRY, L., *Patterns of Anarchy, a Collection oj Writings on the Anarchist Tradition*, New York, Doubleday, 1966.

KUMAR, S., *Non-violence or Non-existence*, London, Christian Action, 1969.

LAING, R. D., *The Politics of Experience and the Bird of Paradise*, Harmondsworth, Penguin, 1967.

LENIN, V. I., *What is to be done?* Moscow Progress Publishers, 1964.

LENSKI, G., 'Status crystallization: a non-vertical dimension of social status', *American Sociological Review*, vol. 19, 1954, pp. 405–13.

LERNER, M., 'Anarchism and the American counter-culture', *Government and Opposition*, vol. 5, no. 4, Autumn 1970, pp. 430–55.

LEVI, C., *Christ Stopped at Eboli*, London, Landsborough Publications, 1959.

LIMPUS, L., *Liberation of Women: sexual repression and the family*, London, Agitprop Literature Programme, 1970.

LINK, A., 'A directory of alternative work', *Peace News*, 1824, 18 June 1971.

LIPSIUS, F., 'Conspiracy means breathing together', *New Society*, 14 May 1970, p. 829.

MCMILLAN, S., 'Postlip Housing Association', *Communes*, no. 37, March 1971, pp. 10–11.

MADER, M., *The Kibbutz—an Introduction*, London, World Zionist Organization, n.d.

MAGUIRE, J., 'For ourselves alone or for social change?', *Peace News*, 1855, 28 January 1972, p. 3.

MAILER, N., *The Naked and the Dead*, London, Panther, 1969.

MANIS, J. G. and MELTZOR, B. N. (eds), *Symbolic Interaction, A reader in Social Psychology*, Boston, Allyn & Bacon, 1967.

MANNHEIM, K., *Ideology and Utopia*, London, Kegan Paul, Trench, Trubner, 1936.

MANNHEIM, K., *Essays on the Sociology of Knowledge*, tr. and ed. P. Kecskemeti, New York, Oxford University Press, 1952.

MANUEL, F. E. (ed.), *Utopias and Utopian Thought*, Boston, Beacon Press, 1966.

MANUEL, F. E. and MANUEL, F. P. (eds), *French Utopias: an anthology of Ideal Societies*, New York, Free Press, 1966.

MARCUSE, H., *One Dimensional Man*, London, Sphere, 1968.

MARCUSE, H., *Reason and Revolution*, London, Routledge & Kegan Paul, 1968.

MARCUSE, H., *Eros and Civilisation*, London, Sphere, 1969.

MARTIN, D. A., *Pacifism: an Historical and Sociological Study*, London, Routledge & Kegan Paul, 1965.

MARX, K. and ENGELS, F., *Manifesto of the Communist Party*, Moscow, Foreign Languages Publishing House, n.d.

MASSO, G., *Education in Utopias*, New York, Columbia University, 1927.

MATZA, D., 'Subterranean traditions of youth', *Annals of the American Academy of Political and Social Science*, November 1961, pp. 102–18.

MAXIMOFF, G. P. (ed.), *The Political Philosophy of Bakunin*, Chicago, Free Press, 1953.

MEAD, M., 'Communes: a challenge to all of us', *Redbook*, vol. 135, August 1970, pp. 50–1.

MILIBAND, R., *The State in Capitalist Society*, London, Weidenfeld & Nicolson, 1969.

MITCHELL, J., 'Women: the longest revolution', *New Left Review*, vol. 40, November-December 1966, pp. 11–37.

MITCHELL, J., *Woman's Estate*, Harmondsworth, Penguin, 1971.

Modern Utopian, Berkeley, California, U.S.A.

MOORE, B. (JR), 'Thoughts on the future of the family', in Lindenfeld, F. (ed.), *Radical Perspectives on Social Problems*, London, Collier-Macmillan, 1968, pp. 104–14.

MORE, S., 'The restless generation', *The Times*, 18 December 1968.

MUMFORD, L., *The Story of Utopias*, New York, Viking Press, 1966.

MURDOCK, G. P., *Social Structure*, New York, Macmillan, 1949.

NEVILLE, R., *Play Power*, London, Cape, 1970.

NEWFIELD, J., *A Prophetic Minority*, New York, New American Library, 1966.

NISBET, R., *Community and Power*, New York, Oxford University Press, 1962.

333

NORDHOFF, C., *The Communistic Societies of the United States, from personal visit and observation*, with a new introduction by Mark Holloway, New York, Dover, 1966.

NOYES, J. H., *History of American Socialisms*, New York, Dover, 1966.

NUTTALL, J., *Bomb Culture*, London, Paladin, 1970.

Openings, 24/25 Wapping, Liverpool 1.

OSTERGAARD, G., *Latter-Day Anarchism: The Politics of the American Beat Generation*, Ahmedabad, Harold Laski Institute of Political Science, 1964.

Oz, Oz Publications Ink Ltd, 52 Princedale Road, London W.11.

PARKIN, F., *Middle Class Radicalism: The Social Bases of the British Campaign for Nuclear Disarmament*, Manchester, Manchester University Press, 1968.

Peace News, 5 Caledonian Road, London N.1.

PETERS, V., *All Things Common: the Hutterian Way of Life*, University of Minnesota Press, 1965.

'Philadelphia Association', *Communes*, no. 34, September 1970, pp. 9–10.

PINARD, M., 'Mass society and political movements: a new formulation', in DREITZEL, H. P., *Recent Sociology*, no. 1, London, Collier-Macmillan, 1969, pp. 99–114.

POLSKY, N., *Hustlers, Beats and Others*, Harmondsworth, Penguin, 1971.

REICH, C., *The Greening of America*, Harmondsworth, Penguin, 1971.

Resurgence, Journal of the Fourth World, 24 Abercorn Place, London N.W.8.

RIGBY, A., 'The British peace movement and its members', University of Essex, unpublished M.A. dissertation, 1968.

ROBERTSON, R. (ed.), *Sociology of Religion*, Harmondsworth, Penguin, 1969.

ROGIN, M., *The Intellectuals and McCarthy: the Radical Specter*, Cambridge, Mass., M.I.T. Press, 1967.

ROSE, A. (ed.), *Human Behaviour and Social Processes: an Interactionist Approach*, London, Routledge & Kegan Paul, 1962.

ROSS, C., 'Equality of Being', *Peace News*, 1855, 28 January 1972, p. 5.

ROSS, L., 'The Newhaven Commune, Edinburgh', *Eclectics*, no. 1, mark 2, October 1971, p. 11.

ROSZACK, T., *The Making of a Counter Culture, Reflections on the Technocratic Society and its Youthful Opposition*, London, Faber & Faber, 1970.

RUBINGTON, E. and WEINBERG, M. S. (eds), *Deviance: the Interactionist Perspective*, New York, Macmillan, 1968.

Rudolph Steiner and the Modern Mind, London, Anthroposophical Publishing Company, n.d.

SABINE, G., *The Works of Gerrard Winstanley*, New York, Cornell, 1941.

SAMPSON, R. V., *The Psychology of Power*, New York, Vintage Books, 1968.

SAMPSON, R. V., *The Anarchist Basis of Pacifism*, London, Peace Pledge Union, 1970.

SAUNDERS, N., *Alternative London*, London, Nicholas Saunders, 1971.

SCHNEIDERMAN, L., 'Psychological notes on the nature of mystical experience', *Journal for the Scientific Study of Religion*, vol. 6, no. 1, 1967, pp. 91–100.

SCHUTZ, A., *Collected Papers, II: Studies in Social Theory*, ed. and introduced by A. Broderson, The Hague, Nijhoff, 1964.

SEGAL, C., '144 Piccadilly', *New Society*, 9 October 1969.

SELZNICK, P., *The Organisational Weapon*, Chicago, Free Press, 1960.

SHARP, G., *Exploring Non-Violent Alternatives*, Boston, Porter Sargent, 1970.

SHARLL, R., 'The search for a new style of life', in DEUTSCH, S. E. and HOWARD, J. (eds), *Where It's At*, New York, Harper & Row, 1970.

SHAW, N., *Whiteway: a Colony on the Cotswolds*, with a foreword by Joseph Burtt, London, Daniels, 1935.

SIBLEY, M. Q. (ed.), *The Quiet Battle*, New York, Doubleday, 1963.

SIBLEY, M. Q., *Revolution and Violence*, London, Peace News Reprint, March 1969.

'Sidcup Commune', *Communes*, no. 33, June 1970, p. 10.

SIMMON, G. and TROUT, G., 'Hippies in college—from teeny-boppers to drug freaks', *Transaction*, vol. 5, no. 2, December 1967, pp. 27–32.

SIMMONS, J. L. and WINOGRAD, B., *It's Happening: a Portrait of the Youth Scene Today*, Santa Barbara, Marc-Laird, 1966.

SLATER, P. E., *The Pursuit of Loneliness, American Culture at the Breaking Point*, London, Allen Lane, The Penguin Press, 1971.

Song of God: Bhagavad-Gita, translated by Swani Prabhavananda and Christopher Isherwood, with an introduction by Aldous Huxley, London, New English Library, 1951.

SPANGLER, D., *Limitless Love and Truth: Continued Revelation*, part I, Findhorn, Findhorn Trust and Universal Foundation, 1970.

SPIRO, M. E., 'Is the family universal?', *American Anthropologist*, vol. 56, 1954, pp. 839–46.

SPIRO, M. E., *Kibbutz—Venture in Utopia*, Cambridge, Mass., Harvard University Press, 1956.

STEIN, M., *The Eclipse of Community, an Interpretation of American Studies*, New York, Harper & Row, 1964.

STEINER, S., 'Communes: life in a selective family', *Honey*, February 1971, pp. 68–9.

SWIFT, L., *Brook Farm, its Members, Scholars and Visitors*, introduced by Joseph Schiffman, New York, Corinth Books, 1961.

TAWNEY, R., *Religion and the Rise of Capitalism*, London, Murrary, 1926.

THOMPSON, O., 'Norfolk Commune', *Communes*, no. 33, June 1970, pp. 9–10.

THRUPP, S. (ed.), *Millennial Dreams in Action*, The Hague, Mouton, 1962.

TURNER, R. H., 'The theme of contemporary social movement', *British Journal of Sociology*, vol. 20, no. 4, December 1969, pp. 390–405.

TWEEDIE, J., 'The faces from another world', *Guardian*, 11 January 1971, p. 9.

TYLER, A. F., *Freedom's Ferment: Phases of American Social History to 1860*, Minnesota, University of Minnesota Press, 1944.

Universal Link, Concept, n.p., n.d.

VAN MENSCH, P., 'Something on the Dutch commune scene', *Communes*, no. 31, February 1970, pp. 10–11.

VIDICH, A. J., 'Participant observation and the collection and interpretation of date', *American Journal of Sociology*, vol. 61, January 1955, pp. 354–60.

WEAVER, M. and WEAVER, V., 'The silence of the Hebrides', *Help*, no. 4, pp. 22–29.

WEBER, M., *The Theory of Social and Economic Organisation*, tr. A. M. Henderson and Talcott Parsons, ed. T. Parsons, New York, Oxford University Press, 1947.

WEBER, M., *The Sociology of Religion*, tr. E. Fischoff, introduction by T. Parsons, London, Methuen, 1965.

WHITNEY, N. J., *Experiments in Community*, Wallingford, Pendle Hill Publications, 1966.

WHITWORTH, J., 'The Bruderhof in England: a chapter in the history of a utopian sect', in Hill, M. (ed.), *A Sociological Yearbook of Religion in Britain*, London, Student Christian Movement Press, 1971.

WHYTE, W. F., *Street Corner Society*, Chicago, University of Chicago Press, 1955.

WILSON, B., *The Youth Culture and the Universities*, London, Faber & Faber, 1970.

Woman, a Journal of Liberation, vol. 2, no. 2, Winter 1971.

WOODCOCK, G., *Anarchism*, Harmondsworth, Penguin, 1963.

WOODCOCK, G., 'Anarchism revisited', *Commetary*, 46, August 1968, pp. 54–60.

'Year of the Commune', *Newsweek*, 18 August 1969, pp. 54–5.

YINGER, J. M., 'Contraculture and subculture', *American Sociological Review*, vol. 25, 1960, pp. 625–35.

YOUNG, J., *The Drug Takers: the Social Meaning of Drug Use*, London, MacGibbon & Kee, 1971.

ZABLOCKI, B., *The Joyful Community*, Baltimore, Penguin, 1971.

Index

International Library of Sociology

Edited by
John Rex
University of Warwick

Founded by
Karl Mannheim

as The International Library of Sociology
and Social Reconstruction

*This Catalogue also contains other Social Science
series published by Routledge*

Routledge & Kegan Paul   London and Boston

68-74 Carter Lane London EC4V 5EL
9 Park Street Boston Mass 02108

Contents

● *Books so marked are available in paperback*
All books are in Metric Demy 8vo format (216 × 138mm approx.)

GENERAL SOCIOLOGY

Belshaw, Cyril. The Conditions of Social Performance. *An Exploratory Theory. 144 pp.*

Brown, Robert. Explanation in Social Science. *208 pp.*

● Rules and Laws in Sociology.

Cain, Maureen E. Society and the Policeman's Role. *About 300 pp.*

Gibson, Quentin. The Logic of Social Enquiry. *240 pp.*

Gurvitch, Georges. Sociology of Law. *Preface by Roscoe Pound. 264 pp.*

Homans, George C. Sentiments and Activities: *Essays in Social Science. 336 pp.*

Johnson, Harry M. Sociology: *a Systematic Introduction. Foreword by Robert K. Merton. 710 pp.*

Mannheim, Karl. Essays on Sociology and Social Psychology. *Edited by Paul Kecskemeti. With Editorial Note by Adolph Lowe. 344 pp.*

Systematic Sociology: *An Introduction to the Study of Society. Edited by J. S. Erös and Professor W. A. C. Stewart. 220 pp.*

Martindale, Don. The Nature and Types of Sociological Theory. *292 pp.*

● **Maus, Heinz.** A Short History of Sociology. *234 pp.*

Mey, Harald. Field-Theory. *A Study of its Application in the Social Sciences. 352 pp.*

Myrdal, Gunnar. Value in Social Theory: *A Collection of Essays on Methodology. Edited by Paul Streeten. 332 pp.*

Ogburn, William F., and **Nimkoff, Meyer F.** A Handbook of Sociology. *Preface by Karl Mannheim. 656 pp. 46 figures. 35 tables.*

Parsons, Talcott, and **Smelser, Neil J.** Economy and Society: *A Study in the Integration of Economic and Social Theory. 362 pp.*

● **Rex, John.** Key Problems of Sociological Theory. *220 pp.*

Urry, John. Reference Groups and the Theory of Revolution.

FOREIGN CLASSICS OF SOCIOLOGY

● **Durkheim, Emile.** Suicide. *A Study in Sociology. Edited and with an Introduction by George Simpson. 404 pp.*

Professional Ethics and Civic Morals. *Translated by Cornelia Brookfield. 288 pp.*

● **Gerth, H. H.,** and **Mills, C. Wright.** From Max Weber: *Essays in Sociology. 502 pp.*

Tönnies, Ferdinand. Community and Association. *(Gemeinschaft und Gesellschaft.) Translated and Supplemented by Charles P. Loomis. Foreword by Pitirim A. Sorokin. 334 pp.*

SOCIAL STRUCTURE

Andreski, Stanislav. Military Organization and Society. *Foreword by Professor A. R. Radcliffe-Brown. 226 pp. 1 folder.*

Coontz, Sydney H. Population Theories and the Economic Interpretation. *202 pp.*

Coser, Lewis. The Functions of Social Conflict. *204 pp.*

Dickie-Clark, H. F. Marginal Situation: *A Sociological Study of a Coloured Group. 240 pp. 11 tables.*

Glass, D. V. (Ed.). Social Mobility in Britain. *Contributions by J. Berent, T. Bottomore, R. C. Chambers, J. Floud, D. V. Glass, J. R. Hall, H. T. Himmelweit, R. K. Kelsall, F. M. Martin, C. A. Moser, R. Mukherjee, and W. Ziegel. 420 pp.*

Glaser, Barney, and **Strauss, Anselm L.** Status Passage. *A Formal Theory. 208 pp.*

Jones, Garth N. Planned Organizational Change: *An Exploratory Study Using an Empirical Approach. 268 pp.*

Kelsall, R. K. Higher Civil Servants in Britain: *From 1870 to the Present Day. 268 pp. 31 tables.*

König, René. The Community. *232 pp. Illustrated.*

● **Lawton, Denis.** Social Class, Language and Education. *192 pp.*

McLeish, John. The Theory of Social Change: *Four Views Considered. 128 pp.*

Marsh, David C. The Changing Social Structure of England and Wales, 1871-1961. *288 pp.*

Mouzelis, Nicos. Organization and Bureaucracy. *An Analysis of Modern Theories. 240 pp.*

Mulkay, M. J. Functionalism, Exchange and Theoretical Strategy. *272 pp.*

Ossowski, Stanislaw. Class Structure in the Social Consciousness. *210 pp.*

SOCIOLOGY AND POLITICS

Hertz, Frederick. Nationality in History and Politics: *A Psychology and Sociology of National Sentiment and Nationalism. 432 pp.*

Kornhauser, William. The Politics of Mass Society. *272 pp. 20 tables.*

Laidler, Harry W. History of Socialism. *Social-Economic Movements: An Historical and Comparative Survey of Socialism, Communism, Co-operation, Utopianism; and other Systems of Reform and Reconstruction. 992 pp.*

Mannheim, Karl. Freedom, Power and Democratic Planning. *Edited by Hans Gerth and Ernest K. Bramstedt. 424 pp.*

Mansur, Fatma. Process of Independence. *Foreword by A. H. Hanson. 208 pp.*

Martin, David A. Pacificism: *an Historical and Sociological Study. 262 pp.*

Myrdal, Gunnar. The Political Element in the Development of Economic Theory. *Translated from the German by Paul Streeten. 282 pp.*

Wootton, Graham. Workers, Unions and the State. *188 pp.*

FOREIGN AFFAIRS: THEIR SOCIAL, POLITICAL AND ECONOMIC FOUNDATIONS

Mayer, J. P. Political Thought in France from the Revolution to the Fifth Republic. *164 pp.*

CRIMINOLOGY

Ancel, Marc. Social Defence: *A Modern Approach to Criminal Problems. Foreword by Leon Radzinowicz. 240 pp.*

Cloward, Richard A., and **Ohlin, Lloyd E.** Delinquency and Opportunity: *A Theory of Delinquent Gangs. 248 pp.*

Downes, David M. The Delinquent Solution. *A Study in Subcultural Theory. 296 pp.*

Dunlop, A. B., and **McCabe, S.** Young Men in Detention Centres. *192 pp.*

Friedlander, Kate. The Psycho-Analytical Approach to Juvenile Delinquency: *Theory, Case Studies, Treatment. 320 pp.*

Glueck, Sheldon, and **Eleanor.** Family Environment and Delinquency. *With the statistical assistance of Rose W. Kneznek. 340 pp.*

Lopez-Rey, Manuel. Crime. *An Analytical Appraisal. 288 pp.*

Mannheim, Hermann. Comparative Criminology: *a Text Book. Two volumes. 442 pp. and 380 pp.*

Morris, Terence. The Criminal Area: *A Study in Social Ecology. Foreword by Hermann Mannheim. 232 pp. 25 tables. 4 maps.*

● **Taylor, Ian, Walton, Paul,** and **Young, Jock.** The New Criminology. *For a Social Theory of Deviance.*

SOCIAL PSYCHOLOGY

Bagley, Christopher. The Social Psychology of the Epileptic Child. *320 pp.*

Barbu, Zevedei. Problems of Historical Psychology. *248 pp.*

Blackburn, Julian. Psychology and the Social Pattern. *184 pp.*

● **Brittan, Arthur.** Meanings and Situations. *224 pp.*

● **Fleming, C. M.** Adolescence: Its Social Psychology. *With an Introduction to recent findings from the fields of Anthropology, Physiology, Medicine, Psychometrics and Sociometry. 288 pp.*

● The Social Psychology of Education: *An Introduction and Guide to Its Study. 136 pp.*

Homans, George C. The Human Group. *Foreword by Bernard DeVoto. Introduction by Robert K. Merton. 526 pp.*

Social Behaviour: *its Elementary Forms. 416 pp.*

Klein, Josephine. The Study of Groups. *226 pp. 31 figures. 5 tables.*

Linton, Ralph. The Cultural Background of Personality. *132 pp.*

Mayo, Elton. The Social Problems of an Industrial Civilization. *With an appendix on the Political Problem. 180 pp.*

Ottaway, A. K. C. Learning Through Group Experience. *176 pp.*

Ridder, J. C. de. The Personality of the Urban African in South Africa. *A Thematic Apperception Test Study. 196 pp. 12 plates.*

● **Rose, Arnold M.** (Ed.). Human Behaviour and Social Processes: *an Interactionist Approach. Contributions by Arnold M. Rose, Ralph H. Turner, Anselm Strauss, Everett C. Hughes, E. Franklin Frazier, Howard S. Becker, et al. 696 pp.*

5

Smelser, Neil J. Theory of Collective Behaviour. *448 pp.*
Stephenson, Geoffrey M. The Development of Conscience. *128 pp.*
Young, Kimball. Handbook of Social Psychology. *658 pp. 16 figures. 10 tables.*

SOCIOLOGY OF THE FAMILY

Banks, J. A. Prosperity and Parenthood: *A Study of Family Planning among The Victorian Middle Classes. 262 pp.*
Bell, Colin R. Middle Class Families: *Social and Geographical Mobility. 224 pp.*
Burton, Lindy. Vulnerable Children. *272 pp.*
Gavron, Hannah. The Captive Wife: *Conflicts of Household Mothers. 190 pp.*
George, Victor, and **Wilding, Paul.** Motherless Families. *220 pp.*
Klein, Josephine. Samples from English Cultures.
  1. Three Preliminary Studies and Aspects of Adult Life in England. *447 pp.*
  2. Child-Rearing Practices and Index. *247 pp.*
Klein, Viola. Britain's Married Women Workers. *180 pp.*
  The Feminine Character. *History of an Ideology. 244 pp.*
McWhinnie, Alexina M. Adopted Children. *How They Grow Up. 304 pp.*
Myrdal, Alva, and **Klein, Viola.** Women's Two Roles: *Home and Work. 238 pp. 27 tables.*
Parsons, Talcott, and **Bales, Robert F.** Family: Socialization and Interaction Process. *In collaboration with James Olds, Morris Zelditch and Philip E. Slater. 456 pp. 50 figures and tables.*

SOCIAL SERVICES

Bastide, Roger. The Sociology of Mental Disorder. *Translated from the French by Jean McNeil. 260 pp.*
Carlebach, Julius. Caring For Children in Trouble. *266 pp.*
Forder, R. A. (Ed.). Penelope Hall's Social Services of England and Wales. *352 pp.*
George, Victor. Foster Care. *Theory and Practice. 234 pp.*
  Social Security: *Beveridge and After. 258 pp.*
● **Goetschius, George W.** Working with Community Groups. *256 pp.*
Goetschius, George W., and **Tash, Joan.** Working with Unattached Youth. *416 pp.*
Hall, M. P., and **Howes, I. V.** The Church in Social Work. *A Study of Moral Welfare Work undertaken by the Church of England. 320 pp.*
Heywood, Jean S. Children in Care: *the Development of the Service for the Deprived Child. 264 pp.*
Hoenig, J., and **Hamilton, Marian W.** The De-Segration of the Mentally Ill. *284 pp.*
Jones, Kathleen. Mental Health and Social Policy, 1845-1959. *264 pp.*

King, Roy D., Raynes, Norma V., and **Tizard, Jack.** Patterns of Residential Care. *356 pp.*

Leigh, John. Young People and Leisure. *256 pp.*

Morris, Mary. Voluntary Work and the Welfare State. *300 pp.*

Morris, Pauline. Put Away: *A Sociological Study of Institutions for the Mentally Retarded. 364 pp.*

Nokes, P. L. The Professional Task in Welfare Practice. *152 pp.*

Timms, Noel. Psychiatric Social Work in Great Britain (1939-1962). *280 pp.*

● Social Casework: *Principles and Practice. 256 pp.*

Young, A. F., and **Ashton, E. T.** British Social Work in the Nineteenth Century. *288 pp.*

Young, A. F. Social Services in British Industry. *272 pp.*

SOCIOLOGY OF EDUCATION

Banks, Olive. Parity and Prestige in English Secondary Education: a Study in Educational Sociology. *272 pp.*

Bentwich, Joseph. Education in Israel. *224 pp. 8 pp. plates.*

● **Blyth, W. A. L.** English Primary Education. *A Sociological Description.*
   1. Schools. *232 pp.*
   2. Background. *168 pp.*

Collier, K. G. The Social Purposes of Education: *Personal and Social Values in Education. 268 pp.*

Dale, R. R., and **Griffith, S.** Down Stream: *Failure in the Grammar School. 108 pp.*

Dore, R. P. Education in Tokugawa Japan. *356 pp. 9 pp. plates*

Evans, K. M. Sociometry and Education. *158 pp.*

Foster, P. J. Education and Social Change in Ghana. *336 pp. 3 maps.*

Fraser, W. R. Education and Society in Modern France. *150 pp.*

Grace, Gerald R. Role Conflict and the Teacher. *About 200 pp.*

Hans, Nicholas. New Trends in Education in the Eighteenth Century. *278 pp. 19 tables.*

● Comparative Education: *A Study of Educational Factors and Traditions. 360 pp.*

Hargreaves, David. Interpersonal Relations and Education. *432 pp.*

● Social Relations in a Secondary School. *240 pp.*

Holmes, Brian. Problems in Education. *A Comparative Approach. 336 pp.*

King, Ronald. Values and Involvement in a Grammar School. *164 pp.*
   School Organization and Pupil Involvement. *A Study of Secondary Schools.*

● **Mannheim, Karl,** and **Stewart, W. A. C.** An Introduction to the Sociology of Education. *206 pp.*

Morris, Raymond N. The Sixth Form and College Entrance. *231 pp.*

● **Musgrove, F.** Youth and the Social Order. *176 pp.*

● **Ottaway, A. K. C.** Education and Society: An Introduction to the Sociology of Education. *With an Introduction by W. O. Lester Smith. 212 pp.*

Peers, Robert. Adult Education: *A Comparative Study. 398 pp.*

Pritchard, D. G. Education and the Handicapped: *1760 to 1960. 258 pp.*

Richardson, Helen. Adolescent Girls in Approved Schools. *308 pp.*

Stratta, Erica. The Education of Borstal Boys. *A Study of their Educational Experiences prior to, and during Borstal Training. 256 pp.*

SOCIOLOGY OF CULTURE

Eppel, E. M., and **M.** Adolescents and Morality: *A Study of some Moral Values and Dilemmas of Working Adolescents in the Context of a changing Climate of Opinion. Foreword by W. J. H. Sprott. 268 pp. 39 tables.*

● **Fromm, Erich.** The Fear of Freedom. *286 pp.*
The Sane Society. *400 pp.*

Mannheim, Karl. Essays on the Sociology of Culture. *Edited by Ernst Mannheim in co-operation with Paul Kecskemeti. Editorial Note by Adolph Lowe. 280 pp.*

Weber, Alfred. Farewell to European History: *or The Conquest of Nihilism Translated from the German by R. F. C. Hull. 224 pp.*

SOCIOLOGY OF RELIGION

Argyle, Michael. Religious Behaviour. *224 pp. 8 figures. 41 tables.*

Nelson, G. K. Spiritualism and Society. *313 pp.*

Stark, Werner. The Sociology of Religion. *A Study of Christendom.*
Volume I. *Established Religion. 248 pp.*
Volume II. *Sectarian Religion. 368 pp.*
Volume III. *The Universal Church. 464 pp.*
Volume IV. *Types of Religious Man. 352 pp.*
Volume V. *Types of Religious Culture. 464 pp.*

Watt, W. Montgomery. Islam and the Integration of Society. *320 pp.*

SOCIOLOGY OF ART AND LITERATURE

Jarvie, Ian C. Towards a Sociology of the Cinema. *A Comparative Essay on the Structure and Functioning of a Major Entertainment Industry. 405 pp.*

Rust, Frances S. Dance in Society. *An Analysis of the Relationships between the Social Dance and Society in England from the Middle Ages to the Present Day. 256 pp. 8 pp. of plates.*

Schücking, L. L. The Sociology of Literary Taste. *112 pp.*

SOCIOLOGY OF KNOWLEDGE

Mannheim, Karl. Essays on the Sociology of Knowledge. *Edited by Paul Kecskemeti. Editorial Note by Adolph Lowe. 353 pp.*

Remmling, Gunter W. (Ed.). Towards the Sociology of Knowledge. *Origins and Development of a Sociological Thought Style.*

Stark, Werner. The Sociology of Knowledge: *An Essay in Aid of a Deeper Understanding of the History of Ideas. 384 pp.*

URBAN SOCIOLOGY

Ashworth, William. The Genesis of Modern British Town Planning: *A Study in Economic and Social History of the Nineteenth and Twentieth Centuries. 288 pp.*

Cullingworth, J. B. Housing Needs and Planning Policy: *A Restatement of the Problems of Housing Need and 'Overspill' in England and Wales. 232 pp. 44 tables. 8 maps.*

Dickinson, Robert E. City and Region: *A Geographical Interpretation. 608 pp. 125 figures.*

The West European City: *A Geographical Interpretation. 600 pp. 129 maps. 29 plates.*

● The City Region in Western Europe. *320 pp. Maps.*

Humphreys, Alexander J. New Dubliners: *Urbanization and the Irish Family. Foreword by George C. Homans. 304 pp.*

Jackson, Brian. Working Class Community: *Some General Notions raised by a Series of Studies in Northern England. 192 pp.*

Jennings, Hilda. Societies in the Making: *a Study of Development and Re-development within a County Borough. Foreword by D. A. Clark. 286 pp.*

● **Mann, P. H.** An Approach to Urban Sociology. *240 pp.*

Morris, R. N., and **Mogey, J.** The Sociology of Housing. *Studies at Berinsfield. 232 pp. 4 pp. plates.*

Rosser, C., and **Harris, C.** The Family and Social Change. *A Study of Family and Kinship in a South Wales Town. 352 pp. 8 maps.*

RURAL SOCIOLOGY

Chambers, R. J. H. Settlement Schemes in Tropical Africa: *A Selective Study. 268 pp.*

Haswell, M. R. The Economics of Development in Village India. *120 pp.*

Littlejohn, James. Westrigg: *the Sociology of a Cheviot Parish. 172 pp. 5 figures.*

Mayer, Adrian C. Peasants in the Pacific. *A Study of Fiji Indian Rural Society. 248 pp. 20 plates.*

Williams, W. M. The Sociology of an English Village: *Gosforth. 272 pp. 12 figures. 13 tables.*

SOCIOLOGY OF INDUSTRY AND DISTRIBUTION

Anderson, Nels. Work and Leisure. *280 pp.*

● **Blau, Peter M.,** and **Scott, W. Richard.** Formal Organizations: *a Comparative approach. Introduction and Additional Bibliography by J. H. Smith. 326 pp.*

Eldridge, J. E. T. Industrial Disputes. *Essays in the Sociology of Industrial Relations. 288 pp.*

Hetzler, Stanley. Applied Measures for Promoting Technological Growth. *352 pp.*

Technological Growth and Social Change. *Achieving Modernization. 269 pp.*

Hollowell, Peter G. The Lorry Driver. *272 pp.*

Jefferys, Margot, *with the assistance of Winifred Moss.* Mobility in the Labour Market: *Employment Changes in Battersea and Dagenham. Preface by Barbara Wootton. 186 pp. 51 tables.*

Millerson, Geoffrey. The Qualifying Associations: *a Study in Professionalization. 320 pp.*

Smelser, Neil J. Social Change in the Industrial Revolution: *An Application of Theory to the Lancashire Cotton Industry, 1770-1840. 468 pp. 12 figures. 14 tables.*

Williams, Gertrude. Recruitment to Skilled Trades. *240 pp.*

Young, A. F. Industrial Injuries Insurance: *an Examination of British Policy. 192 pp.*

DOCUMENTARY

Schlesinger, Rudolf (Ed.). Changing Attitudes in Soviet Russia.
2. The Nationalities Problem and Soviet Administration. *Selected Readings on the Development of Soviet Nationalities Policies. Introduced by the editor. Translated by W. W. Gottlieb. 324 pp.*

ANTHROPOLOGY

Ammar, Hamed. Growing up in an Egyptian Village: *Silwa, Province of Aswan. 336 pp.*

Brandel-Syrier, Mia. Reeftown Elite. *A Study of Social Mobility in a Modern African Community on the Reef. 376 pp.*

Crook, David, and **Isabel.** Revolution in a Chinese Village: *Ten Mile Inn. 230 pp. 8 plates. 1 map.*

Dickie-Clark, H. F. The Marginal Situation. *A Sociological Study of a Coloured Group. 236 pp.*

Dube, S. C. Indian Village. *Foreword by Morris Edward Opler. 276 pp. 4 plates.*

India's Changing Villages: *Human Factors in Community Development. 260 pp. 8 plates. 1 map.*

Firth, Raymond. Malay Fishermen. *Their Peasant Economy. 420 pp. 17 pp. plates.*

Gulliver, P. H. Social Control in an African Society: a Study of the Arusha, Agricultural Masai of Northern Tanganyika. *320 pp. 8 plates. 10 figures.*

Ishwaran, K. Shivapur. *A South Indian Village. 216 pp.*
Tradition and Economy in Village India: *An Interactionist Approach. Foreword by Conrad Arensburg. 176 pp.*

Jarvie, Ian C. The Revolution in Anthropology. *268 pp.*

Jarvie, Ian C., and **Agassi, Joseph.** Hong Kong. *A Society in Transition. 396 pp. Illustrated with plates and maps.*

Little, Kenneth L. Mende of Sierra Leone. *308 pp. and folder.*
Negroes in Britain. *With a New Introduction and Contemporary Study by Leonard Bloom. 320 pp.*

Lowie, Robert H. Social Organization. *494 pp.*

Mayer, Adrian C. Caste and Kinship in Central India: *A Village and its Region. 328 pp. 16 plates. 15 figures. 16 tables.*

Smith, Raymond T. The Negro Family in British Guiana: *Family Structure and Social Status in the Villages. With a Foreword by Meyer Fortes. 314 pp. 8 plates. 1 figure. 4 maps.*

SOCIOLOGY AND PHILOSOPHY

Barnsley, John H. The Social Reality of Ethics. *A Comparative Analysis of Moral Codes. 448 pp.*

Diesing, Paul. Patterns of Discovery in the Social Sciences. *362 pp.*

Douglas, Jack D. (Ed.). Understanding Everyday Life. *Toward the Reconstruction of Sociological Knowledge. Contributions by Alan F. Blum. Aaron W. Cicourel, Norman K. Denzin, Jack D. Douglas, John Heeren, Peter McHugh, Peter K. Manning, Melvin Power, Matthew Speier, Roy Turner, D. Lawrence Wieder, Thomas P. Wilson and Don H. Zimmerman. 370 pp.*

Jarvie, Ian C. Concepts and Society. *216 pp.*

Roche, Maurice. Phenomenology, Language and the Social Sciences. *About 400 pp.*

Sahay, Arun. Sociological Analysis.

Sklair, Leslie. The Sociology of Progress. *320 pp.*

International Library of Anthropology
General Editor Adam Kuper

Brown, Paula. The Chimbu. *A Study of Change in the New Guinea Highlands.*
Van Den Berghe, Pierre L. Power and Privilege at an African University.

International Library of Social Policy

General Editor   Kathleen Jones

Holman, Robert. Trading in Children. *A Study of Private Fostering.*
Jones, Kathleen. History of the Mental Health Services. *428 pp.*
Thomas, J. E. The English Prison Officer since 1850: *A Study in Conflict.* *258 pp.*

Primary Socialization, Language and Education

General Editor   Basil Bernstein

Bernstein, Basil. Class, Codes and Control. *2 volumes.*
  1. *Theoretical Studies Towards a Sociology of Language. 254 pp.*
  2. *Applied Studies Towards a Sociology of Language. About 400 pp.*
Brandis, Walter, and **Henderson, Dorothy.** Social Class, Language and Communication. *288 pp.*
Cook-Gumperz, Jenny. Social Control and Socialization. *A Study of Class Differences in the Language of Maternal Control.*
Gahagan, D. M., and **G. A.** Talk Reform. *Exploration in Language for Infant School Children. 160 pp.*
Robinson, W. P., and **Rackstraw, Susan, D. A.** A Question of Answers. *2 volumes. 192 pp. and 180 pp.*
Turner, Geoffrey, J., and **Mohan, Bernard, A.** A Linguistic Description and Computer Programme for Children's Speech. *208 pp.*

Reports of the Institute of Community Studies

Cartwright, Ann. Human Relations and Hospital Care. *272 pp.*
  Parents and Family Planning Services. *306 pp.*
  Patients and their Doctors. *A Study of General Practice. 304 pp.*
● **Jackson, Brian.** Streaming: *an Education System in Miniature. 168 pp.*
Jackson, Brian, and **Marsden, Dennis.** Education and the Working Class: *Some General Themes raised by a Study of 88 Working-class Children in a Northern Industrial City. 268 pp. 2 folders.*
Marris, Peter. The Experience of Higher Education. *232 pp. 27 tables.*
Marris, Peter, and **Rein, Martin.** Dilemmas of Social Reform. *Poverty and Community Action in the United States. 256 pp.*
Marris, Peter, and **Somerset, Anthony.** African Businessmen. *A Study of Entrepreneurship and Development in Kenya. 256 pp.*
Mills, Richard. Young Outsiders: *a Study in Alternative Communities.*

Runciman, W. G. Relative Deprivation and Social Justice. *A Study of Attitudes to Social Inequality in Twentieth Century England. 352 pp.*

Townsend, Peter. The Family Life of Old People: *An Inquiry in East London. Foreword by J. H. Sheldon. 300 pp. 3 figures. 63 tables.*

Willmott, Peter. Adolescent Boys in East London. *230 pp.*
The Evolution of a Community: *a study of Dagenham after forty years. 168 pp. 2 maps.*

Willmott, Peter, and **Young, Michael.** Family and Class in a London Suburb. *202 pp. 47 tables.*

Young, Michael. Innovation and Research in Education. *192 pp.*

● **Young, Michael,** and **McGeeney, Patrick.** Learning Begins at Home. *A Study of a Junior School and its Parents. 128 pp.*

Young, Michael, and **Willmott, Peter.** Family and Kinship in East London. *Foreword by Richard M. Titmuss. 252 pp. 39 tables.*
The Symmetrical Family.

Reports of the Institute for Social Studies in Medical Care

Cartwright, Ann, Hockey, Lisbeth, and **Anderson, John L.** Life Before Death.

Dunnell, Karen, and **Cartwright, Ann.** Medicine Takers, Prescribers and Hoarders. *190 pp.*

Medicine, Illness and Society
General Editor W. M. Williams

Robinson, David. The Process of Becoming Ill.

Stacey, Margaret. *et al.* Hospitals, Children and Their Families. *The Report of a Pilot Study. 202 pp.*

Monographs in Social Theory
General Editor Arthur Brittan

Bauman, Zygmunt. Culture as Praxis.

Dixon, Keith. Sociological Theory. *Pretence and Possibility.*

Smith, Anthony D. The Concept of Social Change. *A Critique of the Functionalist Theory of Social Change.*

13

Routledge Social Science Journals

The British Journal of Sociology. *Edited by Terence P. Morris. Vol. 1, No. 1, March 1950 and Quarterly. Roy. 8vo. Back numbers available. An international journal with articles on all aspects of sociology.*

Economy and Society. *Vol. 1, No. 1. February 1972 and Quarterly. Metric Roy. 8vo. A journal for all social scientists covering sociology, philosophy, anthropology, economics and history. Back numbers available.*

Year Book of Social Policy in Britain, The. *Edited by Kathleen Jones. 1971. Published Annually.*

Printed in Great Britain by Lewis Reprints Limited
Brown Knight & Truscott Group, London and Tonbridge